Mind, Brain and Narrative

Narratives enable readers to experience vividly fictional and non-fictional contexts. Writers use a variety of language features to control these experiences: they direct readers in how to construct contexts, how to draw inferences and how to identify the key parts of a story. Writers can skilfully convey physical sensations, prompt emotional states, effect moral responses and even alter the readers' attitudes. *Mind, Brain and Narrative* examines the psychological and neuroscientific evidence for the mechanisms which underlie narrative comprehension. The authors explore the scientific developments which demonstrate the importance of attention, counterfactuals, depth of processing, perspective and embodiment in these processes. In so doing, this timely, interdisciplinary work provides an integrated account of the research which links psychological mechanisms of language comprehension to humanities work on narrative and style.

ANTHONY J. SANFORD is Emeritus Professor and Honorary Senior Research Fellow in the Institute of Neuroscience and Psychology at the University of Glasgow.

CATHERINE EMMOTT is Senior Lecturer in English Language at the University of Glasgow.

Mind, Brain and Narrative

Anthony J. Sanford

Catherine Emmott

CAMBRIDGE
UNIVERSITY PRESS

CAMBRIDGE UNIVERSITY PRESS
Cambridge, New York, Melbourne, Madrid, Cape Town,
Singapore, São Paulo, Delhi, Dubai, Mexico City

Cambridge University Press
The Edinburgh Building, Cambridge CB2 8RU, UK

Published in the United States of America by
Cambridge University Press, New York

www.cambridge.org
Information on this title: www.cambridge.org/9781107017566

First published 2012

Printed and Bound in Great Britain by the MPG Books Group

A catalogue record for this publication is available from the British Library

Library of Congress Cataloging-in-Publication Data

Sanford, A. J. (Anthony J.)
  Mind, brain and narrative / Anthony J. Sanford, Catherine Emmott.
    pages   cm
  Includes bibliographical references and indexes.
  ISBN 978-1-107-01756-6
    1. Discourse analysis, Narrative–Psychological aspects.   2. Narration (Rhetoric)–
Psychological aspects.   3. Comprehension.   4. Cognition.   5. Psycholinguistics.
  I. Emmott, Catherine.   II. Title.
  P302.8.S26 2012
  401′.41–dc23
                                                                        2012018827

ISBN 978-1-107-01756-6 Hardback

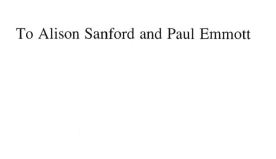

To Alison Sanford and Paul Emmott

Contents

Figures

Tables

Preface

The aim of this book is to provide an interdisciplinary bridge between humanities research on narrative, and psychological and neuroscience work on language processing and comprehension. Narrative requires readers to produce rich and complex mental representations. It offers one of the major means through which the experiences of other people, different cultures and distant times may be conveyed, and expands our virtual experience of the world. Typically, narratives manipulate not only our knowledge of things, but also our impressions of how people feel, judge and react in a multitude of situations. Writers encourage the production of such complex representations through subtle linguistic devices.

It is clear that to understand these many aspects of narrative comprehension, an interdisciplinary approach is required, and that is precisely what we offer here. Alone, humanities and scientific studies have much to say about language and how it is understood, but together, it is possible to make greater progress in examining its use in narrative texts. Thus humanities research has led to many important observations and conjectures about the nature of narrative, and how narrative results in various impressions in the minds of readers, but only a small amount of this work has a real empirical basis. In psychology, much empirical work and theory has been concerned with understanding particular language constructions, but rather less with the global aspects of real narrative. A combined approach means that both disciplines benefit, and our overall understanding of narrative comprehension is much improved. So, the humanities work can provide psychologists with insights into how to handle more realistic and often more complex phenomena than they usually deal with, while psychologists can provide appropriate scientific experimentation and processing theories that make the claims of humanities researchers about reading narratives more tangible and solid. This is the main philosophy behind the present volume.

Our study incorporates an examination of relevant recent work in neuroscience. Apart from the general question of how the brain supports narrative comprehension, there are two specific issues to which we draw attention. First, while many processes of understanding are purely 'cognitive', having to do with using or manipulating a reader's knowledge, writers on narrative have made much of the 'experience' of reading, such as sensory 'feelings' about what is being described, or having emotional responses – so-called 'narrative immersion'. Obviously a purely cognitive model could not accommodate such phenomena, but neuroscience can, because the brain mediates sensory impressions and emotions. Secondly, narratives often deal with matters of social content, where it is important to have empathy with characters and make social judgements. The burgeoning field of social neuroscience is concerned with just such issues, and serves as a means of bringing social dynamics into the study of how narrative affects the reader.

Of course, how a writer portrays things determines how we respond as readers. A lucid description of a scene may highlight the experience of 'feeling' some sensation, or having some image, while an alternative description may suppress such sensations. The writer's rhetorical control over how we process narrative determines what we attend to during reading, what we consider to be important or not, and what images and sensations we have. This is central to the approach we take in this book and is why we describe our model as the 'Rhetorical Processing Framework', offering it as an account of many major phenomena.

The book contains our own original contributions as well as reviews of relevant research by others. Primarily, we hope that it will be of interest to researchers in all disciplines that concern themselves with narrative comprehension. We present material that is also appropriate for courses on the psychology of language at both the advanced undergraduate and specialized graduate levels, and for humanities courses on narrative at these levels.

While much has been written on the psycholinguistic and humanities approaches to narrative, the present book provides an integrated approach. The authors, Sanford, a psychologist with an interest in language processing from both a psychological and neuroscience perspective, and Emmott, a humanities researcher specializing in linguistic aspects of narrative, have worked together for ten years on the project leading to this book, supported primarily by the Arts and Humanities Research Council, and also by the British Academy. We have found it to be a fascinating interchange of ideas, and hope that the rich interdisciplinary insights that this collaboration has given us will also be experienced by our readers.

ANTHONY J. SANFORD
CATHERINE EMMOTT
Glasgow, October 2011

Acknowledgements

This book grew out of the STACS Project (Stylistics, Text Analysis and Cognitive Science). We are grateful to the Arts and Humanities Research Council for providing the principal funding to both authors for this project and also to the British Academy for additional support. Our research assistants Eugene Dawydiak and Lorna Morrow assisted greatly with specific experiments and offered many useful ideas in the discussions we had about this research, as did visiting scientists Yuki Fukuda and Yuko Hijikata. Much of the fundamental work on reference and depth of processing was funded by various grants to Sanford from the Economic and Social Research Council.

Other colleagues, students, friends and family gave us help and support in the writing of the book, for which we are very grateful. Invaluable feedback on various drafts came from Jason Bohan, Ruth Filik, Agnes Marszalek, the late Derek Mathews, Linda Moxey and Alison Sanford. We have also benefited considerably from input relating to specific sections from Marc Alexander, Sally Cochrane, Heather Ferguson, Hartmut Leuthold, Jo Molle, Jessica Price, Christoph Scheepers, Fiona Smith, Patrick Sturt and Bo Yao. Other previous collaborators, especially Simon Garrod and Asifa Majid, have had a strong influence. Encouragement, inspiration and, in some cases, significant practical assistance came from Wendy Anderson, Jan Auracher, Pascal Belin, Lars Bernaerts, Marisa Bortolussi, Jekaterina Bragina, Joe Bray, Michael Burke, John Corbett, Maja Djikic, Paul Emmott, Monika Fludernik, Joanna Gavins, Richard Gerrig, Art Glenberg, Art Graesser, Frank Hakemulder, Geoff Hall, David Herman, Michael Hoey, Lesley Jeffries, Christian Kay, Bill Louw, Max Louwerse, Michael MacMahon, Dan McIntyre, David Miall, Ruth Page, Alan Palmer, Elizabeth Robertson, the late Mary Ellen Ryder, Ted Sanders, Elena Semino, Yeshayahu Shen, Mick Short, Paul Simpson, Jeremy Smith, Rachel Smith, Gerard Steen, Peter Stockwell, Michael Toolan, Jos van Berkum, Willie van Peer, Peter Verdonk, Katie Wales, Judit Zerkowitz, Rolf Zwaan and Sonia Zyngier. We are very grateful to Andrew Stewart, in particular for suggesting that change detection might be used in the context of reading. Many others from learned societies, particularly AMLaP, IGEL, PALA, and ST&D, gave us much useful feedback. We also thank

Alison Bennett, Janet Hampson, Sheena McGill and Pauline Maridor for administrative support, and Marc Alexander and Flora Edmonds for technical support. We are very grateful to Andrew Mathews for reading the full final manuscript, providing fresh and incisive commentary, and also for assisting with the compilation of the bibliography and index. We also wish to thank Anna Oxbury for her diligent and thoughtful copy-editing, the anonymous reviewers who read chapters on behalf of Cambridge University Press, and our editors Andrew Winnard, Sarah Green, Elizabeth Spicer and Christina Sarigiannidou for their guidance.

Finally, we owe a major debt to our partners, Alison Sanford and Andrew Mathews, for providing continued help, support and encouragement while we were writing the book.

1 Narrative and the Rhetorical Processing Framework

The overall goal of this book is to specify the kinds of psychological mechanisms that support the comprehension of narrative. In this chapter, we lay the basis for examining these mechanisms in the rest of the book. An initial question for any approach has to be: what is narrative? As we shall see, there are many opinions about this, but it is possible to specify a relatively simple set of basic features which are generally characteristic of narratives. Following this, we provide an overview of our psychological model, the Rhetorical Processing Framework, indicating how it brings together various phenomena that constitute how we come to understand narrative. In particular, our interest is in the role of stylistic devices that writers use for rhetorical purposes and we investigate the range of mental processes that these devices bring about. This framework is fully explained and developed in subsequent chapters.

Conceptions of narratives

What is a minimal narrative?

Many narrative researchers attempt to specify minimum conditions for what would count as a narrative. Although the exact format of these conditions may differ, there is some consensus that the following factors should be present (e.g., Carroll, 2001; Herman, 2009; Toolan, 2001):

- Events are represented in the text, and/or can be inferred.
- Events or states of affairs are generally chronologically ordered.
- Earlier events or states of affairs contribute causally to later events.

Many narratologists argue that two or more events are necessary for a text to be a narrative, as above, but some regard a single event as sufficient (see Ryan, 2007, for a survey).

Given these three criteria, it is possible to make a basic distinction between some examples of narrative text and non-narrative text, as in (1) and (2):

(1)   Snowball now gave the signal for the charge. He himself dashed straight for Jones. Jones saw him coming, raised his gun, and fired. The pellets scored bloody streaks along Snowball's back, and a sheep dropped dead.

                                      (Orwell (1951). *Animal Farm*, p. 38)

(2)   the neuron (also called a *nerve cell*) consists of several parts: the soma, the dendrites, and the axon. The inside of the neuron is separated from the outside by the limiting skin, the *neuronal membrane*, which lies like a circus tent on an intricate internal scaffolding, giving each part of the cell its special three-dimensional appearance.

              (Bear, Connors, & Paradiso (2007). *Neuroscience: Exploring the Brain*,
                                      p. 28, Bear et al.'s italics)

In the narrative text in (1), there are events and one may assume some temporal sequence, even if the events overlap. Causal relations can also be inferred. Jones shoots *because* he sees Snowball charging, and *in conse-quence*, Snowball is injured. The sheep has died *as a result of* the shooting. In contrast, the expository text in (2) simply provides descriptions with no events being reported.

While both texts require links between the ideas being expressed to be inferred, it is particular links and particular kinds of ideas that supposedly typify narratives. This immediately raises processing questions. How are events recognized and understood? How are relations between events inferred? These issues will be discussed extensively in Chapter 2, which provides a description of psychological research on these topics.

Other typical features of narrative

The minimal specification of features is just that: an attempt at determining the absolute minimum requirements for sequences of clauses to be defined as a narrative. But when we consider a wide range of full narrative texts, other features are evident, and raise many issues regarding how the reader processes narrative. These typical features of narratives include the following:

- Events tend to be specific rather than generic, with references to specific entities and typically some specific spatio-temporal settings (e.g., Ryan, 2007; Fludernik, 2009; Herman, 2009). In a prototypical narrative we might read *Louise ate three eggs that morning*, where the eggs are specific ones, and it is specifically Louise who did the eating. By contrast, in the case of a recipe, for example, *Take three eggs* is a generic statement, in that any three eggs will do, and who is taking them is unspecified.
- Readers feel as if they have entered a different world, as if they are 'immersed experiencers' (Zwaan, 2004; see also Gerrig, 1993). For a fictional world, this will be quite distinct from the real world to different

degrees depending on the type of story, hence there is a varying degree of counterfactuality (Ryan, 1991). Even in an (auto)biographical narrative, there is usually a sense of stepping into a world removed from the reader's current everyday situation.

These features raise the question of how readers set up counterfactual worlds. How do they relate them to reality, and what effects are created? A really substantial issue is what are the processes of narrative immersion? How do we go from words on a page to experiences in a specific context? Other typical features of narratives are:

- People or personified entities are involved in the events (e.g., Ryan, 2007; Herman, 2009).
- The people or personified entities experience the world around them, with their moment-by-moment thoughts, feelings and sensory perceptions being presented at some point in the story (e.g., Emmott, 1997; Fludernik, 1996).

These points raise many questions, but most notably, how do the experiences of others manifest in the mind of the reader?

The *Animal Farm* extract in (1) fulfils these additional criteria. A fictional world is set up with specific characters, settings and events. The characters, although mostly animals, are at least partially personified. They experience the world, reacting according to the situation (implying thoughts), and, in the novel as a whole, they clearly have feelings about things.

These additional features provide a means of distinguishing narratives from other texts by going beyond the criteria of sequentiality and causality. Hence, in an expository text or a recipe, there may be a sequence of processes, without the focus being on the experiences of people as we would expect in a narrative. However, these additional features serve to show the difficulty in defining narrative per se. Different narratologists hold different views on what might be classed as a narrative. Ryan (2007, p. 28) argues for viewing narratives as 'a fuzzy set allowing variable degrees of membership, but centred on prototypical cases that everybody recognizes as stories'.

Another feature that some but not all narratologists hold to be important is:

- A narrative has a narrator.

Sometimes a narrator may be part of the text itself, having a 'presence' in the narrative. This is clearest when the narrator has a distinct personality, perhaps having opinions about the events in the text, and about the characters. Nevertheless, some narratives have no obvious narrator, which makes it difficult to argue for this feature being essential (unless we say that the very existence of a narrative implies that it must have been narrated). A further key feature is:

- A narrative tells a story.

This of course begs the question of what is a story, which we shall discuss shortly. A narrative might, in general terms, be classed as telling a story when it is eventful in the sense that something unusual and interesting happens (Hühn, 2009, 2010).

Taking all these issues into account, the overall picture that emerges from narratologists is that there are a variety of typical features that correspond to everyday notions of narrative. They do not all have to be present, but typically at least some of them are.

A final definitional issue concerns two ways in which the term 'narrative' may be used. In the example from *Animal Farm*, we examined a sequence of clauses for their narrative properties: here, the label 'narrative' is being used for describing types of local connection in a short text extract. At another level, though, the whole novel can be classed as a narrative. The global label 'narrative' can apply even when a text contains other types of clause (e.g., descriptions), if the text is primarily structured around narrative events and/or tells a story.

One of the practical consequences of the diversity of text types within full narrative texts is that to understand how stretches of text cohere, and the effects they have on readers, we need to look at text processing over a wide range of text types. In this book, we shall present a broad-ranging discussion of narrative processing including examples with prototypical event sequences, and other forms, such as descriptions, and the speech of characters.

What is a story?

Linguists and anthropologists have noted that within a variety of cultures, there are conventions that are often upheld in what is in a story (e.g., Colby, 1973; Lakoff, 1972; Propp, 1968). Narratologists have also utilized these ideas, in so-called 'structuralist narratology' (e.g., Barthes, 1977; Greimas, 1983; both first published in 1966). In the 1970s, these observations generated some interest and excitement amongst cognitive psychologists and computer scientists (e.g., Rumelhart, 1975; Thorndyke, 1977). What properties and structures are stories viewed as having in these accounts? Essentially, the idea of these researchers is that a story consists of the following components (based on Thorndyke's (1977) formalism):

- *Setting* (establishing main character(s), location and time).
- *Theme* (consisting of a goal for the main character(s) to achieve, possibly preceded by some specified event(s) which may justify it).
- *Plot* (one or more episodes, in which actions are performed in an attempt to meet the goal or sub-goals; realizing these may be temporarily thwarted by events that block these realizations, possibly leading to further sub-goals and additional attempts).

- *Resolution* (the realization of some event that satisfies the main goal leading to a state – e.g., a satisfactory outcome).

In the past there has been considerable debate about whether a formal version of a story structure (a 'story grammar' or 'story schema') (e.g., Rumelhart, 1975) could be used to distinguish narratives from other types of text. This idea has met with much criticism in terms of the rigid application of a rule-based system to narratives, particularly to more complex narratives (e.g., Garnham, 1983; Toolan, 2001). There is, nevertheless, a key point behind this work which still has relevance to current research. This is that many stories incorporate problem-solving patterns (Hoey, 1983, 2001). Problem-solving arises as protagonists attempt to meet goals. The characters' goals drive the plot forward producing a 'dynamics of plot' (Ryan, 1991, p. 124). This dynamic opens up the possibilities of interest and suspense. An important processing question in relation to story structure, which we will consider in this book, is how precisely do interest and suspense come about?

The Rhetorical Processing Framework

The basic idea in this book is that narrative comprehension can be understood in terms of mental processing operations. This is a fundamental tenet of psychology. Processing operations are things that have to happen in order for something to come about. Our concern in this book is primarily with the *nature* of these processes, but we do not aim to describe in detail the *sequence* of operations that have to take place. The latter would be necessary for a full process model, but our emphasis here is on understanding the processes themselves rather than on exactly how they combine. While there has been a good deal written by psychologists about language understanding in general (see Chapter 2 of the present book), we shall use the typical features of narrative outlined above to explore how processing operations might be derived that could explain narrative comprehension more specifically. In addition, we shall seek to show, by reference to relevant empirical work, how various stylistic devices employed by writers for rhetorical purposes serve to influence processing in ways that correspond to certain of the intuitions of analysts in the humanities.

The framework we propose we term the *Rhetorical Processing Framework*. It encompasses three main strands:

- *Fundamental Scenario-Mapping Theory*: the basic processes by which interpretations can be made at all, including inferences about events and characters, the use of everyday 'scenario' (situational) knowledge to make these inferences, and the representation of counterfactual worlds.

- The *Rhetorical Focussing Principle*: how attention is rhetorically controlled by the writer's style, what it means psychologically to control attention in this way, and how the resulting selectivity determines the types of mental representations constructed, in a way that is central to understanding a text.
- *Experientiality*: the importance of embodiment and emotion as a basis for experiencing narrative, and how this is contained and manipulated by writers in accordance with the Rhetorical Focussing Principle.

Let us briefly outline the three strands further, and use this as a guide to what follows in the rest of the book.

Fundamental Scenario-Mapping Theory

In our first strand, in Chapters 2 and 3, we consider what it means to understand a piece of language at a fundamental level. In Chapter 2, this includes a discussion of inferences in general, and the notion that people set up a model of the underlying situation that is being presented in a text. Following Sanford and Garrod's (1981, 1998) Scenario-Mapping Theory, we discuss the idea that much understanding is accomplished by relating what is being said to background knowledge, and that such knowledge is stored as situation-specific information. It is the boundaries of a particular scenario that limit comprehension and explanation, since otherwise too many inferences would be generated. In Chapter 3, we extend the discussion to include multiple levels, looking at counterfactuals, so central to setting up narrative worlds in general, and, more specifically, to figurative language, a key aspect of all forms of communication including narrative.

The Rhetorical Focussing Principle

The second strand of our framework is to suggest a mechanism of rhetorical focussing to direct the reader's attention. This is a straightforward principle: typically, writers want readers to think about something (call it X), and not about something else instead (call it Y). This is fundamentally important because it is always possible to make a large number of inferences on the basis of a text, yet only a few of those might be relevant or important from the writer's perspective. Many different stylistic devices can be used to achieve such selectivity. We introduce the notion of selectivity in Chapter 4, specifying not only some of these devices, but showing how selectivity is realized. In particular, we introduce the idea of shallow and deep semantic processing in Chapter 5: changing the degree of rhetorical focussing results in changes in the extent to which a text is processed and how much detail of the semantics is used. The Rhetorical Focussing Principle is a psychological version of the humanities ideas of foregrounding and defamiliarization, in which unusual stylistic items are forefronted in attention, and receive a different, more thorough than usual, analysis by readers. These ideas, which we will look at in more detail in the next few chapters, are cornerstones of many peoples' conception of literature, and we believe that the Rhetorical Focussing Principle gives a useful experimental base for these ideas.

The experiential aspect of narrative comprehension

The ideas that narratives lead to 'immersion' in a story world and 'experience' are covered in our third strand, and at first sight these are difficult ideas for a processing framework to deal with. How could a 'mechanism' mediate feelings and images? We will see that it can. Recent work on embodiment in psychology has shown that descriptions of actions and perceptions can create motor and perceptual reactions in readers, while work in neuroscience is showing how this comes to be – effectively by using related parts of the brain. This work is interesting because it is quite closely related to the notion of (having) imagery, but is considerably broader in scope, since it is multi-sensory. We discuss these ideas thoroughly in Chapter 6, ending with the observation that embodiment effects are almost certainly modulated by rhetorical focussing, in the form of different styles of narrative presentation.

Building on the framework

The Rhetorical Processing Framework is applicable to a number of other important phenomena. One major area concerns perspectives in writing, which we examine in Chapter 7. We look particularly at how narratives written with first, second, and third person pronouns can have different effects on readers. For example, when a narrator makes use of the pronoun *you*, it may create a greater sense of involvement for readers. What does 'a greater sense of involvement' mean and can it be demonstrated empirically? Another perspective issue is that of direct and indirect speech. For centuries it has been thought that direct speech, like *Harry said 'I am going to play Quidditch'* is somehow more vivid than the indirect *Harry said that he was going to play Quidditch*. Again, ideas like 'vividness', which seem intuitively to have something to do with the attention-grabbing possibilities of direct speech and seem to provide readers with a more immediate experience, find a natural analysis in terms of the Rhetorical Processing Framework.

Another important experiential issue is the role of emotion when reading narrative, addressed in Chapter 8. This important topic ranges from understanding the emotions of *characters*, through to the role of suspense as a motivator of interest in *readers*. From a cognitive perspective, everyone knows that if a character is goaded in an insulting way by another character, then he or she might become angry or upset. This sort of *knowledge* is purely cognitive – it has nothing to do with feelings directly. On the other hand, there is an oft-made assumption that for a well-written novel the reader may actually *feel* the characters' anger or upset. This is very different from purely cognitive 'knowledge' about emotions, and can be addressed within an experiential account. When issues such as moral values, judgements, moral indignation and ideas of justice are considered, questions arise as to how automatically readers bring such values and responses into play whilst reading, how such issues influence perspectives taken, and, indeed, how they might alter how we actually feel about a character's actions, and the character themselves. These issues raise interesting questions about how writers can depict social situations in such a way as to manipulate the reactions of readers in order to achieve their desired effects. This is a major topic in social neuroscience and we shall report on selected research relevant to narrative comprehension. Finally in Chapter 8, suspense, curiosity and surprise are crucial to creating interest in many types of narrative, and have received some empirical study but need further exploration using psychological techniques in the future.

In Chapter 9 we look at the broader role of narratives in society. To what extent can narratives provide a means of persuading people, a way of changing their attitudes and beliefs? We use the term 'rhetoric' in the book overall to describe the general effects of stylistic features, but the classical sense of the term relates directly to persuasion. It has been suggested that foregrounding devices and methods of creating a feeling of immersion in a story and emotional involvement might increase such persuasive effects. If this is the case, then such effects are controlled by rhetorical focussing. We survey some of the research on this topic, examining how far this idea is supported by empirical research. Another question is whether narratives, in particular literary narratives, have beneficial effects such as making readers more sympathetic to other human beings, creating better people. Again we present some of the relevant empirical research, but these issues are far from settled.

Overall, the Rhetorical Processing Framework provides a number of ways of looking at a broad range of processing issues, including the most fundamental aspects of text comprehension, the attention-controlling properties of foregrounding devices, the experiential aspects of narratives, and the communicative functions of stories in terms of their abilities to entertain and/or persuade. Our central aim is to highlight how stylistic devices are used rhetorically by writers, and the way in which these devices are processed by readers.

2   Fundamentals of text processing

A key question underlying how narrative is understood is, how can *any* text be understood at all? More specifically, we can ask: How does a reader take information from individual sentences and from this material construct a mental model of connected narrative events? How is the content of the text interpreted, how are inferences made, how is general knowledge of the world linked to the narrative as it unfolds, and how is a coherent representation formed in the memory of the reader? This chapter contains an overview of how cognitive psychologists have tackled these questions, and later in the chapter we relate this psychological account to the key humanities issue of narrative interest.

Representing text in the mind

Propositions, text and meaning

An early way of representing text in the mind was as propositions, exemplified by the work of Kintsch and his colleagues (e.g., Kintsch, 1974; Kintsch & van Dijk, 1978), although, as we shall see later in this chapter, the account is not really adequate.

The basic claim is that a proposition captures meaning because it is the minimum assertion that is in principle verifiable as true or false. Consider the sentence *The lion is roaring*. This is in principle verifiable, by listening to the lion. Now consider the sentence *The lion is roaring loudly*. It is easy to see that this example consists of two propositions: the lion is roaring, and the roaring is loud. A slight increase in complexity to three propositions is possible by a simple change: *The huge lion is roaring loudly*.

A proposition consists of a predicator and one or more arguments. The predicator is something that requires further information, provided by the argument(s). The convention, following Kintsch, is to write *The lion is roaring* as a string (ROAR, LION). In this case the predicator (ROAR) needs further information about the entity doing the roaring: it requires the argument (LION). If the lion is *roaring loudly*, then it is the manner LOUDLY that is the predicator, since it prompts us to ask what action is being done in this way: hence in this case ROAR is the argument. So, the two propositions in Kintsch's formulation would be (ROAR, LION) & (LOUDLY, ROAR). Where there are two or more arguments, the predicator shows the relation between them, so for *The lion eats the mouse*, the string is (EAT, LION, MOUSE) with the predicator EAT linking the two arguments LION and MOUSE.

Propositions may be considered the smallest units in which ideas are represented. Even our very basic discussion up to now enables some psychological findings to be described and understood. First, the time taken to read sentences is correlated with the number of propositions that they contain, such that even sentences with similar numbers of words will be read more slowly if they contain more propositions (Kintsch & Keenan, 1973). This straightforward result suggests that readers set up each proposition as a separate piece of information in memory as they read. The second finding is that what is remembered of a text is a function of the structure of the propositions making it up. Consider the propositional pair (ROAR, LION) & (LOUDLY, ROAR). If this sentence was part of longer text, so that memory for it was not perfect, it is more likely that people would remember the simple idea that the lion is roaring than the extra idea that it is roaring loudly. This is because the manner of the lion roaring is dependent on the fact that the lion is roaring – it is a detail and less 'core' to the meaning of the sentence. In reality, experiments carried out to demonstrate this have typically used more complex texts (Kintsch, Kozminsky, Stretby, McKoon, & Keenan, 1975; Kintsch & van Dijk, 1978), but the findings are as we have portrayed them.

These findings offer some support for the idea that people break down text into propositions, that the complexity of a text depends upon the number of propositions contained as a function of the number of words used, and that dependent propositions are less central to understanding than less dependent ones.

Inferences and rhetorical relations

Propositions represent a superficially handy way of breaking down a text into meaningful units, but do not in themselves provide a theory of meaning and interpretation, something that is fundamental to our interest. We shall discuss other approaches that we suggest offer a more satisfactory psychological theory of interpretation shortly, when we introduce Scenario-Mapping Theory (e.g., Sanford & Garrod, 1981, 1998). For the moment, we shall continue looking at the general idea that connections between propositions can be used to capture the underlying structure of texts. The starting point for this is the requirement to *infer* relationships amongst propositions. Not everything that makes up the interpretation of a text is given in the text itself, and so inferences have to be made. Consider the following:

(1a)   Martin crossed the busy road without looking both ways.
(1b)   The ambulance was too late to save his life.

Quite clearly, some process of inference is needed to decide that *his life* is Martin's life, and that (1b) is motivated by what happened to Martin as a result of (1a). We use our knowledge that ambulances are used to rescue injured people, and it can be inferred that an ambulance must have been needed in this instance and that Martin must have been injured while crossing the road. Indeed, many other inferences are undoubtedly made. Importantly, although certain inferences are necessary to properly connect the propositions that make up the text, this information is not explicit, but rather has to be established from our general knowledge of the world. What implicit (inferred) relations fill in the gaps in the propositional structure which is meant to be the memory representation of the text? First we shall look at this question, then go on to look at how such information may be made available for inference.

Rhetorical Structure Theory

Often the relationships between propositions can be complex. For instance, either (2a) could be thought of as the cause of (2b), or (2b) could be thought of as being the result of (2a).

(2a)   Simon hadn't eaten for a couple of days.
(2b)   He started to feel weak and disoriented.

Unless readers realize the causal relation, the sentences will not form a coherent whole. Understanding such relations between different propositions has been a key goal in Artificial Intelligence. The quest after a systematic way of thinking about the problem has led to a huge literature on the notion of coherence.

An important development in this area is Rhetorical Structure Theory (RST) (Mann & Thompson, 1988; see also Hoey, 1983, and Winter, 1977, for a similar framework). RST identifies a set of *rhetorical relations*, that are sufficient to explain the relationships between elements of a text (clauses, sentences, or longer stretches of text) termed *text spans*, thereby linking propositions or sets of propositions by corresponding *relational propositions*. Part of the RST analysis is the specification of what the writer intends by using a specific relation. Consider the *evidence* relation as an example. When evidence is provided the 'satellite' supplies support to increase belief in the nucleus. Consider the example *Andrew thought that Jennifer had left the house* (nucleus). *Her coat had gone* (satellite). The fact that Jennifer's coat is no longer there provides evidence of her departure.

It is not our intention to elaborate on all the posited rhetorical relations, but a short list of selected items, based on Mann and Thompson (1988), gives the general idea:

- *Condition*: the realization of the situation presented in the nucleus depends upon the realization of the situation presented in the satellite.
- *Purpose*: the satellite presents some unrealized situation, and the nucleus presents an activity which realizes the situation.
- *Volitional cause*: the nucleus is some situation, and the satellite is another situation which causes the nucleus, through someone's volitional action.

For a summary of a range of posited rhetorical relations, see the website www.sfu.ca/rst/. Taboada and Mann (2006) and Bateman and Delin (2006) also provide useful overviews. In practice, there is no unambiguously applicable set of rules (i.e., no algorithm) that enables the rhetorical relations to be identified. Their identification is done through human analysts applying standard reasoning to a text in order to try to derive the ways in which parts of it are connected.

RST is really conceived of as a way of analysing text and uncovering the relationships that might provide a good characterization of common patterns in text. What has this to do with human understanding? Well, it might be supposed that when we read, we actually establish these rhetorical relations, even if we don't (normally) have names for them all. Indeed, some rhetorical relations are recognizable from cue expressions (Hoey, 1983; Knott & Sanders, 1998; Sanders, Spooren, & Noordman, 1992, 1993; Winter, 1977). Thus, the *condition* relation may be signalled by the use of *if*, as in *Adam will get stomach ache if he eats that crab apple*. Indeed, the whole notion of cue expressions is based on the idea that they indicate likely rhetorical relations, and ways of indicating local and global structure in text. Whether directly through cue expressions, or indirectly through complex inference, it is generally considered the case that the identification of relations amongst segments of text is key to understanding any text. However, although rhetorical relations play an important part in the *description* of how a text is structured, just how these relationships are *recognized* is a psychological question of processing.

Psychological studies of text-driven inference

As discussed, inferences involve the reader in using knowledge of the world in order to fill in gaps left by the text. Some inferences simply *have* to be made in order to understand most aspects of a message, in line with the discussion of RST, and are for this reason generally known as *necessary inferences*. Necessary inferences arise because of a gap in the coherence of a text. These contrast with inferences that do not need to be made, but which are merely invited by what is being read, so-called *elaborative inferences*. For instance, if we read *There was a thick layer of snow on the ground*, we might infer that it is winter. However, this is simply an elaboration, not a necessary inference for linking propositions. These elaborative inferences have been considered as basically filling out the picture, although such a view scarcely does justice to the problem of comprehension, as we shall see. We begin by illustrating these inference types.

Necessary inferences: linking elements of text

In their now classic experiments, Haviland and Clark (1974) investigated necessary inferences, or, in their terminology, bridging inferences, so called because they form necessary bridges between elements of the presented discourse. In particular, they studied anaphoric reference, the mechanism by which a word is seen to refer to something introduced earlier in a text. An example of their materials is shown below where *The beer* in (3b) is assumed to be part of the previously mentioned *picnic supplies* in (3a):

(3a)   We checked the picnic supplies.
(3b)   The beer was warm.

Haviland and Clark used a method of self-paced reading, in which participants read the materials one sentence at a time, pressing a button when they had understood each sentence. By this means, it is possible to measure how long a person spends reading and understanding each sentence. This measure is an indicator of the ease or difficulty of understanding a sentence in various contexts. Haviland and Clark found that (3b) took measurably more time to process following (3a) than did the same sentence (shown below as (4b)) following (4a) where there is an explicit antecedent (i.e., *the beer* is mentioned in (4a)):

(4a)   We got the beer out of the trunk.
(4b)   The beer was warm.

They concluded that to understand (3b) in the context of (3a), it is necessary to infer that the beer is part of the picnic supplies, an inference made on the basis of knowledge of what might constitute picnic supplies. In contrast, when (4b) follows (4a), *the beer* has already been mentioned, and so no such inference has to be made.

The picture appeared simple in that these results confirmed that bridging inferences were made, and at the same time, this took a measurable amount of time (see also Garrod & Sanford, 1977, and Singer, 1979). However, there turned out to be cases where the time to make such inferences could not be measured. For instance, Garrod and Sanford (1981) found that when a highly predicted instrument of an action was left implicit, and subsequently referred to by a definite description, there was no increase in reading time compared to a case where it was explicitly mentioned. Thus there was no difference in the reading time for the same sentence in (5b) and (6b), following (5a) or (6a):

(5a)   Keith was giving a lecture in London. He was driving there overnight.
(5b)   The car had recently been overhauled.

(6a)   Keith was giving a lecture in London. He was taking his car there overnight.
(6b)   The car had recently been overhauled.

Clearly, to understand (5b) following (5a), it is necessary to draw the inference that the car is what was used to drive to London, and yet the inference seemed to take no measurable time. However, in a similar study, Singer (1979) found that there was a time difference. For instance, he showed that the same sentence in (7b) and (8b) was read more slowly after (7a) than after (8a):

(7a)   The boy cleared the snow from the stairs.
(7b)   The shovel was heavy.

(8a)   The boy cleared the snow with a shovel.
(8b)   The shovel was heavy.

The shovel is a strong possible instrument for clearing snow, and yet a bridging inference time was observed, just as with the earlier work of Haviland and Clark (1974). Why is there a difference from the Garrod and Sanford results? Cotter (1984) used both sets of materials in a single study, and successfully confirmed the difference in the pattern of reading time. The difference appeared to be due to the predictability of the instrument based on the verb: *driving* predicts *car*, but *clearing* does not, by itself, predict *shovel* (see also Harmon-Vukić, Guéraud, Lassonde, & O'Brien, 2009; McRae, Hare, Elman, & Ferretti, 2005).

Results such as these raise an interesting issue: why should some bridging inferences appear to happen very rapidly, so that no measurable time for them is observed? To answer the question, Sanford and Garrod (1981, 1998) put forward the Scenario-Mapping Theory, the idea that texts can evoke substantial representations of situations, and that these representations actually 'contain' the information that represents the bridging inference. It is as though the inference was already made.

Inferences of causality   Making inferences of causality is as necessary for understanding narrative discourse as it is seamless in normal execution. Consider the following pair of sentences:

(9a)   Edward walked near the crumbly edge of the cliff.
(9b)   His body was found down on the beach a day later.

Readers will normally make the standard bridging inferences that the cliff gave way and he fell to his death.

As we saw earlier, causality is at the core of conceptions of how narratives are constructed. Even a single sentence like *The sun came out and the snowman melted* is seen as a causal statement, despite the simple association of clauses suggested by the use of *and*. There is now ample evidence that the time taken to make causal bridging inferences is a function of how obvious the causal relation is. Thus the same sentence in (10b) and (11b) takes less time to read following (10a) than following (11a) (Myers, Shinjo, & Duffy, 1987; see also Keenan, Baillet, & Brown, 1984):

(10a) Tony's friend suddenly pushed him into a pond.
(10b) He walked home, soaking wet, to change his clothes.

(11a) Tony met his friend near a pond in a park.
(11b) He walked home, soaking wet, to change his clothes.

This is prima facie evidence that harder inferential activity takes more time, but more importantly shows that causal inferences are automatically made. Otherwise the difference would not be motivated in any way.

Elaborative inferences

Elaborations have traditionally been thought of as not necessary at all, since they are not strictly required by coherence gaps in the text. Necessary inferences, by contrast, form bridges between ideas distilled from text, and it might be supposed that they only come about when needed. Elaborative inferences have been regarded in two ways. First, as 'filling out the picture' rather than being forced by the need for bridging. Secondly, they have been thought of as providing potentially useful information for future text integration. By making inferences based on plausible predictions of what might be important, it is possible to reduce processing effort later. For this reason, they are sometimes referred to as predictive inferences, or forward inferences.

Consider the following example, taken from McKoon and Ratcliff (1986):

(12) The director and cameraman were ready to shoot close-ups when suddenly the actress fell from the 14th story.

Here, a highly plausible elaborative inference is that the actress died. The inference is not necessary for processing, though it might be argued that it is potentially important to understand sentence (12) in a fuller context. Whether such inferences are made has been tested in a variety of ways, mostly relying on measurements of a phenomenon known as lexical priming. In the present case, lexical priming might be assumed to have occurred if the word *dead* is presented immediately after the sentence and is processed more rapidly than it is after a sentence that does not lead to the 'dead' inference. This is the priming effect. The task given to participants can vary: they may be asked simply to pronounce the word (*naming task*), or to decide whether it is a word or not, where some examples presented would be strings of letters making up non-words, such as *grepe* (*lexical decision task*). Here, priming is judged by participants taking a reduced time to name, or make a lexical decision. Finally, in the *memory probe task*, participants have to decide whether the probe word was presented or not in the preceding sentence. For this task, priming is assessed by a participant taking a longer time to respond *no* to related items that weren't in the preceding sentence (such as *dead*). Priming facilitation has been demonstrated for (12) and similar cases using such methods (see Keenan, Potts, Golding, & Jennings, 1990, and McKoon & Ratcliff, 1990, for methodological discussions).

Such an elaborative inference may turn out to be important for the developing text, or it may not. Keefe and McDaniel (1993), using naming time as a measure and materials from Potts, Keenan, and Golding (1988), found that participants made an elaborative inference that the vase broke after reading (13a). However, if (13a) is followed by (13b), then there is no detectable priming for the probe *broke* after (13b), suggesting that the inference that the vase broke is relatively short-lived:

(13a)   No longer able to control his anger, the husband threw the delicate porcelain vase against the wall.
(13b)   He had been feeling angry for weeks, but had refused to seek help.

In this case, the inference 'broke' was not important for developing a coherent representation of the unfolding text because the focus was on the husband not the vase, and the inference appeared not to persist.

Further work enables the following generalizations to be made. First, the stronger the support for an inference, the more likely it is to be made (Cook, Limber, & O'Brien, 2001; Murray, Klin, & Myers, 1993). Secondly, support for an inference can come from anywhere in a text. Cook et al. (2001) showed that when a sentence leading to an inference is introduced, this may combine with earlier support for the inference in determining that the inference is actually made. Guéraud, Tapiero, and O'Brien (2008) made a similar observation, but also showed that the earlier information could subtly influence the nature of the inference made. The materials introduced a protagonist, followed by a character-trait elaboration in which two alternatives were used. One was a primary character trait, for instance, someone was portrayed at some length as having a short temper and likely to act uncontrollably. In the alternative-trait case, a different aspect of the person was emphasized at some length, for instance, that he or she had had shoulder surgery, and lifting anything caused pain. This was followed by inference-evoking material. For example, in one story, at the restaurant where the person worked, a customer was very rude about his spaghetti to the protagonist.

In the next sentence, she lifted the plate of spaghetti above his head. This was followed by a word-naming task. The words in question in the example were *dump* and *pain*. It was found that the short-tempered trait information caused *dump* to be primed (presumably related to the inference that the protagonist might dump the spaghetti over the customer's head), while, in contrast, the shoulder-surgery trait information caused priming of *pain*. So, the earlier information had an effect, but, most interestingly, the effect was selective. This demonstrates a straightforward control of what specific inferences are made as a result of having encountered the earlier information.

The Guéraud et al. (2008) study suggests that strong supporting contexts lead to more tightly specified inferences. Note that tests of inferences based on priming require specific words to be presented as tests for specific inferences. For instance, in example (13a/b), the probe word *broke* is used to test whether the inference was drawn that the vase broke. Notice that other words would fit the bill quite well too, such as *damaged, shattered, smashed*, as well as consequences such as *shards*. It seems plausible that *broke* is a good probe, but it is only plausible. It is not necessarily the case that the mental representation of what happened to the vase is that the word *broke* comes to mind. In fact, there is work to suggest that the specificity of inferential activity is a function of contextual forces in the writing itself. In one study, Lassonde and O'Brien (2009) examined the specificity of elaborative inference with a variety of texts. In one experiment, they used fairly long texts. It was specified that a boy, Jimmy, new to the district, was playing with some new friends. The kids were throwing rocks, and Jimmy hit the door of a new car. Two target words were used as priming probes: *dent* and *damage*. Using a naming task, priming occurred for both words, compared with a control condition. This shows that one should not think of the elaborative inference as being for one specific word, but rather for a more general conception of some sort. However, it might be expected that the specificity of any inference made would depend upon the specificity of the text leading to that inference. If the concept of 'dent' was made more salient, then perhaps only the probe *dent* would be primed.

In a subsequent experiment, Lassonde and O'Brien (2009) set out to examine this idea. They compared the original passages with ones where there was elaborated writing about the car, emphasizing, for instance, it was *brand new* and *didn't have any scratches* and had *very soft metal that would bend without much pressure*. With these elaborations, priming only occurred for the probe *dent*, and not for the probe *damage*, suggesting that a more specified inference had been made.

This work is potentially very important for understanding the interface between the nature of narrative and processing. Writers write what they do in order to emphasize certain things over other things, in effect, to cause specific inferences to be drawn while suppressing others. Exploring how writers of narrative carry out particular acts of writing to lead to specific inferences is an area ripe for enquiry. While it is central to both humanities approaches and to psychological process models of how comprehension works, bringing these disciplinary areas together is still very much in its infancy.

Interim summary: necessity and elaboration

The findings from psychological work are interesting in a number of ways. As we have seen, there is evidence that sometimes necessary inferences appear to take up measurable time, while in other cases they do not (e.g., Garrod & Sanford, 1981). This strongly suggests that in some cases, reading about a context may cause a representation to be set up in the mind that already contains the 'inference', information that will enable the integration of a subsequent sentence into a mental representation. This idea is central to the development of Scenario-Mapping Theory (Sanford & Garrod, 1981, 1998), to be discussed shortly. This idea stands in stark contrast to the notion that necessary inferences are only made because a gap in coherence has been encountered.

A second point of interest is the fact that elaborative inferences fill out the picture rather than being necessary for coherence. The experimental work discussed suggests that such inferences require quite strong contextual support in order to be made, suggesting that not just any plausible inference will be made for every sentence that we encounter. Indeed, from the perspective of writing style, it invites a proper assessment of how what a writer writes leads to particular, focussed, inferences.

Finally, the idea of elaboration clearly relates to the idea that understanding requires that we access the 'fuller picture' surrounding any depictions at a propositional level. It is this richness that we believe to be the characteristic of language understanding in general. In the next sections, we describe some converging ideas that enable a better conception of how interpretation takes place and meaning is established.

Mental models in discourse comprehension

We now move beyond the idea that meaning may be captured by a series of propositions based on the text and a handful of linking inferences. One fundamentally important idea of how we comprehend any aspect of the world is that we form a 'mental model' of the current situation. Craik (1943) provided the first modern statement of this idea. Later, two books were published in the same year with the title *Mental Models* (Gentner & Stevens, 1983; Johnson-Laird, 1983).

To see how mental models go beyond the simple conception of necessary inferences and single elaborative inferences, consider the following example, adapted from Johnson-Laird (1983, p. 261; see also Goodwin & Johnson-Laird, 2008):

(14)   Andrew, Bill and Claire are sitting at a table. Andrew is to the left of Bill, and Bill is to the left of Claire. On which side of Claire is Andrew?

At first sight, this appears to be a straightforward problem of transitive inference, and the most typical answer given is that Andrew is to the left of Claire. Johnson-Laird's point with this example is that the answer depends upon the mental model adopted by the reader. Thus, the answer that Andrew is to Claire's left is only true if they are sitting on the side of a relatively straight (e.g., square or rectangular) table. If, on the contrary, the table is a round one, then Andrew may in fact be to the *right* of Claire (i.e., if they are positioned all round the table). (This is easy to see by making simple drawings.) So, by simple knock-down argument, mental models of some sort are a reality. Johnson-Laird (1983) provides a broad description of the importance of mental models in thinking, reasoning and language comprehension.

The purpose here is to show how the model that a reader builds determines the answer: the answer is not in the propositions of the text itself. Indeed, for communication to be effective, the writer of a narrative must ensure that the right mental models are formed in the minds of readers at the right time. Forming the wrong one would act as a block to communication. This is a crucial point for explanations of discourse understanding. Following the mental models idea, the question becomes one of what linguistic cues help determine which mental model to adopt, and how mental models might result from the text itself.

As a general account of understanding, the idea of using mental models is very useful, explaining limits to understanding, as well as how understanding is facilitated. In Gentner and Stevens' (1983) edited volume, a range of articles added to this idea by examining human intuitive reasoning in relation to the physical world. For example, Gentner and Gentner (1983) discuss how everyday ideas about the solar system can be used to model the structure of the atom. The relationships within one domain (e.g., gravity holding the planets in orbit) can be used as an analogue of another (e.g., an analogous force from the nucleus of an atom holding the electrons in place). Whole conceptions are used as the basis for understanding new things. Gentner and Gentner also examine how different models might provide different ways of looking at the world, such as when people understand electricity in terms of how water flows or how a crowd moves. They show how the type of model applied can affect the types of inferences drawn.

Mental models explain how one piece of knowledge can be used to stand for another. This notion of a mental model as a mapping of one domain onto another is knowledge-rich. The importance of this richness is discussed by Sanford and Moxey (1999) in their paper 'What are mental models made of?' They claim that a mental model *is* the result of attempting a mapping of elements of a language utterance or a problem description onto pre-existing knowledge representations. This in fact is the central idea behind Scenario-Mapping Theory, which we consider to be a basic notion for discourse comprehension and will now look at in some detail.

The importance of world knowledge:
Scenario-Mapping Theory

Around the same time as Johnson-Laird was developing his ideas about mental models, Sanford and Garrod (1981) described the idea of Scenario-Mapping Theory, and this theory has been in steady development since. The basic suggestion was that mental representations of a discourse are formed by relating what is being read to a situation that the reader knows something about already. Sanford and Garrod see the mapping of language onto situation-specific knowledge as being the mental model itself. The mapping achieves several things. First, it induces a feeling of basic under-standing, since what is being described is grounded in a familiar situation. So, if someone writes *The handsome prince was at the foot of the princess's tower*, then we can recognize the situation and some of its likely concomitants right away. It is not a mere complex of text-based propositions; it is an interpreted piece of language. Secondly, it brings extra knowledge to bear on the comprehension process, since situations that are already known about are comprised of relevant knowledge. And thirdly, it provides a basis for what we expect to find, and enables deviations to be detected. So, if we find, in the context of a fairy story, that *The handsome prince sat down and lit up a cigarette*, this stands out as unusual, because it cannot be accommodated by existing situational knowledge for that genre.

There are large differences between this theory and other processing accounts of how discourse might be understood. The main difference between the Sanford and Garrod approach and that of others who have made proposals regarding how discourse is comprehended (e.g., Gernsbacher, 1990; Kintsch, 1988, 1998) is in its emphasis on using situation-specific knowledge as a controller of processing. Essentially, the theory posits a process based pri-marily on the use of everyday world knowledge as the core engine of understanding. The other theories certainly recognize a role for such know-ledge, but until recently have not placed so much emphasis on it.

The strongest processing assumption of the Scenario-Mapping Theory is that the reader automatically seeks out a known situation (scenario) to which a text is referring, what Sanford and Garrod termed *primary processing*, leading to basic understanding. Wherever possible, text is mapped onto the scenario. When it cannot be, those aspects of the text that are unmapped set off *secondary processing*, in which a variety of component processes might be recruited, including more complex inferential activity, and a search for alternative scenarios. In this section, we shall elaborate upon these ideas fairly extensively, because they provide a foundation for how text understanding is possible. While nobody can doubt that world knowledge plays a crucial role in understanding, the real psychological issue is how and when that knowledge is used, and how it shapes processing.

A core idea behind this theory is that understanding does not occur through combining the meanings of individual words to derive sentential meaning, but that understanding requires at least some recognition of a situation or situations that constitute the basis for what is written. For instance, according to the theory, if a writer says that *Jeremy drove to London*, in the absence of any other information, a mapping will be made to the usual idea of driving to London, which entails the use of a car, rather than, say, a truck or a bus. In other words, language input is interpreted at what might be called the message level. One of a writer's skills from this point of view is to write in such a way as to cause the reader to retrieve the correct underlying situation, enabling basic understanding, and providing a foundation for further understanding. Basic understanding corresponds to knowing the situation that the writer is using as an anchor for his or her writing, and indeed, we would claim that a *feeling of understanding* occurs in the reader when this happens, rather than a feeling of confusion and consequently actively seeking a meaning. (For a discussion of Scenario-Mapping Theory in relation to broader issues of human understanding, see Sanford, 1987.)

Scenario content: in-filling and extended domains of reference

In-filling   As pointed out in relation to inferences and mental models, no text can be thought of as giving a 'complete' description of a situation or an event. It is always necessary for the comprehender to fill out the details in various ways. Indeed, this is one of the cornerstones of the idea of mental models in general. Consider the now classic example of a script for being a customer at a sit-down restaurant (Schank & Abelson, 1977). Scripts are knowledge structures for stereotypical event sequences. If we read the following, there is no difficulty in understanding it:

(15)   Edward went to the Shalimar for a curry. He only left a small tip.

This fragment is intelligible because leaving a tip is typically part of eating in a restaurant. If we understand the way these two sentences are related, it is only because situation-specific knowledge of what happens at a restaurant is invoked by the reader. The important point is that such script information is accessed during reading (15). One of the consequences of this way of arguing is that people should tend to 'remember' that Edward ate a curry, which (15) does not actually say, simply because the eating stage of a restaurant visit normally occurs before the tip-leaving stage. Early experimental work showed that readers falsely 'recall' events and items that were not in the original text (Bower, Black, & Turner, 1979; Pohl, Colonius, & Thüring, 1985). Effectively, the sentences in (15) invoke situation-specific knowledge of what happens at restaurants, and use it to facilitate comprehension.

In-filling by scenario information is in fact exemplified by many different observations. For example, compare the following sentences (adapted from Sanford & Moxey, 1995):

(16a)   Fred put the wallpaper on the table. Then, without thinking, he rested his coffee cup on it.

(16b)   Fred put the wallpaper on the wall. Then, without thinking, he rested his coffee cup on it.

While (16a) is perfectly acceptable, (16b) is not – it is effectively impossible without slow and complex stretching of the imagination. What is the basis of the difference? Quite clearly, it is because putting wallpaper on a table and putting wallpaper on a wall are quite different, even though, at a propositional level, this difference does not emerge. Rather, by recruiting situation-specific information (scenarios), the fact that *on the table* and *on the wall* allow for different orientations becomes immediately clear. The in-filling process creates different mental models (just as there are at least two interpretations possible with Johnson-Laird's table example discussed earlier).

In-filling and definite reference   Another illustration of how situation-specific knowledge enables comprehension comes from aspects of anaphoric reference. Although definite descriptions are typically used to refer to entities that have already been mentioned, it is well established that entities may be introduced into a discourse *de novo* as though they had already been mentioned (i.e., using a definite description) provided they are strongly implicated by the situation being depicted (e.g., Fraurud, 1990). For instance, a courtroom scenario would enable a definite reference to be made to a lawyer, defendant, judge, etc. simply because these characters are part of the scenario. Garrod and Sanford (1983) predicted that if a definite reference was made to a character who was part of a scenario that was established by the text, then this should be read more rapidly than if the character was not part of the scenario. They used materials like (17a/b), which has two alternative titles. (Note that in this example and subsequent examples in the book, alternatives presented to different participants are shown in curly brackets and our own annotations are shown in square brackets.)

(17a)   *In court*
         Fred was being questioned {by a lawyer}.
         He had been accused of murder.
         The lawyer was trying to prove his innocence. [Target sentence]

(17b)   *Telling a lie*
         Fred was being questioned {by a lawyer}.
         He couldn't tell the truth.
         The lawyer was trying to prove his innocence. [Target sentence]

The *In court* title sets up a court scenario, but the *Telling a lie* title does not. Reading times were taken for the target sentence under all four conditions. The results showed first that target sentence reading times were longer when there was no prior mention of a lawyer than when there was, but only in the *Telling a lie* case. In the *In court* case, there was no discernible difference between the condition where the lawyer had previously been introduced explicitly and the condition where this was not the case. So, when there is no supporting scenario, we obtain the classic bridging inference time effect of Haviland and Clark (1974), while in the case where the situation is specified, we do not: this suggests that 'the lawyer' is a concept that is already available as part of the invoked scenario when a court case is introduced. Results of this type led Sanford and Garrod (1981, 1998) to posit that a scenario associated with the situation provides an *extended domain of reference*, in which entities that are not explicitly 'given' by the text are implicitly given in scenarios. Scenarios contain representations of entities that are typically found in situations, as well as relationships amongst them.

Character-types and scenarios

In scenarios representing interactions with people, the theory assumes that role slots exist for those people. In the example of the courtroom scenario, there are default slots for witnesses and lawyers, which is why they can be referred to without making a full bridging inference. Similarly, for the dining in a restaurant situation (from the customer's perspective), there should be role slots for *customer*, and for *waiter*, and possibly others. Typically, if a *main character* in a story, e.g. Bianca, goes to a restaurant to eat, she is also likely to be involved in other activities in the story. When she is mapped into the customer slot of the scenario, the waiter slot is available for mapping also. However, one important thing to note about a waiter is that the character is typically *scenario-dependent* from the customer's perspective. The waiter, if and when mentioned, will normally play a role restricted to the restaurant scenario itself. The whole *raison d'être* of a waiter is to play a particular role as specified by a scenario, unless that waiter is depicted as doing something of more global significance. In other words, the waiter is scenario-dependent in a way that the customer (Bianca) is not. In experimental tasks where people are invited to produce continuations to a presented vignette, continuations generally include references to main characters, rather than to scenario-dependent characters (Anderson, Garrod, & Sanford, 1983; see Sanford & Garrod, 1981, for a fuller discussion).

Scenarios and scenario mapping: primary processing

As described, the basic *structural* tenet of scenario theory is that much of the information that we store about the world is stored as situation-specific representations. What do we mean by a 'situation'? The essential ingredient is that we break up the world in terms of the way we act on it and it acts on us. So, we learn what to expect in the situation of buying something at a shop. As children, we learn about the basic transaction, and who and what is involved in that situation. We learn to recognize the most mundane situations, like how to greet a friend, and the more exotic, like how to recognize what is entailed in a particular class of problem in mathematics (see Sanford & Moxey, 1999, for a broad discussion of the scope of scenarios). In short, situations are construals of the world that are useful for our human activities. The central idea is that we learn these, we learn variants on themes (like different buying-acts in different sorts of shops), and we learn millions of them.

However, two issues that have often arisen in the context of situation-specific knowledge have been 'is there a scenario for everything?', and if not, 'what happens to information that does not fit a scenario? – does comprehension just fail?' We argue that a person does not have a scenario for everything (otherwise he/she would have no more to learn), but that there is one for every situation learned, and that will be a huge number. In case this sounds like too much, note that we can recognize an enormous number of objects from many angles, a huge recognition problem, so why not be able to recognize an enormous number of situations? We shall assume these structures exist in such large numbers.

Scenario-Mapping Theory therefore assumes that knowledge is represented primarily in useful, useable, situation-specific packages (the scenarios themselves). When a text is encountered, the reader is engaged in an attempt to match the text to a scenario. In the event of success, primary processing occurs, as elements of the text are mapped onto the currently active scenario. This is then used as a means of structuring the process of understanding. In the event of failure, comprehension is more difficult, and secondary processing occurs.

This theory predicts that world knowledge will normally be utilized very rapidly during processing. We examine this idea below, showing how the utilization of situation-specific knowledge is so rapid that it can even interfere with the process of assigning local semantic interpretations to sentences.

How quickly is world knowledge utilized?

The primary processing principle presumes that situation-specific world knowledge is utilized as soon as possible during processing of language input. Many other accounts are agnostic about when such knowledge will be used. As we shall see, world knowledge is not only utilized very rapidly, its recruitment can occur even more rapidly than a local semantic analysis of a sentence, with interesting consequences for interpretation.

Event-related potentials

One source of evidence for the rapid utilization of world knowledge is work on *event-related potentials* (ERPs). ERPs reflect electrical activity in the brain, as measured using electroencephalographic (EEG) methods on the scalps of readers (see Appendix 1 for a brief introduction). Of particular interest to us is an ERP called the N400, a negative-going wave that is maximal about 400 milliseconds (ms) after the onset time at which a word is presented. In classic work, Kutas and Hillyard (1980) presented sentences like (18a/b) to readers.

(18a)   He spread the warm bread with socks.

(18b)   He spread the warm bread with butter.

Sentence (18a) contains a semantic anomaly, in that *socks* fails to fit the restriction on what you would normally spread on bread, while (18b) is non-anomalous. They found that there was a large negative deflection peaking around 400 ms from when the anomalous word was presented compared to the non-anomalous control. This is known as the N400 effect, shown in Figure 2.1, and is related to the semantic processing of words.

Subsequent work showed that N400 effects were not limited to semantic anomalies, but depended on the contextual predictability of a word (Kutas & Hillyard, 1984). The N400 is a well-documented phenomenon, and has been investigated in many settings. For now, the important thing is that it shows effects of context on the immediate processing of words, as they are being read.

In an interesting programme of research, Hagoort, van Berkum and their colleagues have extensively studied how a variety of contextual information types influence the N400. One example comes from van Berkum, Hagoort, and Brown (1999). In this instance, as the reader builds a mental model of the situation, words that don't fit the model are temporarily anomalous. So in (19), *slow* is anomalous, while *quick* is acceptable:

(19)   As agreed upon, Jane was to wake her sister and her brother at five o'clock in the morning. But the sister had already washed herself, and the brother had even got dressed. Jane told the brother that he was exceptionally {slow/quick}.

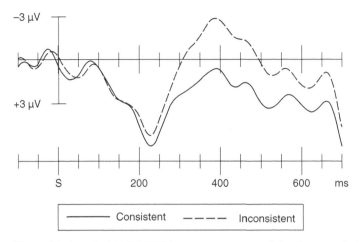

Figure 2.1 A typical N400 ERP in response to a word that is semantically consistent with a context, versus a word that is inconsistent with the context. The latter shows an increased negative voltage peaking at around 400 ms after the point of stimulus onset (S), measured at the Pz electrode. The voltage is measured in microvolts (μV), and, by convention, negative voltage is shown upwards.

There was a greater negativity (N400 effect) for the situation-induced anomaly.

In another study, van Berkum, Brown, Zwitserlood, Kooijman and Hagoort (2005) presented ERP evidence that at least on some occasions, specific words appear to be *predicted* on the basis of context. This experiment used auditory presentation. Consider (20):

(20)   The burglar had no trouble locating the secret family safe. Of course, it was situated behind a big ...

Most people would guess that the next word would be *picture*. In Dutch, the adjective *big* is marked for different genders. Van Berkum et al. (2005) reasoned that if the gender of *big* didn't match that required by the expected noun *picture*, and people were predicting this noun, then there should be a difference between the resultant ERP on the adjective with unmatched gender, and the ERP on the adjective with matched gender. This was indeed the case. Although the effect was not revealed by an N400, there was a different ERP effect, a reliably larger positive-going wave for the unmatched case, in the range 50–250 ms after the acoustic onset of the inconsistent inflection. This is a very early effect, suggesting that a prediction had indeed been made.

Similar results were obtained in a self-paced word-by-word reading study, where the reading time for the prediction-inconsistent adjectives was slower than for the consistent ones (van Berkum et al., 2005, Experiment 3). Other studies have revealed similar effects, though the precise ERP differences vary somewhat from study to study, using different languages and procedures (cf. DeLong, Urbach, & Kutas, 2005; Wicha, Bates, Moreno, & Kutas, 2003; Wicha, Moreno, & Kutas, 2003, 2004). These results rely on prediction occurring, but we have to ask precisely what prediction consists of. At the very least, it is the availability of a concept (and the word describing it) at the scenario level.

Pragmatic normalization and override of local analysis

A different and powerful illustration of the role of global knowledge on processing comes from so-called *pragmatic normalization*. In such cases, knowledge of situations can alter the actual processes of local semantic interpretation, and even parsing. So, there exist some interesting observations that show how local semantic analysis, including assignment of thematic roles, may be overridden and even terminated by the use of pragmatic (world) knowledge. These data therefore raise a problem for a strictly stepwise processing account, in which local interpretations precede more global interpretations. The essential observation of pragmatic normalization is that sentences that are implausible may be falsely recalled in a manner that makes them more plausible. Thus Fillenbaum (1974) observed that unusual sentences such as *John dressed and had a bath* and *Get a move on or you will catch the bus* tended to be falsely recalled in a normalized fashion. In later work, Ferreira (2003) presented people with various sentences, including passive-implausible sentences like *The dog was bitten by the man*. She showed that readers made far more errors in answering questions with this kind of sentence structure than with simple active sentences, confusing the depiction of who did what to whom with the plausible alternative. What is happening here is that the mental representation of the normal state of affairs is actually overriding full local semantic analysis and syntactic role-assignment. In terms of Scenario-Mapping Theory, the phrases of the sentences cause a familiar scenario to be retrieved, and these phrases map into the scenario, resulting in a misinterpreted sentence, because further semantic processing does not occur. We shall explore this idea further in Chapter 5.

For the same reasons, pragmatic normalization can cause people to miss anomalies in sentences. In one of the earliest studies of failing to notice anomalies, Wason and Reich (1979) showed that people consistently found the following sentence acceptable:

(21)   No head injury is too trivial to be ignored.

It is difficult to see the anomaly here, but basically the correct version would be *No head injury is too trivial to be noticed*, rather than *to be ignored*. People's interpretations were tested by asking for paraphrases, and for (21) the investigators obtained something like: *However trivial a head injury is, it should not be ignored*. This makes sense as a *message*, but is not what (21) says.

The interpretation made, we suggest, occurs because of retrieval of a standard scenario regarding size of head injuries and whether they are trivial, and mapping of the noun phrases and verb phrases into the slots in the scenario. Of course, in the example, the structure of polarity (negation) is fairly complex, and so might engender conditions where readers effectively let pragmatics overcome local semantics in forming an interpretation. It is interesting that cases such as this, where the problem hinges on not taking negation properly into account, are quite commonplace in production. An example discovered by one of the authors (AJS) in a magazine article was:

(22)   It is hard to underestimate his contribution.

The intended meaning here seems to be 'it is easy to underestimate his contribution'. Such sentences are sometimes referred to as *depth-charge sentences*, because the clash between expression and intended meaning, if pointed out by someone else, is often discovered after a substantial delay.

Another example of pragmatic normalization comes from an even earlier observation made by Schlesinger (1968, p. 130) on the interpretation given to complex embedded sentences. Consider (23):

(23)   This is the hole, that the rat, which our cat, whom the dog bit, made, caught.

Schlesinger suggested that readers found this easy to understand if they ended up with the interpretation that the rat made the hole, the cat caught the rat, and the dog bit the cat. But in fact the sentence doesn't make ordinary sense at all, since it actually says that the rat caught the hole and the cat made the rat, as the following parse illustrates:

(24)   This is the hole, that the rat, (which our cat, (whom the dog bit,) made,) caught.

Of course, such embedded sentences are somewhat unnatural in English, but that doesn't matter for the present purpose. The point is that local analysis is blocked by easy mapping onto a representation of a commonly depicted situation (i.e., a scenario).

In all of the examples of normalization, the misinterpreted sentence has some processing difficulty associated with it, such as passivization, main–subordinate structuring, complex negation or the notoriously difficult deep embedding. Certainly, such complexities provide the conditions for strong pragmatic influences to play a major role before a full local interpretation has been made. Indeed, such a local interpretation may never be made. These examples show nicely how full semantic analysis does not automatically occur, and that an interpretation that seems satisfactory to the reader can result. That these examples show the interpretations to be wrong is made possible because they are carefully worked out, such that local analysis and world knowledge are deliberately in conflict. Of course, in normal writing, the writer would (or should) take care to ensure this doesn't happen, except, perhaps, for a rare special effect. Indeed, a special effect in writing can be achieved if there is just the right balance between an initial, incorrect interpretation by a reader, and a true meaning. Thus the following example (Johnson-Laird, 1981, p. 122) results from just such a balance:

(25)   This book fills a much needed gap.

Typically, readers do not readily note that it is the book, not the gap, that should be much needed, but when this is noticed or pointed out to them, readers often find it amusing. This example relies on making the dual semantic interpretations approximately equally available, with the asserted one revealed as an ironic mis-paraphrase of what would normally be expected in a book review. Exactly how this balance is achieved by writers is a major issue for further investigation, since many ironic and humorous effects depend upon similar balances.

What the data on pragmatic normalization basically show is that while multiple sources of information (syntax, case assignments, local semantics) are used by the reader for interpretation, not all of these interpretations are completed. Furthermore, local analysis is shown not to necessarily precede the use of world knowledge about what to expect in the situations that sentences appear to be depicting. This is readily interpreted as the operation of the primary processing principle: find a relevant scenario as soon as possible during reading.

Dynamics of scenario-based interpretation

Scenario-based interpretation is dynamic. That is, it changes as the reader processes the unfolding discourse. If an initial scenario has been activated, and a mapping made between the discourse and the scenario, then primary understanding is achieved. But as the text unfolds, it will not be long before the incoming discourse ceases to fit. This could come about in a variety of ways. For instance, if a protagonist is portrayed as being on an afternoon visit to an elderly relative, then a straightforward cue like the phrase *After the visit* would serve to indicate that the visit scenario is no longer relevant as a background, and a new scenario would be activated as soon as the information became available. Such shifts could be indirect as well. For instance, if a protagonist is in a scenario for being at a cinema show, and the cue *Five miles away* was given, this too should indicate that a shift is imminent, provided spatial information is part of the scenario in question. A simple test of a related idea is described below.

Characters, and cues to exit scenarios

For Sanford and Garrod (1981), one of the most compelling pieces of evidence for formulating the Scenario-Mapping Theory was the way in which the ease of processing references to scenario-dependent characters changed when cues suggested that the scenario was no longer the current arena of action for a narrative. Anderson et al. (1983) tested the idea that if a storyline indicated that a main character had exited a scenario, then characters dependent on that scenario became less available for reference as a result. They used materials like (26), in which a time-shift occurs that could either be within the range of time one might expect a scenario to last, or beyond it.

(26)   *In the restaurant*
   The Browns were eating a meal in a restaurant.
   The waiter was hovering around the table.
   This restaurant was well-known for its food.
   {Forty minutes/Five hours} later the restaurant was empty. [Time change]
   He had enjoyed serving all the good food. [Scenario-dependent target]
      [*or*]
   They had enjoyed eating all the good food. [Main characters as target]

It had already been established that while *Forty minutes* is construed as being within the scope of the period that people would spend eating a meal, *Five hours* puts the narrative present beyond eating at the restaurant. This is the factor manipulated in the 'time change' sentence. The alternative 'target' sentences contain anaphoric references to either the scenario-dependent character (the waiter) or to the main characters (the Browns). Participants read passages like these one line at a time, pressing a button when they had finished reading a particular line.

The results showed several things. First, when the time change was beyond a scenario boundary, reading time for that sentence was longer, showing that extra processing was taking place. Secondly, and most important, when the time change was beyond a scenario boundary, reading times for target sentences containing anaphoric reference to the scenario-dependent character were increased relative to those for a within-scenario boundary time change. With targets containing anaphoric reference to the main character, no such increase was observed.

These results fit the view that when a time-shift is indicated that puts the time beyond the temporal boundaries of the scenario, then the scenario is effectively de-activated as a means of interpretation. When that happens, scenario-dependent characters are no longer so readily available for reference. In contrast, a main character, who is not scenario-dependent, does not become more difficult to access, even though the character's mapping into the now-defunct scenario must itself be defunct. These findings are most simply explained if the following assumptions are made. First, individuals are mapped into situation-specific data-structures (scenarios) as they are mentioned in a text (the primary processing principle). Secondly, scenario-dependent characters have representations that are tied to the scenario in question. Third, time cues can indicate that a scenario is ongoing, or is over. If it is over, then that scenario no longer dominates interpretation, and so scenario-dependent entities are no longer so easy to refer to. Finally, individuals who are marked in some way as main characters do not lose a privileged status as a result of the scenario no longer being in focus.

Aspect and sentence processing

Verb aspect differences, such as whether an event is ongoing (has 'imperfective aspect'), or has been completed (has 'perfective aspect'), have also been related to Scenario-Mapping Theory. Consider first a situation with perfective aspect. Stevenson, Crawley, and Kleinman (1994) were interested in the general question of what factors control the ease of anaphoric reference resolution. One type of sentence that they studied depicted the transfer of a physical object, using the simple past tense. For example:

(27a)   John gave the book to Mary.

Stevenson et al. (1994) found that if invited to write a continuation sentence follow-up to such transfer sentences, there were more continuations referring to Mary, at the endpoint of the event, than to John, situated at the start of the event (see also Moens & Steedman, 1988). This result was indeed observed for transfer sentences like (27a) (see also Arnold, 2001; Majid, Sanford, & Pickering, 2007). But what is of interest here is that the result depends upon perceived aspect. Thus Kehler, Kertz, Rohde, and Elman (2008) showed that if this proposition is expressed using the present progressive, as in (27b), then the imperfective aspect is assumed, and in a continuation task, references to John are preferred:

(27b)   John is giving the book to Mary.

This experiment indicates how a direct cue that a situation is no longer ongoing can function in a similar way to an indirect indication such as mentioning the passage of too much time for the situation still to be relevant, as in (26). This study can be viewed as entirely consistent with the scenario study of main and secondary characters.

Other work on aspect is also quite consistent with the Scenario-Mapping account. Thus Ferretti, Kutas, and McRae (2007) were able to show that the availability of an implicit location is a function of aspect. They invited people to complete sentences based on stubs that either suggested an imperfective aspect or perfective aspect, as in (28a) and (28b) respectively:

(28a)   The diver was snorkeling . . .

(28b)   The diver had snorkeled . . .

Completions for the imperfective cases led to more completions that included locations (e.g., *in the ocean*) than was the case for the perfectives, suggesting that such information was more likely to be available in the representation when the event was portrayed as ongoing.

In addition to this production task, Ferretti et al. (2007) also used ERPs to investigate online comprehension. As discussed earlier, the N400 is sensitive to how easy it is to integrate a word into an unfolding discourse representation. If the imperfective makes access to the typical locations of the events easier, then mention of a location should be easier to process. The precise prediction made was that under the imperfective past, a typical location (*in the ocean*) should be more easily integrated (being predicted) than would a less typical location (*in the pond*). The investigators found that the N400 for the location was larger for the atypical than for the typical locations for the imperfective. This strongly suggests that rather specific predictions were being made by the reader as to a likely location for the imperfective constructions. In complete contrast, for the perfective cases, the idea is that the reader is making no such prediction of possible locations, so it should not matter whether the location encountered is typical or not. Indeed, Ferretti et al. found that there was no significant difference in the N400 amplitudes in the perfective case.

So, at a descriptive level, verb aspect influences the ease of processing the locations of events. From a Scenario-Mapping Theory viewpoint, this is perfectly natural, since typical location information may sensibly be supposed to be part of the information available in a scenario, hence accessible for processing with little difficulty. Verb aspect simply acts as a cue to the relevance of a scenario as a data-structure for ongoing interpretation. If the aspect indicates that the event is over, then the details of what happened within that event should be less important than (say) the consequences of the event having taken place. Indeed, this is the interpretation that Ferretti et al. give. These findings are consistent with the earlier work of Anderson et al. (1983) on the effects of scenario-shifting.

What's in a scenario? Functionality and limits on the extended domain of reference

We have shown that certain information is available from scenario-structures (the 'extended domain of reference'), including instrument information for actions, under the right circumstances. We have also shown that default characters are available for reference. Furthermore, default information about the expected duration of event scenarios is used to control what information is readily available, and so must itself be part of a scenario representation. However, two major issues remain: how much information is in a scenario, and how should the limits of what is available be conceptualized? In short, what is the boundary to situation-specific knowledge in any given scenario? This of course defines another problem: what are the limits on primary processing going to be? A simple thought-experiment illustrates the problem. If *Keith drove to London overnight* invokes a 'driving' scenario, what are the limits on the defaults likely to be present? We already have evidence that the term *a car* seems to be available as part of the extended domain of reference. But what about other variants? You can drive the following, for instance: vehicle, car, Aston Martin, BMW, Mazda MX5, van, truck, tanker, bus, armoured vehicle, and so on.

The same point applies to constituents of a default vehicle. Consider the following:

(29a)   Keith drove to London overnight.
(29b)   The engine had recently been overhauled.

Should *engine* (or *wheels*, or *brakes*, or *drive-shaft*, or *brake-pads*) be part of the driving scenario? In fact, when reading times are taken for (29b), it turns out that the reading time is longer than if the engine had been specifically mentioned before (Garrod & Sanford, 1981). In other words, a specific inference, rather than existing scenario knowledge, is needed to accommodate the engine, and that is secondary processing, rather than the primary processing (the latter comprising mapping onto extant default knowledge structures).

The key philosophy behind the idea of scenarios is that they exemplify only situational information that is typically useful and relevant to the user when considering that situation. You don't need to know the entire structure of a car in order to interpret what is means for Keith to drive to London. What's more, the default vehicle descriptor will be *car*. Only in the presence of other cues would some other specification be made or expected. For instance, the first noun-phrase in (30) serves as a controlling constraint:

(30)   Tom the trucker drove to London yesterday.

Here, specifying Tom as a *trucker* might introduce 'truck' as the likely default vehicle. This is an empirical issue, and it may be that other cues would need to be introduced to make certain that 'truck' became the default. In much the same way, an underspecified description should produce a momentary problem in processing. So, given the sentence *Keith drove to London overnight*, then saying *The vehicle kept overheating* would be a very underspecified description relative to the norm (car), and so should lead to secondary processing to establish why it was used. Such additional processing might include holding open an expectation that some alternative vehicle might be specified in the near future.

In general, the idea is that the representations used should be relevant to what people need to know in order to understand a basic situation, and no element should be more or less tightly defined than is necessary. Notice that it is always possible to go into more and more detail in descriptions that start out as simple situations. For instance, *John drove to London* needs only that we have a default of *car*. If it turns out that *John decided to take his Porsche 911*, then this will shift the scenario to one in which 'fast car' expectations, amongst others, are encoded. If we then learn that it kept overheating, and took much longer than expected, then we should start to bring in scenarios about bad car journeys, or breakdowns, or about the consequences of being late, whichever the developing text indicates. What is *not* the case, we suggest, is that all of this information is in the initial 'drive' scenario. What we can see with this example is that two things can go on in terms of developing details:

- From a starting point, changes in which scenario is in focus will alter what information is available at any given instant.
- As a particular 'line' is developed, the grain (i.e., the detail of the representation used) may become finer and finer. This will require shifting to *new* scenarios where this level of grain is relevant (cf. Hobbs', 1985, notion of granularity).

Is there any work that demonstrates effects of the boundaries of representation in scenarios? We outline two areas that are relevant, causal attribution and the process of counterfactual thinking known as 'mental undoing'.

Causal attribution

One approach to specifying boundaries on situations is possible through typical patterns of causal attribution. When an event occurs, what explanations for it come to mind? Consider a situation where a car speeds down a city road and has an accident. What level of description is appropriate about the cause of the accident? The answer is simple: the driver was driving too fast. Although this seems obvious, the question is *why* is this particular reason the best. Other explanations are possible, but they are based on very different considerations. For instance, 'the driver had the accelerator pressed down one centimetre too much', or 'fuel was being injected at too great a rate'. This is not simply a matter of level of detail. Each of these alternatives brings in a different set of background knowledge (different scenarios) and represents an entirely different perspective on the event. Without some reason for one or other of these explanations being made relevant, the interpretations of cause don't make much sense. So, our argument is that scenario knowledge is stored in a way that maximizes the relevance of what is stored to the situation in hand. That a driver is responsible for a car travelling too fast is the most important thing we need to know in the situation depicted, because it is the normative aspect of speed that is important for the situation of observing vehicle speeds in the city, not how speed is implemented mechanically.

The same sort of argument can be applied to a related but different situation. On an icy day, a car skids, mounts the pavement (sidewalk), and hits a pedestrian. What happened? The level of explanation most likely is the default 'must have skidded on ice'. The level of explanation does not include 'the weight of the car on the ice caused a local melting of ice under the area of the tyres which lowered the coefficient of friction making the surface slick'. While such knowledge may be utilized in some circumstances, extra information is needed, we claim, to make it available, because it is a 'physics of slipping on ice scenario'.

It is easy to change the knowledge that is recruited: suppose we are told that a shopkeeper had been washing the floor of his shop with a mop and bucket, and emptied the water on the street. It then froze. In this case, the cause of the skidding would be shifted to 'the car skidded because it hit the patch of ice caused by the shopkeeper's actions'. In short, the cause of the accident is the shopkeeper's action. Such attributions of cause appear to be quite principled. Hart and Honoré (1959), in the context of jurisprudence, where the ascription of cause is a precursor of the ascription of blame, suggest that cause is determined by the identification of an 'abnormal condition'. Each of the causes that we identified in the examples above constitutes an abnormal condition for the situation being depicted. Now there are two intertwined issues at work here: first, the determination of an abnormal condition for a situation, and secondly, a boundary on the level of granularity of a representation for that situation. It is clear that without a boundary on granularity, determining an abnormal condition has no foundation.

Work by Hilton and Slugoski (1987) illustrates nicely how an abnormal event influences causal attribution. They assume that for a depicted situation, a scenario is retrieved, containing the default information about what normally happens in that situation. So the following statements would be understood by being mapped onto the situation of a customer visiting a supermarket:

(31)   Sally bought something on her visit to the supermarket.

This sentence is essentially uninformative, because people normally buy things at supermarkets. It does not require an explanation. By contrast, an abnormal situation would invite further explanation because it would run counter to the default information in the scenario. Hilton and Slugoski show that even this sentence can be regarded as abnormal if it is shown to run contrary to Sally's general behaviour, as shown below:

(32a)   Sally bought something on her visit to the supermarket.
(32b)   In the past, Sally has hardly ever bought anything on her visit to this supermarket.

This abnormal situation triggers the search for a cause. Using various sources of information about the significance of actions, Hilton and Slugoski were able to show that only sources that were rated as informative (i.e., abnormal) influenced the patterns of attributions made. Going back to scenarios, the discovery of an abnormal condition is entirely dependent upon the normative information in the scenario, and that will be in a very specific, situationally relevant, form.

Thinking in the box: mental undoing

There is a further area of study that shows how using a particular scenario to interpret things can circumscribe explanatory reasoning, and this is the area of 'mental undoing', or the use of 'if only' in counterfactual thinking. Kahneman and Tversky (1982) introduced a study in which participants read stories in which a man drove home from work by an unusual route for a change, and was involved in a crash as the lights changed at an intersection. He crossed just as the lights changed to amber, but was rammed by a truck being driven by someone under the influence of drugs. As a result, he was killed. Participants were invited to complete a stem that began *If only*. With this story, the most common continuation was of the type *If only he had taken his usual route*. Others included his crossing on amber, and the drugged driver. Nobody said *If only he had arrived a few seconds earlier*.

In another version, the same events unfolded, except that rather than take a different route, the man left his office earlier than usual. Now the majority mentioned the time of departure, and very few mentioned the route. As Kahneman and Tversky said, the 'if only' continuations were about restoring the abnormal condition to normal, and not generally about any other of the myriad possible things that could have altered the outcome. Counterfactual thinking was entirely at the level of grain of the situation depicted, and in terms of the scenario used to understand that situation.

Both restrictions on causal attribution and on patterns of thinking in mental undoing offer converging evidence for restricted normative representations within scenarios. Scenarios are bounded, even if it is possible to access new scenarios from ones that are currently in use.

Situation models and event-indexing

Our main concern in discussing Scenario-Mapping Theory has been with the importance of utilizing world knowledge in order to interpret language. A somewhat different idea is the psychological notion of a *situation model* (van Dijk & Kintsch, 1983; see also Zwaan, Langston, & Graesser, 1995), another species of mental model. We have used the term 'situation' in our discussion of scenarios, in relation to applying relevant world knowledge to a type of situation (e.g., knowledge of the role of a teacher in an educational situation), but the use of the word in the term 'situation model' is quite different, since there it relates to how knowledge is built up about the *current status* of specific entities, space–time coordinates, etc. within particular texts (e.g., in a specific story, knowledge that Jennifer is a teacher or that Jennifer is in a particular place at a particular time). Readers keep track of continuities and are thereby also aware of discontinuities. This is a major issue with longer texts and therefore has also attracted the attention of text analysts, who describe this knowledge as *text-specific* (Emmott, 1997) and postulate *text worlds*, a term for how the accumulated information from a particular text is built up in the mind of the reader (e.g., Werth, 1999; see also Gavins, 2007). The empirical study of situation models is best illustrated through discontinuities. For instance, if a character is described as being a vegetarian early in a discourse, and later is described as eating a hamburger, there is a discontinuity (see Emmott, 1997, p. 166 for a real text example). Reading times are longer for such a discontinuity than for cases where there is no discontinuity (Hakala & O'Brien, 1995; Myers, O'Brien, Albrecht, & Mason, 1994). Such a finding demonstrates that character information is retrieved readily, and that inferences are not driven simply by local considerations, but by a need to maintain global coherence. However, it should be pointed out that there are limits to such global integration effects, and that they can be compromised if the reader is unmotivated to read, or has a low working-memory span (e.g., Graesser, Singer, & Trabasso, 1994).

The *event-indexing model* (Zwaan, Langston, & Graesser, 1995; Zwaan, Magliano, & Graesser, 1995) has at its core the idea that the situation model constructed for essentially character-based narratives contains information about five conceptual dimensions: properties of the protagonist, time, space, causality and intentionality (the goals of the character(s)). The claims that these factors are monitored has been demonstrated variously for single factors by (this is just a sample):

- For character properties (e.g., Albrecht & O'Brien, 1993; Myers et al., 1994).
- For time (e.g., Zwaan, 1996).

- For space (e.g., Glenberg, Meyer, & Lindem, 1987).
- For causality (e.g., Klin & Myers, 1993; Trabasso & Magliano, 1996; van den Broek & Lorch, 1993).
- For intentionality (e.g., Dopkins, 1996; Suh & Trabasso, 1993).

The demonstrations of monitoring have typically been through the disruptive effects of discontinuities, indexed, for instance, through difficulties in reading.

One important observation by Zwaan, Langston, and Graesser (1995) is that the reading time for an explicit event in a story increased systematically as a function of the number of dimensions with discontinuities that made up the statement (see also Speer, Zacks, & Reynolds, 2007, for relevant brain-imaging work). This shows that all of the dimensions are being monitored at the same time, at least within the limits of their experiments. Of course, this is of significance since it constitutes an important test of the event-indexing model.

It is clear that the event-indexing account is a good general framework in that it attempts to capture story-based information that is used during the very act of interpretation. The most general question that it leads to is what is required in introducing a fact about a character and the spatio-temporal setting in order to guarantee that the information will be available when needed. The same issue applies to all of the dimensions. The event-indexing model also raises interesting issues, such as how and when updates occur.

Secondary processing and defamiliarization

We now turn to some connections between Scenario-Mapping Theory, secondary processing and the language devices used by writers to enrich their writing. To summarize the argument so far: according to the theory, primary processing consists of recovering an appropriate scenario, and mapping elements of the unfolding discourse into this. When such mappings fail, secondary processing occurs and takes many forms. The main ones are:

- Accessing a new scenario, facilitating new mappings of current input onto a new scenario.
- Carrying out other ad-hoc operations to accommodate the input.
- Putting unresolvable input on a 'wait and see' list.

Simple primary processing only produces a very basic aspect of 'understanding' while secondary processing can lead to the reader striving to accommodate, only ultimately leading to understanding in such cases, and in the process potentially producing real interest.

Secondary processing, in the more extreme cases, can be linked to the notion of *defamiliarization* (Shklovsky, 1965), an idea which has had an impact on attempts in the humanities to understand what literary writing, in particular, is doing. Defamiliarization is a posited process by which even the most mundane aspects of everyday life can take on a richer and striking aspect because they are portrayed in an unusual fashion by a writer. Readers may sometimes need to do a 'double take' and re-interpret a scene. We will explore this literary idea further in Chapter 4. Here, we will see how when failures of primary processing prompt secondary processing, defamiliarization may ensue and cause a reader to look more thoughtfully and/or with amusement at either an ordinary or extraordinary scene.

Switching to a new scenario through secondary processing

One failure of primary processing is when information is provided that simply does not fit the scenario that a reader has already established and there is a gross mismatch with the expectations of the characters and/or reader. In such cases, it may be necessary to replace the scenario with a new one. This is often the basis for humour (Attardo, 1994; Attardo & Raskin, 1991; Coulson, 2001; Raskin, 1985; Simpson, 2003), but can also reflect a disorientating reappraisal of a standard scenario, or both. In the following example, we see such potential effects. As the extract opens, a spaceship blows up and so a disaster scenario seems to be appropriate. The incongruity occurs when a green blur appears and asks them if they have a reservation, usually a cue to a restaurant scenario.

(33)   a massive explosion rocked the bridge [...] Four inert bodies sank through spinning blackness. Consciousness had died, cold oblivion pulled the bodies down and down into the pit of unbeing. The roar of silence echoed dismally around them and they sank at last into a dark and bitter sea of heaving red that slowly engulfed them, seemingly for ever.
        After what seemed an eternity, the sea receded and left them lying on a cold hard shore [...] Cold spasms shook them, lights danced sickeningly around them [...]
        A green blur watched them disapprovingly.
        It coughed.
        'Good evening, madam, gentlemen,' it said, 'do you have a reservation?'
        Ford Prefect's consciousness snapped back like elastic, making his brain smart. He looked up woozily at the green blur.
        'Reservation?' he said weakly.
        'Yes, sir,' said the green blur.
        'Do you need a reservation for the afterlife?'
                            (Adams (1986b). *The Restaurant at the End of the Universe*,
                                            pp. 211–212, our underlining)

The mismatch is difficult for the characters to understand, causing surprise and puzzlement. Ford Prefect tries to utilize an afterlife scenario, which could follow on naturally from the disaster scenario and might explain the green blur, although he recognizes that there is a lack of fit with the green blur's question about the reservation. The reader may also be confused at first, prompting secondary processing. There may be a 'wait and see' strategy initially, but, as more evidence is presented (after this extract), the reader can eventually draw the conclusion that the characters actually *are* in a restaurant and that therefore a restaurant scenario needs to be utilized, albeit rather an unusual one. (The reader here has an advantage over the characters, since the book title gives an obvious clue.) In context, the example is humorous and prompts interest.

Scenario under-specification and secondary processing

In (33), the cue to introduce a new scenario (the restaurant scenario) is clear, but the characters ignore it (as might the reader at first) because it is so incongruous. Another option that writers use is to under-specify a scenario, at least initially, providing inadequate cues to retrieve it. There can be reasons for this, such as the portrayal of the perspective of a character who does not fully comprehend the situation which they see in front of them. Sometimes, the author may gradually increase the detail until the reader can use world knowledge to draw on the new scenario. In (34), the first part of the description is under-specified because although specific events are being described on the television screen, the 9/11 attacks in the USA in 2001, the initial cues are limited since the time and place of the television news item are not given and the place description (e.g., *a tall building*) is quite general. As the description builds up, the reader may need to re-evaluate this scene, with secondary processing taking place as world knowledge about 9/11 is accessed.

(34)   'Oh God,' [Chanu] says. 'The world has gone mad.'
         Nazneen glances over at the screen. The television shows a tall building against a blue sky [. . .] A thick bundle of black smoke is hanging outside the tower. It looks too heavy to hang there. An aeroplane comes in slow motion from the corner of the screen. It appears to be flying at the level of the buildings. Nazneen thinks she had better get on with her work.
         'Oh God,' shouts Chanu. [. . .] The scene plays over. [. . .]
         The aeroplane comes again. The television shows it again and again. [. . .]
         The scene switches. 'The Pentagon,' says Chanu. 'Do you know what it is? It's the *Pentagon*.'
         (Ali (2004). *Brick Lane*, pp. 365–366, Ali's italics, our underlining)

From an empirical perspective, this is rather like the classic Bransford and Johnson (1972) experiment, where a vague description of handling household items makes sense and is more memorable if readers are given the correct 'header' ('washing clothes') for the scenario.

Scenario over-specification and secondary processing

The opposite to under-specification is over-specification, where the author provides more information than we would ever normally need. This can also cause a reader to have a 'double take' on ordinary events. This may be due to an over-philosophizing on the part of a character who is treating an everyday scenario as if it deserves the narrative involvement of an extraordinary scenario. In the following case, the ordinary action of putting on a sock is described using an explanation more fitting of a technical account.

(35)   When I pull a sock on, I no longer *pre-bunch*, that is, I don't gather the sock up into telescoped folds over my thumbs and then position the resultant donut over my toes [...] I revealed my laziness and my inability to plan ahead by instead holding the sock by the ankle rim and jamming my foot to its destination, working the ankle a few times to properly seat the heel. Why? The more elegant pre-bunching can leave in place any pieces of grit that have embedded themselves in your sole [...] while the cruder, more direct method, though it risks tearing an older sock, does detach this grit during the foot's downward passage [...]

                    (Baker (1998). *The Mezzanine*, p. 12, Baker's italics)

This type of engagement may match our everyday experiences, but we do not normally spell out our experiences in such detail. Nevertheless, experimental literature of this type can provide real insights into how we respond to the world around us, by verbalizing experiences that are not usually communicated.

Consider the idea that scenarios are bounded in terms of what is represented in them. Scenario shifts can be achieved by steadily presenting information that is beyond the scope of the current scenario. In typical narratives, movements from one scenario to the next will take the reader to different kinds of topics. But in some experimental literature, the whole point has been to exploit the fact that going into more and more detail about something may be unusual in everyday contexts. Specifying detail in a discourse that goes beyond what can be mapped into the initial scenario will lead to secondary processing requiring the reader to find another type of scenario where that degree of detail is typically represented. Doing this iteratively will produce a unique form of narrative.

An empirical study of unusual scenario events
and narrative interest

Narratologists suggest that breaches of our normal expectations, both minor and major, lie at the heart of what a narrative is (e.g., Bruner, 1991; Herman, 2002, 2009). It is the unusualness of the events, or an unusual manner of telling, that make them worth narrating (Hühn, 2009, 2010).

An empirical example of secondary processing in relation to unusual scenario details shows what happens when a scenario-dependent character does something that is out of the range of the scenario. Emmott, Sanford, and Smith (2008) examined how readers would choose to continue simple vignettes like (36a) and (36b) (the slash mark denotes options presented to different participants, the underlining is added here):

(36a)   Jenny had been invited to a reception to celebrate the launch of the new magazine. As she arrived at the party, Jenny saw {someone/the waiter} offering her a champagne cocktail.

(36b)   Jenny had been invited to a reception to celebrate the launch of the new magazine. As she arrived at the party, Jenny saw {someone/the waiter} crouching in the bushes outside.

In (36a), the waiter (or 'someone' that we may assume to be a waiter) behaves in a scenario-dependent fashion, performing an action that is part of the scenario. Given the simple text, the waiter is not given any special significance, but in (36b), the waiter/someone is not doing something that is part of the scenario, but something unusual for the situation, a non-scenario action. The prediction was that in (36a) there would be little if any mention of the waiter/someone, but rather there would be references to other aspects of the scene. However, for (36b), a higher frequency of mentioning the waiter/someone with greater elaborations was predicted. Furthermore, continuations in the latter case were expected to have content that was indicative of extra interest being generated by the ill-fitting action, such as extra information about the character, an indication of a tricky or emergency situation, the main character wondering what was going on, along with signals of surprise and emotion. This is exactly what was found.

Below are examples of continuations containing both scenario-dependent actions and non-scenario-dependent ones (in both cases the materials presented by the experimenters are shown first, and the participants' continuations follow in italics):

(37a)   Ellen loved spending every Saturday afternoon in the town centre. In the department store, she saw the assistant bringing over a new rack of clothes. *They were gorgeous and they had her size, could she really afford it after losing her job? As the till rang the sale through she signed up for more debt.*

(37b)   Heather needed to buy some stylish chairs for her new apartment. At the furniture store, she saw the assistant lying under the table. *She approached [. . .] wondering what on earth the woman was doing under the table. As she got closer, Heather saw fear in the woman's eyes, fear which Heather had never witnessed before.*

In (37a), the experimental material provides a scene that conforms entirely to expectations since the assistant's action is scenario-dependent. Most participants writing continuations to this material did not refer to the assistant at all, but focussed on other aspects of the scene such as interest in the clothes. However, when in (37b), in another experimental material set in a shop, the action of the assistant was made non-scenario-dependent, the participants frequently elaborated about the assistant, often questioning what was going on (*wondering what on earth the woman was doing*), expressing emotion (*fear*), and giving more detail about the assistant (*fear in the woman's eyes*).

These results matched our hypothesis that non-scenario actions of the minor characters would prompt more narrative interest in those narrative characters than scenario actions. We will explore this topic further in Chapter 8 when we examine the topic of suspense.

Summary

This chapter introduced some of the fundamental principles of text processing that form the basis for understanding narratives and many other types of text. The main points we covered were as follows:

- An early way of thinking about a text was simply in terms of the propositions that make it up. In addition, the notion of rhetorical relations indicates how parts of a text cohere. We explored how inferences are made and used to integrate what the writer has expressed with the knowledge and thoughts of readers, examining the distinction between necessary and elaborative inferences. Writers can control the types of elaborative inferences made by the type of context they supply in a story.
- Beyond single inferences is the important concept of mental models and, more specifically, how general world knowledge is utilized during reading. Rather than being expressible in propositions, meaning was shown to depend on mental models. Scenario-Mapping Theory addresses this issue, and makes the claim that world knowledge is organized in terms of situations (scenarios). We introduced the idea that readers map what they read onto their background knowledge. Scenario-mapping explains in-filling and suggests that there is an extended domain of reference in which entities not explicitly mentioned in the text are implicitly given in scenarios. This is a rapid, automatic process, termed primary processing. Sometimes this use of background knowledge can even override local semantic interpretation, as in the examples of pragmatic normalization. When primary processing fails, secondary processing may occur, with the possibility of more complex inferential activity, and a search for alternative scenarios.
- The Scenario-Mapping Theory is meant to be a broadly applicable account of understanding, and we have shown how it offers a ready framework for understanding differences in types of character, shifts in what is being focussed on over time, and what information is readily available for use in comprehending, including level of detail. Scenario-Mapping Theory posits that what is in a scenario is bounded by what that situation-specific knowledge is functionally useful for.

- A complementary idea is that of the event-indexing model. This accounts for how knowledge that is specific to a particular text is handled, showing a distinction between how readers handle continuities and discontinuities relating to properties of protagonists, time, space, causality and intentionality.
- Defamiliarization, the process of looking again at deviant stylistic features and/or unusual aspects of a scene, is regarded by many humanities scholars as a fundamental aspect of responding to literary texts. This can be linked to the failure of primary processing when a reader encounters deviant or unusual parts of a text, hence prompting secondary processing.

3   Multiple levels: counterfactual worlds and figurative language

The psychological work we have presented up to now is primarily based on the idea of a simple, literal interpretation of language. The mapping made from language input onto world knowledge, particularly scenario-based situational knowledge, enables language to be interpreted. Yet often language is multi-layered in that it has to be interpreted in different ways. One example of this is counterfactual worlds: depictions of worlds in which the 'facts' are essentially false, or not realized, or an alternative to reality. These are ubiquitous in language and there has been considerable investigation of them both in linguistics and in narrative studies, but they have not been examined extensively from an empirical point of view. We present a discussion of some of the recent work that has been done to fill this gap. Counterfactuals are particularly interesting, in that representations of both reality and of the counterfactual situation have to be borne in mind, so a simple language-to-scenario mapping is not sufficient to capture such a multiple representation. The problem of multiple representations has received good theoretical coverage in cognitive linguistics work on mental spaces (Fauconnier, 1994) and subsequent work on conceptual blending (Fauconnier & Turner, 1998, 2002). We will draw on this work later in this chapter.

One does not have to look far to find other cases where multiple representations have to be set up in order to comprehend an intended message. This is a crucial issue not only for understanding how a fictional world is comprehended, but also in research on how figurative language is processed. In figurative language, what is said in an utterance or written in a sentence is not meant literally, so figurative and literal levels have to be taken into account in a processing model. We will look particularly at metaphor, which is now generally regarded as being crucial to everyday communication in addition to having a major role to play in literary texts. It is argued that it underlies central aspects of how we think and is also at the root of creativity (e.g., Lakoff, 1987; Lakoff & Johnson, 1980; Lakoff & Turner, 1989). We will focus on psychological accounts of how metaphorical language is understood and examine how it is used both conventionally and creatively.

Our main objectives are to try to elucidate what might be necessary to have a more complete processing model than is possible on the basis of the simpler

45

account of Chapter 2, and to introduce some of the questions that multiple levels raise for the study of narrative processing.

Entering fictional worlds: counterfactual situations in narratives

Although not all narratives are fictional, fiction nevertheless plays a central cultural role from simple childhood stories to sophisticated literary texts. Reading fictional stories provides an example of a major cognitive feat, since it involves sustaining a representation of a counterfactual world over an extended stretch of text. Fictional texts depict worlds in which propositions relating to characters and/or events are in fact false. The characters may never have existed and the events may never have happened. To understand fiction, one has to suspend disbelief, and suppose that the events being depicted actually occur. Only through automatic and possibly effortless suspension of disbelief is narrative immersion possible. On the surface, these comments are just truisms, but there is a major issue of what kinds of psychological processes lead to the suspension of disbelief. At the same time, we need to understand how real-world knowledge is utilized in comprehending counter-factual worlds, since many fictional characters are realistic, and even the most extraordinary fictional characters may perform quite ordinary actions, for which readers need to draw on real-world knowledge. We will examine relevant empirical work on counterfactuals shortly, but first consider the nature of counterfactual situations in narratives. This is a major area of study, with scholars from a range of disciplines, such as philosophy, psychology, text linguistics and narratology, producing a variety of different accounts (e.g., Doležel, 1989; Gavins, 2007; Gerrig, 1993; Pavel, 1986; Ryan, 1991; Semino, 1997, 2006; Werth, 1999).

For our purposes here, a simple overview of some key points will be sufficient. The study of counterfactuals can range from sentence-level examples (e.g., 'If x had happened, then y would have been the case') (Lewis, 1973; see also Barker, 2006) to whole novels. Not only is a fictional world counterfactual to the reader's real world, but within both fictional and non-fictional narrative texts there may be small or large stretches of text devoted to the dreams, fantasies and imaginings of fictional characters or real people respectively (what Werth (1999) has termed *sub-worlds*). Lewis Carroll's *Alice's Adventures in Wonderland* provides a classic example of where a counterfactual world (Alice's dream world) is embedded within another counterfactual world (the fictional Alice's world). In addition to fully developed scenes of this type, every time a text mentions what could have happened, what did not happen, what might happen, what should have happened, or makes predictions about what will happen, counterfactual worlds are set up, although some may be fleeting (see Gavins, 2007).

Counterfactual worlds may depart from reality to different degrees. Alice's dream world (where she changes size and meets an assortment of odd characters) contravenes world knowledge in radical ways. Alice's 'real' world (where she falls asleep on the river bank) is also counterfactual to our own real world (since Alice's 'real' world is fictional), but is less radically different. Some fiction portrays impossible characters or events (for instance, Humpty Dumpty in Carroll's *Through the Looking Glass*, or making sunbeams out of cucumbers in Swift's *Gulliver's Travels*). Other worlds are possible but run counter to supposed reality (such as using owls as a type of mail service in J. K. Rowling's *Harry Potter* series). Suspension of disbelief enables readers to become absorbed in worlds containing many incredible things, but the illusion may fail when everything in a world is either impossible or contradictory (see Semino, 1997, for a discussion of nonsense rhymes), or be challenged where elements from different levels are mixed together (e.g., if a fictional world incorporates a mention and/or appearance of its author or producer/director, as in Hitchcock's films) and where the overall narrative structure is contradictory (e.g., where there are different and incompatible endings, as in John Fowles' *The French Lieutenant's Woman*).

Typically, fictional worlds are a mixture of what is false in that world but asserted as true in the fictional world, and what is true in the real world. For instance, we might encounter a fictional world in which there is a present-day King of France at the centre of a complex political plot. This is plainly counterfactual since there is no current king. But we would still assume that there was an Eiffel Tower in Paris unless told explicitly that there was not, and would be able to use our real-world knowledge to infer that sharp knives still cut, and that aubergines are edible. The idea that we take facts in the real world as holding in a fictional world unless otherwise specifically indicated in the text has been termed 'the principle of minimal departure' (Ryan, 1980).

Counterfactual worlds in narratives require readers to suspend disbelief about imaginary things and at the same time utilize general knowledge from the real world. We will look now at empirical work that demonstrates these processes. Counterfactual worlds also require readers to partition their knowledge, so that information which is true in a fictional world or sub-world may be viewed as false in the real world or at a different level within the fictional world. Later in this chapter, we will look at how the theory of mental spaces captures this partitioning.

Empirical work on counterfactuality

Utilizing counterfactual knowledge   An initial empirical question is whether reading counterfactuals prompts the formation of mental representations that are treated as true in a fictional world, even though they are false in the real world. This has been investigated in a number of ways, including the processing of cartoon-based worlds. For example, in the real world, it is not possible for an angry man to pick up and throw a heavy truck off the road. But, in a fictional world, it is possible for The Incredible Hulk (in green form) to do that. The case of the angry man throwing the truck is anomalous, and in ERP experiments leads to a large N400 anomaly effect (as described in Chapter 2), while the Hulk version is not, and does not lead to a large N400 (Filik & Leuthold, 2008). This simply illustrates how what we already know about a character denoted by a noun phrase may be rapidly utilized during comprehension, i.e., by approximately 400 ms from when the word is encountered. From a psychological perspective, this is of the utmost importance, since it means that listeners are not first detecting a problem, and then using the counterfactual information to fix it. Rather, in this case, they are using counterfactual information effectively as soon as it is available.

The Hulk is a well-known cartoon character, so readers bring expectations about the character to the text. Other work has shown how the development of a novel, cartoon-like, fictional world may have a similar effect. Nieuwland and van Berkum (2006) had participants listen to cartoon-style stories that gave inanimate things animate properties, hence over-ruling standard selection restrictions. For instance, one such fantasy story was about an amorous peanut who fell in love with a little almond:

(1)   A woman saw a dancing peanut who had a big smile on his face. The peanut was singing about a girl he had just met. And judging from the song, the peanut was totally crazy about her. The woman thought it was really cute to see the peanut singing and dancing like that. The peanut was {salted/in love}, and by the sound of it, this was definitely mutual. He was seeing a little almond.

Out of context of this story, *The peanut was in love* would cause a large N400 on *in love* compared to *salted* in *The peanut was salted*. This is because being salted is a normal property of peanuts, while being in love is not. In stories such as (1), this N400 anomaly effect was elicited when the anomalous item (i.e., the animate peanut) was introduced in the first sentence. However, by the time the critical item *The peanut was in love* was encountered, when the fantasy world had been set up, the N400 anomaly effect disappeared. Moreover, the counterfactual meaning was easier to process by this stage in the story: to say *The peanut was in love* induced a smaller N400 than did *The peanut was salted*.

This research shows two important things. First, that a counterfactual world in which, for instance, peanuts are animate, is readily developed by listeners, although it takes a few sentences for such items to become fully acceptable. This is a significant finding, since immersion in a narrative world is such a major element of reading many texts. Secondly, as for Filik and Leuthold's experiment, it also shows that when a counterfactual world has already been set up, this information is used very early in sentence processing and its effect is clearly seen around 400 ms after the critical item is encountered. The brain is finely tuned to respond to the language environment created by a writer. So, these findings are good evidence against the view that local semantic analysis of these items precedes the use of more global contextual information. They fit well with the observations on the pragmatic override of local semantic analysis discussed in Chapter 2.

Drawing on real-world knowledge in counterfactual situations   While in certain respects we might expect readers confronted with a counterfactual item to process it easily once the counterfactual world has been set up, we might also expect them to utilize some real-world knowledge. After all, having knowledge of reality is important to understand that a counterfactual *is* a counterfactual.

Ferguson and Sanford (2008) used eye-tracking to examine how and when different knowledge sources (real and counterfactual) are used during reading. Short materials were used which, in the counterfactual case, introduced the world with an explicit cue (e.g., *If cats were vegetarians*) right from the beginning of the text (so, in contrast to the Nieuwland and van Berkum experiment, there was no need in the counterfactual case to wait for the type of world to be established). Then things were introduced that were either consistent or inconsistent in either the real or counterfactual world. An example material (including options and our added underlining) is shown in (2a/b), with our added explanation below each part:

(2a)   If cats are hungry they usually pester their owners until they get fed. Families could feed their cat a bowl of {carrots/fish} and it would gobble it down happily.

- The situation depicted is real-world consistent ('If cats are hungry')
- Carrots = Real-world inconsistent condition
- Fish = Real-world consistent condition

(2b)   If cats were vegetarians they would be cheaper for owners to look after. Families could feed their cat a bowl of {carrots/fish} and it would gobble it down happily.

- The situation depicted is counterfactual. ('If cats were vegetarians')
- Carrots = Counterfactual-world consistent condition, but real-world inconsistent
- Fish = Counterfactual-world inconsistent condition, but real-world consistent

The main question was whether the counterfactual-world setting in examples such as (2b) would override what would be an anomaly in the real world. In the real world cats do not eat carrots, but is this acceptable in a world where cats are vegetarians?

Ferguson and Sanford (2008) had people read passages like these while their eye-movements were monitored. The number of eye-fixations on words in specific parts of the text, termed regions, was analysed: the critical region in our example was either *carrots and* or *fish and*, depending on the version of the material presented. The cumulative duration of these eye-fixations gives reading times for each region. Various measures of the eye-movements were taken, including the duration of all the fixations made when the eyes first enter a region (first-pass reading time), the duration of subsequent movements in and out of the region (regressions), and the total reading time for the region including regressions. The amount of time spent reading the region and re-inspecting earlier portions of the text by regressions provides an indication of processing difficulty.

For most measures used, it was found that the counterfactual context led to shorter reading times for regions where the key words were consistent with that context (*carrots* in this example) than where the key words were inconsistent (*fish* in this case). In the real-world context, regions with words consistent with reality (*fish*) had shorter reading times than where words were inconsistent (*carrots*). Overall, therefore, it does appear that the counterfactual setting overrides what is normally an anomaly in the real world.

There was an important exception to this pattern. For first-pass reading time, only *part* of this pattern held. For the real-world context, the pattern was the same. However, in the counterfactual context, regions with words that were inconsistent with that context were the ones that had the shorter reading times (*fish* in this case), while those with words that were consistent with the counterfactual setting (*carrots*) had relatively longer times. This pattern for first-pass reading time in the counterfactual case is, of course, what we would normally expect in a real-world context. One interpretation of this, as presented by Ferguson and Sanford, is that even in the presence of a strong counterfactual context, real-world knowledge still exercises an influence, albeit a very short-lived one in terms of influencing eye-tracking patterns. This is perhaps not so surprising when we consider that knowing that vegetarians eat carrots is using real-world knowledge: it is the application of that information to cats that is counterfactual. The result was robust, being found in two further studies in this paper. Note that the effect on reading is very small, and while this does not detract from its importance in understanding what mechanisms are being used in comprehension, it does suggest that under a counterfactual context, accessing irrelevant real-world knowledge is not a great problem for building up a representation of the counterfactual item itself. Ferguson and Sanford suggest that two representations emerge early in the comprehension of counterfactual statements – one of the counterfactual item itself, and one which is true in the real world. These findings illustrate the need for not just one language-to-scenario mapping, but two co-existing ones where counterfactuals are concerned.

A different method was used by Ferguson, Scheepers, and Sanford (2010) to investigate the way in which people *predict* which items (e.g., *fish/carrots*) are likely to occur in a counterfactual world once that world has been set up. This represents a way of investigating how readily counterfactual-world representations influence processing. The technique, the *visual world task*, requires people to listen to sentences while they look at a computer screen. The text materials are sound-recorded and presented auditorily, so that people's eyes are free to look at the screen. On the screen are depictions of objects. During listening, there is no need to look at any particular object(s), though people tend to do so. What they tend to do, in fact, is to look at depictions of objects that are related to the message (e.g., Altmann & Kamide, 1999; Cooper, 1974; Tanenhaus, Spivey-Knowlton, Eberhard, & Sedivy, 1995). The point at which they start to look at one object rather than another can be used as an index of whether people are expecting reference to be made to that object.

The materials used were closely similar to (2a/b) used above, and we shall stick with this example for clarity. On the computer screen, a display of objects was provided. For this example it showed four items: carrots, fish, a cat and a bus. The crucial question was whether people in the process of hearing these materials would look in anticipation toward the carrots in the counterfactual-world case, and the fish in the real-world case, and then later look at the item depicted by the word actually used in each of the four conditions in (2a/b). It was found that the participants looked toward the item that was consistent with the context well before that item was or was not named, and later looked at the item that was ultimately named.

A further result found in this study is consistent with that evident in the Ferguson and Sanford (2008) reading study. After the word denoting the critical object (e.g., *carrots*) had been heard, if it was different from the predicted word that fitted the context, then a shift in gaze toward the entity depicted by the actual word was made more rapidly if it was consistent with real-world knowledge than if it was consistent with what would be expected in the counterfactual context. So, integration into real-world knowledge structures is easier than into counterfactual-world knowledge structures.

Ferguson, Scheepers, and Sanford's results show just how rapidly the counterfactual situation is utilized in comprehension and used for the prediction of upcoming references. The first result illustrates that normal world knowledge, which is highly available, remains available while the counterfactual world is being utilized for prediction, while the second result shows how normal world knowledge remains prominent in order to accommodate recovery from an erroneous prediction.

To summarize the discussion of empirical work on counterfactuals up to now: counterfactual-world statements give rise to mental representations that affect how new text is interpreted, both through what is predicted and what is easy to integrate with the representation. However, there is evidence that a representation based on real-world knowledge also emerges early. We suggest that both are necessary to understand that a counterfactual world is indeed counterfactual. This dual representation idea also allows for real-world knowledge to be used in representations of the full counterfactual world – in line with Ryan's (1980) principle of minimal departure.

Fact, false belief and Theory of Mind in narrative

A special case of counterfactuality occurs when people include the false beliefs of others in their thinking. When a reader adopts the perspective of another person, and uses that person's knowledge, or recognizes that person's emotions, it is said that they have a Theory of Mind (ToM) for that other person (e.g., Baron-Cohen, Tager-Flusberg, & Cohen, 2000). ToM is important for social understanding, and an inability to adopt other people's perspectives has been associated with Autistic Spectrum Disorder (Baron-Cohen, 2000; Leslie, 1994). Ferguson et al. (2010) used cases similar to the following. Suppose that within a narrative depiction, an electric drill is normally kept in a cupboard in someone's house. Now, suppose that some character, say Graham, within that narrative, is unaware that the electric drill has been used by someone else, and has been left lying on the workbench. We now have a dual-perspective situation within the narrative. The interplay of these perspectives has consequences. For example, if Graham comes home wanting to use the drill, he might be expected to go to the cupboard to look for it. If he happens to see it lying on the workbench, he will be surprised. If he did not have his false belief about its location, but knew that it had been moved, he wouldn't be surprised, of course. Readers are naturally good at using false belief information to guide their expectations. Using a visual world paradigm, as described above, Ferguson et al. investigated whether readers would show predictive gazing at objects expected under narrative reality and the false beliefs of a character. A typical passage that participants listened to is as follows. In (3a) the character notices an event in their own 'reality context', whereas in (3b) the belief context is set up because the character has not noticed what is going on (due to being distracted) and is therefore making assumptions.

(3a)   John washed the dishes after his breakfast and left his watch on the table.
        <u>Later, John noticed</u> Victoria move the watch from the table to the bed.
        Later, John wanted to find his watch so he looked on the {<u>bed/table</u>} and yawned.

- The situation depicted is a reality context ('John noticed')
- Bed = reality language input
- Table = false language input which would not correspond to John's belief

(3b)   John washed the dishes after his breakfast and left his watch on the table. While John was distracted, Victoria moved the watch from the table to the bed.
Later, John wanted to find his watch so he looked on the {bed/table} and yawned.

- The situation depicted is a belief context ('John was distracted')
- Bed = reality language input
- Table = false language input corresponding to what would be John's belief

It was found that participants showed a preference to gaze at the location appropriate to the character's beliefs in anticipation of the actual location of the gaze having been specified. These effects began almost 600 ms before the onset of the word specifying where the character was supposed to have looked occurred. As before, shortly after the actual word had been heard, gaze shifted to the location specified by that word.

So, the findings from this study show that a false belief perspective can be used rapidly as a basis for the anticipation of the actions of a story protagonist. This may seem like a fairly necessary conclusion, but we should like to add a caveat to the results, and this concerns the gender of the participants. While the generalization made above holds very well for the female participants, scrutiny of the results suggested that it did not hold for the male participants. So, the female participants were predicting entities in locations belonging to the character's erroneous perspective, but the male participants were not.

There has been great interest in gender-based differences in the capacity to adopt the perspective of another individual (see especially Baron-Cohen, 2002). It has been suggested that there are statistical differences between samples of males and females such that male samples show a bias toward a poorer capacity in this respect. Much of this argument has been based on the use of questionnaires, and these have been criticized by some because of intrinsic biases in the way the questions were structured (e.g., Keen, 2007). However, the data from Ferguson et al. was not questionnaire-based, and provides support for the idea that there are gender differences in Theory of Mind processing. Further evidence of gender effects in reading behaviour using false-belief scenarios is provided by Ferguson, Breheny, Sanford, and Scheepers (2009). We should also point out that the gender effects described above apply only to the false-belief paradigm, and not to the simple counterfactual data, so it really is adopting the perspective of another that is the problem, not just accepting counterfactual conjectures.

Toggling between perspectives: easy or hard?

In narrative worlds we may encounter narrators and characters who have false beliefs, but, as readers, we may be privy to the fact that these beliefs are misguided or without foundation. The small false-belief vignettes used by Ferguson et al. (2010) offer a straightforward example. In a full story, the whole point might be the tension between a character's erroneous beliefs and the reader's knowledge of how things really stand in the fictional world (Booth, 1991). One example is a story set in Holland during the seventeenth-century Tulip Fever period (Moggach, 2000, pp. 209–211), when tulip bulbs became subject to financial speculation and were therefore extremely valuable commodities. In the story, a character called Gerrit falsely believed his master's valuable tulip bulb to be an onion, and sliced it up to go with his lunch. The reader, by contrast, knows that the tulip bulb is really a tulip bulb, and, at the same time, is aware of Gerrit's erroneous belief that it is an onion.

From a processing point of view, such dual-perspective writing causes potential problems. Because of the need to think of the tulip as a valuable bulb on one hand, and as an onion on the other, it might be the case that reading such passages requires extra time because of the need to switch between one perspective and another, as we read and evaluate the impact of Gerrit's actions. Dawydiak, Emmott, and Sanford (unpublished data) evaluated this idea by having people read either a number of dual-perspective passages, or comparable single-perspective controls. An example material, based on Moggach's story, is shown in (4a–g).

(4a)   In a story set in old Holland, a man called Gerrit is tasked with delivering an extremely valuable tulip bulb for his master.

(4b)   To prevent him stealing it, Gerrit is not told about the bulb, and it is tied up in a parcel and hidden among similar parcels in his bag.

(4c)   During his journey, Gerrit gets drunk and starts to open some parcels from his bag.

(4d)   He comes across the bulb, and thinks that it is an ordinary onion.
        [or]

(4d′)   He luckily avoids opening the bulb parcel, but he comes across an ordinary onion in one of the parcels.

(4e)   He looks at the onion, and thinks it would go nicely with his lunch of herring, bread and cheese.

(4f)   He cuts it up into thin slices, and puts these on his bread.

(4g)   In no time, he has eaten everything and fallen into a contented sleep.

Sentences (4a–c) provide the setting and the start of the story. Sentence (4d) is the one that invokes a dual perspective in the form of a false belief held by Gerrit, while (4d′) is the alternative sentence that induces a single perspective with no false belief. Sentences (4e–g) depict actions that have different implications in the single- and double-perspective contexts. The single-perspective story focusses solely on the satisfaction of Gerrit, whereas in the double-perspective version, the reader also has to observe Gerrit destroying his master's valuable bulb. The time taken to read each version, using a self-paced reading paradigm, was the crucial measure.

Surprisingly, there appeared to be no increases in reading times for the dual-perspective passages. This suggests that over short tracts of narrative, where a clear double perspective is brought into play, the text maps onto both perspectives readily, and that toggling between them takes no extra time or an immeasurably small amount of extra time. Alternatively, it might be the case that both perspectives co-exist without toggling, and that co-existence takes no extra time. Of course, it remains to be seen whether long-term immersion in one perspective leads to a detectable processing time when a second (pre-established) perspective is introduced. Clearly, given the lack of an effect on reading time, further investigation is called for.

How multiple perspectives are processed is a considerable issue, and psychological work on it has not been particularly extensive. As we have seen, what evidence there is suggests that both real-world and counterfactual information including false beliefs may be simultaneously available for processing. Furthermore, we suggest that the principle of minimal departure, mentioned earlier, leads to a position where real-world constraints must have a priority realized through automatic accessibility of scenarios containing that real-world information if it is to be readily used during the concurrent interpretation of counterfactuals in a fictional world. It would be of great interest to see how automatically inferences were made on the basis of some narrative situation counterfactual to the real world, and whether real-world facts interfered with or slowed down how rapidly a counterfactual-based inference might be made. For instance, in a world with no vehicles, it is impossible to drive. Such an inference would be readily made, but the question is whether a statement that a character drove somewhere would take longer to process compared to, say, a situation where vehicles do exist, but a particular character didn't have one. There is much to be explored about accessing mundane facts in a counterfactual world.

Counterfactuality represents one type of situation where it is necessary to entertain more than one model: a model that represents reality, and one that represents the counterfactual situation. In fact, the need to represent different states of affairs in co-existing mental models is a typical situation. Amongst other distinctions that are most studied is that between literal and figurative interpretations of discourse, which we shall turn to shortly. Before doing that, let us note that even the notion of two representations being used (reality and counterfactual) is only the start of what might be needed to properly represent what happens when counterfactuals are encountered in narrative. Part of the author's intention might be to draw the reader's attention to the type of counterfactuality in a narrative: it may often be the case that the clash between reality and counterfactuality may set up specific situations that are key to the narrative structure. Consider the case of Gerrit and the tulip. Mistaking the valuable tulip for an onion sets up a tension in the narrative since readers can predict future difficulty for Gerrit and/or other characters. For this to happen, the mismatch itself must be given an interpretation, setting up yet another mental representation of the consequences of the mistake. Awareness of such clashes can create suspense, which we will discuss in Chapter 8.

Mental spaces

Theoretical background

Counterfactuality, including false beliefs, is interesting for many reasons. As we have indicated, from a processing perspective, comprehension of counterfactual situations relies upon at least two separate types of representation: the 'facts' of the counterfactual world, and the facts of the real world. In a mental representation, mappings have to take place into both of these domains, so the picture is more complex than the single language-to-scenario mappings discussed in Chapter 2. The basic ideas remain the same, however. Meaning depends upon interpretation with respect to background knowledge, albeit with more than one source of background knowledge. Multiple representations are the norm rather than the exception, and a general theory of such multiple representations is that of Fauconnier's (1994, 1997) *mental spaces* (see also Coulson, 2001, for a psychologically-based description).

Consider the following case based on a similar example in Coulson (2001, pp. 22–23).

(5a)   Daniel is an actor.
(5b)   He plays a junior wizard in the *Harry Potter* films.
(5c)   But in real life, he is a member of the actors' union.

Clearly, there is a need to partition Daniel's role as a junior wizard in (5b) from his real-life situation, otherwise Daniel would have unusual powers in real life. According to mental space theory, there is a 'base' space for the actor Daniel, and then a 'film' space for his character. Each space contains coherent information and the partitioning prevents any contradiction. Nevertheless a relation is recognized: the actor and his character are *counterparts*, corresponding entities, and links are made between them by *connectors*. Note that on the basis of (5a), an actor scenario becomes accessible, and such a scenario should have slots for the acting that the character does. The junior wizard information is thus separated from the real-world information about Daniel, because it fits a different role-slot.

As Fauconnier points out, the idea is that a new space is set up when utterances concern objects or events that require different background assumptions from those in current use. This was exactly the case we were making in relation to counterfactual worlds earlier. So, following the principle of minimal departure, as far as possible, background knowledge changes will not be made. Although in the films, Daniel plays a junior wizard, so can (eventually) cast spells and perform other magical acts, he still behaves like an ordinary person in other respects.

The need for new mental spaces can be indicated explicitly by what are called *space builders*, or their construction may occur implicitly, because in order to understand something, such a construction is required. Space building includes a variety of language devices, including conjunctions (e.g., *if* – where some hypothetical and possibly counterfactual situation has to be represented). Further examples include modal adverbs (*maybe, possibly* – both of these express a degree of possible current counterfactuality), and expressions of belief (*thinks, believes, asserts*) where the truth of the expressions may be potentially questionable. Others include times and locations other than the assumed present, such as *once upon a time, in May 1900, on Mars*. The way in which readers build new spaces in narrative texts has been explored in text world theory (Werth, 1999; see also Gavins, 2007).

An empirical demonstration of mental spaces

Let us illustrate the processing consequences of having an appropriate mental space structure through the medium of an experiment on understanding causation. Consider the following examples:

(6a)   The streets are wet because it is raining. [Simple causal]

(6b)   It is raining because the streets are wet. [Diagnostic]

While (6a) depicts a simple, natural and physical causation, (6b) is, by contrast, a diagnostic requiring that someone think or otherwise cognize that the observation of wet streets is good evidence to suppose that it is raining. Thus (6b) requires the construction of a mental space in which someone holds the belief that wet streets lead to the (*defeasible*, or potentially incorrect) inference that it is raining. Traxler, Sanford, Aked, and Moxey (1997) used sentence reading time to test the idea that (6b) requires the construction of a more complex representation than does (6a) in order to be understood. They showed that examples like (6b) take longer to read for understanding than does (6a). However, the situation is precisely reversed if an explicit cue, functioning as a space builder, such as *John thought* or *John said*, prefixes the sentences, as in (7a) and (7b). (The cue *John said* is included because it is assumed to imply that John must have thought this if he said it.)

(7a)   John thought/said the streets are wet because it is raining. [Simple causal]

(7b)   John thought/said it is raining because the streets are wet. [Diagnostic]

Traxler et al. (1997) suggest that this is because without the *John thought/said* information, the diagnostic sentence (6b) requires the extra operation of setting up a mental space in which someone is assumed to expect this, while in (7b), since the information is provided, it is easier to comprehend because the extra operation is circumvented. The relative ease of reading (6a) rather than (7a) is explained as follows. In (6a) there is no need for anyone to think this, so there is no requirement for a mental space representing a belief, and in (7a) where it is asserted that someone thought this, the expression of belief is more than is required for a simple factual statement.

This experiment shows that when a new mental space is called for, but not explicitly signalled by a space builder, more processing effort is required, manifesting as longer reading times. This is presumably because the need for a mental space has to be discovered during online processing. When a space builder is used, this process is circumvented, and so processing is facilitated.

Figurative language: processing and rhetorical use

Literal and non-literal meanings

Just as it is important to keep separate mental spaces for reality and for counterfactual situations in narratives, so it is that with figurative language it is important to distinguish what is literally being said from what the intended meaning is. Figurative language covers a multitude of phenomena, including metaphor, metonymy, irony, hyperbole, understatement and euphemism (see Gibbs, 1994; Gibbs & Colston, 2007; Shen, 2006). One important research question in psychology is how this language is processed. If non-literal language is used, do people adopt a strategy involving the following stages: first trying to establish a literal meaning, and then later working out an 'intended meaning' if the literal understanding fails? Or is there a different strategy? We will examine these issues in the remainder of this chapter.

Classically, literal meaning is taken to be what transpires when the meanings of individual words in an utterance are combined under syntactic guidance – the notion of compositionality that is so central to many ideas in formal linguistics. Non-literal meaning occurs when the intended meaning of an utterance is different from the literal, lexically composed meaning, i.e., when it is non-compositional. This led to the general idea, now challenged by most researchers, that in the face of, say, a metaphorical proposition, literal meaning is first established, using compositional principles. According to this view, when the interpreter notes that this does not make sense (its significance does not fit the ongoing act of communication), then a more appropriate non-literal interpretation is established. This literal-first, *standard pragmatic model* is generally ascribed to Grice (1975). As Gibbs (1994, 2002a) has pointed out, the major problem with this account is the tacit assumption that literal meaning is the norm, and figurative interpretations are the exception which supposedly might require extra processing effort. This seems unlikely because figurative language is now recognized as being extremely common in a wide range of communication types, so extra processing would be inefficient. Many experiments have been conducted to test the standard pragmatic model and they have generally shown it to be inadequate for interpreting *conventional* figurative expressions. For conventional expressions, models which provide *direct access* to figurative meanings at an early stage of processing are now generally preferred. Nevertheless, there is recent neuroscience evidence by metaphor researchers which suggests that *novel* metaphors might be processed differently from conventional ones, and some consideration of the underlying literal meaning of a metaphor might be of importance for the inferencing necessary to establish the meaning of a novel metaphor (which would correspond to the idea of secondary processing for literary texts, discussed in Chapter 2). We will look shortly at examples of empirical work in relation to the interpretation of different types of metaphor, following a brief overview of the role of metaphor in everyday language.

Everyday metaphors are commonplace

There is a considerable body of work showing that metaphors are fundamental to the way we think. Indeed, metaphors are so commonplace that it has been claimed that they are one of the main ways that we understand the world, a view championed by Lakoff and Johnson in cognitive linguistics (e.g., Lakoff, 1987; Lakoff & Johnson, 1980; see also Cacciari & Glucksberg, 1994 and Gibbs, 1994, for psychological accounts). A distinction is made by these researchers between *conceptual metaphors* (indicated by capitals), the way that we mentally construct our experience metaphorically, and *linguistic metaphors*, the expressions actually used in texts or speech. Lakoff and Johnson's (1980) examples are now extremely well known in linguistics and psychology and include the conceptual metaphor ARGUMENT IS WAR (with linguistic realizations such as *He attacked every weak point in my argument* and *His criticisms were right on target* (p. 4)) and the conceptual metaphor IDEAS ARE FOOD (e.g., *I just can't swallow that claim*; *That's food for thought* (pp. 46–47)). Conceptual metaphors present a systematic way of thinking about a topic. Lakoff (e.g., 1987, pp. 380–415) and Kövecses (e.g., 2002, pp. 95–98) discuss the example of anger. They suggest that one common conceptual metaphor is ANGER IS A HOT FLUID IN A CONTAINER, giving rise to linguistic examples such as:

- She could only just contain her anger.
- His blood started to boil.
- There was steam coming out of his ears.
- He exploded with rage.
- She blew her top.

According to Lakoff and Kövecses, the body is conceptualized as the container in this conceptual metaphor. As anger builds up, the intensification of the emotion is reflected in references to boiling and steam. Eventually, as the liquid becomes hotter, the containment may fail, with the possibility of an explosion and the lid of the container being blown off. The conceptual metaphor links together various linguistic examples which indicate different stages in the development of anger. Also, this particular conceptual metaphor relates systematically to more general conceptual metaphors, such as the idea that anger is related to heat (e.g., *he lost his cool*) and agitation (e.g., *he was quivering with rage*) and that emotions generally might be held in containers (e.g., *I just can't contain my joy*). (For other depictions of a range of metaphors and metaphorical systems, see Goatly (1997), Kövecses (2002), Semino (2008) and Gibbs (2008), which are also excellent primers on metaphor in general.)

Metaphors consist of two parts, the *source domain* – this is the metaphorical component, like a boiling liquid in a container, and the *target domain* – the non-metaphorical component which is to be understood in terms of the source, such as anger. In general, this is a matter of using a more tangible and conceptually accessible source idea to represent a more abstract target. Background knowledge is drawn on to make the connections, utilizing scenario details. As in Scenario-Mapping Theory, each domain has various slots, so for the above ANGER IS A HOT FLUID IN A CONTAINER example, the source domain has slots for the physical container, the hot fluid in the container, the intensity of the heat, etc. and the target domain has corresponding slots for the body, the anger and the intensity of the anger, etc. The term 'mapping' is commonly used by cognitive linguists for the correspondences between the source and target domains. Although the general idea of utilizing background knowledge is compatible with Scenario-Mapping Theory, 'mapping' in cognitive linguistics means the relations between two conceptual domains in contrast with Scenario-Mapping Theory's use of the term to mean the process of linking conceptual knowledge and language.

Two specific aspects of the use of metaphors are particularly important for our discussion in the remainder of this book. First, according to cognitive linguists, metaphors can often powerfully constrain the way people think. For instance, if arguments are conceived of as war, then it may be more likely that arguments are viewed as confrontational and tactical, rather than being a way of resolving difficulties (Lakoff & Johnson, 1980; Tannen, 1999). Lakoff and Johnson (1980, p. 10) describe the 'highlighting and hiding' function of metaphors, which means that they can serve to focus attention in particular directions, a topic which we will discuss (in relation to other language features) in detail in Chapters 4 and 5. A second point is that metaphors are viewed by cognitive linguists as having an experiential base. Some concepts are understood in relation to other concepts, but Lakoff and Johnson (1980, pp. 56–68) argue that certain basic concepts, such as spatial concepts, are understood in terms of direct experience by the body. They therefore view a conceptual metaphor such as HAPPY IS UP (e.g., *My spirits rose* (p. 15)) as being grounded in our physical experience of posture, since sadness is associated with drooping of the body and happiness with a more upright position. We will return to the topic of experientiality in Chapters 6–8, when we examine psychological and neuroscience evidence for embodiment effects during reading generally (see Gibbs & Matlock, 2008, for a discussion of embodiment and metaphor specifically).

Processing metaphorical language: experimental evidence

While the way that metaphor and other figurative constructions are ubiquitous in language would appear to make a literal-first strategy potentially inefficient, there is no substitute for empirical investigation to determine the processing patterns people actually use. There have been many such studies, mostly aimed at determining what rapid and immediate interpretations are typically made in the face of ordinary figurative language usage. The interest in early, fast processing follows in the tradition introduced in Chapter 2 and in the work on counterfactual worlds discussed earlier in this chapter, where early processes were seen to be diagnostic of many aspects of language understanding.

One classic study illustrates how the literal-first, standard pragmatic model is almost certainly wrong. Glucksberg, Gildea, and Bookin (1982) had participants decide whether simple statements were literally true or false. So, a metaphorical statement like *Some jobs are jails* is literally false. If the standard pragmatic model literal meaning is first established, then a *no* judgement of the literal content should be made easily and the metaphorical interpretation should not interfere with it. Similarly, a sentence which is literally false (e.g., *Some birds are apples*) should easily receive a *no* judgement. In fact, all other things being equal, the time to make a *no* judgement for the two examples should be about the same according to this model. However, the experiment showed that sentences that had obvious metaphorical interpretations caused longer response times to produce a *no* answer, suggesting that the metaphorical interpretation interfered with the literal judgement. This suggests that the metaphorical interpretation is there from the start and such a position is not, of course, predicted by the standard pragmatic model.

One criticism of this interesting finding (Dascal, 1987) is that it may be difficult to determine whether something is literally false, and that while doing so, the participant may recover the metaphorical meaning. However, the results clearly argue against the view that only when a statement is found to be literally false is a search for a metaphorical interpretation launched. Rather, the retrieval of a metaphorical meaning seems to be automatic for simple cases like *Some jobs are jails*. Furthermore, subsequent studies by Keysar (1989) suggest that the conclusions of Glucksberg et al. (1982) are justified. He created materials in which a prior context section provided support for a later statement being literally true or false, or metaphorically true or false. Even with this contextual bias, when a statement was literally true but metaphorically false, or literally false but metaphorically true, verification times were long. In another study, Keysar investigated the time taken to read sentences that followed on from a literal- or metaphorical-supporting context. Reading times were longest when there was a mismatch, regardless of which interpretation was under consideration. Thus readers determine multiple contextually appropriate interpretations, whether they are metaphorical or literal, and metaphorical meaning retrieval is not blocked even in cases where a literal meaning *is* derivable. These data suggest that the traditional standard pragmatic view is incorrect.

Using a different methodology, McElree and Nordlie (1999) presented strings of words, one at a time, such that the final word forced an interpretation of the string into a literal sentence interpretation (*Some tunnels are sewers*), figurative (*Some mouths are sewers*) or anomalous (*Some lamps are sewers*). Participants had to judge whether each word string was meaningful. They were encouraged to make a response by the presentation of a tone: the delay to the onset of the tone varied. The results showed that there was no time difference in the judgements for literal and metaphorical interpretations, suggesting that metaphorical interpretations were not made after a literal interpretation, but occur at the initial stage. These and many similar findings (see Gibbs, 2003, for a discussion) suggest that the literal-first interpretation is untenable for metaphors with conventional meanings where there is adequate context to support the interpretation of metaphors. Therefore for conventional metaphors, the standard pragmatic model, which suggests the rejection of the literal-first information before access to metaphorical meaning, seems untenable, and it seems more likely that a model proposing direct access to metaphorical meaning is correct. There is nevertheless some disagreement about whether at the initial stage of interpreting conventional metaphors there is direct access only to the metaphorical meaning (e.g., Gibbs, 1994) or whether the literal and metaphorical meanings are both activated (Giora, 2008; Giora & Fein, 1999).

Neuroscience evidence supports the direct access model for conventional metaphors, showing that the processing of literal language and conventional metaphorical expressions is not qualitatively different and that metaphorical meanings can be accessed rapidly providing there is adequate context (e.g., de Grauwe, Swain, Holcomb, Ditman, & Kuperberg, 2010; Kazmerski, Blasko, & Dessalegn, 2003; Lai, Curran, & Menn, 2009; Pynte, Besson, Robichon, & Poli, 1996). There have, however, been processing differences found between conventional and novel metaphors, suggesting that initial consideration of literal meaning might be more important for novel metaphors (e.g., Arzouan, Goldstein, & Faust, 2007; Tartter, Gomes, Dubrovsky, Molholm, & Vala Stewart, 2002). This would make sense in terms of Shklovsky's (1965) defamiliarization theory and the notion of secondary processing discussed in Chapter 2. Conventional metaphors can be viewed as being interpreted in a seamless fashion, but novel metaphors may require more processing, which might involve consideration of underlying literal meanings. Indeed, even the classic psychological work by Glucksberg et al. (1982) discussed at the start of this section suggests that for novel metaphors an alternative strategy might be necessary and that this might resemble the literal-first model that Glucksberg et al. were rejecting for conventional metaphors. We will return to this point about the processing of novel metaphors in our consideration of creativity in the following section.

Our discussion so far has focussed on the timing of metaphor interpretation, but neuroscientists have also examined which brain areas are activated during metaphor comprehension. Traditionally, metaphors have been considered to be processed primarily in the right hemisphere, but literal language processing is associated with the left hemisphere. Coulson (2008) has pointed out that this is puzzling, when we take into account the psychological evidence that literal and metaphorical meanings are processed in the same way. Coulson looks critically at the original evidence for the 'right hemisphere theory' (e.g., Winner & Gardner, 1977) suggesting some methodological weaknesses in this research and also indicating that some of this work was conducted on visual metaphors, which may give different results from verbal metaphors. More recent evidence is, by contrast, rather mixed in terms of locating metaphor comprehension in the brain. Some studies suggest the involvement of both hemispheres (e.g., Coulson & van Petten, 2007; Faust & Weisper, 2000), some suggest left hemisphere activation only (e.g., Rapp, Leube, Erb, Grodd, & Kircher, 2004), and some suggest a major right hemisphere contribution (e.g., Sotillo et al., 2005). To account for these different findings, Arzouan et al. (2007; see also Goldstein, Arzouan, & Faust, 2008) have suggested that the brain imaging technologies used in previous studies may not have been suitable for observing the subtle mechanisms involved in interpreting metaphorical language. Arzouan et al. use measuring devices which they argue have better resolution for identifying the relevant brain activity. They find that both hemispheres are involved in both conventional and novel metaphor interpretation, but that novel metaphors (which they draw from poetry) activate the right hemisphere more at particular points in processing.

Creative use of metaphors and similes in narratives

Methods of developing metaphors creatively   Cognitive linguists (e.g., Lakoff, 1987; Lakoff & Johnson, 1980) originally laid emphasis on the metaphorical patterning of conceptual systems, so their focus was generally on *conventional metaphors* which are so much part of the system of thought that speakers and listeners may not be aware of them as metaphors. There has, nevertheless, been recognition within cognitive linguistics (e.g., Lakoff & Turner, 1989) that there can be *creative use of metaphors*, which may be more noticeable. The function of metaphors in extended discourse, where creative use may sometimes be particularly evident, has been studied in detail by corpus linguists and stylisticians (e.g., Goatly, 1997; Kövecses, 2010; Semino, 2008; Semino & Steen, 2008; Steen, 1994).

Even some basic idioms can be used creatively in everyday conversation and in written narratives. In the past, idioms were generally viewed simply as 'dead metaphors', with some psychologists arguing that they are fixed, non-decomposable, expressions functioning like individual words arbitrarily connected to their meanings (e.g., Swinney & Cutler, 1979). However, Gibbs (1994) has challenged this idea and suggested that idioms may be of different types, including those which are non-decomposable and have lost their original meanings (e.g., *kick the bucket*, meaning 'to die') but also many which are more flexible and should not be viewed as 'dead'. In the latter category, some idioms can be modified grammatically, lexically and seman- tically (see Gibbs, 1994, for examples). For example, McGlone, Glucksberg, and Cacciari (1994) suggested that the expression *broke the ice* could be semantically modified into *shatter the ice*. Sanford (1999) illustrated such an idea with the following example:

(8)   The party was not going at all well; people were just sitting around talking to people they already knew. John got out his Fender Stratocaster. It was time to shatter the ice.

In this type of case, McGlone et al. (1994) argue that the literal meaning is used in order to generate the novel meaning. Our knowledge of the literal distinction between 'breaking' and the more energetic 'shattering' can be used analogic- ally to distinguish between the non-literal expressions, yielding interpretations that vary in intensity (i.e., overcoming social inhibitions, in contrast to energet- ically overcoming them). Naciscione (2010) has observed many examples of idiom modification in narrative texts, including the following:

(9) 'I turn over a new leaf every day,' I said [...]
'Well,' said Liz. 'Perhaps a new leaf isn't good enough. <u>Perhaps you</u> <u>need to turn over a new volume?</u>' She was better than I was at carrying metaphor to inscrutable lengths.

(Waterhouse, *Billy Liar*, cited in Naciscione (2010: 147), our underlining).

In the case of more original metaphors, cognitive linguists believe that they are frequently extensions or elaborations of conventional metaphors, so that although they may go beyond standard use, they are generally still rooted in familiar ideas that make them accessible to those interpreting them. For example, Lakoff and Turner (1989) suggest that in creative writing everyday background knowledge can be used to fill (scenario) slots that would not be filled in conventional metaphors and they give the example of Shakespeare's Hamlet *extending* the conventional metaphor of death as sleep by adding the possibility of dreaming from everyday scenario knowledge. Where the metaphor is developed by going beyond the normal scenario slots, they use the term *elaborating*. (See also Semino, 2008; Semino & Steen, 2008.)

Similes (either on their own or in conjunction with metaphors) are often used to introduce highly creative figurative forms (Semino, 2008, p. 17), as we will see in the next section. Similes use overt expressions, such as *like* and *as if*, to make a comparison between two different things rather than suggesting the equivalence relation of metaphors. It may be that the more explicit signalling of similes facilitates the introduction of more complex and novel figurative forms, possibly because it means that there is less chance of misinterpreting the novelty (e.g., by taking it literally). (See Bowdle & Gentner, 2005, and Glucksberg, 2008, for psychological discussions of this issue.)

A further point is that literary scholars have observed that metaphors and similes often form patterns. They may cluster together at key points in a story, and similar or related items may be repeated throughout a text (e.g., Lakoff & Turner, 1989, pp. 70–72; Semino, 2008; Werth, 1999). Repetition is an attention-controlling device which we will examine further in the next chapter.

Creative metaphor use in literary texts: some examples The effect of the above strategies can be better appreciated by some examples from literary texts. In (10), an extract from a short story in which a man is described dying from a heart attack on a beach, original figurative language is used, showing a combination of metaphors and similes (the signals introducing similes are underlined):

(10)   The pain catches him under the arms swiftly and silently, <u>like</u> his own
         father lifting him from behind, surprising him as a child playing in the
         garden. It stiffens him with fright, petrifies him into a shrunken posture
         [...] He lies fallen on the hard wet sand <u>as if</u> turned to stone [...] The pain
         crushes him [...] Words lie motionless in his throat, ready to speak, <u>like</u>
         loaded cartridges in a greased gun-barrel and he unable to reach the trigger.
         He is totally paralysed. Only his eyes record, <u>like</u> a camera still running
         after the tripod has collapsed onto its side.
                              (Leland (1983). *The Last Sandcastle*, p. 91, our underlining)

In this passage, there are a number of conventional metaphorical ideas, such as
pain being an external agent inflicting pressure (*The pain crushes him*), and
paralysis being as if turned to stone. In addition, the body is twice viewed as a
machine (the gun and the camera). More specifically, speech is viewed as the
firing of a weapon (as in *he fired questions at me* in everyday communication) and
visual perception is equated with a camera recording. Yet there are points at which
these figurative forms go beyond everyday conventional use in their level of detail,
such as the mention of the pain being like the man's father lifting him, and the
descriptions of machines that are ready to operate but not functioning properly (the
loaded gun that can't be shot, and the recording camera on the collapsed tripod).
What seems to be happening here is that creativity involves cueing richer scenarios
than would usually be drawn on in a conventional metaphor. These details can be
particularly appropriate to the situation, such as the collapsed tripod reflecting the
fallen man, making it parallel to the specific situation in the narrative.

Indeed creative figurative language can become very elaborate, as in the
following example from later in the same text (again, the signals introducing
similes are underlined):

(11)   His mind still appears to function, but with an already accepted sense of
         isolation, aware that the mechanical systems have packed up, leaving him <u>as
         if</u> locked in a room high up in some deserted building, cemented to the floor,
         with nothing but a screen at one end on which a film is showing, the only
         thing still working, pictures with which he cannot communicate or affect in
         any way. It is <u>almost like</u> a film shot thirty years before of himself as a boy
         upon a beach. The film is dim, scratched and monochromatic with its beige
         sky and ochre sand.
                              (Leland (1983). *The Last Sandcastle*, p. 92, our underlining)

In this case, two conventional metaphors (the body as a machine and the mind
as a machine) are combined to create this specific situation of a mind that
works in a body that doesn't work. The two similes (introduced by *as if*,
almost like) then construct a highly elaborate structure which includes further
figurative items that are relevant to this particular narrative, such as the
locked room, the deserted building, and being cemented to the floor representing isolation and paralysis. Here, the figurative elements become so

detailed that it is almost as if the locked room scenario is being set up as a parallel context alongside the main narrative context, the beach. Again, rich scenario knowledge is drawn on.

The distinction between conventional metaphors and creative metaphors raises the question of how creative metaphors are processed (and the same for similes). One notable feature is that the creative forms break our usual expectations and seem to prompt a noticing response. The striking nature and/or repetition of figurative expressions can make them foregrounded, pushing them into the forefront of the reader's attention, unlike fully conventional expressions. If a metaphor is creative rather than conventional, then secondary processing may occur. This is more time- and resource-consuming, and results in a heightened attention to the language being used, prompting defamiliarization. For novel metaphors, particularly complex ones, readers will normally be expected to recognize the distinct nature of the literal and the metaphorical levels (Gibbs, 1994). This relies upon the recognition of the literal interpretation at some stage. In addition, there are processes of interpretation and appreciation, both described in Gibbs (1994), which involve seeing the point of a metaphor in context and making aesthetic judgements about it respectively (see also Steen, 1994). As discussed in the previous section, there is some psychological and neuroscience evidence to suggest that conventional and novel metaphors are processed differently.

Interpreting creative figurative language can be seen as a problem-solving process which identifies the significance of novel metaphors and similes in the context described. For the machines in (10) and (11), the reader needs to recognize that just as the inability to operate these machines properly is frustrating, so is the paralysed man's inability to move his own body frustrating. The text is given additional coherence, which can provide a sense of aesthetic unity for readers, by the fact that the figurative language echoes what is literally happening in the main narrative. Hence, as we have seen, the collapsed tripod parallels the position of the fallen man, what Lakoff and Turner (1989, pp. 89–96) refer to as an 'image metaphor'. The embedding of references to childhood in the figurative language in both examples reflects the fact that the literal dying man may be seeing his life flash before him and/or reverting to a childhood state of dependency. Also the *dim, scratched and monochromatic* film in (11) can be read as parallel to the deteriorating vision of the dying man. Readers need to recognize the distinctiveness of the parallel literal and figurative levels and their relation to each other.

We have seen that creative language typically builds on conventional metaphors and similes and re-works them into new forms. Some argue that there is also scope for entirely new connections to be made, particularly in cases where image metaphors provide parallels between literal and figurative levels purely on the basis of similar physical properties such as shape

(Lakoff & Turner, 1989), since these can be formed on an ad hoc basis rather than having to be rooted in the language system. When the language departs from conventional usage, in whatever way, there is a defamiliarizing process, in which the language is looked at with fresh eyes. One supposed hallmark of literary language is that not only does the language itself receive greater attention, but it can make us look at described situations afresh, possibly also prompting thoughtful re-appraisal of the real world (Shklovsky, 1965; see also Cook, 1994; Miall & Kuiken, 1994). The following example might prompt this type of defamiliarization since an unusual connection is made between the counters used in the game of Scrabble, and confectionary.

(12)   We play two games. *Larynx*, I spell. *Valence. Quince. Zygote.* I hold the glossy counters with their smooth edges, finger the letters. The feeling is voluptuous. This is freedom, an eyeblink of it. *Limp*, I spell. *Gorge.* What a luxury. The counters are like candies, made of peppermint, cool like that. Humbugs, those were called. I would like to put them into my mouth. They would taste also of lime. The letter C. Crisp, slightly acid on the tongue, delicious.

                    (Atwood (1996). *The Handmaid's Tale*, p. 149, Atwood's italics,
                                                    our underlining)

The link between the similar shapes of the Scrabble counters and the candies is straightforward and is of the image type, but the simile is nevertheless strikingly original, particularly when combined with the earlier words such as *voluptuous, freedom* and *luxury*. This unusual combination can make readers look more carefully at the meaning of a particular passage. The sensual tastes in the candies are set up as a parallel to pleasure in simple literacy. This might normally seem somewhat extreme, but in the fictional story world the degree of appreciation is appropriate because literacy is banned. The unusual simile can give readers some fresh appreciation of what literacy means not only in the fictional world but in the real world, where many people take it for granted. Since the text can be read as a political allegory, the simile can potentially provide an indirect comment on real-world situations where literacy is banned. Hence mappings may be at multiple levels, with the Scrabble–confectionary mapping providing a counterfactual situation which could be mapped onto parallel real-world situations.

Metaphors, conceptual blending and emergent meaning

A development of mental space theory is conceptual blending, or conceptual integration theory (Fauconnier & Turner, 1998, 2002, 2008; see also Coulson, 2001). Conceptual blending accounts for emergent meaning, the way in which new meaning arises as a result of combining together information from mental spaces. One classic example is Grady, Oakley, and Coulson's (1999) discussion of the sentence *The surgeon is a butcher*. Here, there is the additional implication that the surgeon is incompetent, this resulting from a surgeon's finely skilled procedures being performed with the coarse-grained movements of a butcher. This is emergent meaning because this assumption of incompetence cannot be made for the butcher in his own domain. Conceptual blending theory explains this type of example using four mental spaces as follows, with the blended space ('the blend') merging elements from both input spaces:

- Input space (source): Butchery domain (e.g., A butcher cuts flesh)
- Input space (target): Surgery domain (e.g., A surgeon cuts flesh)
- Generic space: Common properties of the two input spaces (e.g., Professionals who cut flesh)
- Blended space: The surgeon cuts flesh like a butcher (i.e., is incompetent)

As Grady et al. (1999) point out, there are some common properties between the source input space (butcher) and the target input space (surgeon), e.g., both professionals cut flesh. The generic space shows these correspondences between the two input spaces. The blend includes the properties inherited from the two input spaces and the emergent content (the incompetence). Note that certain properties are not inherited, i.e., there is no implication here that the surgeon is going to sell the flesh (although Grady et al. suggest that the blend can potentially be elaborated on further).

Grady et al.'s example is conventional in the language, but the same type of conceptual blending can also be seen to underlie novel metaphors and similes. The following example is from an autobiographical account of a man trying to get help after a stroke at home and compares the semi-paralysed man to a commando and a pioneer crossing the Rockies.

(13)   [I] squirmed, commando-style, over the carpet to the head of the stairs [. . .] More squirming and then I was in the spacious living room and there, across the carpet on the floor, was the downstairs phone. I felt like a pioneer who, in crossing the Rockies, finally arrives in California.

(McCrum (1999). *My Year Off: Rediscovering Life after a Stroke*, pp. 12 and 14, our underlining)

Although figurative language which uses activity images as a source space and paralysis as a target space might seem inappropriate out of context, it makes perfect sense when we see it in this example. There is a shared generic space where there is a common element of activity under difficult conditions. The emergent meaning in the blend is that the author must have been significantly incapacitated if he has to describe movement from one room to another using these images of immense activity. In both of these cases, the additional meaning arises because the comparison is being made between two items which are in certain respects parallel, but also vastly different in terms of magnitude (i.e., differences in the surgeon's/butcher's movements in Grady et al.'s example and the scale of the traverse of the room and the landscape in (13)). Metaphors and similes require us to tap into our situation-specific (scenario) knowledge in order to be able to effectively compare and contrast the source and target space items in the relevant contexts.

Blending theory is based largely on assumptions about cognitive processes derived from the analysis of textual examples, rather than empirical work by psychologists (see Dancygier, 2012, for applications to narratives, and Gibbs, 2000, for a discussion of the psychological issues). However, there has been some examination of the idea by Coulson and van Petten (2002) using brain imaging. Drawing on findings from ERP analysis, they observe a continuum of processing effort from literal to figurative. This challenges the idea of a simple literal/figurative divide and suggests that the differences in processing different items might be due to a gradient of complexity and novelty rather than to metaphoricity in itself (see also Giora & Fein's, 1999, graded salience hypothesis for a similar suggestion). The number and complexity of mappings is viewed by Coulson and van Petten as cognitively taxing (see also Lai et al., 2009). Generally, this work supports the idea that conventional metaphors are a part of ordinary language use and processed in essentially the same way as literal language, but still leaves room for the idea that there is a different type of processing for the more complex metaphors.

Summary

Many narratives consist of multiple levels, and for this reason the psychological account of the literal interpretation of language given in Chapter 2 needed to be expanded in this chapter to take account of the processing of these multiple levels.

- One example is counterfactual worlds, where what is proposed is in fact false, but where the reader is invited to suppose that it is true. Counterfactuality is a property of all fictional narrative, as well as being commonplace in everyday life. We described how, during processing, both the counterfactual and the 'real' world seem to be accessed. Based on the empirical findings, we argue, in line with Ryan's principle of minimal departure, that with counterfactual worlds, minimal changes are made to the assumed realities in those worlds, thus real-world knowledge is used even when we are understanding a counterfactual situation. We presented further evidence that when we have to switch between alternative conceptions, the time taken to do this is minimal, suggesting that both conceptions are available effectively simultaneously.

- We discussed the cognitive linguistic concept of mental spaces, a way of separating conceptions that may be contradictory, and we gave an example of an empirical demonstration of these spaces.
- We have provided an overview of empirical evidence which shows that conventional metaphors seem to be interpreted by directly accessing metaphorical meaning, contrary to the standard pragmatic model. However, it seems that novel metaphors may prompt secondary processing, requiring some early consideration of literal meaning. This may result in attention being focussed on the style of delivery and the message content. This, we suggest, corresponds to the literary idea of foregrounding, to be explored in the next chapter.

4   Attention in text: foregrounding
       and rhetorical focussing

Over the next two chapters, we look at the idea that text processing is not a uniform thing. Some parts of a text may be processed more substantially or differently than others, and this is modulated by a number of factors. In short, discourse processing is selective. This is a psychological claim about processing, but it has a counterpart in functional aspects of text structure, in that not all parts of a text, or even a sentence, are equally important. A way of bridging text structure and processing is through what we call the *Rhetorical Focussing Principle*: the task of a writer is to cause a reader to pay particular attention to X, and not to Y. This may be because X constitutes something important, while Y is simply the background against which X happens. It may be that X leads to a set of inferences that the writer would like the reader to make, but that another set of inferences, Y, would be in conflict, constituting a counter-argument. Such an opposition as this is important in political rhetoric. Also, in detective fiction, the writer might want to introduce a clue in such a way that it is just, but only just, encoded by the reader (and thus an instance of the X–Y balance), so that when the story develops the clue can be recognized and used, but does not lead to a strong conclusion when it is first introduced. In the humanities, Rabinowitz (1987) summarizes the issue by saying that a narrative text has:

> [...] a hierarchical organization of details: we do not attend to everything equally [...] the stressed features in a text serve as a basic structure on which to build an interpretation [...] we read with the prior understanding that we are more expected to account for a detail that is stressed [...] than for a detail that is not. (1987, p. 53)

The Rhetorical Focussing Principle raises two questions: what means does a writer have to control the X–Y balance? And how do these means, or devices, work in terms of processing? These questions have been tackled in different ways in the humanities and in the psychology of discourse. First, we explore some of the ideas resulting from commentary in the humanities, and then develop a more psychological argument.

Foregrounding and defamiliarization: definition and origins

Foregrounding is an important notion for the operation of the Rhetorical Focussing Principle and has a long history in the humanities. We have looked briefly at the idea of foregrounding in previous chapters and will now consider it in more detail. *Foregrounding* is the use of either unusual linguistic forms or an unusually high or low density of particular linguistic forms, these being sufficiently prominent to contribute to the overall interpretation of a text, including controlling the attention paid to different parts of it. Historically, the idea of foregrounding derives from work in the 1930s by Havránek and Mukařovský, with the term itself later introduced into English in Garvin's (1964) translation of these writers' works into English (Havránek, 1964; Mukařovský, 1964a, 1964b).

As we have seen in previous chapters, the notion of foregrounding is related to the earlier idea of *defamiliarization*, primarily associated with Shklovsky (1965, originally published in 1917). We will now look at the origins of this idea. Shklovsky was concerned with just what it is that makes literary language special, which he believed it to be. His arguments can nevertheless be applied to a wider range of text types, and offer interesting opportunities for the development of psychological processing accounts. Shklovsky's argument was that perception of things in everyday life is 'habitualized', resulting in 'automatic processing' (our term). For a writer to produce something original, it is necessary to avoid everyday automatic processing, and cause people to look at and think about what is represented in a text in a new and more detailed way than normal. Thus the text 'defamiliarizes' what is being presented, and in so doing offers something rich and dynamic. In the present chapter, we shall look in detail at foregrounding, which involves making parts of a text prominent and favoured for processing. Shklovsky's idea was that by using unusual devices (subsequently termed 'foregrounding'), what would normally be considered mundane could be made to stand out, thereby 'prolonging attention' (p. 22). Overall, Shklovsky's work is significant because it provides an early statement about shallow processing in ordinary reading (shallow processing will be explored in Chapter 5) and the idea of defamiliarization provides an intuitively plausible hypothesis about how readers might respond to novelty in language, with attention being controlled by stylistic devices.

Havránek and Mukařovský continued Shklovsky's approach, examining the range of linguistic devices used. Havránek (1964) uses the term 'automatization', defining it as:

a use of the devices of the language, in isolation or combination with each other [. . .] such a use that the expression itself does not attract any attention; the communication occurs, and is received, as conventional in linguistic form. (p. 9)

Foregrounding, by contrast, he defines as:

the use of the devices of the language in such a way that this use itself attracts attention and is perceived as uncommon, as deprived of automatization, as deautomatized. (p. 10)

The essentially psychological nature of these ideas is revealed by these quotations. Mukařovský (1964a) pointed out that foregrounding devices can be found in language in general, but suggested that a high degree of fore-grounding is a special indicator of literary language (pp. 19–20). Along with some contemporary opinion (e.g., Stockwell, 2002), we believe that fore-grounding is a property of language use in general, since non-literary types of communication, such as advertising, journalism, political discourse, popular fiction, do in fact make heavy use of foregrounding. Indeed, even everyday conversation makes creative use of language by means of foregrounding (Carter, 2004). So although the study of foregrounding has largely grown out of literary studies, it can be regarded as having much broader relevance. These early ideas of defamiliarization and foregrounding have been extremely influential in the humanities, but the arguments for them, while typically well-illustrated with examples, are impressionistic and were not intended to provide a well-worked-out basis for a cognitive model of narrative processing.

From these early beginnings, the notion of foregrounding has become central to the modern study of stylistics, the humanities area where writing style is studied. In addition, foregrounding has become more and more associated with the idea of controlling the processing patterns in discourse. Leech and Short (2007) provide a key survey of types of foregrounding in narrative fiction (see also Douthwaite, 2000; Leech, 2008). Leech and Short (2007) suggest that foregrounding exists at multiple linguistic levels, and they provide numerous examples of different types. A short list includes:

- Typographical devices: for instance, using italics, bold, or other physical properties, such as spacing.
- Punctuation devices: for instance, unusual punctuation or a lack of the usual punctuation.
- Phonological devices: for instance, alliteration.
- Lexical/semantic devices: for instance, coinages, or rare, unusual, or abnor-mally long or short words. Also, unusual metaphors (as discussed in Chapter 3).
- Syntactic devices: for instance, using cleft constructions.
- Discourse devices: for instance, features that deliberately disrupt the normal cohesion and coherence of a work.

Foregrounding is nowadays viewed in terms of *deviation* from some norm (e.g., Leech & Short, 2007). So, for example, in normal typography, italicization

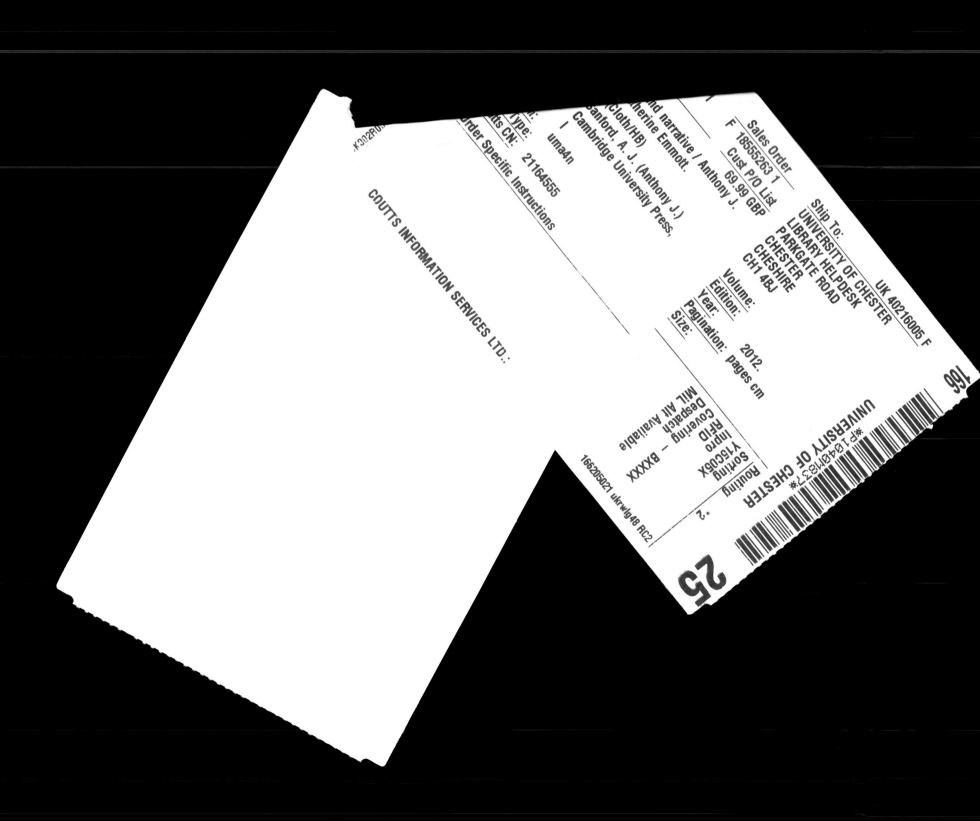

is a deviation, and cleft constructions are rare compared to other syntactic forms for sentences. Some stylistics researchers (e.g., Short, 1996; Wales, 2001) view repetition as a distinct type of foregrounding, but we view repetition as a form of deviation, since repetition can provide an unusual degree of regularity, creating deviation at discourse level.

Leech and Short (2007, p. 41) suggest that all literary foregrounding is a derivative of psychological prominence, and that all psychological prominence results from statistical deviation of some sort. However, the opposites are not the case. Leech and Short point out that all instances of statistical deviance do not lead to psychological prominence of that feature, and all instances of psychological prominence will not have literary relevance. In other words, there is a point at which statistical deviation becomes noticeable to the reader, and even then such deviation will not necessarily have a rhetorical purpose. Our explanation of secondary processing in Chapter 2 works on the same basis: secondary processing will sometimes lead to relatively mundane inferences, but for highly unusual language and/or content, the inferences may be sufficiently noticeable to prompt a literary interpretation. In order to assess deviations, Leech and Short recommend a statistical analysis of texts (see also Leech, 2008). For instance, in order to assess the use of very short sentences as a device, strictly it is necessary to assess the general distribution of sentence lengths within a text, to get an internal norm, or against a corpus of texts within the same genre, to get an external norm. Which baseline is actually likely to be the most relevant is, of course, an empirical issue, but the principles are clear enough.

From a psychological perspective, the brain is generally very good at spotting regularities. Statistical learning takes place when patterns that exist in the world (or a text) are encoded within the brain. Regularities may be identified in incoming discourse, and deviations from 'norms' may be readily spotted (including both rare forms and over-regularities). It is also possible for local norms to be established, such that what was originally a deviation becomes a new norm. For instance, a writer may establish a new norm of using very long sentences, longer than the 'average' a reader might normally encounter. While this may be a deviation at first, it may become established as a new norm. Such patterns occur over the course of tracts of writing. In any given instance, it may be necessary to provide an empirical test of whether a posited exceptional form or posited regularity in writing is in fact detected, and has some effect. We will present empirical methods for assessing the impact of specific linguistic devices on readers later in this chapter and in the following chapter.

Foregrounding in narrative: form and function

Foregrounding can be described in terms of the *form* and *function* of the linguistic devices. Researchers have drawn attention to a vast range of different types of foregrounding devices, but, for reasons of space, we can only provide a few illustrative examples. Detailed lists can be found in Douthwaite (2000), Leech (2008), and Leech and Short (2007). Our examples are provided to show what some of these linguistic devices look like in real texts, and to illustrate some of their possible functions. At this stage, these examples are selected purely on an intuitive basis, picking out linguistic features which a stylistician might point to as potentially significant (based on our own judgement).

As already illustrated, the form of a foregrounded item or passage may be described in terms of the linguistic level(s) at which it occurs, ranging from the typographical and phonological to the discourse level. We can also categorize the form in terms of the type of deviation, depending on whether the writer completely breaks the rules of the language, or uses an existing but unusual item, or uses ordinary items with an unusually high frequency. Each of these possible types of deviation will be looked at in turn.

Breaking linguistic 'rules'   It is quite common for literary writers to break linguistic 'rules', sometimes quite radically in more experimental forms of writing. They may use coinages or break the usual syntactic rules. Punctuation can also be used in unconventional ways or omitted. One well-known example is the final section of James Joyce's (1960) *Ulysses*, where there is no punctuation for forty-six pages (apart from a final full stop). At discourse level, sections, chapters and parts can appear in an unconventional order, as in Alasdair Gray's (1994) *Lanark: A Life in 4 Books*, which begins with Book Three, then moves on to the Prologue and Book One.

Two examples of cases where writers break the usual linguistic 'rules' are as follows:

(1)   Nora Meehan [. . .] was labouring to give birth to her gelatinous, moaning, dankerous baby boy.

(Nolan (1988). 'My Autobiography Entitled
"A Mammy Encomium"', p. 3)

(2)   Back work soon someday.

(Gardam (1984). 'Stone Trees', p. 47)

In (1) there is use of a coinage, *dankerous*, in addition to the rare form *gelatinous*. In seeking to determine what function such foregrounding devices might have, humanities researchers typically rely on their intuitions, suggesting possible functions. So, one possible function of (1) is that affect might be induced by using words with negative connotations. Although *dankerous* is a made-up word, it might have negative connotations due to its resemblance to the words *dank* and *dangerous*.

In (2) the grammatical rules are broken in an obvious manner, since the subject, the verb and the preposition *to* (in 'back to work') are omitted. The suggested function in this case is that the 'broken' syntax is appropriate to the thinking style of the bereaved character, a possibility that may seem more plausible if this example is viewed in its original context, where there are numerous breaches of grammatical rules and discourse conventions (Emmott, 2002).

Unusual items   Even where foregrounded items do not break linguistic/discourse rules, they show deviation from norms if they are unusual, either in the language generally or in a particular context. Foregrounding also includes grammatical and typographical forms which differ sufficiently from the norm to provide a noticeable contrast with the surrounding text. Cleft structures, pseudo-clefts and italics, for example, are used in contrast to the more usual non-cleft structures and non-italicized typefaces (and by convention are generally used as forms of emphasis). The cleft is used mostly for the specific purpose of contrastive focus, as in (3), where the shop assistants are contrasted with the other women:

(3)   all the shop assistants had grey hair and grey clothes. He looked carefully at all the counters. They varied in age, he could see that now, but their hair was uniformly grey. He glanced back at the shoppers. They were wearing varied colours and their hair was of varying shades. It was only the shop assistants who were grey. For some reason, then, all the women who worked dyed their hair grey.

                (O'Donnell (1980). *The Beehive*, p. 27, our underlining)

The pseudo-cleft in (4) has the function of (melo)dramatically revealing the answer to the question 'What is it?', highlighting a plot-crucial revelation.

(4)   And there it was! Mr. Boggis saw it at once, and he stopped dead in his tracks and gave a little shrill gasp of shock [...] There wasn't the slightest doubt about it! It was really unbelievable!

     What he saw was a piece of furniture that any expert would have given almost anything to acquire. [...] here was the fourth Chippendale Commode!

                (Dahl (1990a). 'Parson's Pleasure', pp. 151–153, our underlining)

Unusually long or short sentences can also be used for special effects (cf., Leech & Short, 2007). Shen (2006, 2007) provides examples of figures of speech such as metaphor, oxymoron (oppositions such as *sweet sadness*) and zeugma (e.g., odd coordinations governed by the same verb, such as *she painted her nails and the town red*), arguing that some forms of these figures of speech are strong foregrounding devices.

High frequency of use   Sometimes words and phrases are not inherently exceptional, but are used with unusually *high* frequency in a stretch of text. What is deviant in these cases is the lack of the usual variety of expression. At the phonological level, repetition of specific sounds can occur beyond the usual norm. Alliteration, rhyme, assonance (repeated stressed vowels) and other forms of sound-play are found particularly in poetry, but sound-play can also be found in narrative texts. Words, phrases, clauses and sentences may also be repeated. Some linguists also point to the repeated strategic selection of specific grammatical forms, such as a high incidence of intransitive forms when some transitive forms might normally be expected (Halliday, 1981; Leech & Short, 2007). Toolan (1990) and Emmott (2002) provide discussions of texts where there is pronominal foregrounding, lengthy chains of repeated pronouns including occasions where nouns might more normally be used.

Repetition can be deviant if it goes beyond readers' expectations about how often an item is normally likely to occur in a stretch of text. It can occur at various linguistic levels. In (5), there is a repetition of sounds, with the alliterative /p/ sounds being repeated at the start of each word in a string, and the /ɪŋ/ sounds (represented by *-ing*) re-occurring at the end of each word.

(5)   Mrs. Nora Meehan used lots of <u>p</u>oor, <u>p</u>onder<u>ing</u>, <u>p</u>erplex<u>ing</u> <u>p</u>ommel<u>ing</u>, mov<u>ing</u> Joseph's legs and arms manually.

> (Nolan (1988). 'My Autobiography Entitled "A Mammy Encomium" ',
> p. 4, our underlining)

Here, the repeated sounds in the words may have the function of creating the embodied feel of the forceful and repetitive movements described. Humanities researchers have proposed the notion of 'iconicity', in which the sounds of words are taken as sometimes reflecting their sense (e.g., Fischer & Nänny, 2001; Nänny & Fischer, 1999). As we shall discuss in Chapter 6, when readers encounter written descriptions of motion, motor areas in the brain that are responsible for enacting and recognizing the motion may be activated – so-called embodiment. We shall examine this in relation to the experiential aspect of reading, since we believe it to provide an explanation of why literary writing is often viewed as containing vivid sensual descriptions. Enhanced embodiment effects may well be closely correlated with foregrounding, an important issue for empirical enquiry.

Repetition can also be found at the lexical level, as in the repeated use of the word *dead* in (6), not only in the passage as a whole, but also within a single noun phrase *dead, thrice-dead little Spanish town*:

(6)   And in his battered Ford car her husband would take her into the <u>dead</u>, thrice-<u>dead</u> little Spanish town forgotten among the mountains. The great, sun-dried <u>dead</u> church, the <u>dead</u> portales, the hopeless covered market-place, where, the

first time she went, she saw a <u>dead</u> dog lying between the meat stalls and the vegetable array, stretched out as if for ever, nobody troubling to throw it away. <u>Deadness within deadness.</u>

(Lawrence (1996). 'The Woman Who Rode Away',
p. 39, our underlining)

This repetition of the word *dead* might be argued to be a theme of the work, with different parts of the narrative being given an overall coherence by repeatedly referring to this topic. Empirical work on this could perhaps determine the point at which a topic becomes prominent and whether it is remembered by a reader throughout a work, as a writer keeps returning to the topic.

A further form of repetition is parallelism, which refers to the repeated use of particular structures, including words that might be the same, as in (7) (the repeated word *white*), or just similar (e.g., if a writer was to place various colour words at the start of each phrase).

(7)   [Henry's feet] are <u>white as snow</u>, <u>white as marble</u>, <u>white as titanium</u>, <u>white as paper</u>, <u>white as bread</u>, <u>white as sheets</u>, <u>white as white</u> can be.

(Niffenegger (2005). *The Time Traveler's Wife*,
pp. 457–458, our underlining)

Possibly, the parallel expressions in (7) might create affect by stressing an unfortunate aspect of the scene. The example may have little emotional significance out of context. However, in the relevant text, this sentence occurs when we have been told that the character will lose his feet from frostbite if they remain white. The repetition of the word *white* in this case may be plausibly inferred to represent a situation which is so conclusive that it is hopeless, hence potentially inducing negative affect. This speculation is clearly open to empirical test: do such sentences produce negative affect, in and out of their story context?

Foregrounding as a basis for the empirical study of texts

Linguistic foregrounding is supposed to make items stand out, thereby prompting defamiliarization and hence capturing the attention of readers. The effect of these foregrounding devices needs to be established empirically, rather than simply being assumed. There is clearly considerable variety in terms of both the form and function of foregrounding devices, so how might foregrounding be studied through the application of psychological methods? One critical point is that foregrounding highlights aspects of text. For instance, one common function of foregrounding in narrative text is *local emphasis* (i.e., highlighting a key point, such as a climactic moment in the plot). Within psycholinguistics, one particularly well-studied way of highlighting concepts at the local level is through information structuring.

For example, rather than simply say *Harry was seen running away with the knife*, use of the cleft form *It was Harry who was seen running away with the knife* squarely puts emphasis on *Harry*, perhaps in contrast to anyone else. Similarly, information is emphasized by putting it in the main clause of a complex sentence, while to make information less prominent, it may be put in a subordinate clause. We shall discuss this type of information structuring in more detail later in this chapter, since empirical work on this type of language feature provides a paradigm case of research on attention focus within psycholinguistics.

Writers may also use foregrounding to *highlight globally relevant topics*, termed 'literary themes' (e.g., Louwerse & van Peer, 2002). In addition, foregrounding devices may (perhaps) also be used to induce imagery and affect (for the latter, see Miall, 2007; Miall & Kuiken, 1994). Another major use of foregrounding devices is to present the unusual thinking styles of characters, termed 'mind style' by stylisticians (Fowler, 1996). Halliday (1981) presents one of the most famous examples, suggesting that the heavy use of intransitive verbs in a text may be appropriate in describing a character who lacks understanding of causality. There are many other functions of foregrounding, but this list gives an idea of some reasons why writers use these devices. (See Douthwaite, 2000, for more examples.)

What all of the examples of foregrounding have in common is that they exemplify devices that draw the reader's attention to the text that falls within the scope of the device. This is perhaps the most basic property, and the most general feature of foregrounding. It is also a property that is in principle amenable to investigation by empirical psychology, and one that allows for some interesting theoretical developments that bridge humanities and psychological concepts. First, we look at some of the humanities-based empirical research on foregrounding, before introducing relevant work from psycholinguistics.

Investigations of foregrounding: research in the Empirical Study of Literature

Here we present a selection of the empirical work that has been done in the humanities in order to provide an overview of the approaches used. The studies address a number of different issues of interest. Although this is only a selection, the earlier of these are still very influential on current empirical work in the humanities. We will look particularly at the methodologies of these selected studies. For further examples, see Auracher and van Peer (2008), van Peer (2007), van Peer and Hakemulder (2006) and Zyngier, Bortolussi, Chesnokova, and Auracher (2008).

Researchers in the Empirical Study of Literature tend to seek high ecological validity in materials by selecting real texts, and they generally examine these texts in their full complexity rather than examining specific devices. There are difficulties, however, in terms of creating controlled experiments when there are so many variables. This method contrasts with that of psycholinguistics, described later in this chapter and in the next chapter, where specific, isolated linguistic features are studied in more tightly controlled materials.

Let us begin with van Peer's (1986) empirical investigation of fore-grounding in poetry. He used six poems, ranging from nineteenth-century verse by Wordsworth and Rossetti to twentieth-century modernist writers such as Dylan Thomas and e. e. cummings. Van Peer first analysed fore-grounding at different linguistic levels in these poems, identifying which lines of the poems he himself regarded as more or less foregrounded. In doing so, his aim was to be 'as objective as possible' (p. 58) in his textual analysis in terms of identifying foregrounding devices (e.g., in assessing the statistical deviation of linguistic features), but his judgements of which features might actually be perceived as prominent by readers are neverthe-less subjective. He argued that foregrounding should be greatest where there is a high 'density' of deviance or parallelism occurring simultaneously at multiple levels in a single line, and where devices operate together to support the overall meaning of the text (p. 23). He then examined readers' reactions to the different degrees of experimenter-identified foregrounding in the poems, asking them to judge four main features: memorability, importance, strikingness and discussion value. These categories provide a good insight into how humanities researchers think of the basic attention-grabbing function of foregrounding. Van Peer used readers with a variety of literary and non-literary backgrounds, but this turned out not to influence the results.

Memorability was tested using a cloze-type test, where participants were asked to read the poem, then recall specific words when presented with lines from the same poem with particular words deleted. Importance was established by asking participants to rank lines of the poem in terms of their importance to the overall meaning. Strikingness and discussion value were assessed by asking readers to underline words, phrases, clauses or sentences which they regarded as fitting into these categories. What was to count as striking was left undefined. Finally, discussion value was judged using the instruction for participants to imagine themselves teaching a class of 17-year-olds and finding parts of the poem which were considered to be worthy of particular comment. For each of the variables, van Peer predicted that where his own judgement of the density of foregrounding was greatest, the effect on readers would be greatest in terms of each dependent variable. Importance, strikingness and discussion value yielded results as hypothesized. The test of memory, however, was not so conclusive for all the poems. Van Peer suggested that other factors may interfere with the results, such as primacy and recency effects for items at the beginning and end of the poems, and memory for different grammatical and semantic categories, such as concrete nouns versus abstract nouns.

The main positive aspect of van Peer's work is that he used real literary materials which contribute to the ecological validity of his empirical work, allowing him to explore the full complexity of foregrounding at multiple levels. Nevertheless, we suggest that there are some limitations in his approach due to these materials and methods. Where van Peer's empirical results match his hypotheses, the testing methods are characterized by the subjective responses of participants. Given the subjective nature of the investigator's initial judgements about the possible psychological promin- ence of linguistic features, it seems that there is no objective measure of the impact of foregrounding. Another limitation is that using density of lingui- stic foregrounding as the independent variable makes it impossible to judge the relative effect of each device. While complex interactions may well be important in literary foregrounding, it seems to us necessary to know what effect each factor has in order to fully understand what is going on. A final limitation is that the linguistically foregrounded and unforegrounded condi- tions consisted of very variable material, drawn from different lines in the poems with different content, hence making it impossible to distinguish fully between the effect of differing forms of expression and differing propos- itional content.

In a subsequent study, Miall and Kuiken (1994) adopted a similar approach, but put more emphasis on the connection between affective response and foregrounding, studying narrative texts rather than poetry. They examined four stories, dividing each into short segments, analysing these segments for foregrounding at the phonetic, grammatical and semantic levels, and producing an index of overall linguistic foregrounding per segment. Several studies were performed, with participants' reading times measured on first reading and participants then being asked to rate segments on scales of 1 to 5 for perceived strikingness and affect. Different studies used participants with and without literary training. As in van Peer's work, no differences were found between different types of participant. Overall, the greater the foregrounding, the greater the reading times for the segments used. Also, ratings of strikingness and affect were higher where there was more foregrounding.

Although Miall and Kuiken's methodology differs slightly from van Peer's, several of the points made earlier apply. Again, there is a reco- gnition of the richness of the materials and the complex layering of linguistic features, used for creative purposes and for stimulating affect. Nevertheless, there are methodological limitations due to handling such complex materials. It is not possible to achieve full control of the mater- ials, since expression and propositional content are different. Also, these studies are largely characterized by subjective judgements on the part of the experimenters and the participants. In evaluating the materials, the identification of linguistically foregrounded items by the experimenters was carried out by three judges, who the authors say 'tended to agree' (Miall & Kuiken, 1994, p. 396) on the number of features per level and per segment. Nevertheless, the actual items selected were sometimes different, for example 'one judge might select alliteration of [p] sounds as significant, while another selected [r] sounds' (p. 396). So agreement about what constituted devices of foregrounding was not completely consistent. As in van Peer's work, the issue of the relative weighting of specific foregrounded items seems not to have been taken into account. Also, as Miall and Kuiken themselves point out (p. 397), the link between linguistic foregrounding and psychological effect is only a correlation and does not in itself provide evidence of causality.

More recently, van Peer, Hakemulder, and Zyngier (2007, Experiment 1) attempted to address some of the issues of control raised by these earlier works. They took a single line from a Portuguese poem and created five manipulated versions of the same line, each intended to have slightly less foregrounding than the previous version, producing six versions overall. These were ranked by the experimenters in terms of their judged degree of foregrounding, again, a subjective process. Judges each saw one of these six versions and rated it for six dimensions, as follows: (1) aesthetic appreciation (e.g., whether it is perceived as being beautiful), (2) aesthetic structure (e.g., appreciation of stylistic aspects), (3) cognitive aspects (e.g., what the reader feels he/she has learnt), (4) emotive aspects (e.g., whether the reader feels moved), (5) social context (e.g., likely literary origins) and (6) attitudinal aspects (e.g., whether it causes a change in perspective).

The hypothesis was that the closer the sentence was to its original high-foregrounded format, the greater would be the effect on readers in all these dimensions. However, significant correlations were only found between the experimenter-judged degrees of linguistic foregrounding and the effects on participants for three of the six variables, (2), (3) and (6). Also, even where there was an overall correlation, the different degrees of manipulation of the poetry line were not found to create the neat increments in effects expected. A follow-up experiment was even less conclusive, by the researchers' own assessment (p. 208).

In principle, it is worthwhile to attempt to establish a scale of foregrounding using different versions of the same line, but manipulating even a single line of literary text in this way is not easy and raises issues about how well this process can be controlled. Diluting foregrounding is problematic because it may require extensive changes to the actual meaning of the line, since in these experiments, changes to complex semantic items such as metaphors were involved, as well as formal features. Overall, van Peer et al.'s (2007) work is an ambitious attempt to apply more control to earlier investigation methods, but studying several different aspects of foregrounding simultaneously makes control difficult.

Our final example is of a rather different type of study. Zwaan (1993) investigated the idea that the way in which people read literary texts might be different from the way they read newspaper stories. He related this directly to Shklovsky's (1965) theory of defamiliarization, which, it will be recalled, made the claim that literary writing was distinct from other forms of writing. Zwaan's view was that the difference could be because people read literary texts in a different way from other texts, rather than that differences come from the writing itself. In other words, the effect would be due to the reader's mind-set. He hypothesized that texts would be read more slowly under a literary perspective than a newspaper perspective, predicting a better representation of surface text features in memory under the literary perspective, with better recognition and recall of the text wording. He presented the same pieces of writing as either literary texts or news articles. So, he did not set out to study foregrounding devices as such, but examined instead the attentiveness with which readers read the same text under different perspectives. He introduced the notion of a 'cognitive control system', which he believes to be 'in charge of regulating the basic operations of text comprehension. It can do this by emphasizing some processes and de-emphasizing others. Thereby, it may give rise to a distinctive pattern of cognitive behavior' (p. 2). Zwaan suggested that recall of verbatim wording may not be so important in reading news texts, since the main goal is to ascertain the situation, but that for literary texts, the manner of expression may be of much more interest to readers.

Reading-time measurements showed that when texts were presented as literary texts, they were read more slowly than when presented as news texts. Recognition of words read, and recall of wording by means of a text-completion task, showed a significantly better surface structure memory under the literary perspective. Although Zwaan's findings support Shklovsky's theory, he attributes the results to the reader's approach rather than to Shklovsky's idea that differences reside in the nature of the text.

Interim summary: the humanities approach to foregrounding

Overall, the humanities notion of foregrounding presents a long-standing recognition of the importance of cues in controlling the manner of processing of narrative texts. Although literary interpretations are often based largely on subjective judgements, they provide plausible rhetorical reasons why writers might want to draw attention to certain parts of a text.

The statistical techniques developed by Leech and Short (2007) provide a means of assessing the deviance of linguistic features, but Leech and Short do not explore what they term 'psychological prominence' in any detail. Empirical research within the humanities has been aimed at trying to assess the impact of foregrounding devices on readers, in terms of memorability, impact, affect, etc. This research aims to account for the full complexity of literary texts by examining foregrounding devices 'in situ', often with multiple devices occurring together. Using this type of method, it is, however, difficult to see the effect of any specific device since this method relies on participants' judgements rather than more objective measures. The research that has been done in psycholinguistics on focus addresses these issues, and will be discussed in the remainder of this chapter and the following one.

Psycholinguistic work on foregrounding and attention control

Work in psycholinguistics has explored specific devices for focussing attention, and the effects that they have on discourse processing in the reader. In essence, this work clarifies what the control of attention by foregrounding devices means in terms of mental processes. To begin, we provide an overview of some of the phenomena that are associated with heightened attention to text, based in part on the preceding humanities discussion, which provides general ideas about what might be involved. Given a piece of discourse where more attention is paid to one part than to another, the basic idea of what phenomena we might expect is captured by the oppositions shown in Table 4.1. The oppositions in this table are meant to convey an intuitive impression of some of the issues we shall address, though as we shall see, they also rely on some complex pieces of empirical research. We begin to explore these issues in the remainder of this chapter, studying ease of reference and strength of memory representations in relation to information structuring, and introducing the topic of depth of processing and its effect on the amount of detail stored in mental representations. In the next chapter, we examine depth of processing in greater detail, including a discussion of a growing body of relevant empirical work. In Chapter 6, we explore the concept of embodiment as the basis of the experiential component of comprehension. These ideas represent the crux of our arguments concerning how other aspects of narration, such as perspective, emotion and empathy work (discussed in Chapters 7 and 8).

Let us begin with a discussion of how information structuring influences ease of reference, and, by implication, the prominence and strength of representation of the information being referred to.

Table 4.1 Potential realizations of different levels of attention during discourse comprehension

Greater attention	Less attention
Easier to refer to things	Harder to refer to things
Stronger representation in memory	Weaker representation in memory
Mental representations may be more detailed and semantically deep	Mental representations have less detail and are 'shallow'
More likely to have an experiential component	Less likely to have an experiential component

Basic information structuring: linguistic focus

As discussed, a basic feature of foregrounding is that it is claimed to capture the attention of readers in various ways. In psycholinguistics, there has been a good deal of research on information structuring in sentences, and this forms a good place to start to examine the link between humanities and psychological approaches to foregrounding.

The relative importance of particular parts of a sentence can be signalled through devices of *information structuring* and *prosodic stress*, which control the focus of information within sentences, as is made clear in an extensive linguistic literature (e.g., Chafe, 1994; Gundel, 1999; Halliday, 1967; Jackendoff, 1972; Rooth, 1992). To see how information structuring works in a specific case, consider (8a):

(8a)   It was Harry who left a knife on the table.

This construction consists of a presupposed part, that someone left a knife on the table (Delin, 1992; Prince, 1978), and a new assertion, that *Harry* was the person who left the knife (e.g., Hedberg, 2000; Prince, 1978). Use of the It-cleft structure clearly distinguishes the given from the new information, and enables speakers to 'single out the one element – the clefted constituent – in order to focus attention on it' (Hedberg, 2000, p. 891). Linguistic analyses suggest that the cleft, *It + copula + clefted constituent*, puts the clefted constituent into referential focus. Effectively sentence (8a) answers the question *Who left a knife on the table?*, putting emphasis on *Harry* in contrast to any other individual, hence the effect of clefting is referred to as *contrastive focus* (e.g., Rooth, 1992).

In a similar way, consider (8b), using a pseudo-cleft structure:

(8b)   What Harry left on the table was a knife.

Here, the implicit question being asked is *What did Harry leave on the table?* Here, the given information is that *Harry* left something on the table, and the additional, or focussed, information is that what was left was *a knife*.

Both (8a) and (8b) contrast with the simple declarative sentence (8c), which can answer the more general question *What happened?*

(8c)   Harry left a knife on the table.

These three examples in turn thus put emphasis on *Harry, a knife* and the whole event. The cleft and pseudo-cleft constructions in (8a) and (8b) are said to put *narrow focus* on the parts of the sentence that are clefted. Here, the clefted material is within the *scope* of focus. In contrast, the simple declarative (8c) is structured such that there is *broad focus* over the whole proposition, so the previously clefted material is now outside the scope of focus. One utility of raising the prominence of potential antecedents in the cleft and pseudo-cleft cases is that even when there are several possible antecedents for a pronoun, prominence provides a strong heuristic for the selection of an appropriate antecedent (e.g., Greene, McKoon, & Ratcliff, 1992; Sanford & Garrod, 1981; see Cowles, Walenski, & Kluender, 2007, for a discussion of various factors in the pronoun-antecedent selection process).

A variety of studies have demonstrated that when a word is within the scope of focus, its processing appears to be enhanced relative to the same word when it is not within the scope of focus. For example, Cutler and Fodor (1979) used a phoneme-monitoring task, in which people had to listen out for and respond to the presence of a particular phoneme in a piece of spoken discourse. When the phoneme occurred, participants had to press a button to indicate this. It was found that the response time was shorter for words in the scope of focus than for words outside. Other studies have shown that focus enhances memory for terms within its scope, and also enhances priming (Birch, Albrecht, & Myers, 2000; Birch & Garnsey, 1995; Birch & Rayner, 1997; Foraker & McElree, 2007), and that anaphoric resolution is easier for focussed than non-focussed antecedents (Almor, 1999).

A rather straightforward way of demonstrating the consequences of focus effects is to present participants with sentences, and invite them to write a sentence (any sentence they like) that follows on from the initial sentence in a coherent way. Price (2008; Price & Sanford, 2008) used materials like:

(9a)   It was Harry who mislaid his briefcase. [Cleft form]

(9b)   What Harry mislaid was his briefcase. [Pseudo-cleft form]

(9c)   Harry mislaid his briefcase. [Neutral active form]

With (9a), the focus is on *Harry*, the first noun phrase (NP_1), whilst with (9b), it is on his *briefcase* (NP_2). In the neutral case, (9c), it is not especially on one or the other. Analysis of the continuations produced showed that for examples like (9a), continuations related primarily to NP_1, while with (9b), they typically related to NP_2, as expected. For the neutral case, (9c), continuations relating to NP_1 and NP_2 were closely balanced.

Such findings demonstrate just how syntactic structures control what comes to mind for readers who encounter them. Attention is paid to what is in focus, not what is out of focus. Similar enhancement of processing can be demonstrated by studying how easy it is to process anaphoric references to entities denoted by terms within or outside the scope of focus, and it also turns out that when such enhancement occurs, concepts denoted by other words not within the scope of focus are disadvantaged (processed and read more slowly). To see this, consider an experiment reported by A. J. S. Sanford, Price, and Sanford (2009). This was a self-paced reading study, where it was possible to measure the reading times for sentences that contained a reference to entities denoted by words either within or outside focus. A typical material in the pseudo-cleft form was:

(10a)   What Harry mislaid was his briefcase.
(10b)   It was with the shoes in the hall.
              [or]
(10b′)   He was busy thinking about other things.

Here, (10a) introduces a pseudo-clefted, and therefore focussed item (*his briefcase*), and (10b) and (10b′) are alternative probe sentences that contain pronouns that refer to entities mentioned in parts of the sentence that are either within the scope of narrow focus (10b) or outside its scope (10b′). Comparisons were made between such probe sentences following either the pseudo-cleft (10a), or the cleft (10a′), or a simple declarative sentence (10a″):

(10a′)   It was Harry who mislaid his briefcase.

(10a″)   Harry mislaid his briefcase.

The critical measure was how long people spent reading targets (10b) and (10b′) following these alternative antecedents.

The results are shown in Figure 4.1. Two things are clear. When a word is in narrow focus, it is easier (takes less time) to integrate the sentence in which it occurs with the previous sentence. But more than that, in a sentence where focus is put strongly on one element (i.e., cleft or pseudo-cleft), when an entity that is denoted by a word that is out of the scope of narrow focus is referred to with a pronoun, it is *disadvantaged* in comparison to being referred to by the simple declarative control sentence. Thus selectivity in this case works by both enhancing the processing of references to entities that are in focus, and suppressing or disadvantaging reference to entities that are not in focus. (For related work see Gernsbacher, 1989, and Gernsbacher & Jescheniak, 1995.)

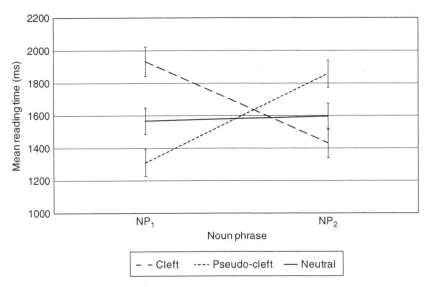

Figure 4.1 Results from A. J. S. Sanford et al. (2009), showing mean self-paced reading times for anaphoric sentences relating to either the first noun phrase (NP$_1$) or the second (NP$_2$) in an antecedent sentence. The antecedent sentences for these anaphoric terms were either of a cleft construction, focussing on NP$_1$; a pseudo-cleft, focussing on NP$_2$; or neutral, with no marked focus structure. Reading times can be seen to be shorter than the neutral control when relating to unfocussed NPs. Thus clefting results in both enhancement of focussed elements and suppression of unfocussed elements.

Subordination and downplaying information   Another common way in which the prominence of certain information may be manipulated is through the use of subordinate clauses. It is widely assumed by psycholinguists and humanities scholars that putting information into subordinate clauses reduces its impact. In terms of the X–Y balance of the Rhetorical Focussing Principle, if X is in a main clause, it is new information and is emphasized, and if Y is in a subordinate clause, it is given information and is de-emphasized. Here we discuss psychological evidence supporting such a view. With sentence (11a), the new information is *John booked the cinema tickets*, and the given information is *Mary finished work*. Focus thus lies on the part of the sentence referring to John's action, which is the main clause (technically the matrix clause). Sentence (11b) simply reverses the order in which the information appears, but the focus is still on the same part of the sentence.

(11a)   John booked the cinema tickets after Mary finished work.

(11b)   After Mary finished work, John booked the cinema tickets.

Subordination has a dramatic effect on continuations produced by participants (Cooreman & Sanford, 1996; Price, 2008). Regardless of the order of presentation, the vast majority of continuations included reference to the character mentioned in the main clause (*John*) rather than in the subordinate clause (*Mary*).

Ease of anaphoric reference follows a similar pattern. Thus Price (2008; Price & Sanford, 2008; see also Cooreman & Sanford, 1996) carried out a reading-time study in which a target sentence like (11c) followed a sentence like (11a) or (11b):

(11c)   He/She wanted to see the new Western.

With the *He* option, the antecedent, *John*, is in the main clause, while with the *She* option, the antecedent, *Mary*, is in the subordinate clause. Mean reading time for a target sentence was substantially shorter when the antecedent was in a main clause rather than a subordinate clause.

So elements of a text that are in syntactically subordinate positions are less available for reference in both of these tasks. In other words, subordination may be used to *disadvantage* information. Indeed, subordination is an important way of burying information that a writer may not wish the reader to pay particular attention to. As we shall discuss in more detail in the next chapter, a number of studies have shown how focus does not just affect reference patterns, but it also appears to affect how thoroughly propositions are processed. This is certainly true for the case of subordination. It is commonly supposed that if one wants people to be less likely to notice part of a message, then the information should be 'hidden' in a subordinate clause. In an experimental test of this intuition, Baker and Wagner (1987) had people evaluate the truth of statements with main/subordinate structures. Consider (12a) and (12b):

(12a)   The liver, which is an organ found only in humans, is often damaged by heavy drinking.

(12b)   The liver, which is often damaged by heavy drinking, is an organ found only in humans.

These examples rely on the use of relative clauses as a means of signalling logical subordination. In (12a), the crucially incorrect statement (*an organ found only in humans*) is in a relative clause, rather than a main clause. In (12b), the crucial statement is in the main clause, rather than the relative clause. When asked to verify the truth or falsity of sentences such as these, fewer people noticed the incorrect statement in (12a) where it is the given, or subordinate, part of the sentence, than in (12b) where it is part of the new (asserted, main clause) information. So, information structuring in the form of subordination modulates how thoroughly propositions are analysed. In the next chapter, we shall discuss this idea and what it means in much more detail, and show how similar arguments for modulating depth of processing apply to the other types of focus discussed above.

General propositional dependencies

Subordination is representative of propositional dependency, an idea introduced in Chapter 2, when we discussed the work of Kintsch and colleagues on propositions.

To briefly recap this idea, consider the following classic example from Kintsch and Keenan (1973):

(13)   Cleopatra's downfall lay in her foolish trust in the fickle political figures of the Roman world.

This complex sentence consists of no less than eight propositions by Kintsch and Keenan's analysis. At the highest levels in the hierarchy, one sees the following:

(14)   Cleopatra had a downfall BECAUSE she trusted some figures.

Now note how other propositions are subordinate to this, and in fact are all details about her trust; for instance, that her trust was foolish depends upon her having trusted, that the figures were fickle depends upon there being figures, and so on. When presented with sentences like (13), and later asked to recall them, the higher-level propositions were better recalled than the lower-level ones.

While there are criticisms of this sort of work (see Sanford & Garrod, 1981, p. 72) it does appear that dependencies influence memory. In other related work, McKoon (1977) had participants read texts, and then presented them with statements, some of which had been in the text, and some not. Participants had to judge whether the statements were in fact from the text, or not. She found that statements that were high up in the propositional hierarchy were verified more rapidly than ones that were low down. The McKoon experiment is interesting in that it showed that people could in fact recognize propositions that were lower down in the hierarchy, even if they typically recalled them less readily, but that it took them longer to do so. This suggests that it is not so much that lower-level propositions are not encoded at all, or encoded less often, but that they are encoded only with a weaker representation in memory, much like the examples of focus discussed previously.

Although this work was part of the earliest detailed investigations of text processing and text memory, it remains interesting. For instance, how would a writer highlight a detail in (13), such as the figures being fickle? With this single sentence example it is difficult to do without adding an intensifying modifier, but by moving the fact of fickleness to its own sentence (main clause status), its recall should be readily elevated, as shown in (15):

(15)   Cleopatra's downfall lay in her foolish trust in the political figures of the Roman world. These people were fickle.

Note that these ideas relate to Baker and Wagner's (1987) work on anomaly detection, discussed in the previous section, since their research showed that anomalies were less detectable in subordinate clauses, which are dependent propositions, than in main clauses, which are higher up in the hierarchy.

Burying information in narrative texts

The psycholinguistic research on subordination and lower-level dependent units provides strong evidence for the idea that writers can use linguistic devices to bury information in a text. The most obvious application of this idea is in political discourse. It has been suggested that political speakers can manipulate their audience by placing information in a subordinate clause or in the middle of a list if they wish to detract attention from that information (e.g., Fairclough, 2000; see also O'Halloran's, 2003, Critical Discourse Analysis research, which draws directly on some of Sanford's earlier work on selective processing).

Although there has been considerable interest in foregrounding in the humanities, there has been relatively little detailed stylistic analysis of background items. Yet the recognition of background is intrinsic to the study of foregrounding. If certain parts of a text are highlighted, others will naturally fall into the background. Mukařovský (1964a, pp. 19–23) points out that it is the overall system of patterning that is important, consisting of foregrounding items made prominent by being set against an unforegrounded background. In this respect, the background is generally just the relief for the foregrounding, but, when used strategically, deliberate backgrounding can, in its own right, be rhetorically significant. Burying information in a narrative is a key strategy for creating surprise endings (Tobin, 2009). In mysteries and detective fiction, it is common to 'bury' clues at the outset, only revealing their key significance at a later stage. For example, Emmott and Alexander (2010) show that in Agatha Christie's *Sparkling Cyanide* there is initial downplaying of the first mention of the character who is later revealed to be the murderer, so that we are less likely to consider him as a possible suspect. On his introduction, this character, Victor Drake, is not mentioned by name and is simply referred to as *a son*.

(16)   In the meantime, the first thing to settle was [Iris's] place of residence. Mr George Barton had shown himself anxious for her to continue living with him and had suggested that her father's sister, Mrs Drake, who was in impoverished circumstances owing to the financial claims of <u>a son (the black sheep of the Marle family)</u>, should make her home with them and chaperon Iris in society. Did Iris approve of this plan?

(Christie (1955). *Sparkling Cyanide*, p. 12, our underlining)

As we have seen, placing information in subordinate clauses lowers attention. Christie makes use of grammatical subordination here by placing this first mention of the son in an *-ing* clause (*owing to ...*), embedded in a relative clause (*who was ...*) describing another character, Mrs Drake. The information is further embedded by placement of the relative clause within the that-clause following the verb *suggested*. At discourse level, this mention of the son is also embedded in text which has the main function of describing another character's circumstances. The chapter in which this quotation occurs is headed *Iris*, and the opening sentence and closing question in the paragraph relate to Iris. We would expect these strategies to make the mention of *a son* less prominent.

On another occasion in this novel, information about Victor Drake's previous occupation as a waiter is buried in the middle of a list. This is information which is revealed as being significant at the end of the book since it explains the method behind the murder, but Christie needs to play down this information about the character's background at this stage.

(17)   'I enjoy myself immensely. I've seen a good deal of life, Ruth. I've done almost everything. I've been an actor and a storekeeper and <u>a waiter</u> and an odd job man, and a luggage porter, and a property man in a circus! I've sailed before the mast in a tramp steamer. I've been in the running for President in a South American Republic. I've been in prison! ... '

                (Christie (1955). *Sparkling Cyanide*, pp. 33–34, our underlining)

The mention of the waiter is here placed between two unskilled jobs to de-emphasize the skills which are subsequently viewed as important (p. 184). We will see in the following chapter that when processing is shallow, readers may not fully absorb the semantic properties of a reference. Here, the information about the waiter is presented to make the discourse point that Victor has had many jobs, but readers may not engage fully with the 'knowledge and technique' (p. 184) that a waiter would possess, which can subsequently be seen as necessary to commit the murder. In addition, the details about running for President in a South American Republic and being in prison at the end of this quotation may be sufficiently interesting to detract attention from the information about the waiter, but this would need to be tested.

The examples from Christie's *Sparkling Cyanide* show that a writer may rhetorically control information in the background as well as the foreground (for further examples, see Emmott, Sanford, & Alexander, 2010). Although detective fiction is a specific type of narrative, the technique of downplaying information to prompt later surprise is a key aspect of many types of narrative (as will be discussed in Chapter 8).

Psychological work on burying

There is some work in empirical psychology that demonstrates a form of 'burying'. We will see here how a specific psychological effect, the 'sounds-like' effect (Sanford & McGinley, 1990), can be reduced by burying it in additional text. We will first explain the nature of this effect before moving on to how it can be 'buried'. The 'sounds-like' effect occurs when a piece of writing means one thing, but 'sounds like' it means something else. Consider example (18):

(18)   A car came tearing around the bend. It almost hit a car.

In this example, although the first and second mention of *car* (i.e., car_1 and car_2) refer to different vehicles, there is a sounds-like effect of them referring to the *same* car. Indeed, when participants were asked to judge whether the pair constituted good English, and, if not, to indicate how it seemed strange, a strong sounds-like effect occurred. Of eighteen participants, all thought it was not acceptable, and fifteen said that it sounded as though the two cars mentioned might be the same one. However, they all clearly stated that they knew it wasn't the same one: that would just not be possible. The following three examples are typical of what was said by participants:

(19a)   *Participant 1*: 'The second sentence reintroduces *car* which has already been mentioned, but it is a different car so it seems odd.'

(19b)   *Participant 3*: 'Slight ambiguity over whether there are two cars.'

(19c)   *Participant 11*: 'Instead of *a car* you would expect it to say *another car*. Although it is not difficult to differentiate between two cars [...] it sounds peculiar.'

Participants were asked to offer corrections that would increase acceptability, and all eighteen produced corrections that were consistent with this reading, typically by inserting the word *another* before the second mention of *car*.

In some ways it is surprising that the possibility of car_1 and car_2 being co-referential is entertained, since there are several things that contraindicate co-reference, including the facts that the pronoun *It* is an anaphor of car_1; car_1 is the agent of the verb to hit and cars do not hit themselves; and the indefinite article with car_2 contraindicates co-reference with an explicitly mentioned entity. In sum, the sounds-like effect shows that interpretations that are ultimately ruled out may have a sufficient impact to cause sentences that give rise to them to be deemed stylistically unacceptable.

In further experiments, Sanford and McGinley demonstrated 'burying' with these materials, investigating whether the sounds-like effect could be reduced or eliminated by simply padding out the second sentence, effectively burying the relevant linguistic features. Obviously, using an extra word to create *another car* in the second sentence would disambiguate, and a simple experiment showed that under such conditions, there was no sounds-like effect. But more intriguing was a condition where there was a simple augmentation that did not produce any disambiguation. The following were contrasted:

(20a)   The car came tearing around the bend. It almost hit a car. [Basic version]

(20b)   The car came tearing around the bend. It almost hit a car despite some skilful and defensive driving. [Augmented version]

A group of twenty participants were asked to evaluate the basic example, and a further twenty the augmented example. The sounds-like effect was markedly reduced by the presence of augmenting material, even though that material does not specifically serve to disambiguate the referents (in that the driving could apply to the driver of either car). The twenty respondents who saw the basic version first also went on to examine the augmented material. Of the fourteen who had reported a sounds-like effect with the basic material, only three thought that the augmented version was as bad or worse, again a significant effect.

One possible explanation is that as reading takes place, processing and interpretation are not strictly incremental, but as one set of constraints is being dealt with, processing continues with the next part of the sentence. In the case of the augmented example, just as the process of checking car_2 is being initiated, processing is also moving on, handling the augmented material. As a result, the overall impact of the possible co-reference is reduced, because the focus of processing has moved over to the driving.

These data open up the idea that simply by continuing with a message, problems with an earlier part of a message may be buried, even if the information content of the message does not in itself solve that earlier problem. There is much to explore here, and we offer this example simply as an instance of how some aspects of burying might be investigated.

Inadvertent foregrounding, inappropriate usage and poor style

The use of foregrounding by a writer is what makes the text into something dynamic by allowing attention to be drawn to some things and away from others. As discussed at the beginning of this chapter, foregrounding devices are closely associated with the use of deviations, including over-regularities. This leads to what stylisticians term a 'toolbox' of useful stylistic devices for writers. However, it is easy to see that the spurious use of foregrounding devices could have an adverse effect on the quality of a piece of writing. For instance, the use of unusual words and heavy repetition can also impede communication if it is used for no apparent reason. Where foregrounding is accidental and distracts listeners from the point being made, we term it *inadvertent foregrounding.* Mukařovský (1964b) pointed to this phenomenon in relation to the inadvertent use of 'an euphonic grouping of vowels in a mathematical treatise' (p. 36). In expository writing there is a difficult balance to achieve in terms of use of lexical repetition. Academic writers may sometimes be advised to avoid repeating words too much, with synonyms being suggested to avoid tedious and awkward-sounding repetition. Conversely, if writers of expository texts use too many synonyms, they can be criticized for unnecessarily shifting the meanings of words that are meant to be co-referential. H. W. Fowler's well-known term 'elegant variation' in *The King's English* (Fowler & Fowler, 1931) was a criticism of this type, since the term 'elegant' was originally used in a pejorative sense. This issue is clearly of importance in academic writing, but is also relevant to creative writers who may redraft their work not only to add strategic foregrounding but also to remove any inadvertent foregrounding which detracts from the effect intended.

In the context of psychological work, Sanford and Moxey (1995) have argued that any regularity that is irrelevant to the pattern of coherence that a writer is primarily attempting to establish is a distraction. There is an assortment of work in psychology that relates to ideas of inadvertent foregrounding, which we will now discuss.

Repeated rhyming

Although rhyme is a key feature of much poetry, inadvertent rhyming can have a disruptive effect on everyday prose comprehension. The effects of repeated rhyming have been shown by Baddeley and Lewis (1981, based on Baddeley & Hitch, 1974), using sentences such as (21):

(21)   Crude rude Jude chewed his stewed food.

Participants were required to read such sentences containing repeated rhyming, and make a judgement as to whether they were meaningful. Meaningless rhyming sentences were either semantically or grammatically nonsensical, as with (22):

(22)   Crude rude Jude queued his stewed food.

They compared the accuracy of such judgements with control sentences where there was some semantic similarity but no rhyming repetition, such as:

(23)   Rough curt Jude ate his boiled meat.

People took longer to process the rhyming sentences than the non-rhyming control sentences. Now these experiments were originally conceived of as an investigation of subvocalization in the reading process, but what they show is that a spurious regularity, rhyming, can serve to disrupt processing when it is not relevant to processing meaning.

Alliterative tongue twisters in silent reading

Alliteration is also a major feature of much poetry and some literary prose, but there is also some evidence showing just how disruptive the effects of inadvertent alliterative repetition (tongue twisters) can be on comprehension of everyday language. McCutchen and Perfetti (1982) had participants read single sentences, and press an appropriate button to decide whether the current sentence was semantically meaningful or not. Sentences could have word-initial bilabial phoneme repetition (e.g., /p/, with the lips closing together), or word-initial alveolar phoneme repetition (e.g., /d/, with the tongue touching the alveolar ridge behind the top teeth), or no such repetition, as in (24a–c) respectively:

(24a)   The press published the poem and promised to pay for permission. [Bilabial]

(24b)   The detective discovered the danger and decided to dig for details. [Alveolar]

(24c)   The investigator found the hazard and chose to hunt for answers. [Neutral]

All three of these are semantically meaningful, and would be given a *yes* response. An example of a sentence that was not semantically meaningful but had a corresponding pattern of alliteration is shown in (25) (corresponding to (24a)):

(25)   The puppies puzzled the peninsula and processed to please for paper.

For both the *yes* and *no* responses, the time to make the decision was longer for the tongue-twister type of sentences than for the neutral type. McCutchen and Perfetti refer to this as the *visual tongue-twister effect*, since the alliteration impedes silent reading (the same label could also be used for Baddeley and Lewis' (1981) 'crude rude Jude' rhyming examples).

Infelicitous pronominal anaphora

An example of a straightforward but commonplace problem of inadvertent foregrounding is that of infelicitous pronoun usage. This will occur when the pattern of foregrounding and attempted pronominal reference do not mesh. The pronoun usage is then said to be infelicitous, as follows (the example, cited by Hirst, 1981, is of unknown origin, but may have been used in a World War II information leaflet about air raids on Britain).

(26)   If an incendiary bomb lands near you, don't lose your head. Put it in a bucket and cover it with sand.

Here, resolution appears to favour *head* over *bomb*. This pattern fits well with expressions occurring within a main clause being more available and accessible than expressions within a subordinate clause. But the fact is that further processing leads us to make an appropriate resolution in each case. So, we have sounds-like effects that can either be regarded as exemplars of poor style or jokes. Interestingly, the same linguistic form can therefore be interpreted in different ways, producing either inadvertent foregrounding (with or without humour) or intended humour, depending on the context.

Repeated morphs

Another kind of repetition, use of repeated words for the same referent, termed *repeated morphs*, has also been demonstrated to be disadvantageous when used inappropriately in everyday language. For example:

(27)   A lorry came down the road, and the lorry was going very fast. As a result, the lorry nearly crashed into a nearby parked car as the lorry careered along.

This kind of repetition is at least in part due to the fact that once a concept is in focus, which *the lorry* is in the first clause of the first sentence, it is more appropriate to refer to it by means of a pronoun. So repeated morphs can provide examples of inadvertent foregrounding, but there are cases when the repetition is acceptable because it serves a discourse-structuring function. So when anaphoric expressions are more specific than is necessary for them to identify referents, they may sometimes function to signal the thematic structure of the text, as shown by Vonk, Hustinx, and Simons (1992). As an intuitive example, they provide the following vignette:

(28a)   Sally Jones got up early this morning.
(28b)   She wanted to clean the house.
(28c)   Her parents were coming to visit her.
(28d)   She was looking forward to seeing them.
(28e)   She weighs 80 kilograms.
(28f)   She had to lose weight on her doctor's advice.
(28g)   So she planned to cook a nice but sober meal.

There is a clear change in theme at (28e), from the visit to her weight. Vonk et al. (1992) suggest that sentence (28e) would sound better had *Sally* been substituted for *She* (an intuition that we agree with) because such an over-specification (in terms of what is required for referential clarity) suggests a change in theme, rather than mere co-reference. Production studies by Vonk et al. (using materials in Dutch) showed that people do indeed prefer to use the more fully specified forms when a thematic change is indicated in a cartoon strip that they are describing.

The consequences of this for comprehension were evaluated using a word probe procedure. Vonk et al. examined the idea that information in the first part of passages with a shift in theme in the middle would be made less available by the use of a fuller referring expression than by a pronoun. This was shown to be the case in two experiments. Other work has shown deleterious effects of using repeat noun phrases as referring expressions where no shift in theme is involved (see, e.g., Almor, 1999; Gordon, Grosz, & Gilliom, 1993; Gordon & Hendrick, 1998; Kennison & Gordon, 1997; Ledoux, Gordon, Camblin, & Swaab, 2007).

Vonk et al.'s argument seems plausible for reference items judged in relation to thematic borders, but there may also be a more general feature at work, especially with multiple repetitions: a spurious but obtrusive regularity that interferes with other processing such as normal comprehension. However, this possibility remains to be examined, since most of the psychological work in this area has been largely concerned with the role of different referring types in the facilitation of comprehension.

Narrative use of sound play, infelicitous anaphora and repeated morphs for creative purposes

As we have indicated, the same linguistic features can be found in both inadvertent infelicitous foregrounding or foregrounding used for creative purposes. Both types can disrupt processing, but the difference lies in whether there is some overall meaningful interpretation. Inadvertent foregrounding might be evaluated as bad style, but foregrounding that does not follow the normal felicitous usage may nevertheless be used by writers for special effects. The disruption caused by such usage allows for more complex processing that may lead to defamiliarization.

First consider alliteration. Although sound play is more common in poetry than prose, we saw in example (5), from Christopher Nolan's autobiography, that literary prose texts can make use of alliteration for possible functions such as highlighting embodied movement and creating affect (indeed, Nolan's story is strongly alliterative throughout). Even alliteration as a tongue twister can be used as a potentially amusing structuring device. For example, in Margaret Atwood's (2005) children's book *Rude Ramsay and the Roaring Radishes*, the entire story has alliterative use of /r/. Both inadvertent alliteration and artistic alliteration can slow processing, but the latter has some added value.

Next consider pronominal reference. Infelicitous pronominal anaphora may sometimes be a feature of poor writing and might therefore benefit from editorial intervention. However, as we saw at the opening of this chapter, writers can make use of unusual, even awkward, stylistic features as foregrounding devices in order to defamiliarize. The sentence below, from a literary writer, has what might normally be judged to be infelicitous anaphora in ordinary writing, but the awkwardness appears to have an ulterior motive, hence might ultimately be judged as felicitous in terms of its overall stylistic purpose in this literary text.

(29)   But who was there except you my darling and I and <u>the Robertsons</u> and the shiny cards and did <u>they</u> do it then?

(Gardam (1984). 'Stone Trees', p. 48, our underlining)

This sentence relates to the thoughts of the bereaved character we saw earlier in example (2). At this point, the scene is at the crematorium. As we read on, beyond this example, it becomes clear that *they* relates to the crematorium assistants since *they* are seen stacking the coffins. In communication generally, it is possible to use pronouns for institutional referents such as these without referring to them with a full noun phrase first (as in the example *I might give some blood today if they want it* (personal letter, Survey of English Usage, cited by Wales, 1996, p. 47); see also Sanford, Filik, Emmott, & Morrow, 2008). However, there is a potential clash in (29) since the pronoun *they* is close to the plural form *the Robertsons*, with apparent co-reference between *the Robertsons* and *they* until we read on. In the context of this passage, nevertheless, this awkward structure might be regarded as wholly appropriate to a funeral scene in which the main character's disturbed perceptions are being presented. Hence, we would not judge this particular example to contain inadvertent foregrounding.

Repeated morphs that can be judged to be inadvertent foregrounding when used by poor writers can be felicitous when used in an appropriate context. If there is some overriding rhetorical function for repeated items, this may make repeated morphs acceptable, even if their use does not follow our everyday assumptions about what is textually and cognitively good style (Ariel, 1990; Emmott, 2002, 2006). We saw literary use of the repeated adjectives, *dead* and *white* in examples (6) and (7). Nouns can also be used repetitively in literary writing. Hence in (30), the repetition of *Mother*, in place of pronouns, might be viewed as appropriate to emphasizing the intensity of the recollected family relationship.

(30)   And <u>Mother</u>? Ah. <u>Mother</u>.
<u>Mother</u> sang. <u>Mother</u> rocked her sometimes, rocked without her sometimes. <u>Mother</u> stayed at home with Mozart, swollen as a sow. <u>Mother</u> played. <u>Mother</u> played.

(Galloway (2003). *Clara*, pp. 26–27, our underlining)

The fact that the same linguistic features may appear both in poor writing and in the artistic breaking of linguistic conventions for literary purposes is clearly a difficult issue for teachers trying to judge the merits of the creative writing of their students. One of the authors of this book (CE) was recently approached for advice from a school teacher about this type of problem, specifically in relation to a pupil providing an unusual mix of tenses in creative writing. There is a distinction to make in such cases in relation to whether a pupil has simply not grasped the normal conventions of language or whether he or she is breaking those rules for creative purposes. This is a matter of pedagogical and literary judgement. Punctuation can raise such questions too. We will see in the next chapter that many authors use grammatically incomplete fragmented sentences for stylistic effect, not just in literary texts. Such incomplete sentences are also used for persuasive rhetorical purposes in newspapers, political speeches and advertising. Even basic punctuation guides (e.g., Allen, 2002) point out the use of incomplete sentences for 'special effect' (p. 57). Teachers need to make a judgement about the borderline between bad writing, where students write incomplete sentences without realizing, and good writing, where incomplete sentences can stylistically reinforce the propositional meaning of a text for creative and other rhetorical purposes. Ultimately, teachers need to have an awareness that rule breaking is possible in creative and persuasive writing, but that the function of the linguistic features needs to be judged in order to assess the merits of the writing.

Summary

In this chapter we discussed the Rhetorical Focussing Principle, the idea that writers aim to focus attention on selective aspects of a text, causing some parts of the text to be processed more thoroughly than others. The following topics were examined in relation to this principle:

- Writers use foregrounding to make certain aspects of texts prominent over others. Foregrounding is achieved through a variety of stylistic devices which rely on deviations from expected forms in writing. Foregrounding is closely associated with the notion of defamiliarization, by which parts of writing transcend the mundane and become focal topics of interest, being looked at in a way that is more thorough than commonplace perception, which is considered to be 'automatic'.
- Within the humanities area termed the Empirical Study of Literature, work on foregrounding tends to have high ecological validity, since full, complex texts are often used as materials. However, this makes it difficult to have adequate control over the large number of different variables. Also, methods tend to rely on participants' judgements rather than more objective measures.
- Turning to empirical psychology, information structuring served as an example for operationalizing some aspects of attention manipulation. In particular, focussed (foregrounded) material has a stronger memory

trace, and leads to more rapid processing during reading. Furthermore, focussed material is more prominent in continuations produced by readers. Material may receive reduced processing (for example when in a subordinate clause), in which case the memory trace is weaker, access is slower and references to the material are less prominent in continuations than to material from main clauses.

- We introduced the idea that foregrounding may lead to 'deeper' processing, to be discussed fully in the next chapter, and also to a stronger experiential component of understanding, to be discussed in Chapters 6–8.
- Finally, patterns of emphasis resulting from 'inadvertent foregrounding' can have an adverse effect on the efficacy of a message, and constitute one aspect of the concept of poor style. However, it is necessary to distinguish between awkward usage which serves no rhetorical function, and foregrounding proper which has a rhetorical function. The latter may involve the creative breaking of rules, which lies at the heart of much accomplished and original writing.

5   Rhetorical focussing and depth of processing

There is growing evidence that foregrounding devices in texts not only make it easier for readers to focus on particular parts of a text, as we discussed in the previous chapter, but also influence *depth of processing* (also termed *depth of semantic processing*). Ordinarily, everyday language use leads to *shallow processing*, but foregrounding and the resulting defamiliarization can produce deeper processing. This is central to the notion of rhetorical focussing. In this chapter, we will look first at the evidence for shallow processing, then move on to examine empirical work which shows how depth of processing is controlled by foregrounding devices.

Shallow processing

When, in the previous chapter, we considered the impact of introducing information in a subordinate clause, we saw that Baker and Wagner (1987) found that factual propositions conveyed in subordinate clauses were less thoroughly evaluated than when the same information was presented in main clauses. This indicates that the processing of subordinate clauses is more shallow, and that shallow processing may be a manifestation of poorer attention. In fact, we believe that shallow processing is a key aspect of selective processing that permeates much ordinary language use.

The idea behind shallow semantic processing is that not all aspects of meaning, including word meaning, are necessarily used during language comprehension, and that those parts of a text that receive less attention do so by receiving a less thorough semantic analysis. Interestingly, a similar issue arose in the psychology of vision, where it was found that not all aspects of a scene are available to consciousness when a person is presented with a picture. Rather, the accessibility of aspects of a scene seems to critically depend on what is being attended to. In vision science, the most common demonstrations of selective availability to consciousness utilize the change blindness paradigm (e.g., Simons & Levin, 1997, 1998). A picture of a scene can be presented to participants for a brief period and then re-presented with some change in it. The original can then be re-presented, and then the changed version again, in a cycle of presentations. A surprising finding is just how easy it is to miss quite substantial changes. Unless the viewer is attending to a particular aspect of a scene, it is easy to change that aspect so that the viewer may be quite unaware of the change. Such evidence is a clear challenge to the idea that a visual scene is perceived as a complete whole, the percept being like the picture. A similar notion of selective processing is applicable to the way that text and speech are processed.

Shallow processing is the term used by Barton and Sanford (1993; Sanford, 2002; Sanford & Graesser, 2006; Sanford & Sturt, 2002), and by it we mean that the meaning of words or expressions are not fully analysed or taken into account during discourse processing. The outcome of shallow processing is an *underspecified mental representation* of the text that is shallow processed. As we will go on to examine, this may mean not utilizing the meaning of a word or not deciding on which senses of a word to select. A further term which is currently used is *good-enough representation*, introduced by Ferreira and Henderson (1999) and made explicit by Christianson, Hollingworth, Halliwell, and Ferreira (2001) (also Ferreira, Bailey, & Ferraro, 2002). The basic idea is that processing may only occur to the extent or degree of detail that is needed for comprehension in a particular situation.

Questioning the degree of completeness of semantic processing

Many accounts of language processing assume that semantic processing is immediate, termed 'incremental', and it has previously been commonly accepted that it is in some way 'complete'. The classic example is that of Just and Carpenter (1980), who argued for immediate processing of words as soon as they were encountered, to the greatest degree of interpretation that was possible. Similarly, MacDonald, Pearlmutter, and Seidenberg (1994) argued for full analysis of sentences, saying that while 'the communicative goals of the reader or listener can be achieved with only a partial analysis of a sentence', they viewed these as 'degenerate cases' (p. 686).

There is certainly a wealth of experimental evidence for incremental semantic processing, although this does not necessarily imply completeness, as we will see shortly. As far as incrementality is concerned, Traxler and Pickering (1996) compared readers' eye-movements in (1a) and (1b):

(1a)   That's the pistol with which the heartless killer shot the hapless man yesterday afternoon.

(1b)   That's the garage with which the heartless killer shot the hapless man yesterday afternoon.

While (1a) makes sense, (1b) is anomalous. Traxler and Pickering found that initial fixations on the word *shot* were longer in (1b) than in (1a), and took this immediate detection of an anomaly as evidence for the immediate accessing and utilization of the word's meaning, which is of course necessary for anomaly detection to take place.

Using a different technique, Altmann and Kamide (1999) had people listen to statements while they viewed a visual depiction of a variety of objects, some of which were relevant and some of which were not relevant to the sentences (the visual world paradigm, discussed in Chapter 3). They found that there were more eye-movements toward objects that were restricted by a preceding verb. An example is the tendency to look at a picture of a cake rather than other objects on display, while listening to a sentence about somebody eating something. These eye-movements were frequently made even before the name of the object had itself been uttered (see also, e.g., Kamide, Altmann, & Haywood, 2003), suggesting that interpretation is predictive as well as incremental. It is as though the full meaning of the verb is retrieved as soon as the verb is encountered (i.e., true incrementality), enabling prediction of which word is likely to occur next.

Despite such good evidence, there are many reasons to believe that complete recovery of meaning in an incremental fashion does not always occur, and is often incomplete, in the sense that the meanings of words may not always be utilized. As we have suggested, semantic representations may be coarse and indistinct, the full meaning of sentences may not necessarily be established, and, in general, the meanings of tracts of text may be mentally underspecified, or may receive an interpretation that is merely 'good enough' for the communicative purpose. Some of the strongest evidence in favour of this comes from a class of semantic anomalies which we will now examine.

Not noticing the evidence: difficult-to-detect anomalies

Most semantic anomalies are very easy to spot: for instance (1b) above, and (2), which we saw in Chapter 2:

(2)   He spread the warm bread with socks.

Here, *socks* simply fails to fit in any way with the rest of the sentence. They are not an instrument for spreading, neither are they a substance that is spreadable on bread. The anomaly simply jumps out at the reader, and is readily recognized at the level of brain activity, as well as awareness (Kutas & Hillyard, 1980). As we saw in Chapter 2, such anomalies produce a classic N400 effect when ERPs are measured. Furthermore, an assortment of eye-tracking studies has shown that when an anomalous word is encountered, it causes very early effects in processing such as longer fixations and regressive eye-movements (e.g., Braze, Shankweiler, Ni, & Palumbo, 2002; Ni, Fodor, Crain, & Shankweiler, 1998).

However, here we want to introduce a class of semantic anomalies that turn out to be very difficult to detect, as in examples (3–5):

(3)   Moses put two of each sort of animal on the Ark. True or False?

(4)   After the air crash, the authorities had the problem of where to bury the survivors. What do you think they should do?

(5)   Can a man marry his widow's sister?

A high proportion of people answer *true* to (3) (the Moses illusion; Erickson & Mattson, 1981), failing to notice that it was Noah, not Moses in the biblical Ark story. Similarly, in (4), answers such as *it should be up to the relatives where they are buried, surely!* occur frequently, even though survivors (who must be alive) should not be buried at all (Barton & Sanford, 1993). Finally, (5) is frequently answered *yes, I think so*, even though to have a widow, the man in question would need to be dead, so the correct answer is certainly *no* (Sanford, unpublished data). In the experiments, all people who were non-detectors expressed surprise and dismay that they had not noticed the anomalies (see Barton & Sanford, 1993, for full details). Another point to bear in mind is that by a variety of post-tests, it is guaranteed that readers possess the necessary knowledge to detect the anomalies: only where people had this knowledge was a failure-to-detect recorded. In short, despite having the basic knowledge that these anomalies are in fact anomalous, people simply fail to *notice* them. It is this not-noticing that offers some of the strongest evidence for shallow semantic processing (Sanford & Sturt, 2002).

What is happening with such difficult-to-detect anomalies? First, they are easy to miss, so are at the borderline of awareness. Secondly, either the full facts about *Moses*, or the full meanings of *survivors* or *widow* are not being retrieved from memory, or, if they are, then they are not being integrated into the reader's representation of the sentence. So, this type of anomaly provides prima facie evidence for shallow semantic processing, as distinct from deep processing, where the full (or sufficient) meaning is utilized. Let us examine in a little more detail what is going on with such anomalies.

Processes underlying failures to detect 'difficult' semantic anomalies

What makes the difficult-to-detect anomalies difficult to detect? Easy-to-detect anomalies like (1b) and (2) generally share the property that the words in question are simply out of place by any standards. That is to say, they simply do not fit either the *global context* (such as the situation of spreading stuff on bread) or the specific *local context* (the kind of stuff you can and do spread on bread). In contrast, difficult-to-detect anomalous words, as in (3–5), have a *good* fit to global context. Thus *Moses* fits Old Testament biblical contexts well, and *survivors* fits an air-crash scenario well, and so on. While these difficult anomalies fit the global contexts in which they occur well, they are of course anomalous at the local level. So, the first important property of difficult-to-detect anomalies is that they fit the global context very well.

An experiment by Barton and Sanford (1993) illustrates the importance of such a good fit to global context. If 'fit to global context' is an important factor in failing to fully utilize meaning, then by changing the global context, it should be possible to manipulate the likelihood of detecting the anomaly. Barton and Sanford (Experiment 3) explored this possibility by contrasting the following cases, using an incidental anomaly detection task (where the reader does not know that they are looking for an anomaly, so that they notice it 'incidentally'):

(6a)   When an aircraft crashes, where should the survivors be buried?

(6b)   When a bicycle accident occurs, where should the survivors be buried?

Pre-testing showed that participants rated *survivors* as more relevant to an air-crash scenario than to a bicycle scenario. Convincingly, an average of 33% of people detected the anomaly in the air-crash case, yet 80% detected it in the bicycle case. The basic idea is that when a word is encountered, it is automatically checked for how well that word fits in the existing global context. Note that the *meaning* of *survivors* as such is not involved in this process; it is simply a matter of whether that *word* fits the context. If word meaning as such were to be involved, then detection of the anomaly should take place. It is simply the fact that the word *survivors* is quite likely to occur in the context of communications about an air crash (e.g., *there were no survivors*).

In another study, Barton and Sanford (Experiment 2) examined performance when the anomaly *survivors* was changed to *surviving dead*. The terms in this (*surviving*, and *dead*) separately fit the scenario well, but together, as an integrated semantic unit, are completely anomalous. Detection of this occurred at the astonishing low rate of 23%, and in an auditory version of the study (Sanford, unpublished data) not one participant noticed the problem! No one thought that *surviving dead* meant *people who had survived but later died*. For other work with similar expressions, such as *tranquilizing stimulants*, see Daneman, Lennertz, and Hannon (2007) and Hannon and Daneman (2004). The overall finding of such studies is that when an anomaly fits the global context well, it is less likely to be detected.

The second important feature of these difficult-to-detect anomalies is that the anomalous words are closely related in meaning to what an acceptable word would be. Thus *Moses* has been shown to be 'similar' in meaning to *Noah* in meaning-rating studies, but less so to *Adam*, which is clearly distinct. As a result, the Moses illusion generally fails if *Adam* is used (van Oostendorp & de Mul, 1990), and will always be expected to fail if, say, *Obama* is substituted for *Noah*.

Shallow processing versus reduced access to awareness

According to the shallow processing hypothesis, an anomalous word will not be detected as anomalous if its core meaning is not retrieved and used; if its core meaning is retrieved, it should be detected. The argument was that in the original *survivors* case, detection occurs only when the core meaning of *survivors* is utilized in comprehension, because that includes the information *is still alive immediately after the event*. However, some expressions that are related to *survivors* do not have *still alive* as part of their core meaning. For instance, *injured* means 'damaged in some way after a traumatic event', but 'being alive' is not part of its core meaning. Rather, *being alive* is a condition of the normal use of the word. In Barton and Sanford's Experiment 1, these core meanings were established in a pre-test by asking a group of people to define what they understood by the words *survivors* and the 'injured set', *injured, wounded, maimed*. Participants were then asked to read short passages, each containing the type of anomaly shown in (6a). The argument was that even if the core meaning of the injured set was utilized, the anomaly would not be noticed, whereas it would be for the term *survivors*. The upshot should be that substituting an 'injured set' term for *survivors* leads to a general reduction in detection rate. This is what was found. While the average detection rate for *survivors* was about 60%, for 'injured set' words (*injured, wounded, maimed*), the rate was only about 18%. This finding, which some people find quite counter-intuitive, is consistent with the shallow processing hypothesis.

Another line of enquiry by Bohan and Sanford (2008) asked whether anomalies are entirely undetected during processing (shallow processing proper) or whether they are detected at a level below consciousness. If the latter occurs, it might have an effect on behaviour but the reader will have a reduced awareness. This has been seen in some previous research. Indeed, using eye-tracking, Daneman, Reingold, and Davidson (1995) showed that there were disruptions to eye-tracking patterns of an incorrect homophone, such as using *hare* when the correct word is *hair*, even though people frequently failed to consciously notice and report the errors. Bohan and Sanford investigated these different possibilities by examining the eye-tracking records of people reading passages like (7), where the context words (*sentence*, or *care order*) determined whether a later anomalous word (in this case *victim*, if *sentence* was used) led to disruption in the eye-tracking record.

(7)   Child-abuse cases are being reported much more frequently these days. In a recent trial, a 10-year {sentence/care order} was given to the victim, but was subsequently appealed.

When an anomaly was detected (judged by the participant making a conscious report and explaining why the word was anomalous), there was disruption relative to the non-anomalous control. However, when an anomaly was present but went undetected, there was no such disruption. So, there was *no* evidence for detection of the anomaly at an unconscious level. (It should be pointed out that offline multiple choice tests were used to confirm that readers had appropriate knowledge that the anomalies were indeed anomalous.)

Of course, with such methods, there is always the question of whether some other method might provide evidence of unconscious detection. Sanford, Leuthold, Bohan, and Sanford (2011) carried out an EEG study using materials like (7), in order to see whether there was any evidence in terms of brain activity for unconscious detection. Since easy-to-detect anomalies lead to large N400 effects, it was possible that the hard-to-detect cases might show the same pattern, and the question would then be whether the N400 effect was present when anomalies were missed. There was no such N400 effect. In contrast, control materials containing anomalies of the classical kind (poorly fitting the context; easy to detect) did show a standard N400.

Hence, the results of the Sanford et al. (2011) study show two things. First, that when an anomaly has a good fit to global context, there is no N400 effect; and second, that there is no evidence for unconscious detection of anomalies, thus supporting the shallow processing hypothesis.

Interim summary: what 'semantic illusions' tell us about processing

The mere existence of anomalies that are easily missed, yet 'known' to readers to be anomalies, suggests that semantic processing is not always deep, in the sense that either the meaning of the anomalous item is not fully retrieved, or there is no integration of the information into the ongoing construction of the discourse representation. This is important, since it opens up the possibility that different ways of constructing a text may influence the extent of semantic analysis afforded a word. The experiments described above show several things:

- Word meanings are not always fully retrieved and used during comprehension – the shallow processing hypothesis.
- There is no existing evidence to suggest that when an anomaly is consciously missed, it is still detected 'unconsciously'.
- When a word appears in a global context that it fits well, it appears likely to receive shallow processing. This must be accomplished without an initial semantic analysis, of course. Rather, some mechanism recognizes how well the lexical item fits a discourse environment, which is some sort of statistical co-occurrence (for instance, *survivors* is a word that co-occurs often with an air-crash situation).

- Finally, it is important to understand that although the deliberately introduced anomalies may be seen as constituting 'tricks', they genuinely reveal failures to process meaning deeply, and are thus a valuable tool. In the next section, we examine aspects of the structure of discourse that lead to deeper or shallower processing, indexed by anomaly detection.

Depth of processing, foregrounding and focus

The next step in our argument is to link depth of processing to foregrounding and rhetorical focus. If foregrounding devices do indeed lead to deeper semantic processing, then this would provide empirical support for at least part of the thesis that foregrounding causes a greater scrutiny of what is portrayed by the language (as suggested by defamiliarization theory).

Attention control: presupposition, focus and emphasis

This class of influences on depth of processing is by far the largest, and related directly to foregrounding and focus. It is noteworthy that many of the materials showing failures of detection have anomalies in positions where the details are presupposed. This may be illustrated by a case that Sanford (unpublished data) has used as a classroom example, mentioned briefly earlier. Students were asked to complete a simple questionnaire about social constraints on who can marry whom in Western culture. Among the items used were:

(8a)   Can a woman marry her first cousin?

(8b)   Can a man marry his stepmother?

(8c)   Can a man marry his widow's sister?

(8d)   Can a woman marry her step-brother?

The crucial item is the third in the list. The answer has to be *no*, because to have a widow, the man has to be dead. Only 40% of students asked this said *no*. Here, the presupposition of the question is that the man is alive in order to be able to marry. With the concept of 'widow' also being out of focus, the anomaly is often missed. As the salience of the notion increases, so does detection rate. For instance, (9) produced a detection rate of 85%:

(9)   If a wife becomes a widow, can her husband marry her sister?

More systematic studies have investigated the effects of information structuring in the form of linguistic focus through the cleft construction, as discussed in the previous chapter. Thus Brédart and Modolo (1988) investigated the influence of the It-cleft structure on the detection of Moses-illusion type anomalies, comparing cases like (10a) and (10b):

(10a)   It was two animals of each kind that Moses took on the Ark. True or False?

(10b)   It was Moses who took two animals of each kind on the Ark. True or False?

Detection rates were much higher for (10b), where the It-cleft places the focus on *Moses*, than for (10a), where the focus is on *two animals*. Thus focus seemed to lead to a more thorough analysis of the term *Moses* than did the neutral simple active sentence. Similar results were obtained when stress was put on the anomalous word using capitals and underlining jointly (Brédart & Docquier, 1989).

Focus was also examined by Bohan, Sanford, Glen, Clark, and Martin (2008). Participants read a set of anomalous materials, varying in whether the anomalous information (that an empty table cannot be vacated) was within the scope of narrow focus, as in (11a), or not, as in example (11b). Detection rates were higher for the focus condition, as shown in square brackets:

(11a)   The restaurant manager regretfully told Mary that they were very busy, and she would have to wait. It was the empty table by the window that was likely to be vacated in about twenty minutes. [77%]

(11b)   The restaurant manager regretfully told Mary that they were very busy, and she would have to wait. The empty table by the window was likely to be vacated in about twenty minutes. [65%]

In (11a), focus is on *empty table*, making the verb *vacated* more obviously anomalous.

In a similar experiment, using the same sort of materials, bold typeface on various words was used as a means of emphasis. For any given presentation, only one word was in bold, but that word could be one of three; additionally, there was a condition where no bold was used at all. A typical material was as follows (with our added underlining and subscript numbers):

(12)   The restaurant manager regretfully told Mary that they were very busy, and she would have to wait. The empty$_1$ table by the window$_2$ was likely to be vacated$_3$ in about twenty minutes.

The subscript numbers indicate the three possible positions for emphasis. Positions 1 and 3 emphasize that an empty table will soon be vacated (the anomaly). These two positions yielded average detection rates of 69% and 67% respectively. The decision to emphasize *window* (position 2) was made because it was expected not to impact on the anomaly, and indeed it produced a lower detection rate of 60%. When there was no emphasis at all, the detection rate was 59%. Thus only emphasis on either the anomaly or the context producing the anomaly results in an improved detection rate.

As we pointed out in the previous chapter, clausal subordination is also closely related to presupposition and focus. It is popularly understood that propositions that are subordinate to others are somehow 'hidden' or 'disguised', and this is reflected as shallower processing. To reiterate briefly what we said there, consider (13a) and (13b) from Baker and Wagner (1987):

(13a)   The liver, which is an organ found only in humans, is often damaged by heavy drinking.

(13b)   The liver, which is often damaged by heavy drinking, is an organ found only in humans.

The subordinate clause of each of these sentences is what is presupposed, while the main clause is what is being asserted. When asked to verify the truth or falsity of sentences such as these, fewer people noticed the false statement (*an organ found only in humans*) in (13a), where it is the presupposed part of the sentence, than in (13b), where it is part of the asserted information.

So, information structuring, through focus and subordination, modulates the depth of processing of words and the analysis of propositions. Similar results have been found for emphasis by typographical devices.

Fluidity, fluency and difficulty

As discussed earlier, defamiliarization entails removing the automaticity of everyday processing, resulting, we suggest, in increased depth of processing. According to this idea, it should be possible to show that under the appropriate circumstances, a text that induces less fluent reading should result in deeper processing, odd though that might sound. Below we report two results that appear to confirm this notion. But if reading becomes too overloaded, for instance through the use of overly complex sentences, then processing may well be more shallow, due to competition over processing resources.

A simple result with fluent reading   One important feature of fluent reading, is that it is rapid. One of the easiest ways to disrupt fluency is through typeface complexity manipulation: some typefaces take much longer to read than others. Would reducing fluency in this way result in an increase in the detection rate for anomalies? On the very simple theory that longer times spent reading a word should be more likely to lead to full recovery of meaning, the answer should be *yes*. Song and Schwarz (2008) reported just such a study, and found that by increasing the difficulty of a typeface, detections of anomalies in questions of the 'Moses' type increased substantially. Simply by reducing fluency, deeper processing had been achieved.

Increasing fluency of processing through information provision There is evidence that not just physical fluency in reading, but increased ease of integration of information can result in shallower processing. In their case-study of the *survivors* anomaly, Barton and Sanford (Experiment 4) investigated whether the processing depth of an anomaly in a question would be influenced by the presence of information that helped readers find an answer to the question. They compared the following versions of the 'survivors' anomaly:

(14a)   *Basic*: Suppose there was an air crash with many survivors. Where should they be buried?

(14b)   *Relevant-augmented*: Suppose there was an air crash with many survivors, most of whom were {Europeans/of no fixed abode}. Where should they be buried?

(14c)   *Irrelevant-augmented*: Suppose there was an air crash with many survivors, which happened last week. Where should they be buried?

In the relevant-augmented case, information is presented about the origins of the survivors, which is superficially relevant to the question. In contrast, the irrelevant-augmented case simply adds when the accident took place which is not relevant to the question. The hypotheses were that detections in the irrelevant-augmented case would be the same as in the basic case, but that in the relevant-augmented case, detections would fall, because of the prominence of additional information relevant to answering the question. In the study, the questions of interest for the empirical study were embedded in a larger set of questions that addressed issues concerning official and personal responsibility. The critical question appeared in only one version for a given person. The results reliably showed that the relevant-augmented case resulted in fewer detections (49%) than the irrelevant-augmented (80%) or the basic (75%). This is a very large effect, and supports the view that providing additional information relevant to answering a question can reduce the depth of processing of at least some elements of the question. We presume that by providing this additional information, there is less additional analysis of the part of the sentence containing the anomaly than there might otherwise be: there is no need to analyse that part any further in order to answer the question, because the shallow analysis has the appearance of being good enough for the purpose of providing an answer.

Syntactic complexity   While slowing people's reading may increase depth of processing, one would expect such a manipulation to have a limit: when disruption causes a very high processing load simply to overcome the disruption, it might be expected that there would be a reduction in anomaly detection, suggesting a reduction in depth of processing. A somewhat more radical way of reducing ease of processing than through typeface complexity manipulations is through syntactic complexity, and this has been shown to have a deleterious effect on the detection of anomalies (Bohan, 2008). Bohan used a set of passages that began with scene-setting information, followed by a question, as shown below in (15). In the example, the anomaly is that negotiations do not take place with hostages, but with the hijackers. In all cases, an extra parenthetical clause in the high-load condition is introduced which separates the main *Wh*-part of the question from the anomaly.

(15)   Pan Am flight 004 from Chicago was forced at gunpoint to land at New York's John F. Kennedy Airport. The emergency services responded quickly and all were in attendance around the international terminal building. [...]

(15a)   *Low load*
Question: Under these circumstances, what difficulties would the officials at John F. Kennedy Airport, who must negotiate the demands of the hostages, be facing when they must ensure passenger safety and possible further threats to airport security?

(15b)   *High load*
Question: Under these circumstances, what difficulties would the officials at John F. Kennedy Airport, who must ensure the safety of their passengers, be facing when they must negotiate the demands of the hostages and possible further threats to airport security?

Participants were asked to read and answer questions of this type (just a few each). They were also alerted to the idea that there might be some (allegedly inadvertent) errors in the text, such as a wrong word, and told that if they noticed one, they were to tell the experimenter. The detection rate was 40% in the low-load condition, compared to 31% in the high-load case. So, the more complex sentence resulted in a lower detection rate. Clearly, it remains to be established precisely what the balance of disruption and depth of processing looks like over a broader range of variables, and this is an area ripe for further empirical investigation. For the writer trying to remove automaticity and increase defamiliarization, getting the balance right is an important part of the art of writing.

Interim summary: results from anomaly detection

The evidence provided in the last few sections shows that noticing an anomaly, and hence depth of processing, is systematically related to variables that might be expected to modulate the amount of processing resource given to different parts of a sentence. With questions where no clue to a potential answer is given in the information provided, processing is deeper than it is when relevant information is provided. When information relevant to an anomaly is put into narrow focus by the use of an It-cleft construction, anomaly detection increases because processing is deeper. And when information is put into a subordinate clause, anomalies are less likely to be noticed. Manipulations of the fluency of reading and integration can also modulate depth of processing. Finally, sentence complexity can decrease depth of processing.

Text-change detection

Anomaly detection is a straightforward way of seeing when the meaning of a word is missed in the context where it appears. More recently, another technique has been exploited that enables a slightly different way of studying which parts of a text are attended to (and hence which can receive deeper processing). This is *text-change detection* (Sanford & Sturt, 2002; Sturt, Sanford, Stewart, & Dawydiak, 2004). It is based on the change-blindness technique devised by vision scientists, and discussed at the outset of the present chapter. Recall that success at change detection can be used as an index of what is being attended to in a visual scene. By analogy, it is possible to show people a short text, which they read, and then after they have read it, show it to them again, sometimes with a small change, for instance with one word changed. The task is to say whether there was a change, and if so, what it was. Although our interest here is primarily in reading, the technique can also be adapted to listening to two successive auditory presentations of a short passage (e.g., A. J. S. Sanford, Sanford, Filik, & Molle, 2005, Experiment 3). The technique is easy to use, and provides a means of examining many factors that might influence depth of processing. We shall use it in several places in this book, since it turns out to be a sensitive tool. But, to begin, as a parallel to our discussion of anomaly detection, we shall illustrate the way in which information structuring influences change detection, and hence depth of processing.

Focus and change detection with written materials

We have seen that information structuring modulates the likelihood of detecting anomalies. Does the same apply to detecting changes in texts? Would the depth of processing afforded words be affected by discourse focus? Sturt et al. (2004, Experiment 2) presented materials like (16a/b), and asked people to read the short passage and press a button when they had read it. The passage was then presented a second time, sometimes with a change to a crucial word in the second presentation. Readers were asked to report any differences in wording that they noticed.

(16a)   Everybody was wondering which man got into trouble.
(16b)   In fact, the man with the hat was arrested.

This is the focussed case. There is narrow focus on *with the hat*, since this is the disambiguating information, which answers the implied question about which man it was. Compare (16a/b) with (17a/b):

(17a)   Everybody was wondering what was going on that night.
(17b)   In fact, the man with the hat was arrested.

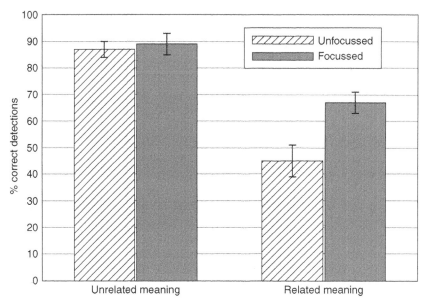

Figure 5.1 Results from Sturt et al. (2004, Experiment 2), showing effects of discourse focus on change detection. Detection of changes was greater for words in focus than for those out of focus, and this difference was largest for changes to words with related meanings.

This is the unfocussed case. Focus is broad, being on the event as a whole, rather than on the hat specifically, which is therefore unfocussed.

In the experiment, on the second presentation, the word *hat* could change to a word closely related in meaning (*cap*) or to a word unrelated in meaning (*roses*), but that does not change the sense of the whole passage.

The results of the experiment are shown in Figure 5.1. First, there is a strong effect of whether the change made was closely related or unrelated to the original word. When the change was to something related in meaning (*hat → cap*), the change was less well detected than for the unrelated case (*hat → roses*). Secondly, for the related meaning case, detection rate was much lower for the unfocussed case (17a/b) than for the focussed case (16a/b). Sturt et al. (2004) interpreted this in the following way. When a change is not detected, this is because the two words (the original one and the changed one) are represented so coarsely that their meanings are effectively indistinguishable. When a change is detected, this is because the meanings of the two words are distinguishable in their mental representation. In the case of *hat* and *cap*, for instance, the words would be indistinguishable in meaning if they are simply represented vaguely as 'headgear' for instance. Note that such a representation would still be different from the meaning of a semantically distant word, such as *roses*, and that the latter would easily be detected (as indeed it is). So, Sturt et al. claim that focus causes a sharper semantic representation to be produced than is the case when a word is out of focus. The basic idea is that meaning can be represented at different levels of specification (*granularity*, cf. Hobbs, 1985), and that words that are within the scope of focus have better specified (finer-grain) representations in the mind. This is the *granularity hypothesis*, and this experiment and other empirical findings support this hypothesis (e.g., A. J. S. Sanford, Sanford, Molle, & Emmott, 2006; Sanford & Garrod, 2005). This idea is still open to further exploration.

A similar pattern of results was obtained by Sturt et al. for cleft sentences. However, using the same paradigm, but this time with auditory presentations, A. J. S. Sanford, Price, and Sanford (2009) extended the observations of Sturt et al. by making a comparison of cleft, pseudo-cleft and simple declarative information structures. A typical material was as follows. Note that in this example and in other text-change detection examples in this chapter and the rest of the book, the arrow denotes a word changing to one of the words after the arrow.

(18a)   Everyone had just got back from a long and tiring swim in the sea.
         What Simon sat down on was the chair ($\rightarrow$ seat/rock) near the beach hut.
         [Focussed]

(18b)   Everyone had just got back from a long and tiring swim in the sea.
         It was Simon who sat down on the chair ($\rightarrow$ seat/rock) near the beach hut.
         [Focus on other element]

(18c)   Everyone had just got back from a long and tiring swim in the sea.
         Simon sat down on the chair ($\rightarrow$ seat/rock) near the beach hut.
         [Neutral]

The results showed that when a change was in focus, more changes were detected than when it was in the neutral declarative sentence. The smallest number of change detections occurred when the word changed was out of focus in a sentence that put strong focus on some other element. So, the results parallel the findings of the study on the effect of focus on ease of interpretation of pronominal reference discussed in the previous chapter (see Figure 4.1), in that both enhanced processing of items that are in focus and suppressed processing of items that are out of focus occur as a result of using cleft structures.

Change-detection effects with typographical devices of emphasis

We suggested that typographical devices are used as foregrounding cues, and have been implicated in the control of attention in discourse, and some of these have been studied using text-change detection. Thus A. J. S. Sanford et al. (2006, Experiment 1) used italics to put emphasis on individual words in three-line passages. As with focus, italics had the effect of increasing change detection on the words that were put in italics. Such effects were observed even on the earliest instances of italics, suggesting that there was no 'strategic learning' involved. The authors concluded that the use of italics served to emphasize the word so treated, and increased the depth of semantic analysis of that word. (Interestingly, changes to adjacent words were not more readily detected, so the effect was quite specific (Dawydiak, unpublished data).)

A writer may split off information by using *sentence fragments* that are words, phrases or dependent clauses which are punctuated as if they were full sentences, even though they are in fact only fragments of sentences (see Emmott, Sanford, & Morrow, 2006a, 2006b, for further discussion). We discussed these incomplete grammatical structures briefly in the previous chapter. Such fragments enjoy widespread usage, occurring in literary narratives, popular fiction and (auto)biographies, as well as being a major device in newspapers and advertising language. They frequently have the effect of extracting dependent information from what would otherwise be a full sentence and giving it main proposition status, as can be seen in (19):

(19)   In all her eighteen years, she could scarcely remember a moment that she had spent alone. Until she married.

(Ali (2004). *Brick Lane*, p. 24, our underlining)

Sentence fragments can also be used for rhythmic purposes. Here, the silent stress (Abercrombie, 1968) preceding the sentence fragment provides an extra beat which may give dramatic impact to the ironic reversal in the fragment.

An item can also be highlighted by placing it in a *mini-paragraph*, an unusually short paragraph (Emmott et al., 2006a). In (20), the author repeats information from the lead-up sentence, presenting the words *The Earth* as a sentence fragment and mini-paragraph. Here the item becomes a topic in its own right after it appears in the fragment.

(20)   He was now six light years from the place that the Earth would have been if it still existed.

The Earth.

Visions of it swam sickeningly through his nauseated mind.

(Adams (1986a). *The Hitchhiker's Guide to the Galaxy*,
p. 53, our underlining)

Are the effects of fragments and mini-paragraphs demonstrable through change detection? Emmott et al. (2006a) carried out a change-detection task comparing detection of changes to a word presented in a fragment attached to a full sentence, as a separate fragment, or as a separate fragment forming its own mini-paragraph. A full example of a material is:

(21a)   *Assimilated into a full sentence*
Peter had tried hard not to go over details of the interview in his mind. He tried not to rephrase his answers, tormenting himself with things he should have said. He tried hard especially not to listen out for the postman every morning, but at last there it was, a brown ($\rightarrow$ white) envelope.

He examined it for a while, before summoning the courage to look inside at his fate.

(21b)   *Sentence fragment, no mini-paragraph*
Peter had tried hard not to go over details of the interview in his mind. He tried not to rephrase his answers, tormenting himself with things he should have said. He tried hard especially not to listen out for the postman every morning, but at last there it was. A brown ($\rightarrow$ white) envelope.

He examined it for a while, before summoning the courage to look inside at his fate.

(21c)   *Sentence fragment, mini-paragraph*
Peter had tried hard not to go over details of the interview in his mind. He tried not to rephrase his answers, tormenting himself with things he should have said. He tried hard especially not to listen out for the postman every morning, but at last there it was.

A brown ($\rightarrow$ white) envelope.

He examined it for a while, before summoning the courage to look inside at his fate.

When the crucial phrase was presented as a separate sentence fragment (21b), and when it was presented as both a fragment and a mini-paragraph (21c), there was an improvement of detection over the case where the phrase was assimilated into the preceding sentence (21a). This certainly demonstrates that processing depth is increased by these formatting devices, as anticipated. However, there was no additional advantage for the separate paragraphing, which one might have expected. Of course, this does not mean that there is *no* effect of using a mini-paragraph, just that the effect is not on depth of processing, and so might not be revealed by change detection. It seems likely to us that the effect of paragraphing may perhaps be detectable by other means, such as tests of retention in memory, or possibly vividness of imagery, but this stands as speculation at present.

Lexical-level statistical phenomena and change detection

The use of low-frequency and/or long words constitutes a deviation from the normal that is a prime candidate for attention capture. In the psycholinguistic literatures on word recognition and eye-tracking, it is well recognized that lexical features such as frequency of occurrence and word length affect the duration of initially fixating a word. Furthermore, it is known from EEG work that low-frequency words produce a larger N400 than higher-frequency words. Sanford, Dawydiak, and Emmott (2006) investigated the effect of word frequency and length on text-change detection. They hypothesized that low-frequency or long words would require extra processing, and so would be more readily noticed in a change-detection task. In the experiment, word changes were to synonyms of the original words.

For the frequency manipulation, word changes could be one of the four frequency types: high → low, low → high, high → high, or low → low (high and low frequency were ascertained by consulting the British National Corpus). An example of these types of changes is as follows:

(22a)   *High → low*
It was a hot summer day and Debbie was pottering about in her garden. She loved (→ adored) taking care of the various plants there. One of her favourites was a big rhododendron bush in the corner. It had a particularly pleasant scent in the evenings.

(22b)   *Low → high*
Benny's parents were really worried that he lacked a clear direction in life. The careers guidance officer had worked hard to find a vocation (→ profession) that would suit him. Unfortunately, Benny wasn't interested in any of the suggestions. He'd rather watch daytime TV than work.

(22c)   *High → high*
Sharon was sitting a stressful exam. In the heat of the moment, she misinterpreted one of the questions. Afterwards, the marker noticed her error (→ mistake) and points were deducted. Luckily, Sharon still managed to pass the exam.

(22d)   *Low → low*
Louise was thinking about investing some of her savings. She thought that the financial (→ economic) benefits of investing in the stock market would be very worthwhile. After talking the matter over with her financial advisor, however, she decided to delay the investment. The box under her bed would have to do for the moment.

The results for changes to the word frequency are shown below:

High → low 67%
Low → high 29%
High → high 25%
Low → low 77%

If a low-frequency word or a high-frequency word is changed to a low-frequency synonym, then it is more likely to be noticed than if it is changed to a high-frequency synonym. This may be interpreted as follows. When a low-frequency word is encountered, it causes processing difficulty, so if it is different from a word that went before, the change will be noticed. However, once a low-frequency word has been encountered, it soon loses its prominence. This is why a low-frequency word that is changed to a high-frequency synonym does not yield an enhanced change detection.

For the word-length manipulation, a parallel set of conditions was used. For brevity, we present in (23a–d) an example of only the word changes; the materials themselves were similar to those shown in (22a–d):

(23a)   Short → short: inn → pub
(23b)   Short → long: clever → intelligent
(23c)   Long → short: competition → match
(23d)   Long → long: financial → economic

Exactly the same pattern accrues for words that are long as was found for words that are uncommon. They too use more processing effort, but the effects are short-lived. The results for changes to word length are shown below.

> Short → short 13%
> Short → long 21%
> Long → short 13%
> Long → long 20%

Although preliminary in nature, these effects may be understood well in Leech and Short's (2007) framework of deviation from the norm. In the Sanford et al. (2006) change-detection study, frequency was simply set up to reflect a real contrast between low- and high-frequency words, using conventional norms. In the case of length, a simple difference in letters and syllables was used to maximize contrasts between long and short. Clearly, a more sophisticated manipulation could be carried out comparing frequency and length for selected words to the norm for the language and/or the norm specific to longer texts containing the words (the external and internal norms which we saw in Chapter 4). This would enable more sophisticated questions to be asked. For example, in a text where the average word frequency is quite low, perhaps a high-frequency word would stand out as being unusual, or perhaps it is only rarity with respect to general usage that counts. In principle, such manipulations may be used to obtain a better analysis of the impact of different varieties of Leech and Short deviation.

Pre-announcements

Another potential highlighting device used is the *pre-announcement*, which signals a speech act or story event which is about to occur (e.g., *then he told me this*; *then this happened*). We are drawing here on a term from Conversation Analysis (Terasaki, 2004), but applying the term to written narratives. This is another device which is used for a particular type of emphasis, being useful for indicating key plot moments, particularly where the significance of the event might otherwise be missed. This appears to be a strategy for putting the information that follows into broad focus, so that the whole event is focussed on. In (24), we see an opening proposition of this type. It prefaces an action which might otherwise seem trivial, but is actually the crux of the whole story (see Emmott, 2003, for a discussion of this story).

(24)   <u>Then this happened</u>: The maid, the tiny, erect figure of the maid in her white-and-black uniform, was standing beside Richard Pratt, holding something out in her hand.

(Dahl (1990b). 'Taste', p. 64, our underlining)

We might expect the event here to be highlighted over and above other events.

In several experiments, we have investigated whether pre-announcements increase the likelihood of detecting change to text that follows (Emmott, Sanford, & Dawydiak, 2007; Sanford et al., 2006). For example, in one experiment, in a simple narrative, a pre-announcement was introduced in one condition, a pre-announcement with an emotional overtone in a second, and a control with no pre-announcement, as illustrated in (25a–c) (underlining is added on the pre-announcements here, but did not appear in the experiments).

(25a)   *Pre-announcement*
I was travelling to a nearby village to meet friends. After driving for 15 minutes, I was approaching their cottage. <u>Then something happened</u>. A sports car drove ($\rightarrow$ moved) out in front of me and nearly hit my car. Thankfully, no damage was done.

(25b)   *Pre-announcement with emotion*
I was travelling to a nearby village to meet friends. After driving for 15 minutes, I was approaching their cottage. <u>What happened next made me furious</u>. A sports car drove ($\rightarrow$ moved) out in front of me and nearly hit my car. Thankfully, no damage was done.

(25c)   *No pre-announcement (control)*
I was travelling to a nearby village to meet friends. After driving for 15 minutes, I was approaching their cottage. <u>It had a thatched roof</u>. A sports car drove ($\rightarrow$ moved) out in front of me and nearly hit my car. Thankfully, no damage was done.

Surprisingly, there was no enhanced detection as a result of either of the pre-announcement conditions. Furthermore, no enhancement was obtained in two other studies where surprise or emotional reaction was used in a similar pre-announcement context. Further exploration of pre-announcements is clearly required. However, taking the lack of effects at face value, one possibility is that when emphasis is indicated by form (italics, paragraphs, syntactic structure), then there is an enhancement of depth of processing, but when emphasis is indicated by content at the propositional level, the same kind of enhancement does not occur. However, we think this a little unlikely: it is effectively saying that a writer cannot manipulate the reader's attention by writing something like *Now, dear reader, pay careful attention to what I have to say next.* This is totally counter-intuitive. An alternative may be that because the material following the pre-announcement is put into broad focus (rather than the narrow focus of clefts, italics, and the like), enhancement of effects at the word level is simply not occurring. We believe the issue is far from settled, and offer what we have as mere suggestions. We think it is possible that an instruction of the type given above, particularly if it is in the form of a direct address (*dear reader* or *you*), may well produce enhancing effects, though this may be because personalizing a message to the reader by direct addressing seems to be a good medium for enhancing attention (which we demonstrate in Chapter 7).

Sentence complexity and change detection

One aspect of style that seems likely to influence text-change performance is sentence complexity. Some accomplished writers are notorious for using quite complex sentences, whereas, for others, such as novice writers, it might be more appropriate to consider this to be poor style. As we saw earlier in our discussion of the detection of semantic anomalies, detection is reduced by high processing load induced by parentheticals (Bohan, 2008). Indeed, using text change, there has been an extensive investigation showing a reduction in change-detection efficiency under conditions of high sentence complexity, where high processing loads ensue. A. J. S. Sanford et al. (2005) explored two kinds of sentential load, finding that complexity reduced the capacity to detect changes.

In the first studies, A. J. S. Sanford et al. (2005) compared complex sentences containing object-extracted embedded clauses, like (26a), with simpler subject-extracted cases like (26b). It is well documented that sentences containing object-extracted relative clauses take longer to process than those containing subject-extracted clauses (e.g., Gordon, Hendrick, & Johnson, 2001; Mak, Vonk, & Schriefers, 2006; Traxler, Morris, & Seely, 2002). Furthermore, (26a) is also intuitively strikingly more difficult to process than (26b).

(26a)   The reporter who the photographer sent hoped for a story.

(26b)   The reporter who sent the photographer hoped for a story.

In the text-change experiments, passages three sentences long were presented for reading, with the crucial changes occurring in the second sentence. Examples are:

(27a)   There is an increasing demand for therapists and counsellors in many areas of life. The child who the psychologist talked to had hurt the woman. It is important that all victims receive a high standard of emotional support. [*High-load* condition]

(27b)   There is an increasing demand for therapists and counsellors in many areas
            of modern life. The child who talked to the psychologist had hurt the woman.
            It is important that all victims receive a high standard of emotional support.
            [*Low-load* condition]

In the high-load condition, detection of changes was poorer than in the low-load condition, as predicted.

A similar effect was found with another type of manipulation, this time based on the object-extracted clauses only. It has long been established that not all sentences with object-extracted embedded clauses are equally difficult. Compare examples (28a) and (28b):

(28a)   The professor who the student had recently met at a party was famous, but
            no one could figure out why.

(28b)   The professor who I had recently met at a party was famous, but no one
            could figure out why.

Intuitively, (28a) is more difficult to read than (28b), for most people. In controlled experiments, both ratings of difficulty and self-paced reading times confirm that sentences like (28a) are harder to process than ones like (28b) (Warren, 2001; Warren & Gibson, 2002; see also Gordon et al., 2001). The only difference between the two versions is that the noun phrase *student* is changed to the first person pronoun *I* in the second example. This difference is known as a difference in *referential load*. Warren and Gibson predicted the observed differences in difficulty on the basis of two arguments: an argument about the relative 'givenness' of full noun phrases and indexical pronouns, and the role that new individuals play in the load that has to be carried while sentence parsing is occurring.

According to the idea of an *accessibility scale* (Ariel, 1990), different types of nominal expressions vary with respect to accessibility of their referents (see also Gundel, Hedberg, & Zacharski, 1993). It has been suggested that the processing load at a noun phrase is related to its referent's expected accessibility, and given the assumption that the referents of first and second person pronouns are highly accessible in context, it is predicted that these pronouns will be easy to process (Warren & Gibson, 2002). On the other hand, full noun phrases refer to individuals that are much less accessible, either because they have not been mentioned recently or at all in the prior discourse (Garrod & Sanford, 1994; Sanford & Garrod, 1981) or most obviously if there is no prior discourse. An alternative explanation is that there is interference between similar elements in memory during the process of retrieving the place in the syntactic structure at which elements are attached (Gordon et al., 2001; Lewis, 1996). Thus Gordon et al. (2001) proposed that one reason why (28a) is more difficult than (28b) is that in (28b) there are different forms of noun phrase (*the professor*, as well as the pronoun *I*), whereas in (28a) there are two full definite noun phrases (*the professor*, *the student*). The similar forms of noun phrase lead to competition, which makes the item more difficult to read; this does not occur in (28b).

For the present purpose, the reasons for the differences are not important. The question is what effect the differences in complexity have on depth of processing as indexed by text-change detection. A. J. S. Sanford et al. (2005) used materials similar to (29), carrying out change-detection measurements at various positions in the second sentence.

(29)   The college frequently held social functions for visiting academics. The
        professor who {the student/I} had recently met at the party was famous, but
        no one could figure out why.

The use of a full noun phrase led to fewer detections of changes than did the use of a first or second person pronoun, in line with the idea that higher load would reduce detection efficiency. Furthermore, the effect of referential load is not simply to make the whole sentence more difficult to read. Rather, the effect is localized to changes made on the embedded verb only. Once again, this fits predictions well (of both the Warren and Gibson account and the Gordon et al. account).

On the argument that change detection reflects the precision of semantic representation, sentential processing load thus reduces precision, while focus and emphasis effects improve precision. In this way, change detection appears to be a suitable tool for investigating the effects of devices that might be expected to modulate the precision of semantic representations, including a wide range of literary devices.

Adopted perspective during reading

One such device is adopted perspective. In addition to sentential phenomena influencing depth of processing, like those described above, there is some recent evidence showing that the perspective that a reader adopts influences change detection. This work fits the intuition that if a reader has a strong interest in certain aspects of what they are reading, then this is more likely to receive deeper processing. In one classic study, Pichert and Anderson (1977; see also Baillet & Keenan, 1986) had participants read short descriptions of houses, while adopting different perspectives such as a burglar's or a house-buyer's. Memory was generally better for some perspective-relevant information, such as furs and jewels from a burglar perspective. Bohan, Filik, MacArthur, and McCluskey (2009) carried out a text-change study using a similar passage, and found that changes to words that were perspective-relevant were more readily detected than the same words when they were not relevant to the adopted perspective. This suggests that the recall data resulted from the degree of processing afforded perspective-relevant material. In a further study, they showed that requiring people to adopt the perspective of one or other character in a short vignette led to enhanced change detection for information about that character. An example of their materials was as follows. (In the experiment, a given participant only experienced one of the changes in each case.)

(30)   John and Jane went to a weekend cookery school. John thought he was good at making cakes {→ buns/sweets} and biscuits. Jane felt she was good at making sauces and soup {→ broth/pasta} but struggled with seafood. The chef was surprisingly a very friendly man who encouraged them both.

Passages were read adopting John's or Jane's perspective. Changes to *cakes* were detected more easily when the John perspective was adopted, while changes to *soup* were more readily detected when the Jane perspective was adopted. While these experiments concern explicitly adopted perspectives based on overt instructions, a similar logic can be used to look at perspectives induced in other ways, as we will see in Chapter 7.

The nature and importance of depth of processing

In this section, we shall consider whether or not shallow processing is exceptional, and whether there are individual differences in processing. We will also summarize relevant work that has been done on text-change detection in relation to the discussions in this chapter (further experiments on text-change detection will be presented in Chapter 7), and indicate future possible research.

The ubiquity of depth of processing effects

The evidence presented for shallow processing is extremely robust. It might be supposed that when readers become wise to the fact that there are anomalies in a text, they will somehow adjust and detect them. But this is not so (witness the case of Bohan and Sanford, 2008, where the task was indeed to look for anomalies). While general task demands can have an effect on the likelihood of detection of anomalies, for instance (Büttner, 2007; Kamas, Reder, & Ayers, 1996; van Jaarsveld, Dijkstra, & Hermans, 1997), performance never approaches 100% correct detections in the experiments we describe here.

Another important question of the same sort is whether some people, perhaps 'good readers', on being confronted by material containing anomalies, will easily spot them. Perhaps missing anomalies characterizes poorer readers because reading imposes a greater cognitive load on them. There is some evidence related to this conjecture, though in general it must be understood that *all* readers are susceptible to anomalies. Hannon and Daneman (2001) manipulated two factors in their materials: how strongly the anomalous words were related to the global context, and how strongly anomalous words were related to what would have been the correct word (e.g., *Moses* to *Noah*). They theorized that two aspects of a person's cognitive ability might influence how good they were at detecting anomalies. First, they argued that a person's ability to detect anomalies would be enhanced if they had high scores on a test of how easily they could access information from long-term memory. Indeed, people scoring well on this found it easier to detect highly semantically related words. Secondly, they showed that people with poorer working-memory scores were less able to detect anomalies when there was a strongly supporting context. Precisely how this works is unclear, but it does show that there is some degree of systematic individual variation.

Hannon and Daneman (2004) carried out a study in which they used locally semantically anomalous phrases such as *tranquilizing stimulants*. They also had their participants complete the Nelson–Denny comprehension skills questionnaire, and found that readers with lower comprehension skill were poorer at detecting such anomalies than high scorers. Hannon and Daneman suggest that this is because the poorer comprehenders were more influenced by the global context, causing a reduction in the depth of processing of local phrase-level semantics. However, one important fact is that all levels of comprehenders missed some anomalies. Indeed, in many years of anomaly research, we have yet to find any individual who was completely (or even largely) immune to the shallow processing phenomenon indexed by either anomalies or change detection.

Shallow and incomplete processing: natural mechanisms

Rather than being a fault in terms of comprehension, we suggest that evidence for incomplete or shallow semantic processing phenomena reflect a number of useful mechanisms that characterize the human comprehension system generally. Some of this can be understood within the Scenario-Mapping framework, as outlined in Chapter 2. According to this account, the primary principle behind comprehension is to identify as soon as possible the basic scenarios that a message is based on. The resulting mappings and activated knowledge structures allow for interpretation to take place with a reduction in processing effort.

One of the opening claims of this chapter was that when an anomaly fits a global context well, then it is difficult to detect. We posited a mechanism by which words are checked for how likely they are to appear in a given situational context, which we will call *contextual co-occurrence filtering*. For instance, the word *survivors* fits well with an air-crash scenario (typically, there are no survivors, might be the message), or the words *victim* and *defendant* fit well with an abuse trial in a law court. The basis for such a mechanism requires exploration, but there is now a vast body of evidence showing how useful for many purposes it is to use lexical co-occurrence information, one of the principal aspects of Latent Semantic Analysis (Landauer & Dumais, 1997; Landauer, Folz, & Laham, 1998). One thing the brain is very good at is recognizing and storing contingencies. Indeed, it is this fact that supports our ability to identify new regularities (parallelisms) and to spot when something is statistically unusual. We suggest that such contingencies in the form of a mental representation of co-occurrence serve to guide the extent of further semantic processing. We also suppose that the process is automatic.

What possible advantages could there be to such a mechanism? First, there is often little need for a reader or listener to even know what a word is in a very restraining context. For instance, the number of word possibilities for the blank below is in fact quite small in this courtroom context:

(31)   The Judge handed down a three year sentence to the ___

There is much redundancy in language, as is particularly the case here. If sentence (31) were spoken, and the blank word were mumbled, it would be unlikely that we would need to ask what it had been. In short, our claim is that situational constraints reduce the need for semantic analysis, so it doesn't happen.

The other side of the coin is the situation where words provide additional information over and above the default roles in the global context. Here it makes clear sense for a semantic analysis of the word to be much fuller. For instance, if the blank above were to be *tearful defendant*, it would be noteworthy, because *tearful* introduces new information. As we have argued, words that would be particularly noticeable would be words apparently not fitting the context at all, for instance low-frequency words that a writer was using for a special effect.

Investigating depth of processing

Control of depth of processing is an important way of allocating processing effort where it is needed, and not analysing all potential aspects of a text in detail. We believe that the processing system is not only limited in the amount of computation it can undertake at a given time, but that limiting processing is an important aspect of language use. For instance, one major fact about language is that there is an effectively infinite number of plausible inferences

Table 5.1 Summary of devices examined through text-change method, with main effects

Device	Effect	Reference
It-cleft/Pseudo-cleft	Focus increases detection	Sturt et al., 2004; A. J. S. Sanford et al., 2009
Discourse focus	Focus increases detection	Sturt et al., 2004; A. J. S. Sanford et al., 2006
Subordinate clauses	Subordination decreases detection	Price, unpublished data
Italicization	Italics increase detection	A. J. S. Sanford et al., 2006
Short sentences/ fragments	Short sentences/fragments increase detection	Emmott et al., 2006a
Long words	Long words increase detection	Sanford et al., 2006
Low-frequency words	Low-frequency words increase detection	Sanford et al., 2006
Complex syntax	Complexity decreases detection	A. J. S. Sanford et al., 2005
Referential complexity	Complexity decreases detection	A. J. S. Sanford et al., 2005
Adopted perspective	Adopted perspective increases detection	Bohan et al., 2009

that can be drawn in a full-length discourse. Inferences must be contained, and we rely on devices of foregrounding in everyday language just as much as in literary language to help control what we attend to and process deeply.

There are plenty of theoretical psychological issues that need to be explored in order to better understand the nature of shallow and deep processing. In this chapter we have championed the idea that shallow (semantic) processing is the failure to retrieve and/or integrate the lexical meaning of a word with the sentence and discourse context. This claim needs examining in more detail. Further, the conscious detection of anomalies and of 'attention grabbers', such as rare or unusually long words, needs to be further explored. Surprisingly, there has been little experimentation in psychology on conscious noticing of textual features, noticing anomalies being an exception.

Given the number of situations where shallow processing has been demonstrated, we can say that it is clearly a widespread phenomenon. Indeed, we would equate it with the relative automaticity of normal language, as identified by Mukařovský (1964a, 1964b) and Havránek (1964). By the same token, it is evident that depth of processing can be modulated by a variety of means, including information structuring and other foregrounding devices which interest stylisticians. The summary shown in Table 5.1 indicates a range of stylistic devices that have been examined, showing how they appear to affect depth of processing. We will also look further at empirical work using text-change detection in our discussion of perspective and the representation of speech and thought in narrative in Chapter 7.

We have explored a range of foregrounding devices in this chapter, but nevertheless recognize that further devices and combinations of devices could be examined and hence view this research as the start of what should be a much more extensive programme of investigation. The literary view of foregrounding is a rich area, and attention control and depth of processing are but two aspects to study. In the next chapter, we move onto the experiential aspect of narrative comprehension, the way that we experience sensations and emotions highlighted by writers. The question is, how can a writer manipulate the intensity of what we experience? Indeed, what is the actual nature of that experience?

Summary

In this chapter, we discussed in detail the notion of depth of processing, the idea that different parts of a text are processed to different degrees. We examined the following issues:

- The idea of shallow semantic processing is that lexical or propositional semantic information is not fully retrieved or utilized during processing. The paragon case of shallow processing is found in difficult-to-detect semantic anomalies. Although recognized by people to be anomalous when pointed out, these are nonetheless easily missed during reading, even when people are aware that there may be some type of anomaly. We presented evidence that such anomalies tend to be missed especially when the anomalous word is similar in meaning to what the correct word should be, and fits the current global context (or scenario) well, even though it is ill-fitting at the local semantic level. Furthermore, there is no evidence to date for 'unconscious' detection of these anomalies, suggesting that processing is indeed shallow.
- Detection of such anomalies is increased when they are within the scope of focus, and when they are presented in more difficult typefaces, suggesting foregrounding may result in deeper processing. This links in with the ideas of Shklovsky (1965) and constitutes one construal of the notion of defamiliarization. Indeed, work that we presented on the effects of modulating the fluency of reading and comprehension are a perfect fit to these ideas: by reducing the ease with which processing occurs, depth of processing is increased, although obviously there is some limit to this.
- Another technique, text-change detection, has been argued as a further index of depth of processing. A large variety of studies show that change detection is enhanced by focus (clefting and discourse focus), and compromised by syntactic and referential complexity, matching and expanding

the results found with semantic anomalies. Using change detection, a wide variety of foregrounding devices have been investigated, including the use of italics, short sentence fragments, and rare or unusually long words. All of these devices increase change detection, suggesting deeper processing. Furthermore, the perspective adopted by readers modulates the detection of changes. In Chapter 7, we shall describe further use of the technique to look at different perspectives induced by pronouns and direct/indirect speech.

6   The experiential aspect: using embodiment theory

A major feature of narrative is the way in which what is portrayed can have a vivid effect on us, even though we know it is not real. As readers we typically have a sense of being 'in' the narrative world. We seem to experience various things depicted in texts, mentally adopting perspectives, sensing movement and being engaged in different kinds of sensory experience, as well as having our emotions affected (e.g., Burke, 2010; Duchan, Bruder, & Hewitt, 1995; Esrock, 2004, 2010; Gerrig, 1993; Miall, 2007). In a work from literary studies, Opdahl (2002, pp. 19–20) comments on the vividness of reading a passage from a Hemingway story:

'You smell or hear or touch or see everything that exists,' [a literary critic] says of the story. 'You even taste Nick Adams' supper of beans and spaghetti' [...] We do not simply translate Hemingway's words into ideas, since this passage is a fictional narrative, which requires us to experience its events vicariously. Instead we *embody* the meaning we read, constructing a model of the author's world so tangible that we can imaginatively enter it. (Discussing Hemingway's 'Big Two-Hearted River', Opdahl's italics)

Psychologists have used descriptions such as 'being transported' into a narrative world (Gerrig, 1993) and 'the immersed experiencer' (Zwaan, 2004) to reflect how the reader seems to actively experience narrative events, the *experiential aspect* of narrative comprehension. The psychological term for the idea that readers draw on some aspects of sensory experience, motor behaviour and emotional experience, while reading, is *embodied understanding*. It has been suggested (for instance, Oatley, 1992, 2011; Zwaan, 2004) that in reading literature, a simulation of the actions, events and experiences depicted runs literally in the minds of readers (see also Feagin, 1996; Preston & de Waal, 2002). The notion of a simulation might be used to capture some of the shared properties of actual everyday experience and our experience during reading. Nevertheless, it is clear that there are also crucial differences between reality and its depiction in writing or other media. For instance, when watching a horror film, we may feel scared of a monster, but, as adults, we do not usually run from our seats as we would if the monster was real (Walton,

1978, 1990). It is possible to keep fantasy and reality apart. Similarly, when we read a description of a character experiencing pain, we may empathize with that character, understanding the character's situation and perhaps even wincing, but we are unlikely to feel the full agony.

In this chapter, we shall examine the contributions of empirical psychology and neuroscience toward exploring the role of embodiment in understanding language. This embodied understanding movement is a burgeoning field (e.g., de Vega, Glenberg, & Graesser, 2008). Work on embodiment has its origins in two fields of enquiry. First, strong arguments have been made that, during language use, meaning has to be grounded in real-world perceptions and actions, and not in a simply symbolic, dictionary-like system (e.g., Glenberg & Kaschak, 2002; Harnad, 1990). Secondly, neuroscience has shown that a capacity to recognize and understand actions depends upon a neural system, the *mirror-neuron system*, that effectively simulates in the brain of the beholder what is being observed in the actions of another (e.g., Rizzolatti & Craighero, 2004).

The main issues to be tackled are twofold. First, what evidence is there that sensory and motor experiences can be induced indirectly, through secondary depictions, and especially through language? This is of course the main question if we are to explain the basis of the experiential aspect of action and event comprehension. Secondly, since it turns out that there is such evidence, we can ask how writers use language to maximize or minimize the experiential aspect in a selective manner. We view this as a further aspect of rhetorical focussing. This second question raises the issue of whether processing using embodiment is a necessary aspect of understanding or a kind of enriching optional extra. From the point of view of research on comprehension in general, it is a possibility that although understanding is rooted in processing based on embodiment, there may sometimes be limits to the degree of embodiment. This is a position which we will evaluate.

Throughout this chapter and at various points in subsequent chapters, we will discuss studies which examine the regions of the brain used in imagined perception and action, making comparisons with the regions used in actual perception and action. These studies examine whether the same brain activation patterns are seen, and whether there is a difference in degree of activation. Given the sense of vividness associated with imagery of different types (e.g., visual, acoustic, taste) and imagined motion by literary scholars, we might expect some resulting embodiment effects in the brain. However, clearly there is a difference between real vision, sound, taste, motion, and so on and their counterparts in imagination, so we might also predict different levels of brain activation when such activation occurs. We describe this experimental work in general terms and also refer to specific parts of the brain where relevant. Readers without a background in neuroanatomy should be able to follow the overall objectives and findings of these experiments and, if interested in the details of specific brain areas, can consult a basic guide to neuroanatomy for further information (e.g., Bear, Connors, & Paradiso, 2007; Crossman & Neary, 2010; Diamond, Scheibel, & Elson, 1985; Felten & Shetty, 2009).

Embodiment and the notion of symbol grounding

In psycholinguistics, the origins of the recent growth of interest in embodiment began with the quest to understand how language conveys meaning. One can discern a shift from abstract notions of symbolic meaning to ones that reflect grounding in the world and processes in the body that might capture this grounding.

In linguistics and psychology, componential analysis has traditionally been used as the dominant way of describing lexical meaning, with the meaning of words being represented as sets of features (see Leech, 1981; Miller & Johnson-Laird, 1976, for discussions). So, for example, the word *man* could be re-written in terms of features as follows:

Man(x) → Male(x) & Human(x) & Adult(x)
where (x) denotes an individual, and & denotes adding properties to form a list.

In much the same way, *father* could be re-written as:

Father(x) → Man(x) & Parent(x, y)
where (x) denotes an individual, and (y) denotes another, in this case, the individual who is the offspring of (x).

This symbolist approach has been useful in many respects in linguistics and psycholinguistics, but it has, nevertheless, been argued that there is a degree of circularity in using verbal descriptors as ways of defining words. This is known as the *symbol grounding problem*, described by Harnad (1990). As an example, Harnad asks us to imagine that we are learning Chinese with no knowledge at all of the language, with only a Chinese–Chinese dictionary as our source of information (this example being a variant on Searle, 1980). Harnad argues that this 'would amount to a merry-go-round' (p. 339) as we move from one meaningless symbol or symbol-string (i.e., a headword or headphrase in the dictionary in Chinese) to another (i.e., a definition in Chinese). The point of this is that meaning has to be grounded in the world itself, and this in turn opens up the possibility that rather than being a manipulation of just lists of features bound together in conceptual relationships, representations of the world itself, such as images and actions, come into play when we interpret the world. Indeed, many words are obviously grounded in the sense that they can only be understood by reference to properties or events in the world. For instance, the *Oxford English Dictionary* defines the word *north* in the following way:

In the direction of the part of the horizon on the left-hand side of a person facing the rising sun; towards or in the direction of the point or pole on the earth's surface which lies on the earth's axis of rotation and at which the heavens appear to turn anticlockwise about a point directly overhead; (also) towards the magnetic pole near this point, to which a compass needle points. (*OED Online*, accessed October 2011, www.oed.com/view/entry/128325)

This definition brings into play our perception. This is quite different from giving a purely verbal definition, for instance, *Opposed to south*, which requires us then to define *south*. Such a verbal definition falls into the symbol grounding problem. Another interesting case is *left*, defined in the *Oxford English Dictionary* as:

The distinctive epithet of the hand which is normally the weaker of the two [. . .] and of the other parts on the same side of the human body [. . .] hence also of what pertains to the corresponding side of any other body or object. Opposed to *right*. (*OED Online*, accessed October 2011, www.oed.com/view/entry/106982)

The initial parts of this definition are more revealing than simply the concluding *Opposed to right* even though, as adults, we understand *left* as the opposite of *right*. In fact, of course, we understand *left* and *right* because we have learnt specifically to associate these terms with certain sides of our own bodies. Hence, when issued with the driving instruction *Turn right* we don't have to stop, ask a sample of people which is their dominant side, and then apply the resulting majority vote to our driving behaviour. But the point is that the meanings of *left* and *right* are understood through using the words to indicate specific sides of our bodies, and therefore can be applied to other bodies or objects, just as the definition says. In this way, the meanings of the words *north/south* and *left/right* are grounded in the physical world. The view of language as embodied understanding is increasingly becoming a dominant approach in linguistics and psycholinguistics (see de Vega et al., 2008, for a useful series of debates about symbolism and embodiment).

Perceptual properties make up a good part of the definitions of objects in general. The same is true of verbs. Consider verbs of motion. It is almost impossible to specify in words the verb *to saunter*, yet it can be adequately described by the characteristic pattern of motion that the joints of a person sauntering make. In an experiment in which light-emitting diodes were fitted to the main joints of actors, when they carried out various styles of walks, such as *saunter* and *trudge*, it was easy for observers to fit the right verb to what they saw (Levelt, Schreuder, & Hoenkamp, 1978). So it would seem to be the pattern of movement that defines the semantics. In much the same way, Malt et al. (2008) found empirically that the word choice of *run* or *walk* in several cultures correlated with biomechanical distinctions between these gaits. These examples, like the examples of *left* and *right*, are interesting, because of the problem of defining the words in other words, or in verbal primitives. There may be advantages to defining the words in terms of actual movements, physical positions and perceptual processes. Indeed, an important development in cognition and neuroscience has been the discovery that concepts seem to activate brain mechanisms that are perceptual, or action-based, in nature. This has led to the idea that concepts are represented in terms of modality-based systems, a view championed by Barsalou (1999; Barsalou, Simmons, Barbey, & Wilson, 2003), and numerous others.

With the explosive growth of neuroscience, which aims to discover the way in which the neuronal systems of the brain support cognitive and emotional behaviour and understanding, it has been possible to explore ways in which language relates to perceptual systems. This is part of a more general venture that includes a fascinating exploration of the relationship between imagination, perception and action, which we shall consider next.

The overlap of conceptualization with perception and action

Many studies in psychology and neuroscience have targeted the kinds of representations that occur when people perceive objects, movements and action. Similarly, much work has been and is being carried out on which areas of the brain are active in acts of perception. Our questions are whether reading about something brings about effects similar to direct perception and, if so, how this occurs. Since the 1980s, there has been a growth of evidence suggesting that a wide range of processing activities may involve the same areas of the brain as those known to be involved in direct perception. This includes using knowledge of objects that is based on sensory input, and actively imagining acts of perception, such as imagining seeing an orange or the movement of a hand. These observations are crucial to building a link between language in use, and the experience to which it is supposed to give rise.

From a neuroscience perspective, one important development was the discovery of so-called *mirror neurons* in macaque monkeys (cf. di Pellegrino, Fadiga, Fogassi, Gallese, & Rizzolatti, 1992). Neurons were discovered that increase their firing rates when the monkey performs object-directed actions; but significantly, they also increase their rate of firing when the monkey observes an experimenter or another monkey performing a similar action. These cells were found in the ventral pre-motor area of the brain, and also in the inferior parietal cortex. Of particular interest is that the cells do not simply respond to observation of an object, or to the sight of a hand mimicking an action in the absence of an object. Rather, the agent, object and action must all be present for them to fire, but this can be induced by performing the action, or by observing the action being performed. The major significance of this discovery is that there is a common code for both perception and action.

Recent evidence using brain-imaging methods, such as PET (positron emission tomography) and fMRI (functional magnetic resonance imaging) strongly suggests the presence of a similar system in humans, known as the *mirror-neuron system* or *mirror system* (e.g., Aziz-Zadeh, Wilson, Rizzolatti, & Iacoboni, 2006; Koski et al., 2002; Rizzolatti & Craighero, 2004). Thus mere observation of actions increases activity in Broca's area of the brain, as does carrying out the actions. Broca's area, although closely associated with language functions, is also associated with the representation of actions, and indeed, the connection between these two functions has led to ideas about language being based in action. This finding has prompted a proposal that observed actions are understood in part through the observer simulating those actions. It has also been considered as providing a basis for imitation, facilitating other phenomena, such as empathy, the capacity to understand how another person feels.

If the observation of action leads to a simulation of action in the same part of the brain as is used in actually executing an action, then a number of other questions spring to mind. These include the idea that stimuli that are merely suggestive of actions and perceptions might lead to simulations of actions and perceptions in the observer. From our perspective, the ultimate question is whether simulations of actions and perspectives may be brought about simply by reading about them. This is the main issue of the remainder of this chapter.

Implication, imagination and reality

There are many situations where pictorial representations induce brain activity normally associated with seeing the objects themselves, or using them. One striking study demonstrated that pictures of appetizing foods activate the same areas of the brain as are involved when tasting actual foods. It was already known that an area in the right insula/operculum is active during tasting appetizing foods (de Araujo, Rolls, Kringelbach, McGlone, & Phillips, 2003; Francis et al., 1999). In addition, a region in the orbitofrontal cortex has been shown to be active for the reward values of tastes (Rolls & Scott, 2003; Rolls, Scott, Sienkiewicz, & Yaxley, 1988). Simmons, Martin, and Barsalou (2005) used an event-related fMRI paradigm (see Appendix 2 for a brief introduction), measuring which areas of the brain became active during viewing foods that were commonplace in American society. These were compared with areas that became active during viewing pictures of commonplace locations, acting as a control. Viewing food pictures for a short time activated a region of the brain which becomes active during tasting food (the right insula/operculum), and also areas representing the reward values of foods. Viewing pictures of locations produced an entirely different area of activation. So, pictures of foods induce activity in areas of the brain associated with taste; hence food magazines plug directly into gustatory areas. Most important, the connection from picture to brain activity seems to be direct and automatic, since subjects were not instructed to imagine what the food tasted like, only to judge whether the picture depicted a food typical of its class.

In much the same way, viewing static images that imply motion activates parts of the brain that are normally recruited for the perception of real motion. Thus Kourtzi and Kanwisher (2000) showed people pictures of athletes, either in mid-movement (such as throwing a discus), or being still, and pictures of animals in motion (such as a dolphin in mid-leap). They found that a brain area normally implicated in the perception of real motion (the medial temporal/medial superior temporal cortex) was far more active when photographs of implied motion were viewed than when viewing photographs of static subjects. So, the interpretation of a photograph as depicting motion appears to implicate areas of the brain that respond to actual motion.

In another situation, Simmons et al. (2007) demonstrated a common neural substrate for the perception of colour and the use of knowledge about it. Subjects performed two tasks while undergoing fMRI. First they performed a property verification task, in which they had to decide whether a physical property or a motor action went with a named object, such as BANANA–yellow, or SCREWDRIVER–turned. Secondly, they carried out a judgement task for colours. They were presented with a set of colour segments, forming a wheel, and had to judge whether the hues increased steadily from lightest to darkest or not. The overall results showed that a region of the brain that was active during colour perception (the left fusiform gyrus) was also active for the colour property judgement task (e.g., BANANA–yellow), but not for the motor judgement task. These data provided evidence for the direct overlap of the brain areas that are active during direct colour perception and information associated in memory with concepts.

In fact, the same logic has been applied to six sensory modalities by Simmons, Pecher, Hamann, Zeelenberg, and Barsalou (2003). The results of this large-scale exercise were interesting. There was clear evidence for heightened activation in the appropriate brain area for the modality probed. However, there was also evidence of other sensory modalities being activated (resulting in what the authors termed 'multimodal' patterns). The authors carried out a rating task, in which the subjects were asked the questions below about items, and invited to score their answers on a 0 (none) – 6 (complete) scale:

(1)   When you experience X (e.g., Tabasco sauce):
         How much of your experience involves SEEING it?
         How much of your experience involves HEARING it?
         How much of your experience involves ACTING ON it?
         How much of your experience involves FEELING it?
         How much of your experience involves TASTING it?
         How much of your experience involves SMELLING it?

The interesting finding was that the distribution of experience reported for a concept over modalities predicted the multi-modal patterns of brain activation well. So, the conclusion was that it was retrieving concepts rather than a specific property alone that determined the pattern of involvement of sensory-specific brain areas. This is consistent with the idea that concepts are at least in part represented by modality-based bundles of information in the brain.

Such demonstrations of an overlap of processing areas with direct and indirect stimuli suggest the possibility of a commonality in processing both types of stimuli, but some caution is required. Consider, for instance, the idea that interpreting a photograph as depicting a movement depends upon the activation of mechanisms used in perceiving real movement. Because movement has direction, if common mechanisms of interpretation are used in common brain areas, then what needs to be established is evidence of overlapping directional processing. Such evidence is not provided by mere evidence of overlapping brain areas. A novel and interesting approach to this problem was undertaken by Winawer, Huk, and Boroditsky (2008), using a motion aftereffect (MAE) method. The MAE is well studied in perception: prolonged viewing of motion in one direction makes a subsequently viewed stationary pattern appear to move in the opposite direction. In two experiments, participants viewed pictures of rightward or leftward motions, the stimuli being, for instance, hurdlers in mid-hurdle or running dogs. After seeing a batch of pictures having a common direction, they saw dots that were in fact moving either left or right. They had to judge whether they thought the body of dots was moving left or right. By careful calibration of these dot stimuli, the task is highly sensitive to any MAE. There was clear evidence that the pictures did indeed induce an MAE, strongly supporting the view that the imagination of motion induced by static stimuli uses the same specific systems that are used in real perception for the detection of direction-specific motion.

Findings of this sort are crucial in our development of an understanding of how the brain deals with direct and indirect sensory stimuli. They also open up a line of research for how narratives may lead to an apparent experience of what is being depicted. The attraction lies in the potential for indirect stimuli, such as language, to bring about experiences of a sensori-motor nature. It is a small conceptual step from the studies of indirect stimuli such as those described above to investigating whether instructing people to imagine perceptual or motor events, or bringing about conditions that facilitate imagination, give rise to a similar activation of relevant parts of the brain, or indeed of the body more generally.

Imagining things

Instructions to imagine things have been shown to lead to a variety of interesting effects. For instance, imagination of effortful movement was investigated by Decety, Jeannerod, Durozard, and Baverel (1993). In this fascinating study, participants performed, and separately mentally simulated, a leg exercise at two levels of work. Heart rate and respiration rate were measured when actually exercising, and shown to increase at first rapidly, and then in proportion to the level of work. When *imagining* the exercise over a similar period, heart rate also increased, though not to the same extent as during actual exercise. Breathing rate also increased, and did so more than it did in response to actual exercise. Wuyam et al. (1995) also found that breathing rate increased during imagined exercise, although only in athletes, not non-athletes. So, mental simulations of effortful action can directly bring about certain aspects of the body's normal response to exercise.

Looking at the nature of simulation itself, it turns out that imagination can indeed activate the same brain areas and representations as direct stimuli can. An example is auditory imagery, where people imagine hearing sounds even though there is no actual sound. In one study (Kraemer, Macrae, Green, & Kelley, 2005) participants listened to music that was modified by the introduction of gaps of between 2 and 5 seconds, which occurred periodically, during which the tunes were interrupted, and continued at the point they would have reached if they had not been interrupted. The music was either familiar or unfamiliar, some pieces with lyrics (e.g., The Rolling Stones' *Satisfaction*), and some without (e.g., the theme from *The Pink Panther* film). During actually listening to music, the primary auditory cortex and the superior and inferior temporal sulcus (STS and ITS) areas are active. For familiar tunes, when listening to the gaps, the STS and ITS were active in the case of music with lyrics. For music without lyrics, the STS was again active, but the ITS was active at a lower level. Levels of activation in all of these areas were very much less for unfamiliar tunes. Participants confirmed that for the familiar tunes, they experienced imagining the tunes or lyrics going on throughout the gaps. Thus the imagination of tunes and lyrics, induced by the gaps, activated brain areas overlapping with those normally involved in processing real stimuli. Furthermore, the study has additional interest in that there was *no* stated requirement on the participants to imagine the music.

Rather, it appeared to be an automatic process not dependent on the will of the participant. The study strongly suggests that actual listening and imagination of a tune might tap into common mechanisms.

Gerardin et al. (2000) investigated real and imagined hand movements, thus comparing brain areas involved in performing an action, rather than observing it, with imagining doing it. The actions were finger flexion/extensions of various types done as a continuous movement. Imagination and motor execution showed overlapping networks, especially bilateral pre-motor cortex, parietal areas, basal ganglia and the cerebellum.

So, there is considerable evidence showing that there is overlap in the areas of the brain that are responsible for actual perception, and the imagination of perception. Imagination may be induced by direct instructions to imagine, or by implicating imagination through indirect stimuli, such as static pictures depicting motion. This directly opens up the issue of how *descriptions* might bring about similar effects, putting us in a position to discover precisely how language stimuli may induce a rich quasi-experience of what is being depicted. We shall consider this next.

Embodiment research in psycholinguistics

Since the mid-1990s, as part of the embodied understanding movement, there has been a growth in experiments showing an involvement of motor and perceptual activity in the understanding of linguistic depictions of events and actions. The strong version of the account claims that understanding *is* embodied, implicating bodily representations and processes even when abstract language is being used. We shall begin by considering some research on the grounded representation of word meaning, and move on to include issues of representation at the sentence and higher levels.

Brain activity for action words and action sentences

Pulvermüller (e.g., 1999, 2001) and his colleagues examined which brain circuits are involved in the representation of verbs denoting actions, such as *kick, bite*, etc. In one experiment, participants were required to classify letter-strings as either words or non-words (the lexical decision task). The interest was in which parts of the brain became active when the words referred to motor activity that is carried out by different parts of the body. It is well known that actions of muscles in the face, limbs, hands and feet are controlled by different, specific areas of the motor cortex. The argument is that if words depicting actions are mapped onto the areas responsible for the actual implementation of these actions, then there should be differential activity in the motor cortex corresponding to these actions.

This is precisely what was found. Using fMRI, Hauk, Johnsrude, and Pulvermüller (2004) similarly demonstrated that the specific areas of the pre-motor and motor cortex associated with actual actions were activated when silently reading action verbs like *lick, pick* and *kick*. While prompting the question of what happens with other classes of word, these results for action-area involvement for action-word meaning are just what would be hoped for to demonstrate that word meanings may be grounded in action.

There has been a little research on the involvement of brain areas in the processing of sentences, rather than single words, depicting actions. Tettamanti et al. (2005) made fMRI recordings of subjects who just had to passively listen to sentences (in Italian), such as *I bite an apple, I grasp a knife* and *I kick the ball*. These action sentences were compared with abstract sentences, such as *I appreciate sincerity*. The fMRI data were interesting. The action sentences activated a left fronto-parietal motor circuit, including Broca's area, already known to be important in both observing and executing actions. The evidence for the involvement of specific effector movement systems, as found by Pulvermüller for individual words, was weaker, but nonetheless, sentences describing leg actions activated areas of the motor system corresponding to the control of leg movements. In contrast, there was more activation in the area corresponding to the control of hand movements for sentences depicting manual interactions with objects. Thus while the case for linking verbs to specific action-systems is strong, and tells us something about the representation of word meaning, things are at present less clear where sentence interpretation is concerned.

Is activation of the areas around the motor cortex automatic when action words are encountered, or is this modulated by the context in which the word occurs? Pulvermüller (2005; Pulvermüller, Shtyrov, & Ilmoniemi, 2005) suggested that the activity is to a large extent automatic, and the Tettamanti et al. results are taken by several investigators as demonstrating that the effects are inevitable when the words are part of sentences. More recently, Raposo, Moss, Stamatakis, and Tyler (2009) challenged such a view, arguing that the motor aspect of action words is not relevant to the comprehension of some sentences. Hitherto, the sentences that were used in experiments had used verbs in a way that literally denoted actions, as in (2a). Raposo et al. (2009) suggested that with sentences where the verb was part of an idiom, as in (2b), motor area activity may not be found.

(2a)   After six minutes, the new recruit kicked the ball.

(2b)   After six months, the old man kicked the bucket.

Raposo et al. carried out an fMRI study comparing brain responses to literal action sentences like (2a), non-action sentences (like (2b), when it means idiomatically that the old man died), and individual words (e.g., *kicked*). They presented a visual probe word a few seconds after participants had heard a sentence, their task being to indicate if the probe was related to the meaning of the sentence. This task is sensitive to the meanings of individual words in sentences (Davis et al., 2007).

The results for the action words by themselves were essentially similar to findings of Pulvermüller et al., showing appropriate motor circuit activation for words viewed passively. With literal action sentences, there was a similar pattern of activity. However, for the idiomatic contexts, there was no such activation. This is supportive of the view that when a literal interpretation of a word (such as *kick* in our example) is not needed, then the motor area activation associated with the use of the literal meaning simply does not occur. Note that, as we discussed in Chapter 3, idioms vary from fixed items such as 'kick the bucket' to idioms that can be creatively varied (Gibbs, 1994), so this result may depend on the type of idioms used as materials. Although this is a challenge to the simplest notions of embodied cognition, where the retrieval of motor information occurs automatically (e.g., Pulvermüller, 1999; Pulvermüller et al., 2005), it could fit into the framework of how motor phenomena might support the experiential aspect of narrative immersion. A writer might not want an experience of kicking to come through if he or she wrote about someone *kicking the bucket* in the idiomatic sense. It is also the start of evidence concerning a major question: are embodiment processes obligatory, or are they a function of relevance to processing requirements?

Action–sentence compatibility effects

Within psycholinguistics, purely behavioural data implicate representations of action in the comprehension of action sentences, and additional work has also explored brain areas involved in comprehending action sentences. Glenberg and Kaschak (2002) introduced the notion of the *action–sentence compatibility effect* (ACE). ACE has been used with descriptions of a variety of motor tasks to check the involvement of motor activity during reading. Consider (3a) and (3b):

(3a)   Close the drawer.

(3b)   Open the drawer.

Glenberg and Kaschak proposed that these sentences are understood by the reader mentally simulating the actions of closing or opening a drawer. Specifically, closing a drawer requires a hand movement away from your body, while opening a drawer requires one that is toward your body. They used an experimental set-up in which participants had in front of them three buttons, arranged in line away from them and in front of them. A participant's finger was placed on the centre button at the start of each trial. When a string of words was presented, participants simply had to judge whether the string made a grammatical sentence or not (on half of the trials, it didn't). If they were asked to move their finger to the button in an 'away' direction to indicate that the sentence made sense, then 'away' sentences (like (3a)) were responded to faster than if they had to move their finger to the 'toward' button. For 'toward' sentences, the opposite was true: here, verification of meaningfulness was faster if the movement was in a 'toward' direction. Glenberg and Kaschak concluded that these effects arise because people are simulating a 'toward' or 'away' movement, and the actual movement of the fingers either is compatible, leading to a faster response, or is incompatible, leading to a slower response.

Similar effects were also observed for 'abstract' transactions, as in (4a) and (4b):

(4a)   You told Liz the story.

(4b)   Liz told you the story.

Here, the direction of *information transmission* is important, being either away from you (4a) or toward you (4b). So, while there seems to be a representation of directionality associated with these sentences, it must be somewhat abstract.

Glenberg et al. (2008) extended these findings. First they replicated the ACE results, and crucially, there was no difference in this effect for concrete or abstract sentences. The second study used transcranial magnetic stimulation (TMS) to index activity in the motor system of the brain. A TMS pulse is a powerful magnetic pulse that can be applied locally to the scalp and can be focussed on specific parts of the brain, momentarily altering activity at the local site. When applied to a specific area over the motor cortex, it evokes a motor response in the muscle that is controlled by that area, the *motor evoked potential*, or MEP. It is known that such MEPs can be modulated by hearing specific sounds in words. For instance, if a TMS pulse is given to the part of the brain controlling the tongue, then a stronger MEP is found in the tongue when a word (in Italian) that uses tongue-trilling is presented (Fadiga, Craighero, Buccino, & Rizzolatti, 2002). Glenberg et al. investigated whether greater modulation of hand muscle activity (specifically the *opponens pollicis*) would occur when participants read sentences depicting transfer than sentences depicting actions other than transfer. Participants read the sentences using a moving window technique, in which the sentence was gradually revealed across a screen, and made a sensibility judgement. The TMS pulse was delivered either shortly after the verb of a given sentence, or after the last part of the sentence. There were larger MEPs for transfer sentences than for non-transfer sentences. Furthermore, there was no difference in MEPs for concrete and abstract transfer sentences, echoing the behavioural findings using the ACE effect. The effects were greatest when the pulse was applied at the end of the sentences, but there was a weaker effect at the verb. Although readers could not have been sure that the sentences were of the transfer type at that point, Glenberg et al. suggested they may be able to predict it given that many of the verbs themselves were verbs of transfer, such as *give*.

What is to be made of these kinds of data? It certainly seems that there is some construction of directionality in the mind of the reader when confronted with these sentences, whether concrete or abstract, and that there is a realization of 'toward' and 'away' movements in terms of activity stemming from the motor cortex. However, it is particularly noteworthy that even an abstract notion of 'away' (as in (4a) above) should give rise to activation in muscles of the hand. This may just be because the hand is being used to implement the judgements. If some other movement were required, such as a movement of the foot to indicate a similar judgement, then on this line of reasoning, an ACE effect should be observed there, and MEPs in the muscles controlling foot movements should also be modulated by 'away' and 'toward' sentences. At the time of writing, this has not been investigated, and so it remains unclear precisely what the relation of effector-specific ACE and MEP effects is to comprehension. However, what is clear is that ACE effects are a reality, and offer good evidence that motoric procedures are implicated in the comprehension of action sentences. We shall continue to present more evidence for this before returning to a discussion of what ACE and similar effects might be indicating.

Using a similar technique to the original ACE paradigm, Taylor, Lev-Ari, and Zwaan (2008; Zwaan & Taylor, 2006) compared sentences depicting actions where a direction of rotation was specified (e.g., *screwed* [clockwise rotation], *unscrewed* [anticlockwise rotation]) or could be inferred (e.g., we can infer that if we read about a character turning up the heat on an oven, the movement is likely to be clockwise). Subjects were asked to continuously turn a knob in order to see a frame-by-frame presentation of each sentence. Example sentences included (5), where the successive frames shown are indicated by / and the options shown to participants are in curly brackets:

(5)   He examined the/pie through/the microwave/window and/turned the/timer./
        The cooking/time needed/to be/{longer [*or*] shorter}.

In this example, it is *longer* or *shorter* that determines the direction of turning the timer. The results showed that people spent less time turning the knob when it matched the direction implicated by the critical word than when the implicated direction was opposite. This is another ACE effect, and was interpreted by Taylor et al. (2008) as showing that motor simulation or *motor resonance*, as these researchers term it, of some sort occurs as a result of reading the critical action. An important aspect of this study is that it shows that it is the whole situation that is critical to signalling a movement direction in context (*longer/shorter* in this case).

Sentences and words implying perceptions

A variety of findings showing embodiment effects similar to those for action have been obtained with respect to *perceptual* mechanisms. For instance, Zwaan, Stanfield, and Yaxley (2002) showed that after reading a sentence like *The ranger saw the eagle in the sky*, people were faster to recognize a picture of an eagle when its wings were extended than when its wings were close to its body. The result, found with a variety of materials, was taken as suggesting that a perceptual representation of a flying eagle rather than a perched eagle resulted from reading the sentence.

In yet another ingenious study, Zwaan and Yaxley (2004) had people judge whether pairs of words were related in meaning. If the words had referents with similar shapes (e.g., LADDER–RAILROAD), then it took longer to indicate *no* than when unrelated pairs did not denote objects of similar shape, as with LADDER–CLOCK, for instance. So shape information is retrieved even when it *isn't needed*, or is indeed harmful to task performance. Furthermore, it was possible to show that this interference effect was localized in the left hemisphere of right-handed participants. It is the left hemisphere where object shape information at the category level is thought to be localized (e.g., Marsolek, 1999).

Research using sentence–picture verification has yielded apparently converging evidence that descriptions at the sentence level can also induce visual imagination. Particularly striking is a study by Yaxley and Zwaan (2007). Consider the sentences:

(6a)   Through the fogged goggles, the skier could hardly identify the moose.

(6b)   Through the clean goggles, the skier could easily identify the moose.

Participants were presented with a sentence like (6a) or (6b), followed by a picture that depicted a mentioned object (such as a moose), or some other object. A match required a *yes* response, and a mismatch a *no* response. On match trials, half of the time the picture fitted the sentence in terms of depicted fuzziness of the image, and half of the time it did not fit. The results showed that for sentences depicting degraded stimuli, the degraded versions were verified faster, while for sentences depicting clear stimuli, the clear images were verified faster. These results suggest that readers mentally simulate the visibility of objects as they interpret sentences that depict differential visibility.

Compatibility effects have been used to show that perceptual mechanisms are involved in processing sentences depicting motion. For instance, Kaschak et al. (2005) used spirals that appeared to be rotating, which induced the illusion of motion toward or away from the participant, or horizontal bars moving up or down a screen to display upward and downward motion. While viewing the displays, participants heard sentences that depicted motion toward them or away from them, or up or down:

(7a)   The car approached you. [Toward]

(7b)   The car left you in the dust. [Away]

(7c)   The rocket blasted off. [Up]

(7d)   The confetti fell on the parade. [Down]

As with the Glenberg and Kaschak (2002) study, participants had to judge whether the sentences made sense (some of them didn't). The outcome was that if the direction of motion of the visual display ran counter to the direction of described motion, then judgements were slower. This was interpreted as showing that the neural systems used for analysing motion were also used in sentence interpretation, thus producing incompatibility effects. While the Glenberg and Kaschak data for 'toward' and 'away' sentences showed motor involvement in interpretation, the Kaschak et al. data suggest perceptual involvement as well. It is of course entirely possible that both perceptual and motor involvement occur together, given the fact that perception itself is intimately linked with the motor system.

In an attempt to directly see whether the areas of the brain involved in motion perception are indeed recruited during comprehension of 'toward'/ 'away' sentences, Rueschemeyer, Glenberg, Kaschak, Mueller, and Friederici (2010) used fMRI. Participants were presented with sentences (in German) depicting 'toward', 'away', and static representations, for example:

(8a)   The car drives toward you. [Toward]

(8b)   The car drives away from you. [Away]

(8c)   The car looks big. [Static control]

On each trial, participants saw a black and white spiral moving clockwise or anticlockwise, or a static input (a scrambled spiral). As they were watching one of these, a sentence was presented auditorily. The fMRI data analysis showed that the area of the brain known to be involved in the processing of visual motion (MT/V5) showed modulated activity for 'toward' sentences as a function of the direction of movement of the spiral (the static display showed no such effects), implicating the involvement of the motion analysis areas of the brain in response to reading 'toward' sentences. However, there was no such effect with 'away' sentences. These data offer partial neuroscience support for the Kaschak et al. (2005) claim, though it is somewhat mysterious that the effect was not obtained for 'away' sentences. Rueschemeyer et al. (2010) argue that their findings suggest that cases of objects moving toward one are often more immediately relevant to the self than objects moving away. In fact, the study showed that areas other than MT/V5 were responsive to 'toward' sentences but not to 'away' (specifically the orbitomedial prefrontal cortex, and the posterior cingulate cortex). Both of these have been observed as playing a role in tasks requiring self-reflection, such as indicating whether a particular adjective fits oneself (Johnson et al., 2002; Kjaer, Nowak, & Lou, 2002). One might speculate that such effects could be exaggerated by using sentences which describe an action more dramatically with potential major impact for the self, such as *The car comes straight at you*, or *The mugger jumps out at you*, but such possibilities remain to be tested. We shall return to the issue of self-relevance in Chapter 7.

In a study of mental imagery related to language, Just, Newman, Keller, McEleney, and Carpenter (2004) carried out an experiment in which they compared fMRI patterns resulting from the comprehension of sentences thought to evoke high imagery, like (9a) and (9b), with ones they term 'low imagery', like (9c) and (9d) (arguably, some of these 'low-imagery' sentences might not produce imagery, but we will use their term). Participants had to verify whether the sentences were true or false.

(9a)   The number eight when rotated 90 degrees looks like a pair of spectacles.

(9b)   On a map, Nevada is to the right of California.

(9c)   Economics deals with the production, distribution, and consumption of wealth.

(9d)   Mammals, including dogs and cats, are vertebrates that hatch their young in eggs.

High-imagery sentences were those which required participants to perform image-handling activities to perform the verification task, such as mental rotation (in 9a) or the evaluation of spatial relations (in 9b). It was already known that explicit instructions to perform mental rotations cause activation in the intraparietal sulcus, implicating this part of the brain as important in visual imagery (e.g., Kosslyn et al., 1993, 1999; Mellet et al., 2000). Just et al. (2004) found that the same areas of the brain were active during the processing of the putative high-imagery-evoking sentences, but not for the low-imagery sentences. The conclusion was that imagery is indeed evoked by the process of verifying the first class of sentence.

The perception and imagination of pain

Descriptions of pain-inducing situations are not uncommon in narratives, and are closely tied to depictions of extreme negative affect. A similar logic of investigation can be applied to the investigation of real and imagined pain as has been seen above with respect to action, perception and emotion. Pain investigators have identified a network of regions in the brain that is active when a person experiences real pain. Crucially, with pain there are two somewhat different things occurring. First, there is the direct sensory experience of pain, and then there is the affective (negative emotional) response to that pain. The brain areas supporting these aspects are different. The primary and secondary somatosensory cortex is activated during the experience of pain itself, while other regions (the anterior insula and anterior cingulate cortex) are more involved in the evaluation of subjective discomfort and response preparation for escaping aversive stimuli. The whole complex is known as the *pain matrix*.

Are any of these areas involved in imagining pain evoked by an indirect stimulus that is not literally painful? We shall address this issue in some detail in Chapter 8 where we deal with emotion, perspective-taking and empathy. For the moment, suffice it to say that there is certainly evidence for some activation in the pain matrix when people are shown pictures of injury being inflicted (such as stubbing a toe, or catching a finger in a closing door). Thus Jackson, Brunet, Meltzoff, and Decety (2006) asked people to adopt a self-perspective and evaluate how painful would be each of the events depicted in such pictures. While the primary somatosensory cortex did *not* show enhanced activation relative to a control condition, the secondary cortex did, along with the anterior insula and the anterior cingulate cortex associated with the emotional response to pain. So there was some overlap with the activations observed with real pain perception, but not completely. This is a finding typical of several other studies.

At the time of writing, there is only a little work on language-induced activity in the pain matrix, despite the intuitive plausibility of narrative depicting pain being a powerful manipulator of a reader's state of mind. However, one interesting study was reported by Osaka, Osaka, Morishita, Kondo, and Fukuyama (2004). In Japanese, there exist a large number of conventional onomatopoeic expressions, and Osaka et al. capitalized on this to examine the idea that pain-related expressions would induce activity in the pain matrix. Participants were scanned (fMRI) while listening as either pain-related expressions were presented (e.g., *zuki-zuki*, 'throbbing pain with a pulsing sensation'; *chiku-chiku*, 'intermittent pain akin to being struck by thorns', etc.), or non-pain nonsense words (like *heyu-heyu*, and *runi-runi*). The words were presented auditorily. Enhanced activity was observed in the anterior cingulate cortex for the pain-related expressions relative to the controls. This is the area responsible for the affective component. However, there was no increased activity in the primary and secondary sensory cortices. So we might say that while the words evoke an affective response, they do not evoke a simulation of the pain experience itself.

This study is noteworthy in its use of onomatopoeic expressions. The expressions used in the Japanese study vividly depict types of pain, and we might expect vivid depictions of other things to produce similarly powerful effects, and not just in Japanese, of course. It would, nevertheless, have been interesting to use non-pain-related repeated onomatopoeic expressions, such as *shito-shito* ('softly falling rain') or *mogu-mogu* ('eating with the cheeks stuffed with food'), as the control, rather than just using nonsense expressions.

The nature of simulation and the theories that embodiment data supports

At this juncture, we should consider two related issues. First, there is the claim that because meaning in language is grounded and embodied (overcoming the symbol grounding problem), then understanding entails embodied processing. Second, there is the question of whether the work on embodiment is useful for a theory of how there comes to be an experiential aspect to narrative comprehension (and appreciation), which is the real issue for the present book.

Embodiment and basic understanding

At the outset of this chapter, we considered the traditional descriptive account of word meaning in which meanings were represented as features, usually described in terms of other words. Following the symbol grounding problem, we saw that meanings need to be grounded in the physical, social and emotional world. This is necessary, and makes a great deal of sense when it is appreciated that much of the learning of words consists in relating them to objects and actions, which have manifestations in the real world, and are accessible through perception and action. The claim that meaning is grounded in action and perception is a huge research area at present, and represents rich territory for experimentation, as we have witnessed in the pages above. It has been claimed that embodied cognition is essential for understanding sentences (in particular by Glenberg). But there is the issue of to what extent simulations are necessary for understanding, or more specifically, whether understanding is even possible in the absence of simulations. It has been suggested that even embodied activity that is irrelevant to a message can occur, leading to the suggestion that embodiment of some sort may be essential to understanding. Some support comes from Masson, Bub, and Warren (2008), who used sentences such as *The lawyer kicked aside the calculator*. The single word *calculator* brings about a preparation of hand action for using a calculator (i.e., getting ready for poking the keys with the fingers). Masson et al. (2008) surmised that if an action was relatively unusual, such as *kicking a calculator*, then part of understanding this sentence would entail retrieving basic information about a calculator such as that retrieved when the single word is used, regardless of the fact that poking the keys is seemingly irrelevant to the act denoted by the sentence. This is indeed what they found. However, equally we have seen that a sentence like *John kicked the bucket* does not lead to motor area activation that occurs with a literal action sentence such as *John kicked the ball*.

One basic problem is that this sort of argument can end up with those who think that simulation (of some sort) is necessary for understanding any sentence having to find what that simulation is. If any claim is made for understanding that is not accompanied by simulation, then the pro-simulation group might well ask 'What is the evidence for *no* simulation?' In many cases either way of approaching the issue is fraught with problems, especially with abstract sentences. For instance, it is difficult to see what functional simulation might underlie the sentence *Mary promised John she wouldn't be late*. If it is an 'away' simulation, this wouldn't seem to help much with capturing meaning.

At the time of writing, researchers have failed to suggest exactly how simulations work in relation to comprehension. What do simulations actually consist of, and how do their real-time characteristics relate to the time it takes to comprehend a sentence? These are difficult questions, and cannot easily be answered by paradigms such as the ACE effect and its variants.

Most of the critique that follows is adapted from Sanford (2008), who suggested three ways in which grounding of meaning might function during comprehension. We will consider cases of action and perception sentences, since these are the best examples given above. First, the strongest version is that simulation is some sort of online, real-time component of comprehension. This is clearest when, in order to carry out a cognitive task, bodily activity of some sort must be fully conducted. This Sanford calls 'full, real-time embodied program running' (p. 185). Consider an example that is not about language comprehension per se, but illustrates the point. Try answering this question:

(10)   What letter immediately precedes U in the alphabet?

Many people answer this by mentally reciting part of the alphabet (e.g., ... *PQRSTU* ...) in order to get the answer 'T'. When 'run-through' of this type occurs, it determines precisely the time needed to decide about the order of alphabetic items (Landauer, 1962; see also Hamilton & Sanford, 1978), due to the fact that we store the alphabet as a motor program to produce the alphabetic sequence. The bodily activity (producing the alphabet subvocally) takes up part of the total time needed to perform the cognitive task. This is a form of full, real-time embodied processing.

While full, real-time embodied program-running may not be a good model for what happens in most language comprehension (though it is really a fair characterization in the case above), it illustrates some problems for the theory that simulation is a necessary component of comprehension. We need to know at what level of detail the simulation runs. We also need to know how long the simulation has to run for in order to support understanding. In addition, we need to be able to show that the simulation takes a time that is a real component of the comprehension process. To our knowledge, these criteria have not been met with respect to embodied language processing.

Of course, a second version is to argue that a simulation does not have to be a full-blown enactment of some motor activity, and that, indeed, this would hardly ever be possible. For instance, to understand the sentence *You close the drawer*, a real enactment would not be possible, and any simulation would have to be a reduced version of the real thing. Indeed, given that people do not usually actually say the alphabet in the tasks discussed above, it is clear that even that example is a somewhat reduced simulation. The question then becomes one of what level of detail a more reduced simulation would occur at.

At an even more basic level, a third and weaker version is that a situation might occur in which the brain-state preconditions for some action or perceptual simulation occur, but the enactment of a simulation of those actions or perceptions does not. This is like knowing which button to press to operate a machine, but not actually pressing it. In fact, this is the same principle as scenario-mapping, discussed in Chapter 2. Access becomes available to relevant knowledge structures, or motor simulation mechanisms, or perceptual simulation mechanisms, but these mechanisms are not actually used unless conditions make such utilization desirable, notably in the interests of certain types of communication. At this level, simulation would no longer be a necessary aspect of comprehension. It would not be a necessary, real-time component of comprehension. Instead, embodied effects become just a possible follow-on to basic scenario-mapping.

Sanford's (2008) arguments were to the effect that to claim that embodiment serves as a component process of comprehension, it is necessary to show that it is a time-consuming *stage* in the process of comprehension. At the time of writing, other papers are starting to emerge that cast doubt on various strong claims concerning embodiment in various different ways (see de Vega et al., 2008, for a range of views). Dove (2009) takes to task the idea of a perceptual representation of concepts in general (one aspect of the embodiment argument). His argument revolves around the issue of how abstract concepts are represented, suggesting that abstract concepts such as *democracy* and *morality* are problematic, since, to him, they do not have any strong link with perceptual representations that might sum up their meanings. By contrast, cognitive linguists argue that the mind is 'inherently embodied' (Lakoff & Johnson, 1999, p. 3).

The limits of embodiment

Whilst those who would like to prove that all understanding has an embodied element may wish to demonstrate that such elements occur in all comprehension, those investigating the experiential aspect of narrative should be more concerned with the contrast between types of writing that cue different types of response. Hence, from the narrative-experience perspective, the *limits* of embodiment during language processing are especially important to study. Because the emphasis has been on finding support for the embodiment hypothesis, there has only been a small amount of work on establishing limits, which we will now discuss.

One simple but compelling study of what might modulate embodiment effects was carried out by Taylor and Zwaan (2008). They utilized the procedure, described earlier, for identifying motor resonance, where participants read a text in which a character moves a knob in a particular direction (e.g., the microwave timer knob in example (5)) and at the same time the participant is asked to turn a knob in the experimental situation. As we discussed, people were found to spend less time turning the knob in the same direction as the imaginary movement than in the opposite direction. Taylor and Zwaan (2008) tested the conjecture that if an emphasis was put on the manner of turning in a subsequent sentence, then the motor facilitation should be enhanced and prolonged, because it is made more salient. They compared the following types of sentence (the successive frames shown are indicated by / and the options shown to participants are in curly brackets):

(11)   The runner/was very/thirsty./A fan/handed him/a bottle/of cold/water/which he/opened/{quickly [*or*] eagerly}.

The term *quickly* modifies the action of opening, but the term *eagerly* qualifies the agent, the runner, and is not focussed on the act of opening itself. Taylor and Zwaan (2008) found that motor resonance here was prolonged in cases where words had a direct bearing on the action itself (e.g., *quickly*), but ceased with words which did not (e.g., *eagerly*). They refer to this as the *linguistic focus hypothesis*, arguing that as the linguistic focus changes, the mental simulation shifts with it.

In another study using the same general methodology (Zwaan, Taylor, & de Boer, 2010), forty critical sentences were presented embedded within a continuous narrative about a bank robbery, making for a more natural stimulus material. In half of the critical sentences, there was a description of an action being carried out that required manual rotation action (e.g., locking a door, turning up the volume on a police radio), and half depicted someone *intending* to act in such ways, with sentences of the following type:

(12a)   He started the car.

(12b)   He wanted to start the car.

The results showed ACE type effects only for the executed actions, not for the intention sentences. This has major implications for narrative theories that examine possible and actual actions, such as text world theory (e.g., Werth, 1999; see also Gavins, 2007) and possible worlds theories (e.g., Ryan, 1991), since this experiment suggests that comprehending a sentence about someone intending to start the car does not bring about a simulation of the action itself.

Zwaan et al. (2010) also examined the effect of different verb forms for actual actions, comparing sentences (in Dutch) using simple past and past perfective, as in:

(13a)   He turned the key in the ignition. [Past]

(13b)   He had turned the key in the ignition. [Past perfective]

ACE effects were obtained for both types of sentences (but see Zwaan et al. for details of effects caused by Dutch language constructions). Other work by Madden and Therriault (2009) examines whether there are any differences in embodiment effects for an event that is ongoing or over. In Chapter 2, we saw that when an event is depicted as ongoing, the representation is different from when that event is signalled as coming to an end. Such a study, using an aspect manipulation, was carried out by Madden and Therriault (2009). They compared past tense sentences with different aspects like:

(14a)   Fred was using his umbrella. [Imperfective]

(14b)   Fred had used his umbrella. [Perfective]

They presented sentences, self-paced, one word at a time. But instead of presenting the word for the critical object (*umbrella*), they substituted pictures of the objects. These could either be a depiction of the object in use (an open umbrella), or a depiction of it out of use (a closed umbrella). Now if the imperfective aspect (indicating an ongoing event) leads to a simulation of the umbrella being used, there should be a disruption to processing if it is depicted in the out-of-use condition (following Zwaan et al.'s (2002) example of the eagle). This was observed: reading times for words just after the picture were long for the out-of-use depiction, and subsequent times to judge whether the sentence made sense were long. For the perfective case (indicating a completed action), these effects were absent. Madden and Therriault concluded that while some sort of simulation might have taken place initially, it quickly subsided in the perfective case. So it seems possible that cueing the end of an event influences the simulation of that event.

There are many possible situations where embodiment effects might be modulated by linguistic descriptions, and it is likely that there will be an expansion of research on this topic in the future. For those of us interested in capturing the experience of narrative, there is no need to suppose that simulations always occur. As we said, it is more important to determine when they occur, and in what detail, and how they may be controlled by choice of expression in writing. Throughout the chapters that follow, we shall draw attention to cases where the experiential aspect of reading might well be understood in terms of such modulations.

Maximizing and minimizing experience in narrative, and implications for process-models of experientiality

Writers of narrative use different types of writing that one would expect to engage processing based on embodiment to different degrees. Sometimes the writer might capitalize on embodiment for some parts of a narrative and other times might suppress it, achieving this by utilizing text types which have different amounts of grain. This is another form of rhetorical focussing. These different text types often co-occur within the same narrative, with the alternation between the text types providing a means for writers to control which parts of a text appear to have a rich experiential representation, and which are more abstract. Even when the impression is given by the writer that the experience is very rich, there is the tricky question of how much of what is depicted we actually experience.

It seems quite clear that some passages are more likely to induce embodiment-based processing of which we are conscious than are others. To show the contrast between passages that might induce high and low experiential effects, first consider one that seems likely to induce embodied reactions due to the sensory detail provided:

(15)   [Harry] swung his right leg over his Firebolt [broomstick], gripped its handle tightly and felt it vibrating very slightly [. . .] Harry kicked off hard from the ground. The cool night air rushed through his hair as the neat square gardens of Privet Drive fell away, shrinking rapidly into a patchwork of dark greens and blacks [. . .] He felt as though his heart was going to explode with pleasure; he was flying again, flying away from Privet Drive, as he had been fantasizing about all summer, he was going home [. . .] Harry's eyes watered in the chill as they soared upwards; he could see nothing below now but tiny pinpricks of light that were car headlights and streetlamps [. . .] his

voice was drowned by [...] the whoosh of the wind in their ears [...] his hands were growing numb [...] Harry's eyes were screwed up against the rush of icy wind that was starting to make his ears ache.

(Rowling (2003). *Harry Potter and the Order of the Phoenix*, pp. 54–56)

This example is rich in sensory descriptions. Emmott (1997) describes passages like this as *contextually framed* text, since, being based in specific spatial locations at specific times, they enable a writer to describe characters having equally specific sensory responses to their environment. Example (15) is part of a longer scene which sustains these sensory impressions, but, even in this short passage, we see the characteristics of writing that is highly likely to induce simulation effects. These include strong action descriptions (*swung his right leg*), and indications of forces required to make movements (*kicked off hard from the ground*). In addition, references to multiple senses are made. And when it comes to the depiction of coldness, there are direct references to feelings, such as creating numbness and aching ears. These are things with which a reader can easily identify, and, given the evidence for embodied responding discussed earlier, would be expected to give rise to simulations. Furthermore, specific perspectives are adopted in the text. Entities adopt a specific shape and size depending on the angle of view, so the gardens become a patchwork of colour and the lights are presented as *tiny pinpricks*, which we can infer to represent the angle of view from a height. Another factor is that there are clear emotional responses. The character reacts with extreme pleasure to his bodily experience of flying. Also the text keys into the positive connotations of *home* and the negative connotations, established in this story, of Privet Drive, a place loathed by the character. We shall discuss emotions with respect to embodiment in more detail in Chapter 8; for the moment, we just note that this descriptive style of writing seems likely to lead to emotion simulation. Finally, in the longer context from which this example is extracted, various other devices can be found that are likely to initiate sensory representations. There is considerable reiteration of the same or connected words which results in emphasis of the sensations (even in this short extract we see the use of several words from the lexical set *cool/chill/icy* and words denoting vigorous movement (*vibrating/rushed/whoosh/rush*)). These are, of course, classic foregrounding devices.

In contrast, it is difficult to see how summary-writing could lead to such effects due to the low level of sensory grain. For example:

(16)   The great war came and went. Silver was a dead market. Her husband's mines were closed down. But she and he lived on in the adobe house under the works [...]

(Lawrence (1996). 'The Woman Who Rode Away', p. 39)

This passage is not set in a specific spatio-temporal context, rather, it is a type of text which Emmott (1997) describes as *contextually unframed*.

Embodied action depends on the human body responding to its environment in a specific context, but there is little scope for such interpretations in this passage. Events take place over a long passage of time and we do not see a specific sequence of actions unfolding at the level of a single occasion. There is no sense of the human experience of war. When the mines are closed down, we do not see any details of the announcement of closure. As the couple live on in the adobe house, we do not see any specific incidents in their daily life.

From a narrative point of view, (16) does not enable us to experience events on a human scale and moment-by-moment basis as we do in our everyday existence. Are there any possibilities for embodiment effects in texts such as these? As we indicated earlier, there is a view that all language might produce embodiment effects of some sort, although some argue against this (e.g., Dove, 2009). Cognitive linguists, for example, such as Lakoff and Johnson (1980, 1999; Johnson, 1987), Langacker (1987, 1991) and Talmy (1988) view the human mind as fundamentally embodied. Cognitive linguists might point in (16) to the movement expressions in *came and went* and the 'down' direction in *closed down* as being interpreted through 'up' and 'down' and 'away' and 'toward' movements, and recall that Glenberg and colleagues found evidence for ACE effects with abstract movements like *You read a story to Mary*. This may be, but we take the view that such effects would be minimal from an experiential point of view, compared to the richness of simulations that might be launched by example (15).

One further point is that the experiential aspect of narrative comprehension must be partial, and not reliant on a full-blown simulation of some event or situation being depicted. We argue that there are limits to the degree of simulation even when readers read the most heavily experiential types of writing, such as (15). Some leading narratologists (e.g., Fludernik, 1996) have argued that although narratives create the effect of mimesis (i.e., we feel as if we are experiencing events directly), this is really just an illusion resulting from the rhetorical skills of writers. The skill of the writer, we suggest, is often in producing the impression of a full-blown experience. For instance, the inclusion of small details which are not plot-crucial has been viewed as a means of making text realistic by Barthes (1968) in a seminal paper 'L'effet de réel' (the 'reality effect'). So a fictional writer may describe a door as green, even though it makes little difference to the plot what the colour was. Such details are highly selective (Ingarden, 1973; Iser, 1978). The writer's art lies in making readers feel as if they are viewing a vividly portrayed scene, but by actually only presenting a limited amount of detailed information. This idea is very different from the notion of there being an accurate simulation of a scene.

From a processing point of view, we can capture some of the issues in Figure 6.1. Essentially, our argument is that language-generated embodiment

| Language depictions → | Motor, sensory and → | Awareness of some → | Constructed experience |
| in narratives | emotional brain activity | of this activity | |

Figure 6.1 Tentative suggestion for possible stages in the constructed experience deriving from language descriptions.

effects are initially created by the activation of brain areas correlated with language depictions (such as emotions, toward/away movement, specific imagery types). These embodiment effects are reflected in consciousness, but as yet, it is quite unclear how or to what extent. For example, with 'toward' and 'away' effects, there may be some conscious representation of this, most obviously in the case of literally moving objects toward or away. With descriptions of rich perceptual and motor phenomena, like (15), there may be conscious representations like imagery, but even imagery is not a 'full' perceptual representation, but rather partial. A good knock-down example of the difference between perception and imagery can be achieved by imagining the word 'regimental'. Is the word in upper or lower case? What colour are the letters? What colour is the background? People are often unsure about the answers to these questions. But one neat illustration is to read out the letters of the word from the image. This should not be too difficult. But now read out the letters from right to left (i.e., in reverse order). This is much more difficult. However, reading the letters backwards from a written example is comparatively easy. To the extent that people believe their image is isomorphic with a physical image, they are being deluded: the belief depends upon a cognitive construction of what is being experienced, presumably based on underlying conscious fragments derived from underlying processes of embodiment. This is reflected in the final stage of Figure 6.1. This is a mere sketch, not a proper theory, although it does posit a relationship between embodiment effects and the experiential aspect of reading narratives. But it serves to highlight some research questions that demand attention:

- Which embodiment effects are mandatory, and which are optional? How does foregrounding increase the likelihood of such effects?
- How do embodiment effects become represented (or constructed) in consciousness? What is the correspondence between embodiment and awareness, and what factors control such correspondences?
- How is 'L'effet de réel' achieved, given such awareness? Note that in Figure 6.1, the third stage could be missed out, the process going straight to the fourth from the second, but this is trivial, since selective aspects of experience will still have to be taken into account.

To answer these questions will require the clever and original use of psychological and neuroscience techniques, coupled with careful consideration of how a writer might try to manipulate the experience of the reader. This promises to be an exciting programme of research, and one that should directly address the issue of how the experiential aspect of narrative understanding works.

Summary

This chapter has taken us through a variety of discussions and empirical investigations of experientiality as follows:

- Although concepts have traditionally been thought of as being represented by component features, it is easily argued that they have to be grounded in social and physical situations in order for meaning to be captured. This is manifestly true of words that denote certain types of actions, refer to entities in the world, or denote certain spatial relations.
- A growing body of evidence has shown that observing actions carried out by others leads to simulations of those actions, involving brain areas which overlap with those that are involved when the observer carries out the action. This mirror-neuron system provides obvious potential for understanding and identifying with the actions of others. Not only do direct observations yield such mirroring effects, they can be induced by depictions that do not directly show states and actions, but rather only imply them. This includes such things as suggestions of motion from static visual depictions, and sentences that suggest actions, perceptions and affect. This is particularly useful as it provides an experiential basis for comprehension that has clear relevance to narrative comprehension in a fuller sense than has hitherto been possible in psycholinguistics.
- At the time of writing, it is an open question whether simulation is necessary for all understanding, and is a component that has to be executed in order for, say, sentence understanding to take place. The evidence is lacking in this respect.
- Regardless of whether simulation is necessary, it clearly occurs in many instances, yet it looks as though it might be maximized by some devices (such as focussing on an action), and possibly minimized by others (such as summarizing). From the perspective of creative writing, the question here is how a writer can manipulate the experiential aspect of reading by manipulating the occurrence of underlying simulation activities within the brain of the reader. This seems likely to be achieved by adjusting the grain of description and by the use of specific foregrounding devices to facilitate rhetorical focussing.

- The relationship between basic simulations and what we are aware of when such simulations occur remains to be investigated. It is likely that much of what is finally the 'experience' of narrative immersion is something of an illusion, and that the impression of a narrative reality is constructed on the basis of fragments of simulations of which we are aware, supplemented by cognitive constructions. These important issues remain to be explored more fully, but at least there has now emerged a good basis on which to build new investigations.

7 Narrative perspective and the representation of speech and thought

In this chapter we turn to the issue of how writers may bring about the adoption of different perspectives by readers, and how this is manifested in discourse processing. There are several ways in which perspective may influence the vividness of a piece of writing, and the capacity to see things from various points of view is an essential part of flexibility in reading. This is another aspect of rhetorical focussing, since different perspectives can control the attentiveness of readers hence determining the type of mental representation constructed.

Let us begin by considering the effect of using first, second and third person pronouns on the type of embodiment experienced during reading of narratives, concentrating in particular on whether these induce readers to adopt internal or external perspectives. These different perspectives would require readers to re-orientate their bodies in their imaginations. After that, we examine how readers interpret descriptive information about a scene as being a representation of perceptions from a particular character's perspective. We also look at how, in some narratives, writers use second person pronouns in order to increase a reader's sense of personal involvement in a text, exploring how this might be achieved. Finally, we shall turn to a major area in narratology and stylistics, that of how speech and thought are presented in narrative. Different modes of presenting speech and thought can lead to information being presented from different perspectives. We examine the difference in depth of processing of direct speech/thought, which is regarded by some scholars as providing a faithful record of what a character said/thought, and indirect speech/thought, where there is a mediating report of a character's discourse by a third party, such as a narrator. We also consider possible differences in embodiment effects that these might bring about.

Linguistic use of first, second and third person pronouns and their psychological consequences

Within narratology, there is a significant body of work concerned with perspective in narratives. Narratologists assume that readers may adopt internal and external perspectives on events in narratives, but the psychological

Figure 7.1(a) Sample visual stimulus – internal perspective. Photograph © Andrew Mathews.

research goes a step further by seeking to demonstrate these different cognitive standpoints in readers. Psychological work reveals some interesting basic phenomena, which will be discussed first. We will then give an indication of how perspective-taking in narrative can be rather more complex, this having implications for further empirical investigation.

Experimental research on pronouns and perspective

A straightforward yet compelling empirical technique to study perspective-taking uses pictures to investigate internal versus external perspectives for simple actions. An *internal perspective* in such pictures is one where the actor is carrying out an action, and seeing it from their own perspective. So given the action 'writing on a sheet of paper' the internal perspective is shown in Figure 7.1(a). In this case, we see the actor's view, looking down at their own hands and forearms performing the action. In contrast, an *external perspective* is what an observer might see if the action were being carried out by someone else, as in Figure 7.1(b). Here, the observer is looking across at a person opposite performing the action.

Figure 7.1(b) Sample visual stimulus – external perspective. Photograph © Andrew Mathews.

Do different linguistic descriptions induce representations that correspond to such perspectives? Brunyé, Ditman, Mahoney, Augustyn, and Taylor (2009) carried out research using pictures of the type shown in Figures 7.1(a) and 7.1(b) to investigate whether descriptions using different pronouns would cause readers to adopt mentally one or other of these perspectives in a systematic way. They examined actions narrated in the first, second and third person, as follows:

(1a)   I am slicing the tomato.

(1b)   You are slicing the tomato.

(1c)   He is slicing the tomato.

Intuitively, one might suppose that the *I* case would induce an internal perspective, and the *he* case an external one. To test this, they had participants read sentences such as these, and then verify whether a subsequent picture matched or did not match the described event (i.e., in this case, a person was either slicing or not slicing a tomato). The pictures that matched could depict either an internal or external perspective, but participants had to say *yes* to a match or *no* to a non-match *regardless of the perspective depicted*. Half of the trials used matching pictures and half used non-matching ones. It was assumed that responses would be quicker if the perspective in the picture matched the perspective adopted mentally. Response times for the *yes/no* decisions showed that for first and second person, responses were faster to internal perspective images than external ones. In contrast, for third person sentences, matches were made faster to the external image pictures. So, perspective clearly results automatically from reading the sentences, since the experimenters did not instruct participants to mentally adopt a perspective.

Brunyé et al. (2009) performed a second experiment to check whether more detailed descriptions of the referent in each case would change the perspectives imagined by the reader. One motivation for this additional study was that they felt that the third person condition in the first experiment might have created ambiguity over who *he* was and hence have impeded taking an internal perspective. In the second experiment, Brunyé et al. added additional discourse context to the sentences before the verification phase. As an example, the first person condition became something like:

(2a)   I am a 30-year-old deli employee.
(2b)   I am making a vegetable wrap.
(2c)   Right now, I am slicing the tomato.

In fact, the third person condition still prompted an external perspective, but the first person condition triggered a different response. This time the responses to the first person sentences were slower to the internal image than to the external, hence showing the adoption of an external perspective, as with the third person case. The second person case showed the pattern of faster responding to the internal image, showing that *you* continued to be interpreted as providing an internal perspective.

These data suggest that readers can apply linguistically driven cues to perspective from the pronoun forms to determine how they construe actions on objects. However, the materials used are very simple and if, in the future, we are to make any generalizations about the interpretation of pronouns in real narratives in general, it is necessary to take account of different writing styles as described next.

Narratological research on pronouns and point of view

Brunyé et al.'s experiments provide a means of testing one of the key issues in narratological research which is the question of whose *point of view* is being presented in any part of a narrative (e.g., Bal, 1997; Fowler, 1996; Genette, 1980; Rimmon-Kenan, 1983; Simpson, 1993; Stanzel, 1984; Uspensky, 1973). A range of perspectives can be set up in a narrative, so that readers may be presented with, for example, a specific character's internal view, an external view of a character, or a long-range panoramic external view. Narratologists often make assumptions about what type of point of view has been established based on textual cues, but a method for examining what perspective has actually been created in the reader's mind is extremely useful, particularly where the text is somewhat ambiguous. In addition to Brunyé et al.'s use of internal and external pictures of a specific character, the method could also be adapted to examine panoramic views.

Because Brunyé et al.'s experiments use very short materials, which may not reflect the full range of text types found in real narratives, some caution is required about making generalizations based on this data alone. Let us look first at their results for third person pronouns. Here, Brunyé et al. find that third person pronouns prompt external views in both experiments. Brunyé et al. distinguish between the materials in their two experiments on the basis of length, assuming that the longer materials are more likely to reflect the properties of real narratives. This may be partly true, but it would be useful also to look at the nature of the text rather than just the length. By inserting appropriate textual cues it may be possible to prompt internal third person perspectives. The following example, describing a dentist and his female patient, provides an illustration of such cues:

(3)   [1] He put his knee up on her chest getting ready to pull, tilting the pliers. [2] Sorry, he said. [3] Sorry. [4] She couldn't see his face. [5] The pores on the backs of his fingers sprouted hairs, single black wires curling onto the bleached skin of the wrist, the veins showing through. [6] She saw an artery move under the surface as he slackened the grip momentarily, catching his breath; his cheeks a kind of mauve colour, twisting at something inside her mouth. [7] The bones in his hand were bruising her lip. [8] And that sound of the gum tugging back from what he was doing, the jaw creaking. [9] Her jaw.

(Galloway (1992). 'Blood', p. 1, our numbering)

The first three sentences do not contain any indicators of internal perspective. However, in sentences [4] and [6], we are explicitly told what the female patient does and does not see, which are cues to adopt her perspective. The angle of view could be tested here with pictures of the type used by Brunyé et al. We might also consider what perspective is produced by sentence [5]. Brunyé et al.'s pictures create an internal perspective by providing a view of the individual's own body, which is one way of signalling an internal perspective. In real narratives, another way is to present descriptions of people or objects in the surroundings of the character, which might be inferred to represent that character's field of view. The detail in the description of the hands in sentence [5] might suggest an internal perspective since the closeness of the dentist's hands could be taken to be appropriate to the point of view of the patient in this dentist chair scenario. This possible interpretation might also be prompted by the reader continuing to adopt an internal perspective after it is established in sentence [4] (if sentence [4] is read as internal). In principle, once an internal perspective has been cued in earlier sentences, more neutral sentences might also be interpreted as internal. It would be interesting to move sentence [1] to a position after the explicit mentions of what the patient is seeing, then use the Brunyé et al. experiment to see whether readers view the description in the sentence from her standpoint, the dentist's, or a third-party observer. There are major embodiment issues here, since the angle of perception potentially affects not only visual images, but also the representation of tactile and auditory details (e.g., the bruising of the lip and the sound of the jaw creaking appear different if we experience them from within the body or from outside).

All of this suggests that cues such as the explicit use of verbs of seeing (or noticing, etc.) and the granularity of the description (in this case the level of detail suggesting closeness) might signal point of view. Other commonly suggested indicators of point of view are deictic expressions (e.g., *come* rather than *go* showing movement toward a character's point of orientation) (e.g., Duchan, Bruder, & Hewitt, 1995). The presentation of a character's thoughts is also commonly regarded by narratologists as a way of cueing an internal perspective. Thought presentation is generally overlooked in the design of experimental materials in cognitive psychology, but is a key aspect of many fictional narratives. We will return to the topic of thought presentation later in this chapter. In the case of all these possible signals, we need to move beyond simply identifying textual features to seeing what effect these features actually have on readers.

So far we have discussed Brunyé et al.'s results in relation to third person pronouns, suggesting that adding internal perspective cues to third person narrative materials might prompt an internal perspective to be adopted, rather than the exclusively external perspectives that they found in their experiments. We will now turn to a consideration of their results for first person pronouns. The first experiment produced an internal perspective effect for first person, whereas the second experiment produced an external perspective effect. Brunyé et al. attribute the difference to the length of text. However, it is possible that both internal and external perspectives may be adopted for longer stretches of first person text, depending on the nature of the text, as explained below.

Consider this example of first person narration which might prompt an internal perspective.

(4)   I noticed a rack of dusty bottles [. . .] But the main ware was something else, something flat, roundish and white. I got close. It seemed to be some sort of unleavened bread. I poked at one. [. . .]

A voice said, 'Would you like to taste one?'

I nearly jumped out of my skin. It's happened to all of us: there's sunlight and shade, spots and patterns of colour, your mind is elsewhere – so you don't make out what is right in front of you.

Not four feet away, sitting cross-legged before his breads, was a man. I was so startled my hands flew up and the bread went sailing halfway across the street. [. . .]

[The man answers a call to prayer]. He ducked into the next room for a minute and returned with a rolled-up carpet. [The man prays.] He returned it to its spot in the next room. He came back to me.

(Martel (2003). *Life of Pi*, pp. 59–60)

There are some potential cues for establishing an internal point of view here, possibly prompting the reader to see events through the eyes of the character. At the start of the extract, we have a verb of seeing linked to the I-narrator (*I noticed*). Also, a specific spatio-temporal situation has been set up, allowing orientational information to be provided. The phrases *right in front of* and *came back to me*, suggest that the I-character is at the 'deictic center' (Duchan et al., 1995). In addition, the field of view is that of the I-character since we are presented with the objects he would see, such as the bottles and bread. The text explicitly says that these objects are what the character noticed, but also the rationale for describing them at this point is that they are new to the I-character not the baker. The underspecified nature of the description (*something*; *It seemed to be some sort of*; *A voice*) indicate the knowledge state of the I-character rather than the other character. The reactions of the I-character are also presented. All these factors might potentially cue an internal point of view, but empirical work of the Brunyé et al. type might provide some evidence of whether the reader is actually oriented to an internal view and whether this extends across the passage. So, for example, when we read *I nearly jumped out of my skin* do we see an external image of a surprised person or do we feel a sense of surprise as from within? As for examples (1a–c), these different readings could yield quite different embodied representations.

Brunyé et al.'s second experiment yielded an external perspective for first person materials. The length of the text was offered as an explanation by the experimenters, but the nature of the materials might provide a better explanation. The reason for the external perspective in the second experiment might be the lack of the internal perspective cues discussed above. In addition, a physical description of a character might prompt us to see an exterior view of that person. The information about age and occupation in the sample material (example (2)) does not seem to be particularly conclusive in terms of creating an external image, but possibly this information sets the character up as being a distinct individual from the reader, hence perhaps blocking the reader from aligning with the character's perspective.

In certain types of writing, an external perspective for first person texts might be more likely than an internal one. For instance, a text may distance a reader from a character by providing the character with a distinct narrative voice. To understand the different types of text, we need to recognize a fundamental distinction made by narratologists. Genette (1980) divides 'point of view', distinguishing between 'Who speaks?' and 'Who sees?', reflecting the fact that an individual might express their perspective (as when giving an opinion whilst narrating) or experience events from a particular perspective (as when seeing events from a particular spatio-temporal perspective). He uses the terms *narrative voice* for the narrator role and *focalization* for the experiencing character role. 'Focalization' can mean not just 'Who sees?' but also 'Who perceives?' (Genette, 1988), since narratives may engage the other senses, as we saw in the dentist example (example (3)), which included references to touch and sound. The I-narrator may take on both these roles, although sometimes one role may predominate. We can say that first person storytelling has the basic structure 'I (narrator role) tell [you] about when I (experiencing role) was involved in certain events', with a time difference likely between the narrating and the experiencing, and with the 'you' addressee being either explicitly referred to or elided. Example (4) puts to the fore the act of experiencing a past occasion, although there is still a narrator relating the story.

In certain types of narrative, the narrator's role can be very obvious if the I-narrator has a distinctive voice (e.g., if he/she uses dialect expressions or swear words which are appropriate to the character) or if the I-narrator explicitly addresses a 'you', with whom the reader might identify. Example (5) demonstrates an I-narrator with a distinctive narrative voice having these features (e.g., the dialect grammar and swear word in *them bastards*, and the *you* address). There is also overt reference to the present time of narration in the words *and still am*.

(5)   As soon as I got to Borstal [prison for young people] they made me a long-distance cross-country runner. I suppose they thought I was just the build for it because I was long and skinny for my age (and still am) [...] You might think it a bit rare, having long-distance cross-country runners in Borstal [since they might escape] but you're wrong, and I'll tell you why. The first thing is that them bastards over us aren't as daft as they most of the time look, and [...] to abscond and then get caught is nothing but a mug's game [...]

                    (Sillitoe (1961). *The Loneliness of the Long Distance Runner*,
                                                    p. 7, our underlining)

This example brings the act of communication underlying narration to the forefront, as the 'I' overtly addresses the 'you'. In this example, if the reader identifies with the 'you' addressee (a role which will be further explored later in the chapter), it seems unlikely that he/she could also identify with the addresser, since the I-narrator appears to be addressing a different person with a different level of knowledge. Hence, an external perspective for the *I* pronoun seems more likely here (with an internal perspective for the *you* pronoun), but would nevertheless need to be tested. In contrast with example (4), the experiencing role is played down here, since although the narrator is describing his past self, there is no account in this extract of the past self involved in events in a specific spatio-temporal context (the quotation is taken from the start of the story before the detailed account begins). This could make an internal perspective for the *I* pronoun less likely since there is less scope for the reader to re-live the experience with the character at this point. Possibly the emphasis on introductory description of the character might also block an internal perspective, since it sets up a character with very specific attributes (young, a runner, in Borstal) who may differ from the real reader.

Brunyé et al.'s experiments show that different effects can be created depending on the choice of pronoun. We will provide a more detailed consideration of the role of second person pronouns later in this chapter. We have suggested that factors other than text length need to be taken into account in explaining Brunyé et al.'s findings and in predicting whether an internal or external perspective is created. Establishing perspective in narrative often depends not just on the use of a particular pronoun, but on other perspective cues.

The examples and discussion in this section provide only an indication of the way that internal and external perspectives can be cued in real narratives. More detailed taxonomies of perspective cues in relation to types of narrative can be found in standard narratological and stylistic works. In addition to those mentioned at the start of this section, see Herman (2002), Hühn, Schmid, and Schönert (2009), Niederhoff (2009a and 2009b), Toolan (2001), and van Peer and Chatman (2001).

Psychological research on physical orientation

The psycholinguistic and narratological research on perspective discussed above relies on the assumption that we can change the orientation of our bodies in our imaginations as we read. Some support for our capacity to do this in real life comes from a behavioural study reported by Kessler and Thomson (2010). They showed an embodied basis for the act of taking the perspective of another in a spatial task. These authors proposed that when asked to take a perspective matching the physical orientation of another person, a mental rotation of one's own body takes place to match that of the other person. They argue for an evolutionary basis of the effect. If another person is looking at something dangerous, for example, and you are facing them, then the dangerous thing will be behind you, and to cope with the danger yourself, you would have to turn to see it (primitive response), or work out that if you were at their orientation, the danger would be apparent (derivative simulated response).

In Kessler and Thomson's experiment, they used a situation in which a participant saw on a computer screen a picture of an avatar sitting at a circular table. In front of the avatar on the table were two objects (a gun and a flower), that could be either on the avatar's right hand or left hand, varying from trial to trial. The table (with the avatar and objects) was rotated either clockwise or anticlockwise and was shown at different orientations in angles up to 160 degrees each way. The participant's task on any given trial was first to take up one of three postures in relation to the computer screen, as instructed: directly facing the screen, at a 60 degree clockwise angle, or at a 60 degree anticlockwise angle. Then they were presented with the display on the computer screen, and cued with one of the objects (a gun or a flower). They then had to press a button to indicate which side of the avatar the object was on (from the avatar's viewpoint). The time taken to do this increased considerably as the angle of the computer image varied from 60 degrees to 90 degrees, suggesting an act of mental rotation.

More importantly, Kessler and Thomson reasoned that if a simulation of actual body rotation underlay the act of orienting toward the other person, then the posture adopted should have an effect on judgement time. If the posture anticipated the direction of mental self-rotation (was congruent), then reaction times should be shorter than if the posture anticipated rotation in the wrong direction (was incongruent). This is precisely what they found. While not directly about reading, the study provides useful evidence of the capacity for orientation to another's perspective.

Focalization, perceptual attribution and processing

In order to construct a spatial perspective, it is necessary to make inferences about the relation between 'Who sees?' and 'What is seen?' As discussed earlier, an individual's experience of embodiment may involve their relation to their field of view beyond their own body. In this respect, a sentence offering a description of the scene can be interpreted as a focalization of a character, even if there is no mention of that character in that sentence at all. To account for this, Bal (1997) distinguishes between the *focalizer* and the *focalized object* (Genette, the originator of the term *focalization*, disputed the need for this distinction in his (1988) work, but we find it useful here). In the dentist example, example (3), sometimes the focalizer and focalized object are mentioned in a single sentence with an explicit reference to perceiving, as in sentence [6] (e.g., *She saw an artery move*), but in sentence [5] only the focalized objects (*The pores on the backs of his fingers*) are mentioned and we have to infer a perceiver (if we read sentence [5] as continuing the patient's point of view). In this respect, Brunyé et al.'s supposedly internal and external images could all represent an internal perspective over a stretch of internally focalized narrative, since the supposedly external images could in fact represent not an external image but an inferred focalizer's view of the focalized object, i.e., being from the perspective of a person looking at someone else's hands.

Bortolussi and Dixon (2003, pp. 188–190) describe the reader's construction of a link between the focalizing character and the focalized object as *perceptual attribution*, pointing out that such attributions can be made either due to explicit perceptual verbs (e.g., *saw, watched, noticed*) or by assessing the likelihood that objects are being perceived by a character. Similar types of inference have to be made in viewing films, in interpreting what Bordwell and Thompson (2010) describe as 'the subjective shot' or 'point of view shot'.

Sanford, Clegg, and Majid (1998) carried out an empirical investigation of such attributions of perceptions to characters. They argued that if the perspective of the named (main) character was adopted, then background information, like *The air was beautifully fresh and clear*, or *In one corner (of the museum), a student was copying an Old Master* should, in the absence of an explicit perceptual attribution, be more likely to be judged to be the perception of the main character than a secondary character introduced through a role description (e.g., a tour guide). They used materials like:

(6)   *The museum*
        {Mary/A woman} was studying the seventeenth-century Dutch portraits.
        {A tour guide/Tom} strolled around the gallery.
        In one corner, a student was copying an Old Master.
        The museum was unusually busy for a weekday.

        Question: Did {Mary/The woman/Tom/The tour guide} notice the student copying the Old Master?

The design allows either character to be the named one, without altering the sense of the text. The question could probe either a named or an unnamed character, and always used a form that made a coherent fit to the possible antecedents. In one version of the story, the background statement of interest had a psychological predicate (*The air was beautifully fresh and clear*), requiring the assumed existence of a person to understand what it means, while in the other shown above, the statement was objective (*In one corner, a student was copying an Old Master*).

Participants simply had to answer the question by pressing one of three keys, labelled *yes, no* and *don't know*. Although logically the only answer is *don't know*, participants responded very differently. They made attributions of awareness on nearly half of the trials, suggesting that character-based perspectives were being adopted. But more significantly, they produced more *yes* responses when the probe was to a named character, at 52%, than to a person given a role description, at 41%. Even stronger results had been obtained previously using a *yes/no* forced choice (Sanford, 1989), with 90% *yes* responses being given to named probes but only 50% in the case of role probes.

These results show a trend that fits what was expected, in that people are, by default, less likely to attribute noticing to the secondary character, and this holds for both psychological and objective predicates. However, the results are based on the requirement to make a judgement. A second experiment probed automatic perspective-taking in the absence of a requirement to make explicit judgements. It has been amply demonstrated that if the content of a sentence in a text follows on from a previous state, then reading times are shorter than if it does not, i.e., if it is unmotivated, even if it is still coherent (e.g., Keenan, Baillet, & Brown, 1984). So, if *the air is hot and sticky*, then the act of someone *mopping their brow* is coherent. However, this is true only if the person doing the mopping is classed automatically as being affected by the hot and sticky air. The conjecture was that a main (named) character would be more likely to be classed that way than a secondary (role-described) character. A typical material in the study (including options) is shown below:

(7)   *The Bank*
         {The teller/Alastair} called the next customer to his window.
         {Margaret/A woman} stood at the head of the queue.
         The atmosphere was {airy and refreshing/airless and oppressive}.
         {He/She} fainted suddenly against a marble pillar. [Target sentence]

Participants read such passages a line at a time at their own rate, pressing a key to get the next sentence each time. The measure of interest was the reading time for the target sentences. As expected, when the background information clashed with the behaviour of the character, reading times for target sentences were longer than if background information was compatible with the behaviour. However, this difference was larger for targets containing the main (named) character, at 390 ms, than for the secondary (role character) where the difference was only 160 ms.

So, it turns out that the actions associated with main characters are more easily understood when they fit background information that is unattributed to any particular individual, and when such background information does not fit the action, comprehension ease is compromised. While there is a tendency for the same to hold for a secondary character, the effect is greatly attenuated. Sanford et al. (1998) claim that this is clear evidence for the main character's perspective being typically adopted as the default.

The use of you in narratives and narrative-style passages

Second person pronoun narration is more unusual than narration using first and third person pronouns, but is nevertheless used by major authors, both in experimental literature and mainstream fiction. This issue has been studied by Fludernik (e.g., 1996), and we draw on her observations here. In certain cases, she regards the use of *you* as being a method of maximizing reader involvement

(Fludernik, 1996, p. 228). This suggested sense of involvement needs to be linked to specific psychological processes in order to be empirically examinable. There is a need for further exploration, but one possibility is that readers may become more attentive if they encounter such a form of address. We saw in (5) how *you* can be used as an address form in narratives. We might regard the reader as identifying with such forms, but for fictional texts, it would be erroneous to say that the 'you' actually is the reader. This is partly because a fictional narrator cannot be said to be addressing a real reader in the real world, since this would involve crossing the boundary between the fictional world and reality. Another reason is that even the real-world author does not normally have knowledge of who exactly will be reading their text on any particular occasion. Hence, the term *narratee* (Genette, 1980, 1988; Prince, 1971) is used to denote this notional addressee.

Providing there is no conflict between the reader's self-knowledge and the information given about the 'you' in the text, identification may be possible. Where the narratee, as indicated in the text, simply has the role of someone supposedly responding to the act of storytelling, the real reader may be able to identify with that role, since that is what the reader is doing anyway. Hence, in (8), the *you* simply has the property of denoting a person listening to the story:

(8)   Have I told you that they were rich?
                              (Ronan (1994). *The Men Who Loved Evelyn Cotton*,
                                                    p. 29, our underlining)

Identification may also be possible where a generic *you* form describes certain experiences in the story that are sufficiently general to be parallel to any reader's everyday experiences, as in example (9):

(9)   It's happened to all of us [. . .] you don't make out what is right in front of you.
                                            (Martel (2003). *Life of Pi*, p. 59)

This is all very well, but when the 'you' has additional properties, there is a chance that there may be a mismatch between the description of the 'you' and the real reader. This is a particular issue for writers if they are to go beyond constructing a 'you' referent that is so general that he/she is totally bland in terms of characteristics. In order to make the narrative more interesting, the writer may wish to add extra features to the 'you' entity. However, Fludernik (1996, p. 230) suggests that, as the 'you' develops extra features, 'the actual reader may or may not recognize herself in the role'. In (10), the *you* reference looks like a generic, but the subordinate clause would exclude any real reader who is very young or cold:

(10)   Unless you are very young, or cold, you must know what it is like.
                              (Ronan (1994). *The Men Who Loved Evelyn Cotton*,
                                                    p. 125, our underlining)

When we look at a case where the 'you' takes on the role of a character in the fictional world, clashes between the properties of the 'you' and the reader may become more likely. The following example begins with a generic *you*, but then appears to transgress the usual separation of the reader from the world of the characters, since the 'you' is clearly in bed with the character Evelyn Cotton.

(11)   I suppose everyone has been in heaven once in their life. It is a terrible thing to look down from that height of ecstasy and know that it doesn't matter if you die now because you will never be happier. [...] From the moment she first kisses you, it is downhill all the way [...] Now, her arms and legs are wrapped around you. Her belly slides softly across yours [...] You have no idea that Evelyn Cotton is pregnant again. That she has no reason for sleeping with you except to revenge herself on Charles Felix [...] That it could have been you or it could have been anyone else. You are still too young and too much of a man to realise that there is nothing special about what you can do in bed.

                    (Ronan (1994). *The Men Who Loved Evelyn Cotton*,
                    p. 22, our underlining)

Bal (1997, pp. 29–30) suggests that in such cases these uses of *you* are still referring to the I-narrator, but that the second person pronoun is used to give the reader a sense of involvement. However, Fludernik (1996) raises the question of whether differences such as gender, (e.g., an older and/or female reader in relation to this young male character), could prevent involvement rather than enhance it. This is an empirical question, capable of being tackled using methods such as change detection and memory probing. It also seems to us very much an open question, since depth of processing might be greater using *you* – if there is a gender mismatch, the aspects elaborated on in the inferential system of male and female readers might be different, given particular texts.

So far, we have examined *you* address in fictional narratives, but second person forms are also found in narrative-style passages in popular expository writing. Generic *you* form is used in the well-being text below to draw the reader into the book before more technical information is presented, and might be argued to make the text more obviously relevant to the reader.

(12)   It's two o'clock in the morning and you're lying in bed. You have something immensely important and challenging to do that next day – a critical meeting, a presentation, an exam. You have to get a decent night's rest, but you're still wide awake. You try different strategies for relaxing – take deep, slow breaths, try to imagine restful mountain scenery – but instead you keep thinking that unless you fall asleep in the next minute, your career is finished. Thus you lie there, more tense by the second.

                    (Sapolsky (1994). *Why Zebras Don't Get Ulcers: A Guide to Stress,*
                    Stress-related Diseases, and Coping, p. 1, our underlining)

Unlike the fictional example in (11), there is no character to identify with in (12) and no specific fictional situation to observe. The reader may need to draw more heavily on personal experience to construct a scene, although personal experience of some degree is also necessary for drawing parallels in the fictional example. In both cases, there is a possibility that using the *you* form will induce deeper processing, simply because the actions depicted may be evaluated against readers' own experiences, as we shall soon explore. Possibly, though, there may be deictic differences in this use of experience. In a classic linguistic account, Bühler (1982) distinguishes between two types of imagination-oriented deixis (termed *deixis am phantasma*): cases where we imagine ourselves repositioned in a location and cases where we bring the imagined object to our current context (as when we imagine how a new item of furniture would look in a room). Where an alignment with a character in a spatio-temporal context is set up, as in (11), the former type seems more likely. Conversely, where there is little specific detail about context, as in (12), readers might bring the situation into their own lives, possibly imagining themselves in their own bedrooms and relating most strongly to the most relevant circumstance in the list offered (*a critical meeting, a presentation, an exam*). One of the skills in writing the popular expository text in examples like (12) is to make such passages sufficiently detailed for the reader to engage with them, but not so specific that readers feel that the *you* address cannot or does not relate to them personally. Empirical work could be carried out, in principle, to examine the extent to which readers focus on certain aspects of the scenario presented, and to see how far they bring in their own autobiographical knowledge when reading.

Personalization: processing consequences of using the second person

One question that has long attracted interest in social psychology is whether the adoption of a personal perspective has any special processing consequences (see Higgins & Bargh, 1987, for a review). For instance, does the reader adopting a self-based perspective have any advantage, or differences, in terms of a broader conception of interpretation? A somewhat disparate literature on so-called *personalization* indicates that there are indeed significant processing differences, and these may explain some of the intuitions that narratologists have regarding the use of different person-perspectives.

Personalization is a way of portraying information such that references are made to the way *you* might feel, how *you* might react, etc., rather than how *a person* might feel or react, which is less personal. There is a considerable psychological literature on the effects of personalization. Of particular interest here is an empirical study of the efficacious effects of personalizing information about the possible side-effects of drugs. Berry, Michas, and Bersellini (2003) carried out work using the following example (amongst others):

(13a)   Epidoxin is associated with some side effects. A substantial proportion of people who take this medicine get one or more of its side effects. Epidoxin can cause convulsions and chest pain. There is also a risk of loss of coordination and blurred vision. It can also cause stomach pains and anaemia.

This non-personalized version was compared with the following personalized one:

(13b)   Epidoxin is associated with some side effects. If you take this medicine, there is a substantial chance of you getting one or more of its side effects. You may get convulsions and chest pain. There is also a risk of you getting loss of coordination and blurred vision. You may also experience stomach pains and anaemia.

In the first experiment, Berry et al. (2003) found that the personalized version resulted in ratings of satisfaction with the information being higher and judgements of the risk to personal health being lower. Thus there were some clear advantages to the personalized version, and a clear effect on interpretation. A second experiment used more substantial descriptions, including information on how to take the drug, and other general advice. This experiment replicated the rating data from the first study, but also used a recall task to test participants' memory under the two conditions. The personalized information was much better recalled, for all categories of information presented. Again, personalization resulted in a desirable improvement in communication, but this time manifested in improved memory.

A somewhat different approach was taken by Fukuda and Sanford (2008), using the text-change detection paradigm. As discussed in Chapter 5, this paradigm is ideal for testing the strength of the memory trace laid down during reading, and also allows an assessment to be made of the granularity of the representation making up the trace. Personalization typically relies on the use of *you* to represent the self, and the most obvious contrast is with third person pronouns like *she*. Fukuda and Sanford also compared the use of *I*. A typical example of the short vignettes used as materials is shown below:

(14)   {I was/ You were/ Sara was} very busy making dinner for {my/your/her} hungry family yesterday. {I/You/She} answered a call with wet hands in the kitchen. The phone was left messy and covered in flour.

Participants saw each material in either first, second or third person. In some cases, changes were made to the verb of the second sentence, for instance *answered → made*. The results showed that more changes were detected in the *I* and *You* cases than in the third person case. So, there is evidence from text-change that second person descriptions (and first person in these sample materials) give rise to deeper processing than third person descriptions.

What is the psychological basis for the effect of inducing a reader-centric perspective? There is a social psychological literature showing that information relevant to the self is processed more efficiently than other types of information. Higgins and Bargh (1987) argued that personal information is more likely to capture attention, and thus be better retained in memory. There have been a number of demonstrations of enhanced recall of adjectives when the task was to evaluate if they applied to the reader rather than for a variety of other judgement tasks, leading investigators to suggest that this is because a check against oneself entails using a self-schema, in which information is richly organized, thus enhancing memory. Consistent with the idea of evaluating information against a rich database in memory is the observation that evaluating adjectives as descriptors of other people with whom one is familiar can also lead to equally enhanced recall (Keenan & Baillet, 1980). So while processing information with respect to the self certainly leads to enhanced memory, so too do other forms of processing when that processing is with respect to something or someone about what or whom the reader has extensive knowledge. There is clearly something special about personalization, and using second person descriptions rather than third person. In writing, one would therefore anticipate that using the second person should lead to better attended and better remembered representations of the discourse. This may, of course, correspond to a subjective impression of descriptions being more vivid, though there has been no direct test of this correspondence.

A recent study by Ditman, Brunyé, Mahoney, and Taylor (2010) has revealed some interesting findings that may relate the advantage of the *you* form to simulation of the type posited by embodiment theory. They argued that if action statements result in a mental simulation under the 'you' perspective, but not (or weakly) for perspectives cued by *I* and *s/he*, then memory retention should be better for the 'you' perspective. This is what they found for memory for actions after ten minutes, and, in a separate study, after three days. However, for non-action events, such as *You are a 35-year-old postal worker*, there is no such effect. They argued that this was because under the 'you' perspective, an action can be simulated, but a description cannot. This effect may not be the same as general personalization, since the advantage only applies to actions. Some caution is required, however. Many important descriptions, such as being in pain or being angry, are scarcely actions, yet it seems likely that some sort of simulation might take place, as we discussed in Chapter 6 and will look at further in Chapter 8. So, it may be the case that simulation, induced by the 'you' perspective, could occur for other personally important descriptions. This remains to be demonstrated, and, when this area is more fully explored, should offer good insights into how personalization and embodiment depend on pronoun-induced perspective-taking.

Self-perspective and other-perspective embodiment effects:
neuroscience evidence

The idea that deeper or more elaborate processing takes place given *you* descriptions as triggers for self-involvement receives some support from neuroscience experiments, in particular from studies that have compared self and other person perspectives on externally depicted events from an experiential (embodiment) point of view. If using a second person pronoun, *you*, causes a reader to process aspects of a discourse more deeply, and to better remember it, then does such a perspective also lead to different embodiment and experiential effects? For example, consider depictions of painful events. Are these more vivid when their depiction leads to a self-perspective being adopted than another person's perspective?

Indeed, the effects of the depiction of pain in this way have attracted several interesting neuroscience studies. What are the differences and similarities in brain activity recruited when imagining how one would feel oneself in a situation, versus imagining how another would feel? In one fMRI study of imagined pain, such perspectives were compared, with interesting results (Jackson et al., 2006). Participants viewed pictures of people with their hands or feet in commonplace painful situations (e.g., stubbing a toe, pinching a finger in a door) or non-painful situations (e.g., using the handle of a drawer). Three different perspectives were used, set up through explicit instructions. In the 'self' condition, participants were asked to imagine that they themselves were being depicted in the target pictures. In the 'other' condition, they were asked to imagine a specific but unfamiliar other person being depicted. In a 'control' condition, they were told that the limb in question was artificial. For the first two perspectives, they were asked to indicate the level of pain being experienced under the appropriate perspective on a scale ranging from 'no pain' to 'worst possible pain'. For the artificial limb condition, they were asked to rate damage rather than pain.

The behavioural findings were that pain felt was rated as more intense for both 'human' conditions (in contrast to the 'artificial limb' control), and, of particular interest here, that the 'self' perspective was rated as more intense than the 'other' perspective, with 'self' ratings being made more rapidly. Although this might seem predictable, note that there is no reason to suppose that one's own feeling of pain would be greater than that of another person. This finding suggests that the perspective manipulation was successful, and that there is some sort of representation of greater intensity under the 'self' perspective. In terms of brain areas showing activation under the different perspectives, both showed activity in the neural network involved in pain processing, discussed in Chapter 6. But there were important differences. The 'self' perspective involved the pain network more extensively in the secondary somatosensory cortex, which is partly responsible for the direct perception of pain (cf. Bushnell et al., 1999), but no activity in the primary somatosensory cortex, where real pain causes activation. Because of the secondary cortex activation, however, Jackson et al. (2006) suggest that adopting a self-perspective is more closely related to one's own actual experience of pain than taking the perspective of a stranger. In the same way, the faster response times for giving ratings suggests that assessing one's own pain is a simpler process than assessing the pain of others. This is important for maintaining a self–other distinction.

In the case of 'other' processing, significant additional activity was reported in several areas thought to correlate with two different functions. The area corresponding to the motivational-affective component of pain (the anterior cingulate cortex) showed an enhanced reaction. This is what would be expected if rather than simulating the pain itself, the negative affect associated with the pain is being simulated in some way. So, in summary, the experience of real pain leads to activation of both primary and secondary somatosensory cortex; in the case of 'self', these effects are restricted to the secondary cortex; and for the 'other' condition, there are no effects in these areas. In contrast, the areas that mediate the motivational-affective aspects of pain are active in the 'other' condition. Support for these findings comes from other studies (e.g., Singer et al., 2004).

Further effects in the 'other' condition relate directly to perspective-taking. There were greater activations in the area known to play a role in perspective-taking and to be responsible for mediating the ascription of agency, namely the right temporo-parietal region and the pre-frontal cortex (see also Decety & Somerville, 2003). This system, involved in perspective-taking, is posited as being generally important for keeping the self separate from the situation of others, which is a key issue in the underpinnings of empathy. We shall discuss empathy and related issues in detail in the next chapter.

The results in general are promising for studying personalized depictions from the angle of social neuroscience (see Zaki & Ochsner, 2011, for a review). One would anticipate that written descriptions of pain being inflicted, or emotional reactions to noxious situations, would elicit generally stronger sensory-related effects for *you* descriptions than would external perspective third person descriptions, though this remains to be established empirically.

Perspective in representation of speech and thought

Up to now we have focussed primarily on personal pronouns in relation to creating the experience of spatial orientation and richness of sensory perception. This section focusses on the depiction of what characters say and think, which can also affect the use of personal pronouns and other deictic forms.

This is a major aspect of narratives not only because of the large quantity of text devoted to speech and thought in real narratives, but also because of important functions such as portraying social interaction, characterization, plot development and the construction of point of view. This topic has a substantial coverage in narratology and stylistics (e.g., Fludernik, 1993; Leech & Short, 2007; McHale, 2009; Page, 1988; Semino & Short, 2004). We will summarize and illustrate it only briefly, trying nevertheless to capture the essence of some of the more important distinctions being made. Furthermore, we shall relate the analyses of narratologists and stylisticians to psychological processes wherever possible.

What a character says or thinks can be reported with various degrees of detail, ranging from a quotation of the words used by the character to a narrated summary (see Leech & Short, 2007, and Semino & Short, 2004, for further details, including a scale of possible forms which has been influential in text analysis in stylistics). We will concentrate in this section specifically on how the perspective can be altered by the use of direct and indirect forms, and study empirically how these affect depth of processing.

Direct and indirect speech and thought: differences in form

Direct speech constitutes a quotation or 'demonstration' (Clark & Gerrig, 1990) of what someone has said, and may include the manner of delivery by that someone, amongst other things. It differs from *indirect speech*, in which a description of what someone has said, rather than a demonstration, is given. To begin, we note that direct speech retains the deictic coordinates of the speaker, but indirect speech shifts the deictic coordinates to those of the reporter:

(15a)   He said, 'I am enjoying this evening's party here.' (Direct)

(15b)   He said that he was enjoying that evening's party there. (Indirect)

In (15b), not only are the quotation marks removed and the reporting clause changed (the *He said* is replaced by *He said that*), but there are shifts in pronouns (*I* to *he*), verb form (*am* to *was*), determiners in time expressions (*this evening* to *that evening*) and place adverbs (*here* to *there*). All of these indicate a plain shift in deictic coordinates, or perspective, to the narrator relative to the perspective of the experiencing speaker in (15a).

These examples are artificially constructed and real narrative will often not include so many deictic indicators in a single piece of speech, since spatio-temporal factors may often be taken for granted in extended narratives. Of course, in fictional narrative, we rarely see both the direct and indirect forms of a particular speech act, unless there is some reason in the narrative to produce a report of what has been previously presented directly – hence, on occasions when we read indirect speech in fiction, we have to imagine what might have been said directly.

Direct and *indirect thought* follow the same pattern:

(16a)   He thought, 'I am enjoying this evening's party here.' (Direct)

(16b)   He thought that he was enjoying that evening's party there. (Indirect)

From the evidence of (15a/b) and (16a/b), indirect speech and thought might be viewed as simple linguistic transformations of direct speech and thought, but it has been shown that rule-based transformations are not always possible (Banfield, 1982) and as we will see below there is flexibility in the forms that indirect speech and thought may take.

Direct and indirect speech and thought: impact and claims of vividness and faithfulness

Many researchers suppose that direct speech is a form of presentation that has more impact than indirect speech. Semino and Short (2004, p. 90), for example, say 'The dramatization of characters' voices is an important part of the effects of vividness, immediacy and involvement of fictional narratives.' Although the narrator quotes a character's words, there is a tie to the character's context in so much as the deictic coordinates are those of the character. By contrast, indirect speech presents us with speech at a level removed from the character's context, with the deictic coordinates of the narrator, the reporting voice. For Leech and Short (2007, p. 276), direct forms are the norm for speech presentation in fiction, so the use of indirect forms is regarded as having a potential distancing effect, in the sense of having less vivid impact. Thought presentation is viewed differently by Leech and Short. They regard indirect thought as the norm for fiction, so that, in their model, direct thought then has a heightening effect, which they argue gives the sense of characters somewhat artificially articulating thoughts to themselves or a sense of sudden strong realization.

Some scholars also distinguish between direct and indirect speech on the basis that direct speech is more faithful to what the character might have actually said. From the point of view of semantics, it has been claimed that these differences correspond to the idea that what is reported in the quotes of direct speech must be an accurate report of what words were actually used, rather than a paraphrase (e.g., Partee, 1973; see also Coulmas, 1986, and Li, 1986, for cultural variants). The same does not apply to indirect speech. For instance, along these lines, (17b) is an acceptable paraphrase of (17a):

(17a)   Mary said that she couldn't go to the meeting.

(17b)   Mary said that she was unable to attend the meeting.

In contrast, such a paraphrase may be viewed as less acceptable when it comes to direct speech:

(18a)   Mary said 'I can't go to the meeting.'

(18b)   Mary said 'I am unable to attend the meeting.'

In this case, being *unable to attend* may carry different overtones from the less formal *can't go*.

Some stylisticians support this view of faithfulness in the case of direct speech, arguing that it carries an assumption of being a verbatim quotation (Leech & Short, 2007, p. 255). Fludernik (1996), Page (1988) and Sternberg (1982) challenge this view, providing examples of direct speech from fiction, including cases of hypothetical speech, such as what might have been said in the past, or might be uttered in the future. Also, they provide examples of cases where speeches supposedly made on separate occasions have been conflated, and cases where the length of utterance does not match the stated duration of the speech. Semino and Short (2004) accept that examples can be found that fail to fit the expected pattern, but nevertheless do not see these examples as necessarily undermining the faithfulness assumption. They point out that, according to their corpus work, examples of non-faithful direct speech (e.g., hypothetical speech) are rare. Although such cases exist, when direct speech is presented, the assumption is that what is said is generally taken by readers or listeners as a faithful representation. Consider a final case, where it is asserted that someone is reported as saying *'I just didn't believe it'*, for an utterance originally in German (cf. Clark & Gerrig, 1990). Now although what is being presented as a verbatim case is qualified as being uttered in a different language (and therefore not truly verbatim), it can be argued that the English translation is considered by a reader/listener to be the most directly corresponding wording. Generally, there seems to be a greater assumption on the part of readers/listeners of faithfulness for direct speech than for indirect speech.

Psychological evidence for differential processing

There is some empirical psychological work supporting a difference in the way that direct and indirect forms are processed. In two recent studies text-change detection tasks were used on direct and indirect speech material (Bohan, Sanford, Cochrane, & Sanford, 2008), and on direct and indirect thought (Thomson, 2009). As an example, in the speech version, one material was:

(19a)   Joan had been searching in her bag but couldn't find her keys. She said to her boyfriend 'I'll just have to wait outside for my flatmate to let me in.' [Direct]

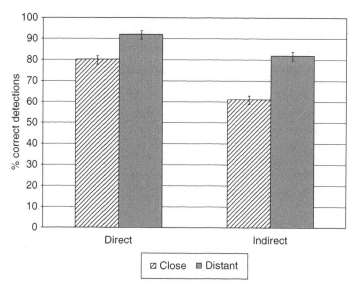

Figure 7.2 Correct change detections as a function of speech type and semantic distance. Direct speech leads to better change detection than indirect speech. There is also an effect of close versus distant semantic change. Data from Bohan et al. (2008).

(19b)   Joan had been searching in her bag but couldn't find her keys. She said to her boyfriend that she'd just have to wait outside for her flatmate to let her in. [Indirect]

The changes used in the example, that occurred on the second presentation, were to the word *flatmate*, that could change to *roommate* (a close semantic change), or *brother* (a distant semantic change). If readers are automatically sensitive to the importance of wording in the direct case, then one would expect changes to be more detectable in the direct case. This result was found, as shown in Figure 7.2. The results for the thought representation experiment are similar. For direct thought, detection rates are higher. These findings are compatible with the idea that closer attention is paid to the actual wording in the case of direct speech and thought, and the underlying mechanism certainly appears worthy of further examination.

The differences between direct and indirect forms may well be brought about because of heightened attention to the actual wording used in the direct case. However, it should be noted that the semantic distance effect still holds in the indirect case. If the effect were due to retention of wording per se, we might expect the distance effect to vanish, or to be greatly reduced. There is little evidence for such a reduction, and we suggest that the enhancement effect is occurring at the level of meaning rather than simply at the actual word level. Nevertheless, there is a strong enhancing effect of using direct speech, as we might predict from Semino and Short's (2004) notion of 'vividness' in direct speech.

Finally, on a methodological note, in these experiments there is a difference in pronoun for the direct case (first person) and indirect case (third person). Given the results for the personalization study, it could be that this alone is the explanation for the enhanced effect under the direct condition. This is because in the direct condition (19a) *I* is used, while in the indirect condition (19b), the pronoun *she* (or *he* in other materials) is used. However, this has been ruled out by a further experiment (Dawydiak, unpublished data), using materials like (20), where the direct speech is either in the first or third person form.

(20)   Tim was telling everyone about {his/his wife's} recent run in with the law. He said, '{I/She} disobeyed (→ disregarded/ignored) the signal to pull over from the policeman and ended up in court the next day.'

Changes were made to the verb in the direct speech, for instance *disobeyed* → *disregarded/ignored*. The results comparing these cases showed only an effect of semantic distance, with no effect of the pronoun at all. So, the enhancing effect of direct speech is not due to the difference in the pronoun.

Embodiment and speech representation

If direct speech is supposed to accurately portray selected aspects of what was said, then how far should that accuracy go? For example, does embodiment enter into the picture? With direct speech, it might be supposed that there is a 'voice in the head', meaning that there is simulation of the speech in the speech production and/or reception areas of the brain. This idea is all the more plausible when the manner of presentation by the person being quoted is demonstrated by a narrator. For instance, compare the three examples below:

(21a)   Harry said 'I don't want to go to any more history lectures.'

(21b)   Harry shouted 'I don't want to go to any more history lectures.'

(21c)   Mary whispered 'I don't want to go to any more history lectures.'

When these are read, do they lead to a simulation of a (male) voice talking normally (21a) or shouting (21b), or to a female voice whispering (21c)? The following real examples from narrative exploit some of the possibilities in relation to a female voice:

(22)   'But I can tell you' – her voice rose to a shrill scream – '*that I'm a lady*!
        What do you think I want with *men*? The beasts! [...]' The pitch of her voice
        had brought a servant to the door.
                (Peake (1985). *Gormenghast*, p. 31, Peake's italics and our underlining)

(23)   And then he remembered her voice again, when she had whispered: 'Who
        would dare to rebel? Who would *dare*?' and then the full, ruthless organ-
        chord of her throat: 'And I will crush its life out! [...]'
                (Peake (1985). *Gormenghast*, p. 44, Peake's italics and our underlining)

In addition to the descriptions of voices, narratives can use typefaces (italics, capitals, etc.), spelling and punctuation to indicate speech characteristics such as loudness, emphasis, regional or foreign accents and hesitations (Clark & Gerrig, 1990; Leech & Short, 2007; Page, 1988). Examples (22) and (23) utilize italics to serve as prompts for paralinguistic features. The example below shows how spelling can indicate a specific style of speaking, in this case alongside explicit descriptions of creaking, whistling and hissing.

(24)   Now they could hear his voice creaking and whistling.
            'Ach, sss! Cautious, my precious! More haste less speed. We musstn't
        rissk our neck, musst we, precious? No, precious – *gollum*!' He lifted his
        head again, blinked at the moon, and quickly shut his eyes. 'We hate it,' he
        hissed. 'Nassty, nassty shivery light it is – sss – it spies on us, precious – it
        hurts our eyes.'
            He was getting lower now and the hisses became sharper and clearer.
        'Where iss it, where iss it: my Precious, my Precious?'
                (Tolkien (2001). *The Lord of the Rings*, p. 599)

Generally, the stylistic research shows that unconventional spelling is limited in terms of accurately representing speech styles (Leech & Short, 2007; Page, 1988), so some reliance on explicit description is often essential.

At the time of writing, there is no clear answer to how readers process the voices of characters. However, on the basis of other embodiment research, there are two clear ways to approach the issue, one behavioural, and one neuroscience-based. Behaviourally, one could present a material like example (22), with a task of indicating whether a word appeared in the text or not. Suppose the word in question was *beasts*, then the answer would be *yes*. But if the voice were presented in a female shrill scream, perhaps verification would be faster than if it were presented in a loud male voice? If so, it would at least be suggestive of simulation of some sort. More directly, would the areas of cortex responsible for processing speech be activated by the direct speech in examples (21–24)?

For studying speech representation, the effects of manner (shouting, whispering) offer a simple and tractable area of study from the embodiment point of view. Usefully, it is known how both timbre and loudness are represented in the brain, for instance (Reiterer, Erb, Grodd, & Wildgruber, 2008), and in principle seeing whether imagined sound is represented the same way should not be especially difficult. There is reason to be optimistic about such an approach. In some relevant but rather different work, it has been shown that readers effectively 'hear' the voices of people depicted as speakers when they are familiar with how those voices sound (Kurby, Magliano, & Rapp, 2009). Participants read scripts that had direct speech for familiar or unfamiliar voices. Memory probes for the scripts were presented auditorily in either appropriate or inappropriate voices. Recognition of the probed material was enhanced when the probe voice matched the actual voice, but only for familiar voices. This provides good evidence that where voices are already known, from auditory exposure, there are indeed 'voice in the head' types of simulation going on (see also Alexander & Nygaard, 2008, for similar observations about rate of speech and its effects on reading). Whether such effects can be achieved through descriptions of voices remains to be seen, of course. A distinctly promising recent result has in fact been obtained. Yao, Belin, and Scheepers (2011) had participants read sentences that were presented in either direct or indirect voice. The participants were concurrently scanned using fMRI. The results showed that the area of the brain responsible for processing speech information was more active in the direct speech situation. Such a finding offers a straightforward and attractive way of investigating how more complex descriptions of speech might modulate any embodiment effects.

Removing indicators of the narrator: free direct speech and thought

We shall now consider some additional ways in which speech and thought may be portrayed, and where there is a dearth of empirical evidence regarding the effects of these forms. In addition to the choice of whether to make speech and thought direct or indirect, writers have the choice of whether to attach reporting clauses, called 'tags', such as *he said/thought* for the direct forms or *he said that/he thought that* for the indirect forms. It is common to avoid repeating these narrator tags when a character makes a series of contributions to a conversation or has a string of thoughts. When the reporting clause is removed from a direct speech example, as in (15a), reproduced below as (25a), and just the bare main propositions are left, as in (25b), the result is called *free direct speech* (FDS) (e.g., Leech & Short, 2007).

(25a)   He said, 'I am enjoying this evening's party here.' (Direct)

(25b)   'I am enjoying this evening's party here.' (Free direct)

Free direct thought (FDT) follows the same pattern, although often omits the quotation marks.

Continued use of free direct speech, as in (26), might potentially appear to readers to be even more vivid than direct speech.

(26)   'You realized Henry had done it?'
         'Of course.'
         'How did you react to this?'
         'What could I do? I didn't want Edith to know it wasn't me [. . .]'
                    (Puccetti (1973). *The Trial of John and Henry Norton*, p. 119)

The narrator's presence might be viewed as less obtrusive in free direct speech than in direct speech because of the lack of reporting clauses, if the narrator is even felt to be there at all. It remains to be investigated whether direct speech and free direct speech have different effects on readers in terms of their impact, but the extent to which recall of wording is similar or different in these forms could be tested using the text-change methodology described earlier.

One potential problem with free direct speech is that the lack of reporting clauses may require readers to do extra processing to infer the identity of speakers, as Bortolussi and Dixon (2003) have pointed out. This might counteract any value in the minimalism of omitting the reporting clauses. In the above example, the identities of the participants can be distinguished because the roles of the lawyer and defendant correspond to the main questions and the answers respectively. Often the roles of speakers are not so obviously distinct. For this reason, it is common to mix free direct speech utterances with some direct speech utterances over longer stretches of discourse, thereby providing some tags amidst the untagged forms in order to make the identity of the speakers clear.

For free direct thought, one might again expect the free form to have more impact. However, without the reporting clause and possibly with no quotation marks, there can sometimes be a problem of distinguishing whether a sentence is to be interpreted as speech, thought, or main narrative. In the following text, the author gets round this problem by presenting the thoughts in italics, the convention having been set up earlier in the book.

(27)   The curator lay a moment, gasping for breath, taking stock. *I am still alive.*
                    (Brown (2003). *The Da Vinci Code*, p. 17, Brown's italics)

Without the italics, readers could draw on deictic information (the shift to *I* and the present tense) to signal the shift, but such cues may not always be provided and, even when they are, taking account of them might slow reading time.

Major hybrid forms: free indirect speech and thought

Other ways of portraying speech and thought that have emerged in the narratology literature are *free indirect speech* (FIS) and *free indirect thought* (FIT), often referred to together by the superordinate term *free indirect discourse* (FID). Free indirect thought is viewed as particularly important in narrative text because it is a major way of presenting a character's internal consciousness, a key aspect of narrative writing. Free indirect speech and thought are generally viewed as hybrid forms (e.g., Leech & Short, 2007), in the sense that they portray a mixture of features relating to the narrator and the character. This is demonstrated in (28), an example of free indirect thought, which appears in sentences [2] and [3].

(28)   [1] At the same time, she felt a little trembly in her chin and cheeks. [2] What the hell was this? [3] What the hell would she have done if she'd found anything?

        (Harris (1989). *The Silence of the Lambs*, p. 373, our numbering)

The presentation of thought in sentences [2] and [3] is 'free' because the writer omits the reporting clauses ('she thought') in each case. These sentences are indirect because the deictic forms reflect the *narrator's* reporting perspective rather than the character's present perspective (they are 'backshifted' to the narrator). This is evident in the past tense use of *was* rather than *is* in sentence [2], and the use of *she* to describe the character rather than *I* in sentence [3]. The hybrid nature comes from the fact that free indirect discourse often has a sense of immediacy that we would normally associate with direct discourse, despite reflecting the narrator's standpoint. In (28), the two profanities (the repeated *What the hell*) might be viewed as more characteristic of direct quotations than indirect forms. In some cases, free indirect speech/thought may include some non-backshifted forms alongside the backshifting. The *this* in Sentence [2] of (28) is not backshifted. Even the question form is indicative of direct discourse, since it would not be possible to insert the indirect tag *she thought that* in Sentences [2] and [3] with English grammar as it stands. (See Fludernik, 1993, for an extensive study of the features of free indirect discourse.)

    Why do writers use these hybrid forms? The advantage of the backshifting is that it allows the presented thoughts to run relatively seamlessly on from the main narrative, avoiding the sudden switch of deictic coordinates that we saw in the previous section in (27). The possible disadvantage is that full backshifting seems less immediate, but this is partially compensated for in these hybrid forms by keeping some elements that are sufficiently vivid and performance-based to be characteristic of direct discourse (e.g., profanities, rhetorical questions, etc.) and having the possibility of retaining some unbackshifted forms.

Because of its ability to merge characteristics of direct and indirect forms, there is an unresolved debate in narratology and stylistics over how free indirect discourse should be categorized and how readers interpret it. Some scholars take the style primarily to reflect the voice/thoughts of the character or primarily the narrator's perspective (different types of 'single voice' hypothesis). Other analysts have put forward a 'dual voice' hypothesis, arguing that free indirect discourse intermingles the voices of the character(s) and narrator. For a range of perspectives on single and dual voice hypotheses, see, for example, Bakhtin (1981), Banfield (1982), Cohn (1978), Fludernik (1993), Leech and Short (2007), Pascal (1977) and Toolan (2006). Distinguishing between a character and a narrator can often be important because some narrators (e.g., omniscient narrators) can be more reliable than characters (characters often have a limited self-perspective tied to a specific spatio-temporal context, which can cause them to lack knowledge or have faulty knowledge, which the reader may need to take into account).

Leech and Short (2007) place free indirect discourse between direct and indirect discourse in terms of impact and faithfulness, since it is viewed as having properties of both types. This possible mingling of voices is clearly more complex to investigate empirically than the simple cases of direct and indirect speech/thought we examined earlier. Nevertheless, there have been some attempts to assess the dual voice notion empirically in the humanities. Sotirova (2006) and Bray (2007a) performed sets of experiments in which readers were asked whether they interpreted specific sentences of passages of free indirect discourse as originating from the character(s) or the narrator, or both. The results for both sets of experiments were inconclusive, although this perhaps reflects a genuine ambiguity in these forms (e.g., Simpson, 1993).

Some humanities scholars attribute empathetic effects to some instances of free indirect thought and ironic effects to some instances of free indirect speech (e.g., Fludernik, 1993). In the latter case, the perceived voice of the reporting narrator (for those researchers who acknowledge that voice) can be viewed as providing a distancing perspective which can be used for ironic purposes. However, a preliminary empirical study by Bray (2007b) made him question whether it is the linguistic features or the content of the sentences which is primarily responsible for the effect in the real narrative examples he examined, so was inconclusive.

Summary

Perspectives constitute a major feature of narratives. We have examined the theoretical aspects of perspective both from a humanities point of view, and the empirical work of experimental psychology. While the former offers a rich set of ideas, the latter is starting to provide ways of conceptualizing what perspective means in terms of processing. Hopefully, future development will lead to a fuller psychologically based picture of narrative perspectives. In this chapter the following points were made:

- Perspectives can be cued by the use of pronouns (first, second and third person). The psychological evidence showed how the perspectives these pronouns engender are different and understandable in terms of a reference system in the real world. The psychological work is rather limited by the simplicity of the language materials used, and it is clear that in real narrative, things may be more complex. However, in principle, many of the ideas in humanities analyses may be tested using experimental methods, and we have offered a few examples.
- The use of the pronoun *you* as a way of addressing the reader in some fashion is particularly interesting, because it has been equated with heightening reader 'involvement' in some manner. Psychological work on personalization shows that such usage can increase memory for and depth of processing of what is written, and this relates to a body of work in social psychology.
- Other issues of perspective arise in the use of direct and indirect speech and thought. The intuition that direct forms are somehow more 'vivid' than indirect forms finds support and explanation in experiments showing increased depth of processing with direct forms, and in newly emerging evidence that direct forms may be related to embodiment effects (and hence to the experiential aspects of reading).
- The various forms of speech/thought presentation used in writing are often complex, and it may not always be straightforward or even possible to classify particular pieces of text as being in one form or another. Although there has been considerable work done on the different linguistic forms, there is a long way to go before a full processing account is developed.

8   Hot cognition: emotion, empathy and suspense

Cognition refers to acts of perceiving, understanding and thinking. This category of mental activity was classically considered separate from emotion and motivation (or 'conation'). We use the expression *hot cognition* to refer to the way emotion and feeling interact with cognitive activities, that is, how cognition is coloured and modified by feelings. The term originates from Abelson (1963), who used it in relation to computer modelling. For us, the term refers to the way in which human feelings are linked to embodied cognition.

Up to now we have only briefly mentioned emotion in our discussion, touching upon the topic with respect to foregrounding and embodiment. Without invoking emotion, a large part of the general character of narratives would be overlooked. In this chapter we first look at emotional judgements and feelings elicited by writing. Then, we examine the extent to which we empathize with characters in stories. Finally, we move on to suspense and other emotions induced by story structure such as surprise and curiosity. The over-arching question is: how do writers bring about deep emotion-related processing? Questions of how writers control readers' processing are central to the Rhetorical Processing Framework. Although full answers are some way off in this case, ways of finding them are becoming clearer.

Background: theories of emotion

Character-based narratives gain much of their force and interest from the portrayal of emotion in characters, and often invite us to appreciate how a character must feel as a result of the things that happen to them. We assume that readers experience emotions as they read, but there is much debate over the nature of emotions. We will begin with some theoretical background to show different views about what emotions are, before moving on to consider empirical research which investigates emotions in relation to reading.

Broadly speaking, emotion theories can be divided into two main types: *cognitive appraisal theories*, which emphasize the role of an experiencer's judgement (appraisal) in assessing the emotion-stimulating situation; and *somatic feeling theories*, which highlight the role of an experiencer's body (Greek *soma*) in producing an emotion, either automatically or with less emphasis on intervening judgement than in appraisal theories. This is a simple binary presentation of the two main approaches, but in reality there are many variants of each, and a number of the modern versions of these theories both involve an element of judgement and treat the body as significant, as we shall see. The judgement and embodiment components of these theories are important for when we come to look at the psychological work on emotions in relation to reading, because two major experimental approaches are to look at judgements of readers about how emotion-eliciting situations affect characters and to examine embodiment effects in readers.

Cognitive appraisal theories and action tendencies

The notion of *appraisal* is currently particularly associated with Frijda (1986, 2007), who draws on Arnold (1961). Arnold distinguished between perception, which has an object, and emotion, which relates the object to the perceiver. The judgement about this relation is the appraisal. In general terms, this involves assessing whether an object is 'desirable or undesirable, valuable or harmful' for the perceiver (p. 171). Arnold gives the following example to distinguish between perception and emotion. She suggests that she may perceive two cars travelling toward each other and may not be touched personally by the observation. However, if she judges that the cars might crash and knows that there are people in the cars, then she will feel emotion. The appraisal enables the perceiver to evaluate an action or object, since the same action or object can have different meanings. For example, another person touching our arm can be appraised positively, negatively or neutrally depending on our view of the person touching us and the situation (Oatley, Keltner, & Jenkins, 2006, p. 11). Frijda (1986, 2007) provides an extremely detailed model of emotion, which includes this appraisal component. The appraisal not only determines the nature and personal relevance of a potential emotion-stimulating event, it also allows an assessment of how urgent and serious the event is, and can take into account any social factors that might prompt inhibition of a response. Commonly, there are also physical responses mediated by the autonomic nervous system, including heart rate, respiration, blood pressure, blood vessels, sweating, electrical conductivity of the skin, tears, etc., which contribute to the intensity of the emotion but, according to Frijda, are not essential prerequisites. Other possible elements include inner subjective states (e.g., 'I feel sad'), possible actions (e.g., running away in fear) and changes of plan.

For Frijda and Arnold, although the appraisal is important in assessing the situation, it is *not* the emotion itself. For Arnold (1961), the emotion is the sense of being drawn toward or away from an object, what is termed an *action tendency* (p. 177). This action tendency may have a physical form, with possible muscle tension, gestures and facial expressions. Frijda also uses this term, suggesting that the essence of an emotion is, literally, 'being moved' (1986, p. 231). This is interesting in connection with the psychological work on embodiment that we will examine in this chapter, because that work includes the idea that emotions include movement toward or away from different emotion-stimulating entities. Although appraisal theory is not generally classed as a somatic theory (because the emphasis in appraisal theory is on explaining the appraisal itself), there is at its very core an embodiment assumption.

Somatic feeling theories and facial feedback

In appraisal theories, although the body is important, the physiological reaction generally follows the appraisal. In some somatic feeling theories, by contrast, the emphasis is on bodily changes precipitating an emotional response, for some emotions at least. Damasio (2000, 2003, 2006) is particularly associated with this type of idea. He suggests (2006) that 'the essence of a feeling might not be an elusive mental quality attached to an object, but rather the direct perception of a specific landscape: that of the body' (p. xxiv). Likewise, Prinz (2004) describes emotions in his book title as 'gut reactions', using this expression to directly implicate the body in triggering emotion. Damasio (2006) recognizes emotions which are not cognitively mediated at the initial stage, terming these 'primary emotions' (p. 131). He defines 'primary emotions' as 'innate, preorganized' responses in early life. He believes that humans and animals may be pre-wired to respond to specific types of stimuli or configurations of stimuli in terms of their size, sound, motion, etc. Damasio assumes that this type of response utilizes the limbic system in the brain, particularly the amygdala. Damasio describes this type of response as 'Jamesian', likening it to the classic idea of William James (1890) that when we see an entity such as a bear, our body reacts, and then we *subsequently* feel scared due to our experience of the body's response. In Damasio's model the reaction may be before we even realize that it is a bear since the response may be simply to size, sound, etc. Only subsequently is consciousness involved in the process, in the form of a feeling.

Another type of somatic feeling model is the facial feedback hypothesis (e.g., Izard, 1971; Tomkins, 1962). The idea here is that even without an originating emotion-causing object or event, changes to the body, specifically the face, can prompt changes in affect. The strong version of the hypothesis is that the facial expressions of an individual can by themselves create emotion in that individual, and the weak version is that such expressions can increase or decrease existing emotions. A classic technique to demonstrate this is the pen-in-the-mouth reading test (Strack, Martin, & Stepper, 1988), in which facial expressions similar to smiling or pouting/frowning can be produced according to the position of the pen – the pen being used so that the subjects do not realize the nature of the expression they are forming. This task reliably produces differences in affect when reading. While in the induced-smile state, people reported a greater intensity of felt humour in response to cartoons, while an induced-frown leads to lower intensities of felt humour (see Strack et al., 1988, for details of other examples of how the procedure influences emotional experiences).

The idea of facial feedback seems counter-intuitive since it involves the facial expression causing (or inhibiting) the emotion, rather than vice versa. Nevertheless, there is substantial scientific evidence for this (see McIntosh, 1996, for a review). Some of the early psychological research on this phenomenon also suggests humanities applications, in terms of the potential for sound play in writing to produce similar effects. Zajonc, Murphy, and Inglehart (1989) deliberately constructed examples to include specific sounds. In one case, they used German passages with many /ü/ sounds which cause the facial muscles to adopt positions usually occurring in negative facial expressions, and found the passages produced greater negative affect than passages without these features. We will see that not only do modern-day embodiment researchers utilize facial feedback to trigger mood in their experiments, but that emotional responses to language require engagement of the relevant muscles, meaning that emotional responses to a passage of language can be inhibited if the facial muscles are positioned for a contrary mood state.

Both the facial feedback hypothesis and Damasio's idea of primary emotions, as discussed above, provide examples of theories that do not rely on consciousness at the initiating stage. However, as we indicated earlier, many emotion theories contain a mix of a cognitive component and a bodily element. Damasio (2006) views 'secondary emotions' (p. 134) as being typical of adulthood. He believes that when we experience emotion in adulthood, such as when we see an old friend or hear that someone has died, there is an initial 'conscious evaluation' of the person or situation, which leads to an acquired dispositional response, in addition to the automatic response by the amygdala and other limbic areas which produce a physiological response. The mention of a cognitive evaluation sounds like a form of appraisal, but, unlike in appraisal theories, the personal relevance of the stimulus in this model of secondary emotions appears to arise more from conditioning than from considered judgement. Damasio also suggests a third mechanism which bypasses the body, the 'as-if-body-loop' (2006, pp. 155–158), which might provide an alternative path in cases of extensive paralysis and which he believes could account for empathy. This relies on mirror neurons and previous embodied experiences, but he believes the nature of the emotional response might be fainter in this bypass mode (2006, p. 155).

Overall, these theories show different balances between cognitive elements and embodied responses. In the experimental work that we will discuss later in the chapter, judgement and embodiment are investigated separately in order to test specific research questions, but clearly a general model of emotional response to narratives needs to take account both of readers' assessments of potential emotion-stimulating situations and the bodily responses when readers feel moved by a piece of writing.

Emotion and narrative: humanities background

Emotion has always been a topic of importance in literary study, but when specific groups of researchers initially became interested in cognitive approaches to reading, the study of affect was largely side-stepped since the interest was at first focussed on models from the knowledge-engineering approach of artificial intelligence (see Burke, 2006, for a critical review). Nevertheless, there have been a few researchers who have emphasized the need for an approach that links cognition and emotion. Miall and Kuiken (1994; see also Miall, 2007) have been central in pointing out that the affective impact of literary language is a crucial area of study. Their view has been that foregrounded language may induce emotion, e.g., in the use of metaphors, soundplay and repetition of words that have emotional impact through their content, aesthetic appeal and/or rhythmic impact. In Chapter 4 (e.g., examples (1), (4) and (7)), we saw some instances of foregrounding which might induce affect, and discussed empirical work in the humanities by Miall and Kuiken. Burke (2006, 2010) and Tsur (2008) have also played a significant role in highlighting the importance of affect in reading literature and have discussed the potential emotional impact of a wide range of stylistic features. This area is clearly a major possibility for future work in psycholinguistics and neuroscience, where researchers can identify whether foregrounding can prompt and perhaps even intensify an affective response in the brain. Burke (2010) also suggests, based on his own intuitions and those of other literary critics, that there may be a feeling of bodily motion when we read emotional passages in narratives. Cognitive linguists recognize the use of movement metaphors in discussing emotions generally (e.g., Lakoff & Johnson, 1980) and in literary texts (e.g., Gibbs, 2002b; Kövecses, 2000; Lakoff & Turner, 1989). The link between emotion and movement finds support in the empirical work on embodiment which we discuss in this chapter.

Before examining embodiment research, we will look at the key topic of how readers of narratives make judgements about the emotions of characters. Oatley (1992, 2011) has pointed out that understanding the emotional significance of events in narrative is often crucial not only for recognizing the complex personalities of some characters, but also because emotions can be linked to the goals of characters and can explain key plot moments. Many readers, when asked in questionnaires about their reading experiences, report subjective experiences of emotion (Burke, 2010). The scientific research aims to supply objective measures of the affective response to texts.

In reviewing this scientific research, we need to be aware that there may be different ways of introducing emotion in narratives. Use of explicit mentions of emotion are one obvious means of communicating affect that are used in psychological research, but there has also been a recognition by psychologists that emotions may need to be inferred from a situation. The medium of presenting a story can make a considerable difference to the way in which characters' reactions are presented. In films, which we will discuss in more detail later in this chapter when we look at suspense, we often hear and see direct audio-visual representations of characters, which may include extreme close-ups of facial expressions, so we may rely on our real-life methods of interpreting expressions (e.g., G. M. Smith, 2003; M. Smith, 1995). Although written text does not have the direct audio-visual impact of film, it has multiple ways of representing emotion. In addition to explicit narratorial statements and descriptions of situations which might be inferred to prompt emotion, there may be references to emotions in the conversations of charac- ters, descriptions of the facial expressions and movements of characters, and descriptions of actions resulting from emotions. Some of these written descriptions can be highly ambiguous out of context (e.g., a smile may be of happiness or malice), so text-world knowledge (Werth, 1999; see also Gavins, 2007) may be essential for contextualizing them and readers may need to make Theory of Mind judgements (e.g., Zunshine, 2006). Unlike much film, written text, as we saw in Chapter 7, can also take us into the minds of characters, allowing us to overhear their thought processes. This may provide information about their emotions and may also allow readers to align themselves with the perspective of a particular character, a topic to which we will return when we examine empathy later in the chapter.

Empirical work on judging the emotions of characters

Psychologists have found that working out the detail of how emotions are attributed to characters by readers is complex, even for the simplest stories. Certainly, conventional psycholinguistic experiments have shown that an appropriate piece of writing can invoke knowledge of the emotions of a character at some level (e.g., de Vega, Diaz, & Leon, 1997; Gernsbacher, Goldsmith, & Robertson, 1992; Gernsbacher & Robertson, 1992; Gygax,

Garnham, & Oakhill, 2004; Gygax, Oakhill, & Garnham, 2003). For example, Gernsbacher et al. (1992) used stories similar to (1a):

(1a)   Joe worked at the local 7–11 [store], to get spending money while in school. One night, his best friend, Tom, came in to buy a soda. Joe needed to go back to the storage room for a second. While he was away, Tom noticed the cash register was open. From the open drawer Tom quickly took a ten dollar bill. Later that week, Tom learned that Joe had been fired from the 7–11 because his cash had been low one night.

Each of Gernsbacher et al.'s stories implied an emotional state and in this case they suggested that readers might form a representation that Tom would feel guilty. Using a self-paced sentence-by-sentence reading time procedure, Gernsbacher et al. (Experiment 1) looked at reading time for continuation sentences, such as examples (1b) and (1b′):

(1b)   It would be weeks before Tom's <u>guilt</u> would subside.

(1b′)   It would be weeks before Tom's <u>pride</u> would subside.

In addition to *guilt–pride*, Gernsbacher et al. investigated a wide range of pairs of emotional states, including also *bored–curious*, *shy–confident*, *sad–joyful* and *restless–content*, with stories relevant to one of the emotions in each of the opposites. Reading times were faster for emotion statements that matched the implied emotion in the story, as in (1b), than for mismatched ones like (1b′), suggesting that readers had built the implied emotions into their mental representations. In a follow-up experiment (Experiment 2), Gernsbacher et al. explored the issue of whether the difference in reading times was due simply to the negative–positive polarity contrast in the pairs (e.g., *guilt* is negative affect and *pride* is positive affect) rather than to representations of specific emotions. Here, the researchers were addressing the question of whether participants reading negative materials such as (1a) above are simply responding to the general sense of something bad happening. Instead of the previous negative–positive pairs (e.g., *guilt–pride*), they used pairs which they judged to be negative–negative, such as *guilt–shyness*. Since there was still a significant difference, they argued that the readers did have mental representations of the emotional state of the characters which went beyond negative or positive valence.

   Gygax et al. (2003) built on this experimental paradigm to examine further the nature of readers' representations of emotions, using more finely tuned sets of words. They addressed the issue of whether readers of narratives can do more than simply infer so-called basic emotions, such as anger, happiness and sadness (e.g., Oatley & Johnson-Laird, 1987). Gygax et al. were also interested in whether one specific emotion (e.g., 'guilt') was evoked, as suggested by Gernsbacher et al., or whether more general information about emotions was inferred. Participants were given the same materials as in Gernsbacher et al.'s work and asked to carry out a sentence completion task (Experiment 1a). So after reading a material such as example (1a), participants were asked to complete the sentence *Tom felt . . .* Each participant could give between one and ten answers. Gygax et al.'s idea was that if, overall, participants found a variety of emotions consistent with a particular material, the emotion was unlikely to be specific. An example of one of the materials, with the words generated by the participants, is as follows. The numbers in parentheses (for the first eight items) relate to a second experiment (Experiment 1b) where participants were given the generated words and asked to rate the likelihood of the main character feeling the emotion (represented as a mean rating on a 7 point scale, where 1 = 'not very likely' and 7 = 'very likely'). The word used in the original Gernsbacher et al. experiment is given first.

(2)   Russ had just graduated with a degree in archaeology. As a graduation gift, his uncle sent him on an expedition to the Yucatan. While there he went into the jungle to examine ancient Mayan pyramids. In one pyramid, he noticed a rock that looked strangely like a handle. It was protruding from a smooth wall. He walked toward the rock to get a closer look. Russ felt . . .

     Generated words: Curious (6.84), excited (6.36), nervous (4.52), scared (4.10), intrigued (6.89), anxious (4.15), interested (6.57), amazed (4.52), privileged, like it was fate, inquisitive, fascinated, hopeful, it was too strange to be true.

The researchers found that participants in Experiment 1a generated a number of different emotions, going beyond basic emotions, and that participants in Experiment 1b (see example (2) above) gave similarly high ratings to very different emotions. They took this to confirm their hypothesis that more general emotional information was involved rather than a specific emotion. Subsequently (in Experiment 2), Gygax et al. tested different emotion terms in a self-paced reading experiment, again using Gernsbacher et al.'s stories. They tested *matching* words, which were Gernsbacher et al.'s original words (such as *guilt* for the story shown in example (1a) above); *matching synonyms*, which were words that were judged to be the closest synonyms to Gernsbacher et al.'s words; *matching similar* words, which were emotion terms with the same polarity as the matching words, although differing in several dimensions, but still rated (in Experiment 1b) as likely to occur; and *mismatched* words, which were Gernsbacher et al.'s perceived opposite emotions.

One of the materials used for Experiment 2 is shown below. After reading this material, different participants were given sentences containing the words *depressed* (matching), *miserable* (matching synonym), *useless* (matching similar) and *happy* (mismatched) and their reading times measured.

(3)   'How many things like this can happen in one day?' Don asked himself.
        First, he was beaten out of a new job by a younger man. If that wasn't
        enough, on the way home, he wrecked his car. Then, when he got home, he
        found out his wife wanted a divorce. All he could do was sit in his living
        room and stare into space.

Mismatched words yielded significant differences, but there were no significant differences between matching words, matching synonyms and matching
similar words.

Subsequently, Gygax et al. (2004) used longer passages (each with a few
extra sentences), which gave more detailed information about each character's state of mind, but without mentioning the key word. They showed that in
a rating experiment (Experiment 1), people's assessment of the protagonist's
likely emotion became better defined, although matching emotions were only
chosen 63% of the time (as opposed to 100%) for these longer passages,
compared to 49% with the shorter passages. More importantly, these differences had no effect on reading times (Experiment 2). In later experiments
(2004, Experiments 3 and 4), they re-designed the materials in order to
compel participants in each case to make emotional inferences to link
together different parts of a story which would be incoherent without the
inference. This may have some relevance for how readers make plot inferences in real stories. When it was necessary to make emotion inferences to
establish coherence (in contrast with reading the standard short materials), a
rating experiment (Experiment 3) showed that there was an increased likelihood of readers selecting specific emotion words. However, for a reading
time experiment of the same design (Experiment 4), there was no significant
difference for the three matching conditions.

Overall, these results are rather mixed. Gygax et al. (2004) concluded that
generally people do not infer specific emotions, but that they may be more likely
to do so with longer stories or when they need to do so to make inferences to
determine coherence. However, there are different interpretations of these
results. It is possible that individual readers may make specific inferences,
but that different readers may be making different specific inferences. For
example (2), we might imagine different readers interpreting the material using
different scenarios. If a reader sees the events as part of a suspense narrative in
the *Raiders of the Lost Ark* style, then being scared (one of the responses to (2))
might be possible, but this seems less likely for a story that is simply about a
professional archaeologist making an unusual discovery. Achieving consensus
on the nature of the emotion might perhaps depend less on the length of the
material than on clarifying the nature of the scenario, where different interpretations are possible. Gygax et al. (2004) acknowledged that individual differences provide a plausible explanation, but argued that an examination of their
reading time distributions does not support it for these experiments.

Another possible explanation, which Gygax et al. (2003, 2004) do not seem to consider, is that individual participants might make multiple specific emotion inferences. In example (3) above, parts of the material seem to suggest a possible interpretation of uselessness (e.g., wrecking his car), whereas other parts might suggest interpretations of miserableness/depression (e.g., staring into space). (The lack of distinction between the matching synonyms may be, though, because some of these really are largely indistinguishable in everyday speech, e.g., *happy* and *pleased* in the (2004) experiment.)

Gygax et al. (2004) used longer materials with 'the idea that readers need more contextual information to become more engaged in the text and consequently to infer the main character's goals and actions more specifically' (pp. 616–617). This makes sense in terms of exploring empirically whether specific emotions can be activated, but does not necessarily replicate real texts. Up to a point, it is a reasonable assumption that lengthier texts can build up additional background knowledge about a character and hence potentially increase commitment to that character. Nevertheless, short episodes and vignettes in real texts can, on occasion, have the potential to be extremely moving. In longer texts, a writer might sometimes reinforce a particular emotional message to direct readers (e.g., by use of foregrounding devices such as metaphors and repetition of emotion words) and might thereby place the focus on a specific emotion. This could, perhaps, achieve more specific responses than seen with the Gygax et al. materials. However, many highly literary texts rely on the opposite effect. One of the hallmarks of much literature is that it deals with very complex emotional states. Emotions may be presented in an ambiguous way by writers, or supposedly conflicting emotions may compete. In designing materials for psychological experiments, positive and negative emotions may be viewed as mutually exclusive, but in real texts, such emotions often intermingle. Even popular fiction, such as crime novels, can rely on such juxtapositions of conflicting emotions for character presentation and plot purposes. Hence, the way we respond emotionally to real narrative texts may ultimately depend on the nature of the writing.

Embodiment and affect

The reading time experiments in the previous section only show the time taken to integrate a verbal description of the emotions to produce a coherent representation of the text. The experiments do not tell us whether or not readers have any embodied representation of the feelings of the character. Rather than experiencing the emotion of the character, the experiments just show that people have knowledge of what the relevant emotion is, in terms of being able to label it. On the basis of this type of data, it could simply be the case that the inference made constitutes *cold cognition*, simple *knowledge* of how one might *describe* the emotion, which is completely different from *experiencing* an emotion. Recent work on the embodiment of emotion aims to address this issue by using different testing methods. With these empirical techniques, emotion embodiment effects can be observed even in the simplest materials. The effects that we will see constitute examples of hot cognition phenomena, in that they directly implicate affect itself, as felt, rather than simple knowledge of affect, in comprehension.

Demonstrating affect by means of compatibility effects

In Chapter 6, we saw examples where embodiment effects such as quasi-perceptual and motor action states could be induced by language. Likewise, it appears that actual emotional states can be induced when readers understand sentences that have emotional overtones. A good demonstration of this relies on a variant of the action–sentence compatibility effect (ACE), described in Chapter 6. Recall that the basic assumption of this work in relation to motor actions (Glenberg & Kaschak, 2002) was that readers mentally simulate actions when reading sentences. Hence, if readers encounter a sentence about a movement toward them, they will respond more quickly if they are asked to push a button that is positioned toward them rather than away from them. A real-life movement that is compatible with that of the mental simulation is easier than one that is incompatible. The same principle applies in research on emotion embodiment. In the context of language, Havas, Glenberg, and Rinck (2007) reasoned that if people were already in a negative emotional state, then it should be more difficult to process sentences having positive affect, since these would be incompatible if *actual emotion* was the result of reading the sentences. If the effects of prior emotional state actually interact with the processing of emotionally toned language input, then a hot cognition effect must underlie it. Similarly, if people were already in a positive emotional state, it should be harder to process negative emotion sentences. Examples of positive (4a) and negative (4b) affect sentences were:

(4a)   The college president announces your name, and you proudly step onto the stage.

(4b)   The police car pulls up behind you, siren blaring.

In order to get readers into a positive or negative emotional state, the experimenters utilized facial feedback by means of the simple pen-in-the-mouth induction procedure (e.g., Strack et al., 1988) before testing for compatibility effects by asking the participants to read emotionally toned sentences. Rather than creating a prior mood by asking participants to smile or frown, the induction procedure manipulates the facial muscles to produce this type of effect without the participants being aware of it. The induction technique involves holding a pen in the mouth using only the teeth to induce upward-turned lips, which in turn brings about positive affect in the person doing it. As we saw earlier, feedback from the position of the muscles is interpreted as an affective response by the brain. In contrast, holding the pen only in the lips induces a frown, which in turn gives rise to negative affect.

Participants in Havas et al.'s (2007) research were asked to hold the pen in either lips or teeth during which time they were presented with sentences for evaluation. There were two main experiments. In the first, they were asked to press buttons to indicate whether the sentences were 'pleasant' or 'unpleasant'. The results showed that when the pen-induced affect matched that of the sentence, judgements were faster, indicating a compatibility effect. In a second experiment, subjects were asked simply to say whether the presented sentences were easy or hard to understand, thus removing the relevance of emotion from the task. Even so, similar results were obtained. Thus it appears that the emotional tone of the sentence was an implicit part of understanding it, even when there was no need to appreciate the emotional tone. This in turn suggests that affect is automatically represented for sentences with affective valence, and that affect is represented in a common system whether it is 'pen' induced or language induced.

Another line of enquiry stemmed from observed effects of blocking facial mimicry on the ease of recognizing emotional expressions on people's faces. Basically, if the pen-in-the-lips manipulation (the one which induces a frown) is carried out, then recognizing happy faces is compromised (Oberman, Winkielman, & Ramachandran, 2007). Applying this logic to sentence processing, Havas, Glenberg, Gutowski, Lucarelli, and Davidson (2010) used whole sentences depicting positive or negative events, similar to (4a) and (4b) above, and explored the consequences for muscles that are active during the expression of positive and negative feeling. Positive sentences led to activity in the muscle group responsible for smiling (zygomaticus), and negative sentences led to activity in the corrugator muscle (responsible for frowning). The most interesting manipulation directly incapacitated the muscle responsible for frowning, the corrugator, which made it more difficult to comprehend negative affect sentences. Havas et al. (2010) tested participants who received a treatment of botulinum toxin (botox) which reduces frown lines on the forehead. People were tested for reading times for sentences with positive and negative affect before the treatment, and after two weeks when the toxin prevented them from being able to frown (because corrugator activity was blocked). At this stage, reading times for negative sentences showed a statistically significant increase, while times for positive sentences showed no such increase. The explanation is that understanding a negative affect sentence is made more difficult if the muscle responsible for a concomitant of understanding that sentence – frowning – is compromised. This is provided as evidence that brain events leading to the muscle response are an automatic part of comprehending the affective polarity of sentences.

An EEG study lends support for the view that induced emotion interacts with the processing of emotional language, offering further support for a hot cognition embodiment effect. Pratt and Kelly (2008) induced positive and negative affect in participants by discussing with them fabricated printouts of the participants' EEG records. One printout showed a very noisy, disorganized EEG pattern, and was explained to the participants as meaning that the person might not be suitable for the experiment because they might be stressed or anxious. Such manipulated feedback is known to induce mood-states, in this case negative (Anshel, 1988; Nummenmaa & Niemi, 2004). The other type of record showed a very smooth, clear EEG record, described as meaning the participant was 'ideal' for the experiment; this induced a positive mood. Following the manipulation, mood was checked by questionnaire. Then participants saw a series of words, which were positive (e.g., *kindness*) or negative (e.g., *hatred*). They had to judge whether the words were positive or negative on each presentation. Pratt and Kelly found that ERP electrodes in frontal scalp regions of the brain distinguished positive and negative words around 400 ms after the stimulus had been presented. There was a larger N400 for positive words compared to negative words in the frontal electrode region when participants were in a positive, but not negative, mood. These findings demonstrate that people process affective language differently when in positive and negative moods, and lend support to recent views that emotion and cognition interact during language comprehension.

The embodiment effects described above indicate a fairly direct involvement of mood in the comprehension of positively or negatively valenced statements. But note that the stimuli are expressed in the second person, and as we saw in Chapter 7, such a presentation style tends to cause the reader to adopt a personal perspective during processing them. In the next section, we shall see evidence to suggest embodiment effects with other perspectives.

Affect, compatibility effects and irony

There is some earlier work that is also consistent with embodiment effects, but somewhat less directly. This research involves third person depictions. The effects are interesting, partly because they have been used recently to investigate the possibility that irony can be used to intensify emotive impact. The background to this study is as follows. In social psychological work on the automatic encoding of affect, some investigators have found that participants liked stimuli more when their arms were performing an action like moving something toward them (Cacioppo, Priester, & Berntson, 1993; Förster & Strack, 1996; Solarz, 1960), the argument being that if something constitutes an approach movement, then the object being approached is literally seen as more approachable and affectively positive. Chen and Bargh (1999) conjectured that the reverse causal pattern would be true: automatic evaluation of something as positive or negative would automatically facilitate approach (toward) movements, or avoidance (away) movements. They were asked to classify words as good or bad in meaning, using 'toward' and 'away' movements of a lever. Reaction times were shorter for 'toward' movements for positive words compared to negative, and were shorter for making 'away' movements for negative words compared to positive. These effects are consistent with an embodied reaction to negative and positive stimuli.

Some more recent work has built on these observations, leading to an examination of the affective component of irony. Filik, Hunter, and Leuthold (2009) presented people with positive and negative valence sentence pairs, in which the final word (indicated with our added underlining) reinforced the affect:

(5a)   *Positive valence*
         George had just found out that he had been promoted.
         He celebrated his <u>success</u>.

(5b)   *Negative valence*
         Susan heard that Roger had cheated on her.
         She immediately filed for <u>divorce</u>.

Materials were presented one word at a time, and after half a second, the final word changed from white to blue or green. This was used as a cue to indicate that people should either move a slider toward themselves, or away, as quickly as possible. They showed that if the sentences were of positive valence, then moving toward was facilitated, while for negative valence, the opposite was true. To get this effect, the whole passage had to be presented. Simply presenting the last word by itself had no such effect.

On the basis of this, irony was explored by means of sentence pairs like (6a–d):

(6a)   *Non-ironic – positive*
         John finished the race way ahead of the other competitors.
         His friend laughed and said to him, 'You are so <u>fast</u>!'

(6b)   *Non-ironic – negative*
         John finished the race way behind the other competitors.
         His friend laughed and said to him, 'You are so <u>slow</u>!'

(6c)   *Ironic – negative (criticism)*
         John finished the race way behind the other competitors.
         His friend laughed and said to him, 'You are so <u>fast</u>!'

(6d)   *Ironic – positive (praise)*
        John finished the race way ahead of the other competitors.
        His friend laughed and said to him, 'You are so <u>slow</u>!'

They found that there was a very strong compatibility effect for the irony manipulation, but a statistically insignificant one for the simple manipulation. The authors concluded that there is a weak compatibility effect for simple affectively valenced statements, but a much stronger effect for ironic statements. Clearly irony is a case of double perspective, as discussed in Chapter 3, but how the strength of affective effects relates to single versus double perspective in general remains to be seen, although the work of Filik et al. (2009) is promising in this respect.

Gender differences in emotional responses

Application of similar methodologies has produced interesting results suggesting a gender difference in style of emotional responding. Mouilso, Glenberg, Havas, and Lindeman (2007) tested the idea that women and men would differ in their preparation for action as a result of encountering emotional material. The logic was that moving a lever in an 'away' direction with force corresponds to an aggressive state, while pulling a lever toward the body is consistent with an affiliative response. The argument was that women would be more likely to be prepared for affiliative responses, while men would be more prepared for aggressive responses. Participants were presented with sentences that depicted sad and angry situations, or neutral sentences, as well as strings of words that did not make sense. They had to decide whether each presentation made sense or not. Half of the time, a *yes* answer required an 'away' movement ('aggressive' response), and half of the time it required a 'toward' response ('affiliative'). The findings were that, following angry sentences, the 'away' responses were facilitated, but only for men. In contrast, following sad sentences, the 'toward' responses were facilitated, but only for women. These data are interesting, but again show the broadness of the category of elicited 'away' and 'toward' responses. Nevertheless, the findings do fit the idea that aggression is somewhat enhanced in males, while sympathy and affiliation is enhanced in females. Certainly, there is some evidence that, on average, men and women differ in certain ways in how they respond to emotional stimuli. For example, presented with depictions of negative stimuli, such as loss, pollution and illness, women responded with greater defensive reactions, including stronger negative facial displays, heart rate deceleration, and increased startle responses than did men (Bradley, Codispoti, Sabatinelli, & Lang, 2001).

Another study indirectly tested the idea that women are more likely to react with fear to certain situations, and men more likely to react with anger and aggression. Wallbott (1988) presented clips of actors, and participants were requested to guess the emotion being portrayed. For emotions of sadness and fear, recognition accuracy was greatest for the women actors, while anger was more accurately recognized in male actors. It is important to recognize that the gender differences that we are discussing are in the main small, and that men and women tend to respond in very similar ways to most situations. However, the differences are statistically significant, and should be highlighted as a possible source of preferences in reading literature, and of patterns of reaction to depicted situations.

Glenberg, Webster, Mouilso, Havas, and Lindeman (2009) examined gender differences in reactions to depictions of various situations within the embodiment framework. The studies utilized the observations from the ACE effects that being in an emotional state congruent with sentence content facilitates sentence comprehension. Men and women read sentences that depicted different emotions, such as:

(7a)   You shout at the pushy telemarketer who had the nerve to call during dinner. [Angry]

(7b)   You see a cat running across the street too late to avoid hitting it with your car. [Sad]

(7c)   Your lover chases you playfully around your bedroom. [Happy]

Reading times for the sentences showed that angry sentences were read slower than sad ones (of corresponding length) for both males and females, but that this difference was reduced in the male group.

A subsequent experiment was based on the idea that if an emotional state has a strong representation, then it will take longer to shift to a new emotional state. In terms of reading times, if a woman reads a sad sentence before reading a happy sentence, the time to read the happy sentence should be longer than if the previous sentence was also a happy one. Also, if a man reads an angry sentence, then a subsequent happy sentence should take longer to read than if it followed another happy sentence. Finally, these predictions should not hold for the other gender. This is precisely what was found. Thus the data support the view that emotional state has a direct effect on language comprehension, and that in men responses to anger are strong relative to women, while in women, responses to sad depictions are stronger.

These data suggest that there are some fairly basic differences between males and females in terms of emotional responding. However, it must be understood that none of it suggests that males are never sympathetic and affiliative, or that females are never aggressive in their responses to affect-ively charged sentences. Rather, it is just that these responses appear to be exaggerated in different ways in males and females.

Returning to the issue of embodied emotion during reading, the findings are encouraging for the idea that there is a real affective experience brought out by language. One might question whether the experience of affect in response to encountering an affective sentence is a necessary part of under-standing the sentence. Affect is not part of the denotation of sentences like (4b) above, and so on a classical semantics is not part of the meaning of the sentence. Yet at the utterance level (spoken or written) it can be a major part of interpretation. The answer may lie in depth of processing: the more the context in which an utterance occurs focusses on the emotional content, perhaps the more likely it is that the embodiment effect will occur. There is virtually no evidence about this in relation to emotion at the time of writing. However, a report by Niedenthal (2007) makes an interesting initial connec-tion between deep and shallow processing and embodiment effects with emotional words. She reports a study in which participants had to make simple judgements about single words. In the shallow processing condition, participants simply had to judge whether the words were printed in upper or lower case. In the deep processing condition, they had to judge whether the word was related to an emotion. Emotion words generated emotion-specific facial activation only in the deep condition, where emotion information was most relevant. This study is interesting, being one of few demonstrations that it is not mere exposure to the word that leads to a bodily response, but rather, it is evaluating the word at an appropriate level that leads to it. The other, to reflect back to Chapter 6, was the study by Raposo, Moss, Stamatakis, and Tyler (2009), showing that an action word occurring in an idiomatic context does not induce the same kind of lexically related neural activity as the word in use in an action context.

Interim summary: emotion and reading

The work discussed so far in this chapter presents two very different, but not incompatible, approaches. Readers need to make judgements about the emo-tional states of characters, whether or not they share these states. The work of Gernsbacher et al. (1992), Gernsbacher and Robertson (1992) and Gygax et al. (2003, 2004) shows how readers can attribute emotions to characters even when no explicit mention of emotion is made. This means that readers appear to be including information about the emotions of characters in their mental representations, a finding which has significance for mental modelling approaches such as situation models and text world theory. The work on embodiment and emotions by researchers such as Havas et al. (2007) has the rather different aim of examining whether emotion is actually felt by readers. Even the very simple materials used in these experiments show evidence of embodiment effects. Thus, in a real sense, there is an involvement of the emotion system in reading emotional material (hot cognition), rather than the utilization of stereotyped knowledge of emotions (cold cognition). The findings are fairly basic at the time of writing, and there has been virtually no consideration of the modulating influences of foregrounding, such as may be found with natural discourse. However, what has been found is promising for future research.

Empathy: an introduction

The capacity to infer emotion, and to feel how another person might feel, in some sense, is fundamental to the notion of empathy, and empathy is a topic that holds a central place in some conceptions of narrative. In this section, we offer a brief exploration of the notion generally, then examine its significance in humanities work on narrative. We then move on to examine empirical work on empathy in the following section.

Key notions

Empathy is typically regarded as the capacity to share the experiences and feelings of others, often characterized as the ability to put oneself in the shoes of another person. However, the whole notion is more complex than this simple characterization (see Decety & Ickes, 2011, for a review).

At the most basic level, it can mean simply a parallel experience of an automatic nature, which may be physical and/or emotional. Davis (2007) includes the apparently innate tendency of newborn babies to cry on hearing another cry, and also motor mimicry, where an individual imitates another's movements, as when gestures and body position are reflected in conversational participants or when we flinch at an object hitting or about to hit another person. 'Mimicry' in this sense is not a deliberate replication of movements, but an unconscious echoing of another person's actions or anticipated response. The concept of emotional contagion (Hatfield, Cacioppo, & Rapson, 1993) describes the automatic mimicking of another person's moods or emotions, such as when we feel depressed when a friend in our presence is also depressed, or when a crowd's emotion becomes heightened as each person feeds off the emotions of the others. Unlike role-taking described below, there may be no real understanding of the other person's situation, since the response is a purely automatic emulation of emotion. Beyond mimicry, Schmitt and Clark (2007, p. 469) use the term 'physical empathy' for cases which involve 'a painful sensation such as one might feel when viewing another's deplorable surroundings or evidence of severe bodily suffering'.

By contrast, empathy proper may be an 'advanced cognitive process', according to Davis (1994, 2007), if it includes some assessment by an observer of another individual's situation, that is, how their emotions and actions are situated. He argues that this can cover role-taking, which may involve imagining another's perspective to the extent that the observer's own egocentric perspective is suppressed. However, he suggests that on other occasions, it may be that the observer is triggering similar relevant memories of their own, without any need for the observer to suppress their own perspective. Davis (2007) points to research by Batson, Early, and Salvarani (1997) which supports these differences. When instructed to observe a distressed person in a film, there was less discomfort on the part of the observer if they were told to imagine how that other person was feeling than if they were asked to imagine themselves in the same situation. Davis et al. (2004) reported that 'imagine self' instructions led to more reports of self-related thoughts than if participants were asked to imagine how another person was feeling.

Davis (2007) distinguishes between parallel emotions and reactive emotions, both of which may result from empathy. For parallel emotions, the observer replicates the target's feelings (unconsciously or consciously), whereas for reactive emotions, the observer has an affective response which may be different from the target's own but nevertheless is a reaction to the target's state (e.g., compassion or discomfort at a distressed target). This corresponds to the idea that empathy may be *with* or *for* a target (Zillmann, 2006a). Sometimes the response may be purely cognitive rather than affective, being a judgement of the target's state of mind, rather than an emotional reaction (Davis, 2007; Schmitt & Clark, 2007).

Zillmann (2006a) claims that empathy may involve observing another person's expressive response (facial/bodily expressions, actions, etc.) but may also anticipate such a response based on an assessment of circumstances. Even when directly witnessing a response, circumstances may also need to be taken into account to judge the nature of that other person's state of mind due to the potential ambiguity of expressions. Conversely, the same circumstances can be reacted to in different ways by different individuals, so expressions can also clarify the nature of the response to the situation.

For Zillmann (2006a), emotional reactions must be 'hedonically concordant' to be classified as empathy, meaning, for example, that we respond to joy with joy, or pain with pain, not the opposites. Although terms such as 'negative empathy' and 'counter-empathy' are used for non-concordant cases, Zillmann argues that these are confusing because this suggests that there is some empathetic response, whereas in fact there is an absence of empathy in these cases. Hence, he refers to observers responding 'anti-empathetically' in non-concordant situations. He also thinks that moral judgement underpins empathy. This means that we may feel positive emotions for a liked individual who succeeds, but not a disliked one who succeeds. We will explore this further in discussing relevant empirical work on empathy below.

Zillmann (2006a) points out that there can be mixed responses from an observer to a situation. He gives the example of an observer watching a disliked individual fall off a bicycle. The automatic reaction may be to cringe at the fall, which would be physical empathy in Schmitt and Clark's terms. If the observer believes him-/herself to be unobserved there might then be an anti-empathetic response with some feeling of pleasure at the misfortune of another ('schadenfreude'), a positive sensation at seeing the disliked individual fall. However, if the observer is observed by others, then any expression of glee would normally be drowned out by what Zillmann terms 'dispositional override', a suppression of the response, although there might still be some inner feeling of glee. If the disliked individual turned out to be seriously injured, then a further dispositional override might create pity and this might be regarded as empathy.

Empathy is generally identified as being different from sympathy (e.g., Feagin, 1996), although there is in fact considerable overlap. Schmitt and Clark (2007) see empathy as a prerequisite for sympathy, if we interpret empathy in the broad way described above. Sympathy does not necessarily require any sharing of the emotions of another person, but it does require some understanding of the consequences of a situation for an individual. So a counsellor might not share the emotions of a bereaved person, in terms of feeling any grief, but might be expected to provide some expression of sympathy and recognize the bereaved person's special circumstances. Studies of sympathy focus heavily on the overt expression of sentiment and concern (genuine or otherwise), which is viewed as a way of maintaining and developing social cohesion (e.g., Schmitt & Clark, 2007). Nevertheless, some models of empathy also include such interaction and also practical responses such as altruism and the decrease in negative emotions (e.g., Davis', 2007, 'interpersonal outcomes' and Hoffman's, 2008, 'prosocial behavior'; see also Keen, 2007). We will return to this topic in the next chapter, when we consider the effects of reading in terms of possible real-world consequences.

Empathy for characters in real narratives

Empathy is of central importance in the understanding of many real narratives (Feagin, 1996; Keen, 2007), since such involvement on the part of the reader may provide a key motivation for reading. Empathy creates interest in the characters and their future actions, and it can reinforce a distinction between different types of characters (e.g., major and minor, heroes and villains).

In order to create empathy for a character, a writer will generally need first to communicate information about that character's emotional state, as discussed earlier in this chapter. However, there may be cases where characters are themselves unaware of the situation inducing empathy and are not displaying emotion. Zillmann (2006b) points out that it is possible to empathize with characters who are oblivious to their special circumstances. Zillmann refers to an example from a Hitchcock film where characters are walking, unaware, toward an open manhole. Zillmann suggests that we may feel anticipatory fear on their behalf and that this could be classed as empathy *for* them (as opposed to *with* them). Of course, what we feel may be a reflection of simulating falling in an anticipatory way. Another possibility is that we simply do not know whether a character is experiencing emotion or not because this is not directly reported to us (e.g., if the character's response is underspecified or the character is absent from the scene). In such cases, empathy may be based entirely on our assessment of the situation affecting the character. A combination of these factors may also be possible, i.e., we feel joy or concern for a distant individual who is not yet aware of good or bad news.

One issue that has particularly concerned researchers in literary studies is that of whether a reader's ability to empathize is facilitated by sharing the characteristics of the character (see, for example, Stockwell, 2009). We will term this 'autobiographical alignment' (the term 'identification' is common, but this is used in so many different ways, that we will not adopt it here). There is sometimes an assumption that readers who have the same autobiographical characteristics as characters may be able to relate better to these characters. Up to a point, this may be true. We might see shared background in terms of gender, age, race, ethnic and religious groups, etc. as providing topic interest (Campion, Martins, & Wilhelm, 2009), since the interests and concerns of the protagonist might overlap with those of the reader (e.g., dieting, clothes and finding a partner might be of particular relevance to single female readers of Helen Fielding's *Bridget Jones's Diary*). Readers might also find role-taking easier if they have previously experienced particular circumstances or can imagine being in a similar situation in the future. (We will look at empirical work which attempts to gauge the significance of this type of connection in the next chapter.) Nevertheless, if narratives depended on autobiographical alignment, it would be difficult to explain female interest in books with an all-male character list, such as William Golding's *Lord of the Flies*. Indeed, as Keen (2007) points out, readers may even feel empathy for characters who are non-human, such as the rabbits in Richard Adams' *Watership Down*. Literary specialists often point to the universal themes of great works, meaning that they deal with topics which are supposedly common to humanity in general, such as love, fear, striving, etc. In these circumstances, autobiographical alignment may depend on a much looser type of connection, where a situation in a narrative is seen to echo a similar experience in the reader's real life, by stripping away surface features of both and matching essential characteristics (Schank, 1999).

As we discussed earlier, moral judgement is important in determining whether empathy will occur in real-life situations. In reading, there are several stages at which moral aspects are important. One issue is the moral stance of readers prior to reading, since this may determine how readers will evaluate stories, and the moral judgements that they may make. J. K. Rowling's *Harry Potter* stories, for example, which have been very popular, have nevertheless prompted protests from conservative Christian groups in the United States who are morally opposed to any representation of witchcraft (DelFattore, 2002). We will see recent empirical work on moral stance in the next section.

A second issue is the way we respond to good and bad characters in a story, such as heroes and villains. As we will see shortly, moral approval influences how a reader might empathize with a character. This may match well with plot structures in popular fiction, such as thrillers, where the presentation of characters is heavily polarized, but literary works often rely on highly complex presentations of moral issues. In such cases, we may be presented with characters who are partially flawed and/or who may behave reprehensibly, but whom we are encouraged to view positively overall, since the writer pushes us toward downplaying the deficits or taking special account of mitigating situational factors (e.g., Booth, 1991; Stockwell, 2009, p. 166). A reader's assessment of complex characters may also change over the course of a story, as the characters' personalities develop, as the perspective shifts to allow us to enter into the inner worlds of different characters, or as new plot information is revealed to us. Moreover, great literature may present moral dilemmas where there is a mixed empathetic response to a character. For example, we may feel some loyalty to a character on the basis of their earlier close portrayal in a story, but subsequently have grounds for moral repugnance (e.g., the portrayal of Hanna in Bernhard Schlink's (2008) *The Reader*). A consideration of literature therefore moves us beyond a notion of characters filling simple good/bad slots in a plot, to the idea that a writer may present characters in a way which may reflect the moral problems that readers encounter in their real lives, hence explaining why readers feel that literature has relevance to their real lives.

A third issue of interest is the possible moral consequence of empathizing with characters. Empathy researchers (e.g., Zillmann, 2006a) suggest that we tend to feel greater empathy for individuals who are close to us rather than distant. Narratives can give us accounts of individuals who might normally appear quite outside our normal scope of experience and bring them closer to us, hence potentially broadening our range of empathetic experience. This raises the question of whether readers can be morally changed by reading, in ways which may be judged either positively or negatively. These possible moral effects are much disputed. We will discuss the debate on the effects of empathy in the next chapter.

Mind, brain and empathy

There is ample evidence that the observation of others performing actions or experiencing sensations activates the representation of actions or sensations in the observer. As we have noted, these effects may be a matter of degree. For instance, the evidence presented in Chapter 6 showed that to imagine oneself in a pain-inducing situation activates the secondary somatosensory cortex involved in the actual perception of pain. Observing pain in others may have less effect, but certainly activates some of the brain circuitry involved in experiencing pain inflicted on ourselves. Similarly, the observation of a disgusted face is sufficient to engender activity in the part of the brain of the observer that is responsible for mediating disgust (Wicker et al., 2003).

In general, the observation of such simulation effects over a wide range of situations suggests a good basis for understanding what someone else is feeling. Indeed, such a view has been promoted for a very long time. Importantly, however, simulation can only take us so far in understanding empathetic reactions, as the earlier discussion suggested. When narratives depict the good and the evil in the form of characters, it is to be expected that a reader's moral stance and attitude toward the protagonist will play a role in their reaction as a reader. There is some evidence that automatic appraisal of conventional morality occurs, that morally relevant information is actively sought, and that a reader's reaction can influence the flow of inferential activities that occur during reading. There are several other interesting issues: for instance, can and do readers empathize with characters even if these characters are portrayed as behaving reprehensibly?

Reactions based on a normative moral framework

Recent evidence suggests that morally based judgements during reading occur very rapidly, and are automatic. Murphy, Wilde, Ogden, Barnard, and Calder (2009) carried out an experiment investigating the use of knowledge of morality during the reading of stories that bring into focus moral issues. Stories were presented to readers a line at a time using self-paced reading, enabling reading times for critical sentences to be measured. A typical story consisted of a portrayal of a young wife who, being alone with her husband's best friend, notices that he is attractive. She has the opportunity to seduce him. The target sentence portrayed her thinking about it and either deciding that it would be the right thing to do (moral mismatch) or the wrong thing to do (moral match). Reading times were longer for the moral mismatch cases.

A second part of the manipulation was to have readers carry out a secondary task, to manipulate processing load, while reading. 'No-load' participants simply read the materials. 'Low-load' participants attempted to remember a string of three letters (e.g., S-D-V) presented at the start of each passage, while 'High-load participants' attempted to remember a six-digit sequence (e.g., 372815). The idea was that only an automatic process would survive the high-load situation (e.g., Bargh & Chartrand, 2000; Bargh & Tota, 1988). While the high-load case caused an increase in reading time, it did not affect the difference between the fit and misfit to morality targets. So, Murphy et al. (2009) conclude that moral processing is not made on the basis of principled logical reasoning, but rather that automatic responses are used in making (at least initial) moral judgements. We should perhaps caution against drawing the conclusion that people are inherently moral: what is happening in this experiment is that people are having to accept a sentence that reflects a moral norm (for instance, committing adultery is not the right thing to do). This is equivalent to verifying a normal observation (like judging *a waiter brings a menu* to be a normal thing to happen in a restaurant), and really does not address deeper issues of what moral judgements a reader actually makes. However, several other pieces of work implicate moral judgement proper, as we will go on to examine.

Clashes of moral stance: evidence from ERPs

A somewhat more direct test of the early involvement of a person's moral stance in processing ethically loaded statements comes from a study using the N400 component of ERPs as an index of processing. Van Berkum, Holleman, Nieuwland, Otten, and Murre (2009) had people make judgements of the acceptability of statements like these:

(8a)   I think euthanasia is an {acceptable/unacceptable} course of action.

(8b)   Watching TV to relax is {wrong/fine} in my opinion.

(8c)   If my child were homosexual, I'd find this {hard/easy} to accept.

The research was conducted in The Netherlands and the critical statements were designed to either be consistent with or clash with the moral values of members of a relatively strict Dutch Christian party. Two groups of people read the statements, referred to by van Berkum et al. (2009) as the strict Christian (SC) group, and the non-Christian (NC) group. The two groups were expected to have very different views.

The results showed that for both groups, the words that clashed with their moral stances led to an early (approximately 200 ms) positive wave effect in the ERP, and also to a small N400 effect. Van Berkum et al. view this as evidence for an early effect of moral stance on processing meaning, since moral stance information shows an interaction with meaning processing as soon as 200 ms after the occurrence of the word that violated the attitude. In addition there was an enhanced late positive potential for words that clashed with values, an effect that has been associated with emotional valence (negative or positive), by Cacioppo, Crites, Berntson, and Coles (1993). So, the results show that moral stance affects processing very rapidly, and has a slightly later effect reflecting the emotional reaction to the match or mismatch of values and the statement of content.

Processing the reprehensible: using and seeking motivations

Recent work using brain imaging provides a rather more sophisticated angle on the immediacy of bringing in the moral judgement dimension during reading. This evidence strongly supports the idea that when we read of someone doing something that would be typically judged as bad, we immediately attempt to discern their knowledge and motivation, providing the basis of making a moral judgement about their behaviour. As discussed earlier, work using fMRI found particular areas to be involved when stories are read that depict a character's mental state. The same regions that appear to support Theory of Mind knowledge in contexts that have nothing to do with moral judgements per se are also recruited, but show stronger effects when explicit statements about an agent's beliefs are provided, enabling the judgement of the moral status of some related action (Young, Cushman, Hauser, & Saxe, 2007; Young & Saxe, 2008). For instance, one material used by Young et al. (2007) involved a character who either knowingly or unknowingly poisoned a friend by putting in her coffee a toxic white substance which was either thought to be sugar or known to be dangerous. Clearly, the moral judgement that the character is behaving reprehensibly depends upon the reader's recognition of the character's knowledge at the time of the action (see Baird & Astington, 2004, for a fuller discussion from a developmental perspective). The fact that recognized brain areas supporting the representation of an agent's state of mind become active during reading consolidates this picture.

Young and Saxe (2009) used these findings as a basis to examine a more subtle question. This is: when an agent causes something to happen which is, or could have been, a bad thing, do readers automatically question that agent's prior knowledge, so as to be able to make a moral attribution? Indeed, they found that in the absence of prior information, the same brain areas were activated as with the situation where the prior knowledge of the agent was explicitly stated in situations where moral judgements were relevant. Where outcomes had no perceivable moral content, however, there was no such effect. Although this work makes the assumption that the activation of particular brain areas is associated with a particular psychological process (the so-called 'reverse inference'; see Poldrack, 2006), this work is extremely suggestive. Furthermore, in the absence of behavioural data on the issues of spontaneous search for an agent's prior knowledge in morally loaded situations, the data represent the best analysis to date.

Induced reader attitudes and processing: participatory responses

An important part of our experience as readers of fictional narrative is to react to the frustrations and dangers that unfold as we read, with these attitudes often depending on our moral stance. Allbritton and Gerrig (1991) introduced the idea of *participatory responses*, or *p-responses*, to describe reader reactions to situations being depicted in narratives. These reactions include hopes and fears for the characters. So, if danger is imminent for a protagonist, a reader might well wish the protagonist to escape the situation. For instance, in a short story Polichak and Gerrig (2002) discuss, a young boxer, portrayed in heroic terms, goes down hard in a match. At that point, a p-response may occur in which the reader mentally wills the boxer to 'Get up and win!' On the other hand, if a villain looks likely to succeed at some nefarious activity, then the reader may very actively and consciously wish this not to happen.

Gerrig and his colleagues (Allbritton & Gerrig, 1991; Gerrig, 1993; Polichak & Gerrig, 2002; Rapp & Gerrig, 2006) have carried out a number of experiments to investigate whether p-responses are in fact made during reading, and what impact they have on text processing. Consider Allbritton and Gerrig's (1991) case where a character is rushing to catch a plane in order to get to a job interview. In a *positive outcome* case, the outcome to fit the requirement is that of catching the plane. A *positive preference* on the part of an involved reader for the outcome of catching the plane would be engendered if the protagonist, Margaret, were running late, and hoping to make the plane. But a *negative preference* on the part of the reader would be engendered if the story introduced a fact that, unknown to Margaret, the plane was inadequately looked after, and would plunge into the sea after take-off. In contrast, consider a *negative outcome* case, for instance, where it is made clear at the outset that Margaret did in fact miss the plane. In this case, a positive preference (p-response) for her catching the plane is in conflict with the actual negative outcome. By the same logic, where it turns out that the plane was doomed to crash, a negative preference as a p-response would be congruent with the actual negative outcome. Experiments using materials of this type showed that where there was a mismatch between the preference and outcome, participants were slower to respond when asked to verify what outcome had occurred in the story, showing an influence of the p-response on text processing.

In another set of studies Rapp and Gerrig (2006) systematically manipulated the likelihood of an outcome occurring as a story unfolded, and independently manipulated the desirability of the outcome, considering what we might take to be normal moral judgements. An example given by these authors concerns the question of whether a character will win a Senate Race. A context can either make it probable that he will win the race or probable that he will lose, as in:

(9a)   The New York Times put his efficient campaign several points ahead in its final poll. [Success-biasing context]

(9b)   The New York Times put his lackluster campaign several points behind in its final poll. [Failure-biasing context]

Over a set of materials, it was shown that these biasing contexts worked, in that people judged the outcomes as likely success or failure.

The other variable was to engender a reader desire for success or failure, based in this example on moral issues:

(10a)   Charles worked hard to help the underprivileged and underrepresented have a voice in government. [Reader desire for success]

(10b)   Charles was corrupt, taking bribes and giving favours to companies that polluted the environment. [Reader desire for failure]

In one investigation, participants were presented with each story, the first sentence of which was a statement inducing desire in the reader for success or failure, followed by a success- or failure-biasing statement. Finally, there was an outcome sentence (e.g., *Charles was elected / not elected*). The task was to press a key indicating *yes*, if they agreed that the outcome 'would happen next', or *no* if they thought it would not. Participants did respond *yes* more often than *no* to outcomes that matched the biasing context. However, and most interesting, this effect was modified by the reader-desire status. Where reader desire did not match the outcome, the rate of *yes* responses was lower than where it did. This is clear evidence for the involvement of p-responses in reading the passages, because preference interferes with judgement of likelihood of an inference.

These results could mean that what one wishes were the case interferes directly with one's capacity to reason about how likely an outcome will be (a loss of rationality). Alternatively, and perhaps more plausibly, the results could reflect a difference in selectively attending to different sources of information. Probably what makes us judge a plausible inference as likely is our concentrating on those aspects of the situation that would bring about the plausible outcome. Kahneman, Slovic, and Tversky (1982) have studied the basis of making likelihood judgements extensively, and they showed that the availability of information supporting an outcome directly influences the judgement that an outcome is probable (Tversky & Kahneman, 1973). The availability of information can be altered by focussing on particular things. For example, Kahneman, Krueger, Schkade, Schwarz, and Stone (2006) investigated people's judgements of whether they thought they would be happier if they were richer. They found that when people consider the impact of any single factor on their well-being, they are prone to exaggerate its importance – what they call a 'focussing illusion'. In the present context, it is possible that a clash between desire and a plausible outcome results in the plausible outcome being considered from the point of view of desire, and so desire modifies a judgement of plausibility.

A further experiment by Rapp and Gerrig (2006) used reading times as an index of processing. This technique allowed a test of whether desire actually influenced the time-course of accepting a plausible inference. Obviously, if the p-response is at loggerheads with what is normally considered important in accepting a plausible inference, then the plausible inference should take longer to integrate into the reader's representation of what happened than if there were no clash. Rather than make an explicit judgement, readers simply read the passages one line at a time, using self-paced reading. When an outcome matched the initial bias, reading times were faster than if it did not. However, a further major finding was that when an outcome did not match reader desire, reading times were elevated over when it did. This shows again that p-responses occur, and that they create difficulties for the integration of sentences when an outcome is portrayed, even if it has a high pragmatic likelihood based on real-world knowledge. This study is very convincing, showing that what the reader *wants to happen* momentarily interferes with understanding what is *actually* likely to happen. At once, we can see that p-responses are a reality, and affect processing quite directly.

Perceived fairness and altruistic punishment

Moral judgement has been studied quite extensively in relation to the perception of fairness, using neuroscience methods. What happens when bad outcomes occur for characters whom we perceive as being fair in their behaviour, compared to those whom we perceive as being unfair? Do we empathize to the same extent with people whom we perceive as being unfair? Obviously, one might be able to appreciate the point of view of an individual who appears unfair, despite one's p-responses. However, one's reactions when something bad befalls a person who is behaving reprehensibly might well be different from those occurring when something bad happens to a person who is, say, a victim in a story. This issue has been examined in real contexts in work on so-called *altruistic punishment*. The theory of altruistic punishment (e.g., Boyd, Gintis, Bowles, & Richerson, 2003; Fehr & Gächter, 2002) is based on the idea that when a person breaks some norm of behaviour, then people will be effectively rewarded by seeing that person punished. The punishment of such behaviour is seen as a way of maintaining the coherence of society. The altruistic component comes in because it is further assumed that a person may punish another in this way, and find it rewarding, even though it may be costly in some way to that individual to do so (the philosophy of 'this hurts me more than it hurts you'). It is thus altruistic with respect to society.

These ideas were used to motivate a study of the effects of perceived fairness in others on empathy, using brain-imaging methods. Singer et al. (2006) measured brain responses using fMRI of individuals empathizing with individuals whom they either liked or disliked. Liking and disliking was manipulated by having the participant and experimental confederates play a complex investment bargaining game. The confederates could engender either trust or mistrust in themselves by the other player, the participant in the experiment, by playing in a fair or unfair way. This manipulation led participants to like or dislike a confederate.

Having induced the like/dislike pattern, the participants' brain responses to pain induced in themselves, in the liked confederate, and in the disliked confederate, were measured. Pain was induced electrically on the back of the hands of each of the three people involved. A cue indicated to the participant which of the three would be stimulated on each of a short run of trials. In this way, it was possible to compare the participant's reaction to receiving the stimulation with reactions in the participant to seeing the painful stimulus applied to the liked or disliked confederate.

Empathy-related activation occurred in the pain-related brain areas (insula, anterior cingulate cortex) when the stimulus was applied to the liked confederate. This is in line with the research reported in Chapter 6. However, for the disliked confederate, this effect was considerably reduced in the male participants, suggesting a lack of empathetic responding contingent upon whether the confederate was liked or not. However, it is interesting to note that this reduction was *only* evident in the male group, and was virtually absent for the female participants. On this evidence at least, the effect of perceived fairness of a confederate did not modulate brain responses in the female group.

Further observations within the altruistic punishment framework were made with respect to the reward aspect. Singer et al. examined brain activity in the areas known to be associated with reward processing (the ventral striatum/nucleus accumbens and orbitofrontal cortex; see, e.g., deQuervain et al., 2004). Their question was whether the punishment of the unfair confederate would yield evidence of activity (or greater activity) in those areas. Once again, such activation was observed in the male but not the female group. Singer et al. also collected ratings of the participants' desire for revenge on the unfair confederate. Men showed higher ratings of desire for revenge than women, and the brain activity in the reward region was correlated with the level of reported desire for revenge, but only for the men.

What has this study got to do with reading? Nothing directly; the empathy-inducing situation was not a verbal description. However, it is certainly grist to the mill for the idea that the moral dimension influences our perceptions and experience of what is happening to other individuals. It remains to be established whether observations such as those made by Singer et al. can be induced by *reading* about fair and unfair individuals receiving their comeuppance. However, given the ubiquity of themes of malevolence and revenge in most areas of literature, it is clearly an issue for exploration. Given studies discussed earlier showing apparent seeking of information by readers to enable the moral classification of actions (Young & Saxe, 2009), the outlook is promising. Of course, the other point is the gender difference in brain activity and desire for revenge. This may have consequences for distinguishing interest in 'male' and 'female' literature.

To summarize, empirical work in psychology and neuroscience in this area leads to a number of important conclusions. Simulations induced by perception and imagination provide a basis for a person feeling the way another person does. However, the extent of the simulations is modulated by both how close the person being observed is to the observer, and also by the extent to which the actions of an observed person fit with the moral attitude and general understanding of the observer. Indeed, p-responses have been shown to interfere with the making of plausible inferences when there is a clash between the observed and the attitude of the observer. These modulations are of major importance to understanding social cognition in general, and one can expect to see many further studies in this general area in the near future. Although many of the studies reported are not directly concerned with reading narrative per se, they strongly suggest that effects induced by reading should follow the same pattern. The empirical gap needs to be filled, however.

Reactions over the course of protracted narrative: suspense, curiosity and surprise

In discussing the work of Gerrig and colleagues on participatory responses, we have seen how emotion may play a central role in relation to the overall shape of a story, in terms of creating desires for or against specific outcomes. In this section, we look further at how emotion is created over protracted narrative, since it can make a major contribution to a reader's enjoyment of the plot of a story and be a key reason for reading a story.

Fundamental notions: the work of Sternberg

Sternberg's influential work describes narratives in terms of their structures of curiosity, surprise and suspense (e.g., Sternberg, 1978, 2003). His framework suggests how different types of text engage readers, and it has been used extensively in subsequent empirical research. His account relies on a classic distinction between two types of temporal sequence in narratives: the order in which the events are supposed to have taken place in the underlying story and the order in which the discourse recounts these events (e.g., Chatman, 1978). As he points out, events do not need to be presented in the order which they occurred and explanatory information, which he terms 'exposition', can be withheld until later in a story. If a reader knows that information has been withheld until later by the narrator, this can create *curiosity* about what has happened prior to the current time period of the narrative. The detective story is an obvious genre which plays on such curiosity, in respect of a previously committed crime. More generally, Sternberg points out that whenever there is an 'expositional gap' in a narrative, such as when a major character is introduced without full background, this can drive the reader forward to find out more. A further category is that of *surprise* where information is suddenly revealed later in a story, but the reader has not been previously alerted to a gap so is not expecting the new information. Often the prior narrative has been rhetorically set up to lead the reader down a 'garden path' and yet to make the surprise subsequently credible (in addition to Sternberg's work, see Emmott, 2003; Emmott & Alexander, 2010; Emmott, Sanford, & Alexander, 2010; Jahn, 1999; Tobin, 2009). Another of Sternberg's categories is that of *suspense*. In this case, the information is presented in the order it supposedly occurred, but there is uncertainty about the future course of events which makes the reader eager to hear more. In the everyday sense of the word, suspense can be linked with story situations creating extreme tension, where, for example, there is a major threat to a character. More generally, interest in what happens next is the primary motivation for reading narratives. Sternberg sees the principles of curiosity, surprise and suspense as three key aspects of reading, since curiosity relates to interest in what has been introduced in the past, surprise relates to a clash with a reader's expectations about the present, and suspense relates to speculation about what will happen in the future. Indeed, he suggests that these three factors are so important that they should be classed as 'Narrative Universals' (Sternberg, 2003).

The psychological model of Brewer and Lichtenstein

Brewer and Lichtenstein (1981, 1982) introduced a psychological model, the structural-affect theory, utilizing Sternberg's ideas (see also Brewer, 1996;

Brewer & Ohtsuka, 1988; Jose & Brewer, 1984). Brewer and Lichtenstein (1981) use the following examples to demonstrate the basic principles of curiosity, surprise and suspense. In (11a–d), we see the underlying event structure, presenting the events in the sequence that we might expect them to occur in if placed in chronological order.

Underlying event structure

(11a)   Butler puts poison in wine.
(11b)   Butler carries wine to Lord Higginbotham.
(11c)   Lord Higginbotham drinks wine.
(11d)   Lord Higginbotham dies.

In (12a–d), we see the events rearranged to prompt curiosity so that a puzzling event is placed first, then an explanation given later:

Curiosity discourse structure

(12a)   Lord Higginbotham dies.
(12b)   Butler has put poison in wine.
(12c)   Butler carried wine to Lord Higginbotham.
(12d)   Lord Higginbotham drank wine.

The event in (12a) may create curiosity about the reason, later explained by (12b–d).

In (13a–c), there may be an element of surprise because the butler's action of poisoning the wine has not been mentioned at the outset.

Surprise discourse structure

(13a)   Butler carries wine to Lord Higginbotham.
(13b)   Lord Higginbotham drinks wine.
(13c)   Lord Higginbotham dies.

In (14a–c), the basic format for suspense is to show the character, Lord Higginbotham, in danger and create tension while the reader awaits the outcome. Brewer and Lichtenstein's example below shows the suspense unresolved, since the outcome is not specified. Suspense may also be resolved by a character dying or escaping, either way removing the uncertainty.

Suspense discourse structure

(14a)   Butler puts poison in wine.
(14b)   Butler carries wine to Lord Higginbotham.
(14c)   Lord Higginbotham drinks wine.

Clearly there is a considerable difference between these short examples and a real narrative such as a Hitchcock film, and we would not expect the above structures to prompt much, if any, emotion in the form above. There is more to creating an affective response than simply changing the event order, a point which we will return to later. However, these examples show up the different discourse structures clearly.

Brewer and Lichtenstein (1982) use Berlyne's (1960, 1971) model of 'arousal' to account for the way that readers respond to stories of different types. Berlyne's work in particular has attracted the interest of those studying suspense (e.g., Vorderer, Wulff, & Friedrichsen, 1996) so we will describe its use for this purpose. Much of Berlyne's work was conducted with simple stimuli (e.g., pictures of simple shapes in different configurations) and he himself describes his results as tentative, but his model nevertheless provides a simple and appealing framework for testing responses to narratives. Berlyne (1960) bases his model of arousal on the assumption that the sudden removal of an aversive state, leading to a sudden drop in arousal, may be rewarding. He terms this the 'arousal jag'. He explains this using the Wundt curve which shows a sudden drop in arousal when a maximum threshold of stimulation has been reached, reflecting the point at which satiety occurs. This may help to explain the somewhat odd fact that readers/viewers appear to enjoy suspense-ful narratives which might be regarded as potentially distressing. Some suspense theorists suggest that the point at which suspense is resolved may lead to an arousal jag of this type, as the reader feels a sudden relief. In his later work, Berlyne (1971) reiterated this model, but also proposed a second distinct mechanism, the 'arousal boost', whereby a reward may come from the steady increase in arousal before the maximum threshold is reached. Suspense theorists (e.g., Vorderer et al., 1996) use this second mechanism to suggest that the suspenseful build-up might itself be arousing and that some readers/viewers (those who particularly enjoy this type of tense event sequence) might find the bodily changes stimulating even though they might be normally associated with negative emotions. Berlyne (1971, p. 136) suggests that when the arousal-boost mechanism is in operation, the 'inter-mediate, rewarding' level of moderate arousal needs to be maintained by arousal-raising and arousal-moderating factors operating simultaneously. In some cases, there may be a combination of the two mechanisms at work, producing an 'arousal-boost-jag'.

Berlyne's work on simple visual stimuli may be suggestive for narrative processing, but did not, of course, provide evidence for how narrative texts are read. Brewer and Lichtenstein provide a framework for studying narra-tives by taking the three categories of suspense, surprise and curiosity, and providing postulated affect patterns (Brewer, 1996, p. 111), as follows. Suspense arises due to a major initiating event occurring that creates uncertainty about the future outcome of the story. This uncertainty is then sustained by the writer over a stretch of text and is eventually resolved. The hypothesis is that for the reader there will be a sudden rise in suspense as the initiating event occurs, which continues to grow for some time as the tension builds up, then eventually drops suddenly as the situation resolves. To create surprise, a writer withholds an event for some time, then reveals it. In this case, the hypothesis is that until the revelation there is no surprise response, then as the revelation is made we would see surprise peak suddenly, then rapidly drop. For curiosity, a writer presents a crucial event which is not fully explained, then after some time provides further explanation. The hypothesis is that the reader feels a rise in curiosity, then this remains at a moderate level over time, then curiosity drops suddenly as the reader's questions are answered. Brewer (1996) does not consider different versions of these patterns in real narrative texts, but we might expect the exact nature of the response to vary depending on how suspenseful, surprising and puzzling writers make the events, and for the suspense and curiosity patterns there would be variability depending on the length of time writers maintain the situation of uncertainty and puzzlement, respectively. In addition, the relative suddenness or gradualness of the resolution in the text could affect the time period over which the reader's affect eventually drops. Brewer's patterns suggest three separate strategies and some researchers may attempt to link particular types of affect with particular genres, but many real narratives use all of these strategies. Although curiosity is an obvious factor in detective fiction (as readers puzzle over the crime), there is also frequently suspense (e.g., when a murderer threatens to kill again) and surprise (e.g., when the murderer is revealed) (Emmott & Alexander, 2010).

Of these three types of affect, suspense has been particularly extensively studied, especially in the context of film. A number of key factors that create suspense have been suggested, based on the analysis of suspenseful texts (e.g., Brewer, 1996; Carroll, 1996; Gerrig, 1996; Tan & Diteweg, 1996; Vorderer, 1996; Wulff, 1996; Zillmann, 1996). First, there is the situation. The main point, as we have seen, is that there is uncertainty about the future. This may be a significant event which causes major risk to a key participant, but the risk may also be to a key place or object, or a valued objective may be placed in jeopardy. Usually the expected outcome will be a binary choice between success or failure, judged by the reader's knowledge of likely end results. There is usually a high probability of a negative outcome occurring, but there is no certainty since then readers/viewers would resolve themselves to a negative outcome and not feel the same involvement. Secondly, there is a judgement of significance. The outcome needs to be important to the reader/viewer, in terms of the significance of the events themselves and whether the reader/viewer cares about the character. The reader will generally be wishing for a positive outcome for a liked character, but there may be occasions when a reader/viewer may desire a bad outcome for a disliked character.

The p-responses of Allbritton and Gerrig (1991) provide insights into suspense, since these reflect the desires of readers for certain types of outcome. Finally, there is the time course of the suspenseful sequence of actions. Events are usually unresolved over an extended period to create tension, e.g., the build-up may be lengthened by cross-cutting between scenes or showing events moving slowly or being interrupted.

Brewer and Lichtenstein (1981) had people make judgements about surprise and suspense in short stories that the experimenters wrote themselves, each about two pages in length. Three base forms of the narratives were produced, describing routine activities: (1) a man driving home from work; (2) a man wandering on the beach; and (3) a gardener clearing leaves in his yard. Then for each of these base forms an additional five manipulated versions of these narratives were constructed, including a surprise version and four different suspense versions, yielding eighteen materials in total. In the manipulated versions of these narratives, (i) a significant initiating event and (ii) an outcome event were inserted, as follows:

- In (1), the driving story, (i) a 10-minute bomb is activated in the car and (ii) the bomb explodes just after the driver leaves the car and enters his house.
- In (2), the beach story, (i) an underwater earthquake triggers a tidal wave heading for the beach and (ii) the tidal wave hits the beach, but the character is just out of reach.
- In (3), the gardening story, (i) a car driver dumps a sweepstakes ticket in a litter bag onto the yard and (ii) the gardener finds the ticket.

For each story, the 'suspense-standard version' consisted of all the base narrative events plus the above initiating and outcome events in chronological order, with the initiating event toward the start of the story and the outcome event toward the end. In the additional suspense versions, three different manipulations were made: (a) the chance of a negative outcome was heightened; (b) the reader was told the positive ending at the outset; and (c) the story was left without an outcome. In the 'surprise version', the initiating event was withheld until after the outcome. Readers made ratings for suspense (described as concern about what would happen) and surprise as segments of each narrative were read, in addition to various evaluative ratings, such as liking for the narrative and whether the narrative seemed like a story.

The results for this experiment were as follows. The suspense ratings for the suspense-standard versions were significantly higher for all three narratives than for the base narratives and the suspense ratings dropped dramatically at the point of resolution. Against predictions, the attempt to heighten the likelihood of the negative outcome ((a) above) did not yield any significant differences from the suspense-standard version. Inserting information at the start of the story about a positive outcome ((b) above) produced suspense ratings that were significantly lower than the suspense-standard version on two of the three stories. The surprise versions all yielded significantly higher surprise ratings at the point where the surprising outcome was presented, but were the same as the base narratives elsewhere (the drop in surprise was not measured). For the evaluative judgements, base narratives were judged less story-like than any other versions (below the 'barely a story' threshold), suspense-standard versions were judged significantly more story-like than base versions, and suspense-no-resolution stories ((c) above) were judged significantly less story-like than the suspense-standard stories. The surprise narratives were also judged significantly more story-like than the base narratives. In all cases, the suspense and surprise narratives were preferred to the base narratives.

Brewer and Lichtenstein's experiments provide an interesting study of readers' reactions to different narrative structures, but are limited in a number of respects. One is the reliance on structural factors alone in determining what constitutes a story. The base narratives were judged as below the 'barely a story' threshold because they gave accounts of daily events that lacked exceptional happenings, but some of the great works of literature might be judged 'barely a story' if evaluated on the basis of these criteria. People read stories to observe many other features such as characterization, the relations between characters, and philosophical content, not just suspense and surprise. It is perhaps not surprising that given the lack of these other factors in the materials, versions of the materials which mentioned bombs, tidal waves and lottery tickets were viewed as more story-like than the base materials, but this does not in itself fully explain how readers become sufficiently interested to create a tense situation.

Work on texts leading to predictive inferences provides one explanation for such interest. Campion (2004) identifies *predictive text*, as in (15a), which leads readers to speculate about what happens next by drawing *predictive inferences*, as in (15b). He shows that these inferences are stored in memory as *hypothetical facts* which create the expectation that the subsequent text will either show the events occurring as predicted or will provide an explanation of an alternative outcome. So readers are likely to predict that the ship has sunk or will sink, but alternatives are possible.

(15a)   Predictive text: It was a pitch black night and a gigantic iceberg floated in the ocean, emerging by only 5 m. The helmsman was inattentive, but the ship advanced toward the iceberg and ran into it, causing a terrible noise.
(15b)   Predictive inference: Maybe the ship sank.

By contrast, deductive text, as in (16a), allows a deductive inference arrived at by logical operation which makes the deductive inference (16b) certain.

In the example below, all trees over 8 m are uprooted and the oak is 15 m, hence the oak must be uprooted. If the text does not follow this logical pattern, it will be viewed as contradictory.

(16a)   Deductive text: A violent storm blew across the country and caused a lot of
         damage to forests. At Albert's, all trees that were more than 8 m tall were
         uprooted. Albert's most beautiful tree was an old, majestic, 15 m tall oak that
         embellished the park entrance.

(16b)   Deductive inference: The old oak was uprooted.

Campion, Martins, and Wilhelm (2009) have found narrative texts which contain predictive inferences to be rated as more interesting. To create a more suspenseful text, this type of prediction, *maybe the ship sank*, also needs to be supplemented by Allbritton and Gerrig's (1991) p-responses which provide a preference for a specific outcome (e.g., 'I hope it doesn't sink'), and it is possible that there may be some sense of pulling the ship back from danger (Polichak & Gerrig, 2002). In addition, Gerrig and Bernardo (1994) suggest that the reader might treat the situation like a problem space (e.g., 'How can the helmsman stop the ship sinking?') and (Gerrig, 1996) consider desired counterfactual situations ('replotting') after the outcome has occurred (e.g., 'It would be better if the helmsman had been attentive.'). Gerrig points out that these types of response show the reader actively participating in the creation of a tense situation, rather than just passively responding to narrative structures in the text.

Another limitation of Brewer and Lichtenstein's (1981) work is that it relies on subjective reports by readers. An alternative is to use physiological measures, such as observations of facial expressions and body posture, heart rate and blood pressure monitoring, and measuring the electrical conductivity of the skin (see de Wied & Zillmann, 1996; Mattenklott, 1996, for details). Zillmann, Hay, and Bryant (1975) had been more successful than Brewer and Lichtenstein in creating materials that produced different levels of suspense, achieving this by altering the degree of danger and also the extent of the distress shown by protagonists. They found heart rate to increase significantly according to degree of suspense, and to fall suddenly and reliably on resolution of the suspense. The decline was statistically significant in all cases, and more pronounced with high degrees of suspense. Appreciation ratings increased as levels of suspense were raised, particularly in the case of resolved suspense, supporting Berlyne's 'arousal jag' theory. More recently, Auracher (2006) finds that reading extracts from highly suspenseful novels can have a significant effect on heart rate, skin conductance and peripheral blood volume, with textual manipulations involving changes in perspective making a difference to the degree of the effect.

*Cumulative suspense and emotional contagion in film
and media studies*

In real narratives, high levels of suspense often seem to be achieved by cumulative effect of a succession of suspenseful scenes, rather than just the single initiating event suggested by Brewer and Lichtenstein. In film studies, G. M. Smith (2003) examines films such as *Raiders of the Lost Ark* and Hitchcock's *Psycho*, showing how a series of minor tense moments can build up to a highly suspenseful sequence or major surprise ending, which might gain in effect from the arousal caused by the earlier minor tense events. G. M. Smith's work is descriptive rather than empirical, but is nevertheless broadly in line with the empirically based observations of Zillmann and Frijda. Zillmann (1978, 1996, 2003) lays emphasis on the time span within which physiological responses of the body resolve. Zillmann's 'excitation transfer theory' suggests that due to this lingering physiological arousal, individuals may still have some residual effect when they meet a later stimulus and can then transfer this 'residual excitation' to that later stimulus. Road rage is an obvious case, where a minor traffic incident can apparently cause significant violence, but the real cause may be a combination of this specific stimulus plus earlier arousal from previous stimuli. For Zillmann, the positive/negative nature of the original stimuli does not matter, so, for example, potential football hooligans in a frenzy of excitement might sometimes become more violent if subsequently provoked when still in this state. Frijda (1986, 2007) makes similar observations about the development of mood. G. M. Smith (2003) draws directly on Frijda's work in developing his descriptive observation of what he terms 'mood cues'. So in *Raiders of the Lost Ark*, the startle reflex is drawn on when spiders fall on the hero's head, which we might expect to contribute to overall arousal as the sequence progresses. Humorous incidents could possibly have the effect of raising overall arousal, based on Zillmann's model, which suggests that positive/negative valency is irrelevant to increasing activation. Alternatively, following Berlyne's model of the 'arousal boost', humorous incidents could alleviate tension, making it more bearable, thereby allowing cumulative presentations of suspense and ensuring that the viewer does not stop watching. G. M. Smith's descriptive model needs empirical investigation, but nevertheless provides an interesting hypothesis about how scriptwriters might build up tension in films.

M. Smith (1995) and Coplan (2006) suggest that narrative films may be more likely to produce emotional contagion in spectators than real events, because attention in narrative films can be manipulated by techniques such as extreme close-ups combined with slowing of the pace of the narrative to focus on the face. Coplan and M. Smith believe that emotional contagion may be used by film makers to complement other types of response such as empathy and sympathy, but that also emotional contagion may be used in ways that are incongruent with the other types of response to produce a complex overall reaction. M. Smith suggests that in Hitchcock's film *Saboteur* there is a conflict of this type, since the protagonist is a repugnant character, but when he falls to his death from the Statue of Liberty, we see extreme close-ups of his expression of terror which may prompt a similar expression in the reader and hence sympathy for him. Clearly this claim would need to be tested in relation to this specific film incident and other similar ones (Coplan, 2006, pp. 33–36, provides a related example). Some psychological research has revealed individual differences in response to facial expressions and bodily reactions in films. Laird et al. (1994, p. 235) showed participants short clips from the films *Crocodile Dundee*, in which a crocodile jumps out of the water toward the viewer, and *Dead Calm*, in which a heavy block with a hook on it comes suddenly toward a man's head. In both cases, the actor leaps back in reaction. Laird et al. report that:

Some subjects responded to these segments by jerking their heads and bodies backward, in unison with the actors, while other subjects sat essentially motionless. (p. 235)

When it occurs, this type of bodily reaction of the viewer might be said to be a reflex, and some film theorists suggest that these types of reflex might be one mechanism that maintains the viewer's general level of arousal, contributing to the overall emotional response (Coplan, 2006; M. Smith, 1995).

The paradox of suspense

In the work described up to this point, it has been assumed that suspense arises from genuine uncertainty. However, researchers have noted a 'paradox of suspense' (Carroll, 1996; Gerrig, 1996), which is that suspense can arise even when there is no apparent uncertainty, either because readers/viewers are told the ending at the start of the narrative, or because they know the ending from previous encounters with the story. Carroll (1996) reports seeing *King Kong* at least fifty times and still feeling suspense. Repeated enjoyment of suspenseful films might be explained because viewers become immersed in empathizing with a character and the character does not know his/her own future, so we experience the fear that the character feels, although several other suggestions have been made. Hoeken and van Vliet (2000) examined the paradox of suspense by manipulating event order, in line with Brewer and Lichtenstein's model. They found that on first reading a story, suspense about an outcome could be achieved whether or not subjects knew the outcome. They used the following opening sentence from P. D. James' story *Devices and Desires*:

(17)   The Whistler's fourth victim, Valerie Mitchell, was his youngest: fifteen
        years, and she died because she missed the bus leaving at twenty to ten from
        Easthaven for its ride to Cobb's Marsh.

(cited in Hoeken & van Vliet, 2000)

This was manipulated so that a parallel version was created which did not reveal the murder until the end. Using appreciation ratings, it was found that participants found the story equally satisfying in both conditions.

The researchers suggest, though, that in place of uncertainty, a different account might serve as an explanation. This is Sanders' (1994) theory in which perspective is posited as a source for the creation of suspense. Sanders uses mental space theory (Fauconnier, 1994) to suggest that information supplied by the narrator is compartmentalized in a mental space and kept separate from a character's perceptions. This model might lead readers to suppress the narrator's details about the outcome (or their previous knowledge of that outcome) when viewing events through the character's perspective. Tobin (2009) makes a similar suggestion using conceptual blending theory (Fauconnier & Turner, 2002), which we discussed in Chapter 3. This type of compartmentalization is difficult to imagine actually occurring, but is perhaps not all that different from the suspension of disbelief required to believe in fantastic creatures and situations which we know do not exist, or to feel fear at circumstances which we know to be fictional (Walton, 1978, 1990).

A more mundane explanation of the paradox of suspense is that when we are told the outcome at the outset, we still get some satisfaction from curiosity as to how this outcome will be achieved, as Hoeken and van Vliet (2000) suggest in their study. For repeated exposure to a story, we might forget the exact details due to the time intervals between readings/viewings or we may simply enjoy the repeated re-enactment of a dramatic situation. Hence theories which depend entirely on emotions arising from the withholding of events (as in Brewer and Lichtenstein's work) may need to be supplemented by theories which show readers/viewers responding emotionally to fearful events, regardless of knowledge of the plot outcome. Empathy may provide one explanation, but suspense can also be felt when a character is oblivious to their own danger, so it might be the case that viewers are sometimes feeling *for* rather than *with* the character, as suggested by theories which assume that we may respond by empathetically witnessing potentially dangerous situations as well as by empathizing with characters' emotions (e.g., Tan, 1994, 1996; Zillmann, 1991, 1994, 2006b).

The paradox of suspense remains an interesting problem in need of a proper explanation. We favour the idea that suspense is really determined by many factors, including event withholding, the presence of p-responses (which do not require the character to know their situation) and empathizing with a character, with each of these factors playing a role when this is possible. For instance, note that p-responses may be automatically made, even if we know what the outcome will be. The automaticity of emotional contagion, empathy and sympathy is obvious, though ultimately, it may be possible to become unresponsive (hardened). If such multiple determination is indeed the case, then a more flexible theory of suspense needs to be formulated and tested. It is entirely possible that certain kinds of suspense persist over multiple exposures, but others simply do not. These are interesting issues for further exploration.

Summary

In this chapter we have examined some of the affective issues that arise while reading narratives, including knowledge of characters' emotions, embodiment effects in readers, empathy and suspense.

- Using standard cognitive techniques, it is possible to show that people infer the likely emotional state of characters during reading (as in the work of Gernsbacher and colleagues, or of Gygax and colleagues). Similarly, it is possible to show that people take into account conventional moral thinking in judging reported behaviours.
- However, these cases rely on the reader using their *knowledge* of typical emotional and moral responses rather than on having their *feelings per se* manipulated by the text. The difference is that while the first might be called cold cognition, the second, involving feelings proper, is hot cognition. Yet having feelings is central to readers having real emotional reactions, anger, disgust, pleasure, etc., in the face of a narrative. And of course it is an essential ingredient of empathy, reactions typified by expressions like 'I feel your pain.'
- Neuroscience-based work on embodiment has shown a variety of brain areas that are involved in the direct processing of painful stimuli are also activated when another is observed as being in pain. We discussed a number of examples of this sort that lay a foundation for the experiential aspect of emotion coming into play when understanding things happening to other people.
- We reviewed the role of moral stance in the reactions readers have to the situation of others, ranging from p-responses to direct activity in a variety of brain areas. Outcomes that readers would prefer, for moral reasons or reasons of justice, were shown to interfere with the making of rapid plausible inferences which are so central to comprehension. The involvement of moral judgement affects the way readers view bad things happening to reprehensible people, as indexed by measures of brain activity. Some interesting gender differences emerged here.
- Our survey of factors influencing different patterns of emotional response led to the issue of suspense, which can often last over a long tract of narrative. Ideas of how to characterize suspense involve withholding information while the reader is motivated to obtain closure. However, an

important idea is the 'paradox of suspense' – why can we get feelings of suspense even when we have read a story several times, or seen a film more than once? This causes problems for simplistic notions of withholding information from readers, and suggests that as readers we can enter a narrative world at some level as though it had not been encountered before. This is an area that needs further enquiry. It seems likely that suspense is multiply-determined, and future models must produce a fuller picture of which factors are present even on repeated exposures (and why, and what the limits are), and which ones are present only on first exposure (if any are restricted in this way).

- According to the Rhetorical Focussing Principle, writers should be able to modulate all the effects described in this chapter through the stylistic devices of writing, such as foregrounding. There has been some investigation of this idea in the humanities (e.g., Miall, 2007), but within psychology this exciting area has not been explored and is open for future research.

9   Narrative's social impact: persuasion and attitude change

So far, our concern has been with how readers understand and experience narratives in terms of inferences, attention and embodied responses. We now turn to the effects that narratives may have on their readers' attitudes and beliefs, a topic which has relevance for personal moral development and in promoting social values. The term 'narrative impact' (Green, Strange, & Brock, 2002) is used to describe these potential effects of narrative, such as changing the opinions and even the behaviour of readers and film viewers. In this chapter, we discuss how such changes might be achieved both as a result of deliberate strategies to affect attitudes and beliefs, and as by-products of reading. We look first at overtly persuasive texts which have the explicit aim of influencing people, examining particularly courtroom narratives which aim to convince listeners of guilt or innocence. We then consider narrative texts which embed deliberate persuasion for educational purposes within the telling of an entertaining story, referred to as entertainment-education. Next, we will examine narratives which are written for artistic and enjoyment purposes, such as literary texts and popular fiction, which might have an influence on the beliefs and moral stance of their readers. Finally, we will see how autobiographical narratives might have an effect on their authors, focussing particularly on the idea that expressive writing might have health benefits.

In all of these areas, it is necessary to establish whether there is any real evidence for any claimed impact, and, if there is, how best to characterize it. As will be seen when literary texts and popular fiction are considered, the everyday public have strong views about reading, such as the idea that certain literary texts are of sufficient quality to 'improve' their readers and may therefore be of social value. Indeed, some psychologists with an interest in narrative also hold this opinion. Such views have social significance because they can determine public policy. However, it is necessary to distinguish between ideas that are expressed with little or no supporting evidence and those which have been examined empirically. Within literary studies, there are discursive works that present ideas about the practical effects of reading, and these ideas may provide useful hypotheses for future empirical examination. Nevertheless, it is important to be aware that although some of these discursive studies base their ideas on socio-historical research of the presumed effect of specific books and films on groups of readers, they sometimes rely on little more than speculations and anecdotes to support their claims of actual effects. Even where the impact of narratives on attitudes and beliefs has been tested, by Empirical Study of Literature researchers and in cognitive psychology, it is still important to critically examine the design of experiments. It is also necessary to be cautious in drawing conclusions from studies of correlations: if a correlation is found between, say, reading narratives and empathy, it may be that empathetic people choose to read narratives rather than that narratives make people more empathetic. Moreover, it is rare for empirical work in this area to provide evidence to show whether or not effects are long-lasting. Such issues may be glossed over in empirical reports, but have huge implications for public investment in reading and writing programmes.

Narratives and overt persuasion

We have used the term 'rhetorical' in this book so far to describe the effects of stylistic devices generally, but 'rhetoric' in the classical sense relates to persuasion. We will begin by considering narrative texts which are specifically designed to persuade, and where the audience is clear that this is the intention and is expected to judge the persuasive force of the material presented. Courtroom discourse provides a good example, since the whole point is to convince an audience of the truth or falsity of a story. Narratives can be found in the elicited storytelling of courtroom questioning, in the summaries of courtroom professionals, such as prosecution and defence lawyers, and in the legal case rulings which give an overview of judgments which may sometimes provide precedents for subsequent cases (Atkinson & Drew, 1979; Brooks, 1996; Bruner, 2002; Farber & Sherry, 1996; Gearey, 2005; Gewirtz, 1996a; Jackson, 1988, 1990; Mertz & Yovel, 2005). Let us first consider ideas about how legal narratives might be presented in order to make them more persuasive. In principle, certain stylistic devices might be expected to have rhetorical focussing effects which might enhance the persuasiveness of legal discourse. We will then turn to empirical work which examines stylistic devices in legal contexts.

Narrative design of historical and legal accounts

Coherence and credibility   One question about legal storytelling is whether the shaping of a story, that is, the coherence of a narrative, can make an account more or less convincing. This applies both to the connections made between sentences (e.g., the use of causal connectives) and the overall structure of the text (e.g., whether there is a specified end result). Some of the ideas in this area derive from work in historiography, the study of historical writing, where there has been a move since the 1960s to emphasize the important role of narrative form in presenting historical accounts (e.g., Burke, 2001; Carr, 1986a, 1986b, 2008; Danto, 1985; Munslow, 2007; Polkinghorne, 1988; Ricoeur, 1983–1988; White, 1973). Historical storytelling, like legal storytelling, depends on giving shape to events for which the evidence might be confused, incomplete and apparently contradictory. White (1980) has shown how the nature of historical narratives has developed over the ages to increase their overall narrative coherence ('narrativity') and potentially their ability to persuade readers of a particular view of history. White discusses texts from the Middle Ages that provide a contrast to much modern historical writing in terms of their presentation, since they lack the sophisticated shaping of the narrative that we would nowadays expect. By looking at these earlier forms of writing, we can see what properties modern historical narratives have. White explains how annals simply list events which happened in each year. Annals may have some narrative sequence (in cases where an event clearly follows on directly as a consequence from another), but little else. There may be little obvious connection between many events, however, and no highlighting of which are the key events, and sometimes little or no information about outcomes. Chronicles can be more sophisticated as narratives since they may not only make connections, selectively emphasize events, and give a better indication of outcomes, but can also represent people, institutions and countries as agents with intentions rather than presenting events as just happening to people. Modern histories are generally the most narrative-based since they have the properties of chronicles, but also have more shaping to the text, with more of an overall moral conclusion about the success or failure of particular groups of individuals.

Although narratives may satisfy human needs to see coherence in events, there is debate about the extent to which they may distort by imposing too much form on sequences of events where the evidence for what happened may be very fragmentary and where there is no clear beginning, middle or end in reality. White believes that narratives provide a false sense of structure, providing 'illusory coherence' (1987, p. ix). He suggests that there is a discontinuity between the ad hoc nature of real-life events and the shaped historical accounts which he views as having formats associated with literary narratives, not reality. By contrast, Carr (1986a, 1986b) has suggested a 'continuity theory' which views everyday life as primarily narrative based, so that historical accounts then mirror the way that people account for their lives as they live them. Even if narrative is regarded as forming the basis by which people judge how their everyday lives will develop, this can, of course, still potentially provide a distorting bias. Taleb (2007) argues that in everyday life people have a 'narrative fallacy', his term for the tendency for individuals to over-interpret and prefer 'compact stories over raw truths' (p. 63).

So, narrative might therefore be seen as both potentially facilitating the structuring of everyday experience, but also as possibly having negative consequences through overstructuring and oversimplifying it. In courtroom situations, legal narratives may be shaped to make a story sound more credible, but this might be of concern if added coherence makes an account sound more convincing when actually there is factual inaccuracy and/or a weak underlying argument. Some of the techniques that might be used to enhance credibility include:

- Selective inclusion or non-inclusion of key facts in the case in order to support a particular argument (e.g., the different arguments of the prosecution and defence, or in order to justify a specific judgment).
- Added background detail in order to encourage sympathy for or empathy with particular individuals.
- Added causal connectives, such as 'in spite of this' or 'as a result of this' to emphasize details that might be potentially incriminating and/or to give a sense of increased control of the narrative by the narrator.
- The insertion of specific statements to make explicit certain conclusions that would otherwise have to be inferred (e.g., 'x was ten minutes' walk away at the time of the shooting, therefore x could not be responsible for the shooting').
- More careful structuring of the discourse to increase clarity and/or to increase the appearance of narratorial control (e.g., greater use of spatio-temporal signals; changes to the chronological order of presentation; more explicit use of structures that indicate a beginning, middle and end).
- The inclusion of speculation where facts are uncertain. Hypothetical narratives may be added to a prosecuting or defence lawyer's summary where there are gaps in actual knowledge to suggest a possible course of events (e.g., 'x was the only person known to be in the room when the stabbing took place, so x must have committed the crime', where there are no witnesses to the latter point). Strong modals such as 'must' may be used, when the evidence only suggests 'may'.

Even where the narrative is not explicitly shaped in these ways, the fact of using a narrative structure at all can be argued to distort events. Dershowitz (1996) points out that our experience of crime stories may potentially carry over to our interpretation of court narratives, but that they are fundamentally different. Crime stories may make use of the 'Chekhov's gun principle', where a gun mentioned in an opening scene may be assumed to be relevant to a later scene. However, as Dershowitz points out 'life is not a dramatic narrative' (p. 99) and such connections cannot be assumed in the courtroom.

Dershowitz discusses the case of the American sportsman O. J. Simpson, who was tried for the murder of his wife and had an alleged history of abusing her. Dershowitz reports that the prosecutor tried to strengthen his case by arguing that in a large proportion of instances where a man kills his wife, the killing is preceded by abuse, whereas the defence argued that only a very small number of wife abusers escalate to murder. Dershowitz argues that the prosecutor was trying to show a narrative progression, with the abuse supposedly leading to murder, but that the defence was trying to show that no such conclusion could be reached because 'real life [is] filled with coincidences, randomness, and illogic' (p. 103).

To summarize, aspects of narrative, including both the narrative form itself and added embellishments, have been considered by legal scholars to have a possible effect on persuading courtroom audiences. We will look shortly at whether empirical work supports these ideas, after discussing further the way in which narratives may potentially be weighted toward the perspective of particular participants by the addition of added details.

Perspective, emotion-inducing detail and possible sympathy/empathy
As mentioned, one aspect of narratives which may have persuasive impact is the use of emotion-inducing detail, since there is a possibility that this might cue sympathetic and/or empathetic responding to an individual presented in a story. We saw in Chapters 6, 7 and 8 that many narratives bring events to a human level when they report a story embodied in a particular spatio-temporal setting and/or reflect the point of view of a particular narrator or character. As far as legal narratives are concerned, we know that they can be told from different perspectives because not only will prosecution and defence lawyers put different emphasis on selected aspects of a particular story, but also different rulings can come from different courts for the same case (e.g., the original ruling and a subsequent appeal court ruling).

There is empirical work by cognitive psychologists on whether the presentation of background detail and the use of additional elaborations may have an effect on the conclusions drawn from legal narratives, as we shall see shortly. This idea is in line with a descriptive study by the legal scholar Jackson (1990), who provides a study of English legal case histories in which he argues that storytelling evaluations might have biased legal judgments. His opinion here is based on the nature of the narratives, the end results of the court cases and his own views about what judgments should have been made. As an example, he discusses the judgment in the case of *Miller* v. *Jackson* where the Court of Appeal looked again at a case in which a village's cricket ground had been closed down by a High Court judge because a new resident had complained that the cricket balls landing in his garden were dangerous.

Jackson suggests that the Court of Appeal judgment, which ruled in favour of the cricketers, provided a narrative including highly positive and colourful background details about the traditions and practice of cricket which were, in Jackson's view, not directly relevant to the legal point at issue, but which might have prompted empathy for the cricketers. In contrast, the presentation of the complaining 'newcomer' to the village gave little personal detail, apart from the fact that he was objecting. Adding detail is a natural part of everyday and artistic storytelling, but there is potential for unduly weighting sympathies in legal cases. Jackson also looks at a series of English cases where he argues that similar legal decisions were inconsistent (even though English case law requires the judgments of classic cases to provide a benchmark for later similar cases) and attributes the differences to the portrayal of the individuals in the narrative stories, such as sympathy being created for elderly ladies by explicit descriptions of their circumstances (irrelevant to the legal point, but nevertheless potentially influential in weighting the case). The point being made here relies on Jackson's own judgement, hinting at possible negative effects of narratives if storytellers provide a distorting bias. As Brooks (1996, p. 16) points out in relation to legal narratives 'storytelling is a moral chameleon, capable of promoting the worse as well as the better cause [. . .] it is not, to be sure, morally neutral for it always seeks to induce a point of view'.

In addition to the possibility of weighting a specific legal story in a particular direction in order to change the sympathies of an audience, there is also the issue of whether a personal narrative inserted into the courtroom proceedings might affect the jury. In the United States, the use of 'victim impact statements' has been particularly controversial (Gewirtz, 1996b; Scarry, 1996). These narratives of victims (either those directly affected or survivors' relations) have been used at the stage of sentencing to highlight the damage inflicted, including the psychological effect of crimes. So in legal cases, the narratives of victims can be used to draw attention to their side of the story in cases where otherwise the main focus of attention would be on the narrative of the accused. The last phone calls of the 9/11 victims were apparently used for such purposes in court (as discussed in the television documentary *9/11: Phone Calls from the Towers*, broadcast on the UK's Channel 4 on 6 September 2009). Here the aim is to add a narrative voice that would not otherwise have been heard.

Hoffman (2008) points to the need to counteract 'here-and-now' biases where an individual in court may otherwise elicit more empathy than a dead victim, as in some child abuse cases, where, say, a nanny or a young mother may be on trial. Hoffman (2008) explains that traditionally legal scholars believed that the law should be 'cleansed of emotion so that reason and logic can prevail' (p. 450), but that now there is some recognition that 'emotions inevitably influence not only legal judgments and decisions by jurors and judges, but at times law's very substance' (p. 450) (see also Bornstein & Wiener, 2010; Gewirtz, 1996a). Hoffman points out that certain lawyers believe that empathy can allow a deeper understanding of people's needs and thereby reflect the spirit of the law, but that there is controversy about this, with other lawyers feeling that this should only be the case under very exceptional circumstances. Hoffman argues that in particular human rights cases, such as classic legal decisions in the USA in the 1950s concerning the effects of racial segregation, 'empathy narratives' were essential in allowing fair judgment of the effects of segregation on victims. He suggests that empathy for a group of victims may be facilitated by enabling empathy with individuals who can then be seen to represent the group. The use of 'empathy narratives' does, nevertheless, raise questions about how such narratives are used in courtrooms in general. Critics have questioned the extent to which their impact may unfairly depend on how articulate the victims are and even on personal factors such as whether or not they have a family who might in consequence also be deemed to have suffered (Scarry, 1996).

Clearly, there are legal issues here concerning what information should be relevant in order to make a legal judgment, but there are also empirical issues in relation to whether and to what extent changes to narrative perspective are able to influence judgments.

Empirical work on overt persuasion in legal situations

Cognitive psychologists have investigated the question of whether coherence and added elaborations can add to the persuasive force of legal stories and thereby influence legal decisions. Voss, Wiley, and Sandak (1999) describe an experiment examining participants' responses to texts simulating summaries of cases made by a prosecuting attorney. For each case, participants read either the 'baseline' summary or one of three versions with changes made to the text, then answered questions about their judgement of the degree of guilt of the accused, their confidence in their judgement, the quality of the summary they are presented with, its convincingness, and the strength of argument of the lawyer. In producing the manipulated versions of the texts, a 'causal disruption' version included weakened causal links, a 'chronology disruption' version contained jumbled sentences to change the order of main events and background information, and a final 'incomplete' version omitted certain peripheral and case-relevant details from the baseline account. It was found that the causation disruption and chronology disruption versions showed significantly lower guilty ratings than the original baseline version. The incomplete version was not significantly different from the baseline. Confidence in judgements was generally high, with the baseline condition yielding the highest confidence levels. The causation disruption and chronology disruption versions produced poorer judgements of narrative quality, convincingness and strength of argument of the lawyer than the baseline and incomplete versions.

The overall idea of this experiment is interesting, and seems to yield some evidence that changing the format of presentation can affect the perceived credibility of a narrative, for two of the manipulated versions, the 'causation disruption' and 'chronology disruption' ones. It may seem strange that the 'incomplete' versions did not produce judgements that were significantly different from the baseline, but obviously this depends on the nature of the information omitted. In the sample material presented in Voss et al.'s (1999) account of the experiment, some of the details left out seem incidental to the issue of guilt. Even where details are relevant, there may be shallow processing occurring, as discussed in Chapter 5, so the overall conclusion might carry more weight for persuasive purposes than would specific supporting points. This aspect of the experiment might benefit from further research which makes use of the depth of processing framework to judge which details of a narrative readers are attending to.

Although the causality disruption manipulation produced an overall effect, it appears to be rather an odd mix of different changes which make it difficult to assess the effect of particular features. In some parts of the text, explicit connectives and explanatory phrases such as *Despite this fact* and *This evidence indicated* were removed, potentially affecting the way in which evidence was signalled as being relevant to the overall conclusion. In addition, some explicit conclusions were not drawn from the evidence. A rather different, but nevertheless interesting, change was to introduce/replace modal expressions such as *must* with *may* and to add *probably* to hedge the force of these statements (e.g., *[x's] bat must have been used [as a weapon]*, *[x's] bat may probably have been used [as a weapon]*). Other changes in the 'causality disruption' condition seem to have more to do with content, even though the experimenters were supposed to be keeping this constant (e.g., in a car accident, the action of the driver getting out to check on an injured girl was replaced with the driver getting out to check on the car). Overall, there are some stylistic changes here that are particularly worth investigating, but they need to be separated out from each other, with the content remaining as similar as possible.

Subsequent research has built on the above experiment. Voss and van Dyke (2001, Experiment 1) used the 'chronology disruption' manipulation with strong and weak evidence, but found no significant difference between the strong/weak versions and the baseline version. They concluded that this type of disruption only appeared to make a difference when the evidence was ambiguous, as in the earlier Voss et al. (1999) experiment.

Voss and van Dyke also performed a version of Voss et al.'s 'causation disruption' manipulation, this time separating out some of the factors which had previously been handled together. They compared (Experiment 2a) the reading of baseline versions of a prosecutor's summary with versions adding modal expressions to decrease certainty about the accused's role (e.g., by adding *probably*, *apparently*, and changing *was* to *could have*). The narratives were judged as being of significantly lower quality and convincingness in the more uncertain version, and guilt ratings were also lower at a borderline significance level. In a subsequent experiment (2b), Voss and van Dyke introduced uncertainty in relation to incidental background detail that was not relevant to the crime, and still found the same pattern of results. It may seem odd that participants are taking account of the uncertain status of information which is not crime-relevant, but they may be responding to the overall sense of authority of the prosecutor's statement. The authority of a speaker is regarded by rhetoric scholars as a key aspect of much persuasive discourse (e.g., Cockroft & Cockroft, 1992).

Voss and van Dyke also separately added potential emotion-inducing statements to the prosecutor statements to see how this affected the assessment of the crime. This was done first (Experiment 2a) by making statements about the accused (e.g., that he was 'ruthless') and by making the crime seem more dramatic (e.g., that the accused *burst* into the location of the crime, and was *gesturing frantically*). This affected perceptions of the quality and convincingness of the narrative, but had no significant effect on guilt judgements. They also tested the effect of emotion-inducing statements about the victim's plight (e.g., that he was *shocked, trembling*, etc.). This might be expected to increase sympathy and/or empathy for the victim, thus leading to higher guilt judgements about the accused, but, surprisingly, guilt judgements (as well as judgements of the quality and convincingness of the narrative) were lower. Voss and van Dyke suggested that the inclusion of this type of descriptive information about the victim had 'backfired', but it is unclear why this would be the case. Possibly such statements might have a different effect when included in the victim's own evidence or a victim impact statement.

This work suggests that coherence (e.g., in terms of sequencing and the use of causal expressions, explicit conclusions, etc.) is a factor in increasing plausibility. In later research, Allison, Brimacombe, Hunter, and Kadlec (2006) found that the increased use of explicit spatio-temporal information, which might also be seen as a coherence device, in simulated witness narratives leads to judgements that the narratives are more credible. Voss et al.'s work also shows that modal expressions appear to be able to increase or decrease credibility depending on whether they make the discourse seem certain or uncertain. This is somewhat disturbing if we consider situations where more certain expressions might be used for key crime-relevant statements which are based purely on hypothesis. Voss et al.'s findings regarding added extra detail are puzzling, since highlighting the plight of the victim had a counter-intuitive effect. Overall, there seems to be plenty of scope for investigating these issues further, and for additional work such as seeing how far a judge's direction about which factors to focus on might influence the depth of processing of information in courtroom narratives.

Entertainment-education: embedding persuasion in an entertaining story

So far we have been examining acts of persuasion where both the speaker and the audience are aware of the persuasive intention of the message, but it is also possible to bury persuasive material in a story designed for entertainment purposes. The term 'entertainment-education' is used by some researchers to cover the 'process of purposely designing and implementing a media message to both entertain and educate, in order to increase audience members' knowledge about an educational issue, create favorable attitudes, shift social norms, and change overt behavior' (Singhal & Rogers, 2002, p. 5). In this definition, persuasion is viewed as arising from a deliberate intention, but other researchers extend the term also to include cases where persuasion is unintentional, as when a storyline is added purely for entertainment purposes but where it also has unintentional educational effects (e.g., de Graaf, 2010; Moyer-Gusé, 2008).

In cases of deliberate persuasion, a major device has been to design television dramas or films to include plot elements and/or characters for promoting issues such as alcohol and drug control, AIDS education, family planning, safety for agricultural workers, women's rights, anti-racism, etc. (see Singhal, Cody, Rogers, & Sabido, 2004; Singhal & Rogers, 1999, 2002; Slater, 2002, for reviews). Although this may seem like a recent innovation, Slater (2002) points out that moral messages date back at least as far as Aesop's fables and are prevalent in religious texts such as the New Testament's parables. Singhal and Rogers (1999) report the use of specially prepared narrative films in Latin America and Africa, which resulted in dramatic increases in relevant behaviour, such as people enrolling in adult literacy classes after viewing a film about characters benefiting from increased literacy, and also rises in visits to family planning clinics after audiences watched films having a sex education storyline (see also Slater, 2002). The film makers drew on social learning theories (e.g., Bandura, 1977) which suggested that the behaviour of viewers might be changed more readily in the required direction if characters with positive moral attributes or behaviours were seen to have positive outcomes, and the opposite for characters with negative moral attributes and behaviours. Specially devised films of this type have been used mainly in Third World countries and with immigrant workers in other countries, but this type of entertainment-education can also be seen in scenes embedded in soap operas and in technical training films in countries such as the USA.

Slater (2002) points out that such media entertainment has to be carefully designed to avoid having inadvertent effects, such as rejection of the message or misinterpretation. In the case of one 1970s situation comedy in the USA, a parodied racist character was taken seriously by some viewers who shared the racist attitudes and felt that the character provided a voice for their views (Singhal & Rogers, 1999). Slater suggests that films showing characters in the process of change might be more successful in encouraging change than simply supplying role models who already have the desired attributes or behaviour, but this needs empirical testing. He also points out that the effect of placing the moral message in the main storyline or secondary storyline requires further investigation, as does the effect of moral epilogues and post-viewing discussion programmes. Separate research by Hanauer and Waksman (2000) on fables shows that explicit moral points can facilitate enhanced integration of information and can produce a convergence of responses toward an interpretation provided by an author.

Much research has been directed at the processes by which change may occur. One idea is that the persuasive effect of entertaining narrative texts may lie partly in the degree of immersion of readers or film audiences in a story. Green and Brock (2000) use Gerrig's (1993) notion of 'transportation', or becoming absorbed in a story, as a framework for testing this hypothesis (see also Green, 2004). Previously, persuasion research had been dominated by models such as the Elaboration Likelihood Model (Petty & Cacioppo, 1986) which suggest that persuasion results from increased attention to crucial points in an argument, providing a framework for explaining attitude changes due to logical appraisal of the presented material. The Elaboration Likelihood Model is useful for explaining explicit persuasion, but is of less relevance to entertainment-education where attention is primarily focussed on enjoying a story. For entertainment-education, Green and Brock suggest a Transportation Theory, which includes the following possible processes.

- First, immersion in a narrative may make readers/viewers less aware of real-world concerns and might therefore give them less opportunity to formulate counter-arguments to the embedded persuasive content of the story, hence making it more difficult to resist attitude change.
- Secondly, immersion in a story may simulate direct experiences, providing a powerful means of prompting new attitudes.

• Thirdly, immersion might produce sympathy for and empathy with story characters, so that characters' experiences and beliefs have a strong influence on readers/viewers.

Green and Brock tested their theory with written stories using a Transportation Scale which aimed to show the degree of immersion of readers. They assessed the degree of transportation by a questionnaire asking the reader about issues such as the amount of mental imagery produced by the story, the self-reported degree of involvement in the story, the emotional effect of the story and the degree to which the real-world context intrudes on the reading experience. In a series of experiments, they showed that highly transported participants are more affected by attitudes expressed in a story.

Green and Brock also attempted to measure whether individuals who were highly transported were less questioning of the story. Using a novel technique which they term 'Pinocchio circling' (after the fictional character whose nose grew when he told a lie), participants were asked to circle any 'false notes' in the story they read, such as contradictory information or details that did not ring true. The results showed that highly transported readers found significantly fewer 'false notes' than those who were less transported. This seems to support the idea that immersion in a narrative world prompts fewer counterarguments. Also, Green and Brock investigated whether changes to the task might affect the degree of transportation. When participants were asked to focus more on 'surface' elements of the story, such as highlighting words that would be deemed difficult for younger students, there was a slight, but not significant, effect on transportation.

In principle, these attempts to manipulate immersion are interesting because they suggest that becoming involved in a story world might be a different process from observing the wording of a narrative, the latter being the key issue in the depth of processing work discussed in Chapter 5. Indeed our own research also suggests a distinction, since we saw in Chapter 5 that attempts to increase story interest by adding pre-announcements or expressions of surprise did not affect depth of processing as measured by attentiveness to wording changes. Subsequent work by de Graaf, Hoeken, Sanders, and Beentjes (2009) has built on Green and Brock's method of circling specific language items, in this case asking participants to identify spelling and punctuation errors. The task was intended to disrupt smooth reading and was found to decrease participants' attentional focus (in the sense of whether participants reported that their attention was captured by the story). In the same experiment, a separate group of participants were asked to perform a different distraction task which involved selecting one sentence in each of the story paragraphs which they thought could be omitted without disturbing the storyline. De Graaf found this to weaken the sense of presence in the narrative world rather than reported attentional focus, and she argues that these may be separate dimensions of narrative transportation.

A scale of readers' self-reported immersion has also been produced by Busselle and Bilandzic (2009). They refer to the scale as measuring 'narrative engagement', and with it they examined various aspects of the reader's or viewer's experience, incorporating, but also going beyond, Green and Brock's transportation indicators. Busselle and Bilandzic used the statistical method of factor analysis to interpret responses to a broad-ranging set of questions about narrative engagement on topics such as sympathy, empathy, understanding of characters' motives, sense of loss of time and self-awareness (or conversely, distraction from the task), sense of presence in the narrative world, feeling of narrative involvement, and ease of understanding the story. From the analysis, they identified four aspects as important indicators of narrative engagement: narrative under-standing (ease in constructing a mental model of the narrative), attentional focus (meaning in their research, lack of distraction from the real world context due to an intense sense of self-absorption in the narrative world), emotional engagement (feeling for and with characters) and narrative presence (the feeling of having entered a narrative world). According to their analysis, these four aspects of narrative response all correlated with enjoyment. In addition, attentional focus (as defined by these researchers), emotional engagement and narrative presence all correlated with story-related attitudes, suggesting some persuasive impact, but not with their notion of narrative understanding, in the sense of ease of constructing mental models.

De Graaf (2010, Experiment 1) relates specific aspects of story involve-ment to belief change. She altered the structure of narratives to create suspense, following Brewer and Lichtenstein's (1981, 1982) structural-affect theory, as described in Chapter 8. She found that readers who read suspense-ful versions agreed more with story-consistent beliefs than those who read non-suspenseful versions. Nevertheless, her analysis indicated that it was the structural differences rather than their emotional effect that were linked with greater agreement with story-consistent beliefs. In spite of these results, she believes that empathy in suspenseful situations might be a major affectual factor that prompts belief change, suggesting that her suspenseful materials in this experiment may not have adequately prompted empathy with the main character.

Individual differences in the personality traits of participants might also influence the role of affect. Appel and Richter (2010) investigated this possibility. They used Maio and Esses' (2001) notion of 'Need for

Affect', this being the characteristic of seeking out emotional situations and trying to intensify the emotional experience in these situations. Appel and Richter found that participants who scored higher on Need for Affect tests experienced a greater sense of transportation than readers with lower scores.

This work on narrative transportation and engagement is centred on the effects of simply reading a specific text or viewing a specific television programme or film. However, researchers in the entertainment-education field have suggested that persuasion might also be enhanced by post-reading and post-viewing activities such as group discussion (e.g., Larson, 2009; Slater, 2002). Although books are often read privately, they become a source of discussion in book groups, either in specific groups or nationally (see Swann & Allington, 2009, for reports on the national use of a story about immigration in book groups in the UK). When television programmes are shown nationally in countries such as the USA where there are multiple media influences, the persuasive impact might be enhanced by implementation strategies such as repetition of the message through multiple channels and screenings, and associated promotions, such as free gifts and celebrity endorsements. Also the use of online chat rooms, the encouragement for viewers to form their own local groups and specific calls to action (Larson, 2009) may influence persuasive impact. However, even if the repetition of a message and additional promotional techniques may sustain a message for a longer duration than reading a book or viewing a television programme or film, the limited duration of many media campaigns may not be sufficiently long to support individuals in maintaining lifestyle changing behaviours over extended periods. Larson's (2009) case study is of the use of such strategies to encourage a single specific action, namely encouraging women to attend a mammogram screening. But it is a different matter to change behaviour in such a way that it creates a sustained lifestyle behavioural change, such as encouraging changes in diet and exercise to tackle the problem of obesity. Slater (2002) has proposed a *stages-of-change model*. This is based on Prochaska, DiClemente, and Norcass' (1992) account of addiction changes that specifies the stages of precontemplation (no intention to change or unaware of the need for change), contemplation (consideration of possible change), preparation (plan for making changes), action (make changes), and maintenance (continuing to make changes). This model may also explain why some individuals are more susceptible to change, since the effect of a persuasional message may be different depending on the stage of change an individual has reached. The management of long-term change arising from entertainment-education and the effects of repeated persuasion on individuals already partly influenced by a particular idea are major issues for further research.

Literary texts and popular fiction: can they change readers?

General debates about possible effects on readers

Literary narratives and popular fiction are commonly held by the general public to have positive or negative effects. On the positive side, it is often taken for granted that reading literary classics is a character-improving and socially valuable activity. Public libraries are funded on this basis, financial support is given to literature students, and reading groups are organized in some prisons in the United States and in Britain. As Keen (2007) reports, when surveys show that reading is declining, there is concern that this will have an adverse effect on good citizenship. Conversely, some individuals and societies believe that narratives can have a subversive effect. Western books have sometimes been banned in certain countries, with reading only taking place under the guise of other activities and/or at considerable personal risk (e.g., Lamb, 2002, and Nafisi, 2004, for accounts of book groups organized in Afghanistan under the Taliban, and in Iran respectively). This suggests that these books are regarded as potentially dangerous by those who have banned them. Book banning occurs in specific schools in the United States due to parental concerns and ideological stances, as described by DelFattore (2002) in relation to religious objections to children's books (e.g., to J. K. Rowling's Harry Potter series for its portrayal of witchcraft). Films are often thought to have moral effects too. In Britain, Stanley Kubrick's film *A Clockwork Orange* was withdrawn from public cinemas for a 27-year period due to fears that it was inciting copycat violence.

Public views on the practical effects of reading seem to be based on little, if any, empirical evidence. In a study centred on the effects of reading novels, Keen (2007) has questioned whether reading really does have the effects attributed to it. She takes issue with the 'empathy-altruism hypothesis' of developmental psychologists (e.g., Eisenberg & Strayer, 1987) in relation to reading. This hypothesis is that empathy leads to socially desirable effects in the real world, such as greater compassion and reduced aggression to other people resulting in practical support and assistance. As mentioned in Chapter 8, the term 'prosocial behaviour' (Hoffman, 2008) is also used by psychologists for these types of practical effects. These psychological theories of Eisenberg and Strayer (1987) and Hoffman (2008) describe real-life situations where the empathizer is assessing and possibly reacting to an individual, the empathizee, often with the result being of direct benefit to the empathizee. For instance, an empathizer may feel sympathy for the empathizee and provide practical assistance. There is a different situation in reading fictional narratives because the immediate empathizee is a character, i.e., a mental representation of a textually described entity. When reading fictional narratives, the reader cannot directly assist characters, so any real altruism can only take the form of practical moves toward similar people in the real world. (Allbritton & Gerrig's, 1991, theory of participatory responses, discussed in Chapter 8, does, nevertheless, provide a model of how we might feel an urge to help a textually described character or pull that character back from danger.) In theory, real altruism might result after reading about a fictional character from a developing country, empathizing with that character, and then donating money to a relevant charity or having a more positive attitude on meeting real people from developing countries. If this happened, the empathizer's contact with the fictional character in the text would involve some change to the mental model of the reader, such as a change in moral stance, prompting prosocial behaviour to a third party at some time interval from when the text is read.

Keen accepts that there are a few documented cases where fictional books are regarded as having made a substantial difference to humanitarian campaigns, such as the influence of Harriet Beecher Stowe's *Uncle Tom's Cabin* on the eradication of slavery, but she questions whether this is in any way the norm. She suggests that many books might have neutral effects, with some types of reading (such as popular fiction) being little more than entertainment, and she also argues that negative effects (such as those arising from pornography) might counterbalance any positive effects of literary works, making it difficult to justify reading as a prosocial activity overall.

Keen's work is largely discursive, with a few anecdotal studies of real readers from which it is difficult to draw generalizations. Her work nevertheless provides a refreshing critique of ideas about the value of reading that are taken for granted by the general public and by many literary researchers. Her book challenges the supposed link between reading and altruistic benefit for a real-life third party, but we need to be aware that she is putting the emphasis on the most extreme type of case, since altruism, in the sense of directly related practical action to help another, is not the only potential social effect. Readers are often concerned to change themselves rather than to change others.

Hakemulder's (2000) book *The Moral Laboratory* provides a broader set of suggestions for a range of possible changes that could occur from reading literary narratives. These might include enhanced ability to make inferences about the consequences of events and human behaviour, awareness of the complexity of moral problems, awareness of fresh perspectives on common human problems, stimulation of ethical reflection and role-taking, in addition to any more substantial practical effects such as changing beliefs and prompting moral behaviour. We will look later at Hakemulder's empirical research to see the extent to which he manages to provide evidence for such possible changes. In principle, he is suggesting that reading literary narratives might enable us to develop mental tools that can be used as a precursor to ethical and moral reasoning, rather than that all literary books have a direct effect on the opinions and behaviour of readers. In this respect, the moral effects of reading books might be different for readers at different stages.

This may link in with Slater's (2002) stages-of-change model, providing a more sophisticated picture of possible change than a simple all-or-nothing model. Books might have a cumulative effect and also books might interact with other factors such as co-occurring real-life events or discussions, in order to change opinions or behaviour. Hakemulder's (2000) review of prior research suggested that discussing a book in addition to reading it was more effective than just reading a book, as found in the work of Slater (2002) and Larson (2009) just discussed. Hakemulder's review seeks to separate out these factors, in the interests of identifying the effects of reading alone. This type of distinction allows better controlled experimentation, but we should nevertheless remember that it is very common to discuss books, not only in educational settings, but also in book clubs, which are now a major social phenomenon (Swann & Allington, 2009), so there are important reasons for investigating reading in conjunction with other pre- and post-reading activities.

Types of texts

Empirical researchers need to take account not only of the ways that readers might be influenced, but also of the types of text. Much work in the humanities deals with texts which have the properties of being 'narrative', 'fiction' and 'literature' (e.g., Dickens' *David Copperfield* would be all three), but each of these labels makes different claims about the text. This can be significant in terms of the type of effects we might predict texts to have. Also, when it comes to empirical studies, the interest in specific aspects of a text will determine what type of texts are selected in the empirical design. Table 9.1 shows some of the distinctions which might be made.

Firstly, it is possible to contrast narrative text with other types of text. Narrative texts may be contrasted with argumentative texts, to gauge whether a story with an embedded moral point is more or less effective at changing beliefs than a text presented in argumentative form. Here the issue is how events are connected together and whether or not the text 'brings to life' specific characters, as we would expect in a narrative. We will see this explored in our case study of Hakemulder's work in the next section. Secondly, a narrative text can be presented to readers in different forms, such as with changes in perspective in a story. In this case, the issue of study is the balance of focus on one character or another. We examined the effects

Table 9.1 Possible text type distinctions to be made when carrying out empirical work

Narrative	Non-narrative, e.g., argumentative text
Narrative$_1$ (e.g., perspective$_1$)	Narrative$_2$ (e.g., perspective$_2$)
Fiction	Non-fiction, e.g., (auto)biography, history, law, newspapers
Literature	Non-literature, e.g., popular fiction

of changes in perspective in relation to first/second/third person presentations in Chapter 7, and the discussion of legal texts earlier in this chapter has also shown that a specific set of events might be told from different perspectives. It will be seen in the following section that Hakemulder and other researchers have manipulated texts with the aim of changing the perspective in order to see what effect this has on the beliefs of readers. A third area of investigation is the distinction between fictional and non-fictional texts. Here the issue is whether events are imaginary or real. Some researchers, such as Oatley (2002) and Keen (2007) believe that fiction may have special properties in providing a safe haven for experimenting with ethical issues. This argument may have an obvious point in the case of political allegories, such as Orwell's *Animal Farm*, where real-world details are set aside which might otherwise be difficult for writers to address directly and for readers to engage with, or might detract from the general point being made. The claim is, however, made more broadly than just in relation to such texts, with the suggestion that fiction per se may have special properties.

Oatley (2002, p. 63) claims that 'fiction has a laboratory quality. We experience it in a place of safety away from the ordinary world.' Oatley's argument relates specifically to how readers handle the emotions of texts, since he suggests that 'emotions in fiction can be experienced at different distances, not kept too far away so they do not touch us, nor too close so that they overwhelm us' (p. 64). We will return to Oatley's research in a case study of his empirical work in the next section. Keen (2007) suggests that fictional texts as a category might provide greater opportunities than non-fictional texts for empathy since they might be perceived as reducing the need for any direct action in the real world. Her ideas have been influential on humanities researchers, but we need to look critically at what evidence she presents. She claims to demonstrate this point with anecdotal reports of students' responses to two non-fictional fund-raising documents compared with an extract from Alexander McCall Smith's novel *Morality for Beautiful Girls* which contains an appeal for help from one of the characters. She finds that the majority of her students respond more empathetically to the fictional text. However, the study seems fundamentally flawed. Apart from the lack of any numerical data about the responses, Keen points out that the two non-fictional texts contain indicators that they are of dubious origin and hence may have aroused the suspicions of the students on this basis. Fund-raising letters are, anyway, a specific genre containing a direct appeal for action which might put people on their guard. Other types of non-fiction, such as a cancer patient's published autobiography, might present accounts which might make no direct demands on a reader in terms of action, but might nevertheless evoke empathy and provide a means of learning about a situation without experiencing it first hand. Of course this debate presumes a distinction between fiction and non-fiction, but in reality much fiction incorporates elements derived from autobiography, and conversely supposed non-fiction may contain fabricated elements.

Another category of text is literature. The term 'literature' implies a quality judgement, in contrast, for example, to popular fiction which is not generally regarded as having literary qualities. Discussions about the nature of literature inevitably lead to discussions of the literary canon. This is the body of texts which is at any point in time regarded as being of sufficient quality to be classed as literary. There is a fair consensus of agreement in literary studies that there are no defining formal features of literature, since judgements about literary value are social in nature (e.g., Eagleton, 1983). Individuals may have very different views on whether a text is of quality or not, and societal views may change radically from period to period. Nevertheless, the canon is normally regarded as being what the literary establishment considers to be literature at any particular point in time. This view of the canon gives experts the responsibility for determining which texts have quality. There is, however, debate about this.

Miall (2007) argues that the question of what constitutes literature should be determined by empirical means, determining how actual readers are responding to texts. He believes that literature is responsible for triggering certain types of feelings in readers. Miall and Kuiken (2002) suggest a four-part framework for categorizing the feelings prompted by literary works. They include what they term 'evaluative feelings' (e.g., overall enjoyment of a text), 'narrative feelings' (e.g., suspense, curiosity and empathy), 'aesthetic feelings' (interest in the formal features of the work, such as its stylistic properties, see also Kneepens & Zwaan, 1994; Tan, 1996) and 'self-modifying feelings' (those feelings which have the power to change the reader). This provides a useful model for examining the effects of literary reading, although the first two types of feeling do not appear to be exclusive to literary works, as Miall and Kuiken point out. As we saw in Chapter 8, popular fiction works, such as thrillers and detective stories, also prompt emotions such as enjoyment and suspense/curiosity.

Miall and Kuiken's idea of the possible self-modifying effects of reading literature can also be found in other academics who view literature as having the power to change its readers. Cook (1994) suggests that many literary texts may have 'schema refreshment' as their primary function, providing readers with new ways of looking at the world. Cook argues that although non-literary texts can also change schemata, literature's importance is that its main function is to challenge our world view. This 'schema refreshment' hypothesis has been a popular idea with humanities researchers. Nevertheless, Cook's idea is simply a hypothesis based on textual analysis and speculations about how texts might prompt significant schema changes, not on any evidence of how real readers actually respond to literary texts. Keen (2007) argues that if literary texts have any effect at all, they can have negative effects as well as positive ones, questioning the extent to which literature is elevated in status in terms of how it might affect the reader (although again, this is not based on any convincing empirical evidence). Semino (1997) and Jeffries (2001) point out that the value of some literary texts may lie in their ability to reflect the experiences of readers rather than change them, in which case 'schema reinforcement' might be as applicable as 'schema refreshment', but this again is speculation. Hakemulder (2000, p. 15) thinks that literature may be able to 'boost' the effects of narrative writing because of the way in which it represents complex emotional experiences. He proposes a mechanism based on defamiliarization. He suggests that the emotions of literary characters might demand more reflection than those of stereotyped characters in popular fiction, due to the complexity of presentation. Nevertheless, the experiments in his book do not directly deal with this type of contrast.

Shortly, we will examine empirical research which has looked directly at issues of quality, including Miall and Kuiken's explorations of their notion of self-modification. Although an exalted role is often suggested for literature in terms of its power to change us and it may be that quality of writing can have a 'boosting effect', we should remember that the empirical research on entertainment-education (as discussed earlier in this chapter) suggests that even non-literary stories, such as the storylines of soap operas, can have the ability to modify our attitudes and beliefs.

Empirical work on the personal and social effects of reading and writing

There have been empirical investigations of the effects of reading. In addition to questioning whether there is any practical effect at all from reading/ viewing narratives, and whether it is positive or negative, we need to consider who is affected (i.e., the writer, the reader or a third party). The type of effect also has to be taken into account, from changes to the ability to reason and respond emotionally to changes in opinions and behaviour (as outlined in Hakemulder's different categories). It is necessary to recognize that readers might be more or less receptive to persuasion through narrative at different stages in the process of change (as indicated by Slater's model) and that texts might lead to practical effects either cumulatively or in conjunction with other factors such as discussion of a text.

As far as the texts themselves are concerned, we need to consider how a text may direct the reader's judgement (e.g., by setting up particular perspectives) and whether distinctions such as the narrative or non-narrative categorization of a text, or its fictional or non-fictional nature, or its literary quality really make any difference.

Let us now examine case studies of empirical work which aims to answer some of these questions. There is a significant amount of research in this area so the studies we examine are a selection to show the nature of this type of work. The IGEL Society (the Society for the Empirical Study of Literature and Media) provides a major forum for experimental research of this kind. See also its journal launched in 2011, *Scientific Study of Literature*.

Does narrative fiction have greater moral effects on readers than argumentative non-fictional text? Hakemulder's (2000) book *The Moral Laboratory* was discussed in general terms earlier, but we will now look at the nature of his empirical work. His book is a classic study which focusses specifically on whether texts have moral effects on readers, and has influenced much current research in this area. He uses literary narratives for some of his materials and frames his general discussion in terms of the effects of reading literature (e.g., he focusses on this in his sub-title). Nevertheless, it is difficult to draw any conclusions from his empirical work about literature as such, because the experiments in this book do not directly contrast literary materials with narrative writing of lower quality. We will look here instead at his investigation of the distinction between the narrative fiction mode in contrast to an argumentative non-fictional text.

Hakemulder investigated whether stories might create belief changes over and above any belief changes prompted by an argumentative non-fictional work. He did this by requiring readers to perform virtual role-taking. In Experiment 2, his experimental materials consisted of a chapter from a novel ('the story'), and a non-fictional chapter from an argumentative work ('the essay'), both dealing with the topic of the position of women in Islamic fundamentalist countries. The story contained characters, and Hakemulder argued that this provides readers with the opportunity to 'experience for themselves' (p. 100) the position of the women, through empathetic responding. By contrast, the essay used only general statements, with no characterization. Participants read either the story or the essay, and were asked to provide ratings to questions about their beliefs after reading the text. A control group performed this rating exercise before reading the text. The questions were on the following topics: (1) beliefs about others, such as how the participants would behave if in the same position as the Algerian woman in the story; (2) solidarity with the women in the story, such as whether they favoured giving such women asylum; (3) beliefs about factual information about Islam, such as how widespread it is worldwide and regarding the position of women generally in Islamic countries; (4) social distance, such as attitudes toward Muslims; and (5) cultural intolerance, such as attitudes toward specific Islamic practices. There was also a bogus task of identifying stylistic features to avoid putting too much emphasis on the questions about attitudes (this was deemed necessary because in an earlier version of this experiment (Experiment 1), a number of students had guessed the purpose of the experiment). The results for Experiment 2 were: For topic (1), only one out of the four questions yielded a significant difference in attitudes between the story and both the control and the essay (the essay and the control were approximately the same). Topic (3) also produced significant differences for one out of the two questions for the story (again the essay and the control were approximately the same). Topics (2), (4) and (5) did not reveal any significant differences for any of the questions asked.

In this experiment then, many of the questions did not show any significant effects. Nevertheless, to get any difference to any questions at all is potentially interesting, since this means that even a single chapter of a story and an essay read in laboratory conditions appear to have had at least some effects on the readers' attitudes. Bearing in mind Slater's (2002) stages-of-change model, it might be argued that we would not necessarily expect all participants to be equally receptive to a text at any particular stage in their intellectual development. Indeed, in some respects, it might be worrying if readers did fundamentally change their attitudes every time they read a text.

Overall, there is some evidence from Hakemulder's work that stories may sometimes have greater moral effects on readers than argumentative text, but there is need for further testing across a range of texts. Hakemulder's results need to be treated with caution because, as he points out himself, the materials were natural texts and hence varied in many respects apart from the fact that one was a story and one was an essay. In addition, one was fictional and one was factual, a distinction we will return to later. Furthermore, although broadly on the same topic, there was no exact match, and the quality of the writing style cannot be directly equated (so the literary nature of the story might have had a 'boosting effect' but it is impossible to say without comparing it with a non-literary story of the same content). Another point about this work is that there is no real assessment of specific participants' attitudes before and after reading the texts. The comparison of the story group is with the essay group and the control group, but participants in these groups might have had different attitudes to start with, particularly considering that the subject matter concerns religious and gender issues.

Can changing perspective in narrative prompt greater empathy or sympathy?   Hakemulder (2000) has also examined the effect of changing narrative perspectives in relation to whether this leads to greater empathy. His Experiment 3 overcame some of the control problems of the experiment discussed above by presenting students in the two experimental groups with the same text, but with different reading instructions. Hakemulder drew on earlier psychological research (Gregory, Cialdini, & Carpenter, 1982), suggesting that if we imagine *ourselves* in a scenario, there is a greater likelihood of belief change than when we do not (note that this relates to the idea that personalization influences depth of processing and memory, as discussed in Chapter 7). He used the same story chapter as in Experiment 2, but gave participants either an empathy-building instruction or a placebo instruction, plus a control. The empathy-building instruction was 'Try to imagine, while you are reading, that you are in the position of the main female character. Imagine you see what she sees, you feel what she feels, and try to imagine that the events are all happening to you yourself. Please read slowly and try to link the story events with related personal experiences.' By contrast, participants in the placebo group were asked to read the story and mark the structure of the text with a pen or pencil. As in Experiment 2, the control group answered the questions before reading the text. Hakemulder expected the placebo instruction to have an effect, but the empathy-building instruction to have an even stronger effect. The same questionnaire was used as in Experiment 2 (with some minor modifications). For topic (1), Hakemulder's predictions were confirmed for three of the four questions, with the empathy-building group being significantly different from the control (the placebo instruction was sometimes as effective, sometimes less effective and sometimes not effective). For topics (2–5), none of the questions produced significant differences for the empathy-building group. The results, therefore, were rather mixed.

In principle, this experiment is interesting because it shows that in some cases reading effects might be enhanced by combining reading with overt instruction on how to read. Although in some natural solitary reading we do not normally have someone telling us how to read a book before we start, there may be more instructions on how to read when the book is a prescribed text for a class or reading group. The fact that there was sometimes an effect due to the placebo instruction is also interesting, because many literature students read set texts by annotating the structure as they read. Nevertheless, there is still the issue of whether we are really observing change here. Again, the results are assessed by comparing the end attitudes of participants with those in other groups, but this does not actually show each participant's attitudes before and after the experiment, hence does not chart the degree of change in each participant (bearing in mind the possibility of different attitudes to start with).

Experiment 3 used an explicit reading instruction to direct the reader, but as we have seen in Chapter 7, stylistic features might push readers toward seeing a story as if they are sharing the point of view of a character, so empathy could be boosted in a natural reading situation by the properties of the text itself. Hakemulder's Experiment 4 aimed to show this. He made minor changes to the style of literary narratives in order to change the focalization structure, such as changes from first person presentation to third person external presentation. This change from first to third person references had an effect on readers who responded significantly more leniently to a character who was an adulteress when they had read the narrative as a first person story than as a third person story, as judged by story evaluation questionnaires. This is what might be expected on the basis of the effects of personalization (see Chapter 7). Other manipulations of a second text did not have a significant effect, but this may be because the stylistic changes were less clear-cut in terms of changing the focalization format.

Earlier work by van Peer and Pander Maat (1996) separated out different aspects of focalization in order to assess the effect of these features on sympathy for characters. Participants were schoolchildren who were pre-sented with five different versions of a text, including not only manipulations for first and third person, but also inserted thoughts to change the third person representation to an internal perspective (as discussed in Chapter 7, third person perspectives can be either internal or external). The perspectives were aligned with two different characters, a husband and a wife having an argument. Sympathy was judged by asking participants which of these char-acters they sympathized with. The experimenters expected that there would be more sympathy for the character whose point of view was represented. Generally, this was the case, but the manipulations for linguistic features alone (first/third person manipulations) were limited and the experimenters were surprised that they did not observe more powerful effects considering how important focalization is in many narrative texts. Also, in one case the manipulations had the opposite effect to those intended, aligning the perspec-tive with the character whose point of view had not been represented. Van Peer and Pander Maat suggest that the readers' sympathies might also be affected by real-world attitudes, such as gender stereotypes, which might in such cases override attempts to manipulate perspective.

Hence, there appears to be some evidence to indicate that perspective manipulations can affect empathy/sympathy, but the direction and magnitude of the effect is not always predictable. In our earlier discussion of Voss and van Dyke's work on empathy in constructed courtroom discourse, we saw that the results were also against predictions, with attempts by a lawyer to gain empathy/sympathy for a victim leading to lower guilt ratings of the accused. Although there are many ideas about how empathy/sympathy is cued in literary studies, it seems that there is a need for further empirical work to determine how these emotions are triggered to different degrees, and whether they may reach saturation points resulting in attempts to induce them becoming counter-productive.

How effective is fiction in changing real-world beliefs? As we have seen, the empirical research on entertainment-education indicates that films about fictional events can be used as a mechanism for persuasion. Experiments by Prentice and Gerrig (1999) and Green and Brock (2000) suggest that written fictional texts can have at least a short-term effect on beliefs. Prentice, Gerrig, and Bailis (1997) showed that false information had an impact on students' beliefs when the setting was unfamiliar to students, but not when it was familiar, suggesting that students were more vulnerable to the false information in the former case. However, this effect was not replicated by Wheeler, Green, and Brock (1999). Other factors such as the disposition of participants to process information thoroughly and familiarity with the story topic have also been demonstrated in some studies (e.g., Green, 2004; Green & Brock, 2000; Wheeler et al., 1999).

Appel and Richter (2007) have examined whether written fictional stories might also have a long-term effect on readers' beliefs. They utilize Hovland, Lumsdaine, and Sheffield's (1949) notion of a 'sleeper effect', which is the idea that belief change caused by reading fiction might not only persist but also increase over time (see also Kumkale & Albarracin, 2004). Previous models such as the Elaboration Likelihood Model (Petty & Cacioppo, 1986) had included the assumption that the effect of persuasion by means of fiction would decline over time, since readers would not continue to think systematically about the fictional world to the same extent after reading. Appel and Richter offer a different model, arguing that the sleeper effect may arise in situations where persuasion is combined with a discounting cue that indicates that the source of the information is unreliable. They suggest that as the discounting cue is forgotten over time or disassociated from the false information in the message, the belief may increase for the false information.

Appel and Richter tested this using a fictional story from previous studies by Gerrig and Prentice (1991) about a kidnapping, with the text translated into German and set in Germany since the experiment was conducted there. Two versions of the story were used, one including a number of false statements about the real world (e.g., exercise weakens your heart and lungs) and one version replacing these false statements with accurate statements (e.g., exercise strengthens your heart and lungs), in addition to a control. Participants were given a questionnaire and asked to rate to what extent they agreed with these statements and how certain they were about their beliefs. Participants were tested immediately after and two weeks after reading the story. They found long-term persuasive effects to be stronger than short-term effects in two respects: the participants held stronger beliefs and were more certain about their beliefs after a two-week gap. Appel and Richter see their work as compatible with the Transportation Model of persuasion discussed earlier (e.g., Gerrig, 1993; Green and Brock, 2000), since they believe that the fictional nature of the text might neutralize critical evaluation of the relevant statements.

Does narrative fiction enable readers to simulate social situations and thereby improve their personalities?   As we have indicated, the 'improving' nature of reading narrative fiction is an idea that is very much in circulation. Oatley (2008; Mar & Oatley, 2008) makes the argument that reading narrative fiction is the operation of the mind's 'flight simulator'. Through simulation of complex social interaction, we come to understand such interactions more deeply, the argument goes. The analogy is further extended by Oatley, who argues that 'if one wants to learn to fly, it may be a good idea to spend time in a flight simulator' (2008, p. 1030). The idea is, then, that people who spend time reading narrative fiction will become more skilled socially than those who do not.

Mar, Oatley, Hirsh, dela Paz, and Peterson (2006) set out to test this prediction. They compared people who were taken to be habitual and frequent readers of narrative fiction with people who were not. The index of such 'exposure to print' was the Author Recognition Test, or ART (Stanovich & West, 1989), in which the names of narrative fiction writers and non-fiction expository writers were presented, and the participants had to indicate whether each name presented was a real author or not (some were not in reality). This test is known to reflect early reading ability (Cunningham & Stanovich, 1997) and to predict real-world reading (West, Stanovich, & Mitchell, 1993), amongst other things.

The question was whether people who scored high on the narrative fiction names in the ART would show a higher score in measures of empathy, or sensitivity to social situations. Three basic measures were used: a self-report test (the interpersonal reactivity test; Davis, 1980); a test of judging people's mental states from pictures showing a variety of eye-gazes (the 'Reading the mind in the eyes' test; Baron-Cohen, Wheelright, Hill, Raste, & Plumb, 2001); and a test in which unscripted videos of social interactions were shown, and participants had to make a judgement about the social relations amongst the characters (the interpersonal perception task; Constanzo & Archer, 1989).

The results showed a positive correlation between exposure to narrative fiction and performance-based measures of social ability, as the experiments had predicted. Furthermore, there was a negative correlation between exposure to non-fiction and social ability. So, apparently it is not reading per se that matters here, it is reading narrative fiction. These findings could not be explained through any other obvious variables.

So, does reading narrative fiction bring about better empathy-based social skills? This cannot be concluded. For instance, at its simplest, people with better social skills may prefer to read about things that portray social skills in operation, while people who have a 'general knowledge' orientation may prefer to read expository texts about science, politics and philosophy. The authors of this work acknowledge such a fact, although they take the relationship that they established as meaning that the possibility that reading narrative fiction improves social skills remains a compelling idea. However, on the basis of this study, such a conclusion is more rhetoric than fact. Mar et al. (2006) discuss many interesting issues in this paper. It is clear that the debate will continue and is in need of further empirical investigation. Certainly stories have the capacity to place readers in situations that they would not personally experience, allowing experience-by-proxy (Oatley, 1999).

An issue that needs further study is whether non-fictional narratives have the same effects as fictional ones with respect to the development of social skills. (Auto)biographies often provide stories of exceptional people in exceptional circumstances, and can offer a rich vein of human experience from which readers may be able to learn. It is not clear to us why Oatley attributes the social effects of reading entirely to fictional narratives. Possibly his argument that fiction provides a 'safe zone' for personal experience (see earlier) is behind this, but narrative non-fiction may also be relatively 'safe' in contrast to real-life experience. Compare, for example, the experience of reading a fictional account of a cancer patient's treatment, the experience of reading a factual account of a patient's treatment in a biography or autobiography, or actually witnessing or undergoing the treatment in real life. Both types of reading might be hypothesized to require less direct personal emotional involvement than real-life experience, but both might nevertheless provide the possibility of important insights.

Does literature have particular ability to change its readers?   In our discussion above, we introduced Miall and Kuiken's (2002) idea that literary texts might lead to 'self-modifying' feelings, i.e., that they might cause readers to change their self-concept in some way (see also Kuiken, 2008; Kuiken, Miall, & Sikora, 2004; Kuiken, Phillips, et al., 2004; Miall, 2007). In a number of empirical studies they have investigated this using a 'self-probed retrospection' method (originally designed by Larsen & Seilman, 1988), where the experimenters ask readers to mark a literary text as they read it, with readers noting passages which they feel have particular emotional resonance. After completing reading the text, participants are then asked to think aloud about some of the passages that they have marked, with the protocols being taped and subsequently transcribed. This is regarded by Miall and Kuiken as a less intrusive method than conventional 'protocol analysis' where participants think aloud as they read a passage for the first time.

From analysing the self-reports, Miall and Kuiken argue that readers appear to sometimes experience a fresh emotion which they have not previously experienced, providing a novel understanding of a situation. Readers may 'self-implicate' (Kuiken, Miall, & Sikora, 2004) by using the generic *you* pronoun to include their own reaction when discussing events in the story (e.g., '[A] passage like this makes you realize that some day, perhaps something like that will happen to you because you know how close it could be for you' (Kuiken, 2008, p. 61)). Such observations may also be elaborated on during the course of the protocol in ways that show the readers' self-perceptions shifting. Kuiken, Phillips, et al. (2004) find individual differences in the number of self-modifying feelings reported in response to selected passages in a specific literary story, with readers with higher degrees of absorption (as measured by the Tellegen Absorption Scale (Tellegen, 1982)) reporting a greater number. These investigators do not directly contrast literary texts with popular fiction, so the issue of whether literary writing has a different effect from other types of writing is not demonstrated. They do, however, show that the way that readers become involved in the world of a literary text is important.

A study by Djikic, Oatley, Zoeterman, and Peterson (2009) attempted to show how 'art' (literary narrative fiction) might change readers' personalities by contrasting a literary work with a non-literary version. Whereas Miall and Kuiken were looking at the effect that specific passages have on readers in terms of their own self-reports of thoughts prompted by the text, Djikic et al. (2009) aimed to find evidence for an overall effect of a text on specific personality factors using questions and checklists. Participants were given material from an English translation of the short story *The Lady with the Toy Dog*, by Anton Chekhov. This story deals with an adulterous love affair between two married people. Djikic et al. used this content to present two versions of the story. In one version, the story was presented in its original (literary narrative fiction) format. In the other version, experimenters presented the same story, fabricated as a courtroom interaction (i.e., non-literary narrative (supposed) non-fiction). The two versions were equated on length and readability. Hence, it was possible to compare the two materials for the effect that they had on readers.

To do this, all readers were initially presented with a series of questions from the Big Five Inventory (cf. John & Srivastava, 1999), and an emotions checklist. The Big Five Inventory poses a series of questions about how people see themselves (e.g., talkative, friendly, etc.), and assesses extroversion, conscientiousness, agreeableness, emotional stability and openness. The emotions check-list comprised a list of ten emotions (e.g., fearfulness, contentment, etc.) and participants were required to rate themselves in terms of how much they felt each emotion at the moment of testing.

The basic idea was that there would be more changes in the measures made by these tests following exposure to the literary version than to the court case version, though the test was rather open-ended in terms of the direction changes might take and the differences in changes across different participants. After participants read one of the texts, the questionnaire was re-administered. It was indeed found that there were more changes following the literary version than the court case version, though the directions of changes were not systematic over individuals. Arguing that everyone is different in the way they might change as a result of encountering literature, this work might be seen as evidence that the literary text has more impact than the court case presentation. However, Djikic et al.'s experimental materials differ in more than one respect in terms of the category of text to which they belong. The title of their article focusses on 'art', presumably meaning the literary quality of Chekhov's writing, but their sub-title refers to 'fiction', what we would take to be the imaginary nature of his story, in contrast to the (supposed) factual nature of the court case presentation. Also, the experimental materials are obviously of different genres since one is in the style of courtroom discourse and one is a short story including descriptive passages. Without further control of the materials, it is not possible to determine whether the quality of Chekhov's writing, its fictional status or genre differences are having an effect on readers.

Does writing autobiographical narratives improve the health of authors? Narration appears to cause otherwise fragmentary states of affairs, motivations, plans and goals to become coherently unified, whether this is veridical or illusory. This prompts the question of whether being the producer of narratives of our own, personal experiences has any psychological effects on us as producers, such as making our lives seem more coherent. Indeed, the empirical work of Pennebaker and colleagues suggests that writing can actually have health benefits for writers. Ramírez-Esparza and Pennebaker (2007) claim that there is a substantial body of published work supporting this idea, citing meta-analyses showing weak to moderate effects of expressive writing. One interesting method used by Pennebaker and colleagues has been to ask a number of individuals to write about their deepest thoughts and feelings about a traumatic event in their lives for fifteen to thirty minutes per day for one to five days (Pennebaker, 1997a). Another group provided a control by writing about more superficial topics, such as day-to-day activities. In Pennebaker and Beall (1986), students' visits to the university health centre were monitored before and after the writing study. The visits of those writing about emotional trauma were reduced by half in the two months after writing in contrast to those in the control group, and physiological studies showed immune function to be enhanced (see Pennebaker, 1997a, b, for reviews; also Pennebaker & Chung, 2007; Sloan & Marx, 2004).

Pennebaker and colleagues have focussed on using computer techniques to analyse the grammatical and vocabulary use of writers. Their studies show that predictors of health are as follows: (1) high levels of positive emotion words, and moderate levels (not high or low levels) of negative words (Pennebaker, Mayne, & Francis, 1997); (2) increases in the use of causal words (e.g., *because*) and perception words (e.g., *understand*) across the span of a study (Pennebaker et al., 1997); (3) switches in the use of different pronouns during the study, such as switching from '*I*-focus' to '*we*-focus' or '*them*-focus', or vice versa (Campbell & Pennebaker, 2003). The results for emotion words make sense in terms of writers taking a positive approach, but were against predictions for negative words, where it might be expected that a low use of negative expressions might be beneficial for health. Pennebaker et al., however, rationalize this on the basis that moderate use of negative words might reflect the author engaging with negative issues rather than repressing them completely. The use of causal and perception words was as predicted, since this may reflect the ability of writers to link events and draw conclusions from them. The use of pronouns shows that any change is beneficial, with no noticeable effect in a specific direction (i.e., in terms of a switch from singular pronouns to plural or vice versa). Campbell and Pennebaker argue that this may reflect the ability of writers to change orientation in terms of presenting themselves and others, which may have health benefits. Overall, the links here are with a particular style of writing rather than with narrative structure in itself. Also, as Campbell and Pennebaker point out, the correlation simply shows that there is a connection between these linguistic features and assumed health, not that writing in this style causes good health. Thus the writing style could reflect improvement that was due to other causes.

Expressive writing therefore appears to have health effects, but this raises the question of whether writing in narrative form can have specific benefits. Pennebaker and Seagal (1999) speculated that this might be the case:

the act of constructing stories is a natural human process that helps individuals to understand their experiences and themselves. This process allows one to organize and remember events in a coherent fashion while integrating thoughts and feelings. In essence, this gives individuals a sense of predictability and control over their lives. Once an experience has structure and meaning, it would follow that the emotional effects of that experience are more manageable. Constructing stories facilitates a sense of resolution, which results in less rumination and eventually allows disturbing experiences to subside gradually from conscious thought. (p. 1243)

So, the suggestion is that the increased coherence produced by narration somehow produced a sense of reduced uncertainty and of understanding. The idea that stories allow a means of providing a coherent notion of autobiographical experience is also a key notion in studies of the self (e.g., Linde, 1993, 2005; Polkinghorne, 1988). Of course, whether the whole narrative corresponds to reality or contains illusory coherence remains an issue. Perhaps this is less important when the emphasis is on reducing distress in people, as in clinical applications (e.g., Gergen & Gergen, 2007), than when attempting to verify what happened, as in the case of a law court narrative.

In spite of the appealing nature of this idea, Ramírez-Esparza and Pennebaker (2007) state that Pennebaker's group have not succeeded in linking the narrative form itself, as opposed to expressive writing in general, with improved health. Also attempts to see whether better storywriters show greater benefits have not been successful. This may, however, be due to the criteria that they have used and/or the whole idea that a third party's judgement of quality might be connected to how the writers themselves respond to their own stories. In Graybeal, Sexton, and Pennebaker (2002), judgements of the quality of stories were made on the basis of whether the story had a moral message and whether it was a good read. However, since the whole point of the exercise is for writers to explore their own feelings, it seems odd to judge the stories on the basis of factors which make the story accessible to an audience. Possibly factors such as the ability to integrate events into a more coherent account and see events from different narrative perspectives, which are both assumed to have therapeutic value (e.g., Gergen & Gergen, 2007), might provide alternative ways to study the possible benefits of story-writing.

Summary

In this chapter we have examined the social impact of narratives, examining a range of types of narrative which might have a persuasive effect on readers, possibly prompting attitude change. The main issues we have examined are as follows:

- Narration is a two-edged weapon when used for persuasive purposes in relation to events in real life. On one hand, it can relate things to one another so that they form a clear unified whole. On the other hand, doing so may involve filling in gaps in ways that are not strictly warranted, resulting in ideas that are coherent, but that may distort reality. This applies to the presentation of information in courts, expository arguments in general, historical description and producing narratives about oneself.

- Courtroom discourse has been examined to see how effective it is in persuading a jury of guilt or innocence. There is evidence that increasing the coherence of a text can increase its plausibility. This has been shown empirically by manipulating the sequencing of events, the use of causal expressions, and the occurrence of modal expressions suggesting a higher degree of certainty, in addition to inserting explicit conclusions. There is, nevertheless, a need to explore further the effects of adding extra descriptive information about participants, and it would be useful to examine how the judge's directions might affect the depth of processing of courtroom evidence, using the types of techniques (anomaly detection and text-change detection) discussed in earlier chapters.

- Persuasive material can be embedded within entertaining narratives, termed 'entertainment-education' within media studies. This is now common in films and television programmes in order to promote social messages, such as advice about health. There is sociological evidence that entertainment-education can be effective in changing attitudes and behaviour. Much research evidence in psychology has been directed toward understanding the processes by which changes might occur. The idea that the degree of immersion of readers in a narrative affects the degree of persuasion has been shown in a number of experiments. There is still, however, further research needed on how attitudes and behaviour can be changed on a long-term basis.

- There is much public debate about the possible positive and negative effects of reading stories. In particular, it is suggested that literary narratives may be character-improving. Conversely, books may be banned on the basis that they are supposed to have a corrupting influence. Many of these claims made by the general public are based more on rhetoric than evidence, but there is now a considerable body of relevant experimental investigations by researchers in the empirical study of literature and cognitive psychology. The experimental work has studied issues such as the relative moral effect of narrative fiction compared to argumentative effect, the effects of changing perspective in a narrative on empathy/sympathy, the effectiveness of fiction on changing real-world beliefs, the possible influence of narrative fiction on the personalities of readers and whether works of literary quality have particular ability to change their readers. There is some evidence of effects in all these areas, although results are sometimes rather mixed and it is not always clear what particular aspect of the text (i.e., its narrative form, its use of rhetorical focussing devices, its fictional status or its literary quality) is responsible for these effects.

- The health benefits of writing narratives have been extensively examined. Pennebaker and colleagues have investigated the health effects of expressive writing, where individuals are required to make daily autobio-graphical reports about traumatic events in their lives. A correlation has been found between writing and health, but this does not give conclusive evidence of a causal relation. Although this team of investigators has suggested that the narrative format might be a factor in giving writers greater control over their lives, they admit that they have not been able to provide empirical evidence of this link.

- Overall, the social impact of narratives is an important practical area of research. Further research is needed to understand the processes under-lying the effects of reading and writing, in particular the long-term effects. This is necessary to guide public policy on funding reading and writing programmes.

10　Final comments

Throughout this book, we have presented a study of the interface between psychological accounts of discourse comprehension and humanities-based discussions of narrative. Our Rhetorical Processing Framework has been used to integrate an extremely broad range of topics relating to narrative processing. Much of mainstream psycholinguistics deals with issues such as how syntactic parsing occurs and how basic meaning is established, but as soon as one considers anything but the most basic minimal definition of narrative discussed at the start of Chapter 1, it becomes necessary to extend the range of psychological issues examined. Most narratives include characters in social situations, and so narrative becomes a microcosm of human activity in general. Readers get a sense of being immersed in a narrative world, and a feeling of experiencing physical sensations and emotions, as well as having moral attitudes toward characters. The experiential aspect is thus crucial to our framework. We have also extended the range of processing issues by examining how writers rhetorically control how their narratives are told. The use of particular stylistic devices is important for focussing attention, which serves to control the types of mental representation that readers construct.

Our Rhetorical Processing Framework, as presented in this book, has three key strands. The first strand, fundamental Scenario-Mapping Theory, provides what we consider to be the most broadly embracing psychological account of how words manipulate the kind of knowledge brought into comprehension, and the nature of that knowledge (specificity, scope and its limitations, such as what information will typically be readily available). We argued that scenario-mapping is the most basic form of understanding, the recognition of situations, following the earlier work of Sanford and Garrod (1981, 1998). The basic processes of scenario-mapping have been extensively investigated empirically, but there are still many issues which are worthy of further exploration. For example, we suggested that when a language-to-current-scenario mapping fails, this disrupts the smooth nature of primary understanding, driving more complex secondary processing and leading to defamiliarization. We examined this in relation to unexpected events occurring to scenario-dependent characters in Chapter 2. These unexpected events appeared to stimulate interest in readers, but nevertheless the wide range of different ways in which writers can manipulate expectations needs more empirical investigation. In addition, in Chapter 3 we presented initial explorations of the use of everyday knowledge in situations where counterfactual worlds are set up, but clearly the many different types of counterfactual situation in full, complex narratives need further study.

The second strand of our framework is the Rhetorical Focussing Principle. The claim is that when writers write, they want readers to think about and make ready inferences about X, not about Y. If X is more important than Y, then too much emphasis on Y would be distracting. An important part of writing is the control over the flow of attention that is engendered in the reader. Writers use attention-controlling devices, such as clefting, unusual vocabulary items, metaphor, sound play and graphical emphasis. Just how these devices work is, of course, a key issue. The Rhetorical Focussing Principle proposes that the familiar ideas of ease of anaphoric reference and strength of representation in memory have to be extended through the modulation of the depth of processing, a proposal that is central to this book. According to the idea of depth of processing, foregrounding devices lead to more semantically detailed representations based on language input than is possible with neutral or 'buried' forms of presentation. The experiments we presented in Chapters 4 and 5 showed that foregrounding devices do indeed modulate depth of processing. Depth of processing is an important concept because it provides a general way of accounting for the relationship between devices in writing and the processing consequences that they have, in terms of tractable psychological ideas. Beyond that, depth of processing provides a starting point for studying situations where it is claimed that a writer is manipulating the 'vividness' or 'directness' of the impressions a reader has from the writing. We illustrated this in Chapter 7 through both the issue of personalization in narration (the use of *you*), and the long-standing and important distinction between direct and indirect speech and thought. The key idea here is that the notions of 'vividness' and 'directness' need not be nebulous concepts, but may be understood in terms of depth of processing.

In our explorations of rhetorical focussing, we have had most success in dealing with stylistic devices of emphasis, such as clefting and italics. We were surprised that some explicit forewarnings of the need to attend (e.g., *Then this happened*), did not seem to influence depth of subsequent processing. This whole class of forewarnings requires more exploration, because one would expect such devices to have attention-controlling effects.

These two elements of our framework, scenario-mapping and rhetorical focussing, are essentially cognitive in nature, being concerned with how reading leads to meaning representations of various sorts. The experiential aspect of narrative comprehension, the third strand in our framework, has traditionally been regarded as more mysterious. However, since the recent accumulation of psychological discoveries about embodiment, this has changed. Ideas of immersion in a narrative world and experiencing a seemingly physical sense of rich perceptual and motor descriptions find a potential basis in embodiment effects. The important relationship for understanding the effects of writing is between sensation and language. In Chapter 6, we presented a review of a great deal of evidence showing how the comprehension of statements about movement and perception seem to entail some sort of simulation of how those movements or perceptions are processed in the brain. Embodiment effects seem to come about simply by reading descriptions of actions and perceptions, but the full details of this are far from established.

Some psychologists believe that embodiment effects always occur, and that they represent the only way meaning may be understood. Others believe that embodiment effects may occur, but are not the sole means of 'understanding' action and perception statements. We incline toward the latter point of view. We also believe that embodiment effects (or at least, their role in our consciousness as we read) may be amplified or minimized by how writers express themselves (see Zwaan, Taylor, & de Boer, 2010, for a similar view). Thus, the modulation of embodiment effects would seem to be another aspect of depth of processing, and should fall under the Rhetorical Focussing Principle. There is little work on this, but we think that the study by Yao, Belin, and Scheepers (2011) is suggestive for future research. These investigators (see Chapter 7) showed that direct speech more greatly activated brain areas that correspond to speech processing than did indirect speech, which we consider to be an observation of major significance. This means that, to an extent, we may be really hearing voices as we read. Could similar differences be found for, say, brain activation for action statements that were presented in either a foregrounded or unforegrounded way? The possibilities here are very exciting.

Another interesting thing about embodiment effects is that they relate closely to the idea that when reading of a character being in pain, we might 'feel their pain'. There is a big difference between simply having the knowledge (i.e., a cognitive condition) that the other person would feel uncomfortable in some situation and actually 'feeling' uncomfortable. While the evidence for a direct feeling of pain is not there, it is clear that parts of the brain involved in the reaction to actual pain are active in many such situations. This has led to observations concerning how a person might react to another who is unpleasant, or perceived of as immoral. This has implications for the study of empathy and its limits, and recent work in social neuroscience, cited in Chapter 8, has begun to address these issues. Of course, much of this work has not used texts, but rather other more direct forms of depiction. There is a great potential for studying the effects of text in this regard, and that is precisely what is needed. All in all, a greater connection between psychological and neuroscience studies of empathy in general, and how writers might manipulate this in texts, must be in the sights of front-line future research. Possibly collaboration between scientists interested in the humanities and creative writers might provide the best tool for investigating scenario-elicitation, rhetorical focussing effects and the use of writing devices to control the experiential effects of reading.

A further theoretical issue we would like to touch on is the role of consciousness in processing narrative. Once we introduce the experiential, we inevitably have to deal with consciousness, relating this to the special conditions of narrative. For instance, how does rhetorical focussing influence what we are aware of? In our account of rhetorical focussing, we discussed the problem in terms of ease of reference, strength of memory representations, depth of processing and embodiment effects. Although embodiment effects bear an undoubted relation to what we are aware of, the possible role of awareness remains relatively untouched by discourse psychologists, though there may be tacit assumptions about it in humanities work. It seems worth exploring, but the early history of psychology was bedevilled by problems when introspection was used, so the exploration will not be easy.

The applicability of psychological and neuroscience research to the overall functions of narrative should not go unobserved. Entertainment is a primary function of many narratives. Although the theory of suspense requires more substantial development, the fact is that we do find many narratives interesting (Chapter 8). There is a balance here between the enjoyment of unusual events and the enjoyment of familiarity. Unusual events motivate storytelling, but stories are also rooted in the familiar, which has its own satisfaction. We build alternative worlds using familiar everyday knowledge. We often also like hearing the same stories repeated, even though we may remember, from previous tellings, how the story develops. We have argued that scenario-mapping is a fundamental of understanding. By relating new concepts to the familiar, we have a basis for more complex understanding. But more than that, we believe that scenario-mapping is responsible for a *feeling* of understanding. An interesting question is whether there is any evidence that both scenario-mapping and narrative formats satisfy some basic neural process. Though there is no evidence that we are aware of that the brain responds favourably (in the sense of being satisfied, or comforted) to familiarity of basic scenario-mapping and repeated narrative events, it is an open question for investigation.

Enjoyment is one key function of many narratives, but narratives may also have other functions such as persuading people to change their attitudes and behaviour (Chapter 9). Rhetorical focussing by means of stylistic foregrounding may play a role in the effectiveness of narrative as a persuasive tool.

The study of anomalies and text change, as described in Chapters 4 and 5, might be used to investigate the use of linguistic features such as modal verbs and adverbs (*can*, *must*, *probably*, etc.) to see whether and how these might contribute to explicit persuasion, as in legal discourse. These techniques might also be used to study whether placing information at different points in a paragraph or in longer stretches of text serves to raise attention or bury information. For narratives which may persuade through entertainment, the role of narrative immersion seems crucial and this might be further examined using the psychological and neuroscience research on the experiential aspects described in Chapters 6–8.

We have attempted a broad coverage in the present book, combining psychological and neuroscience work with issues raised in the humanities. We believe that the psychological and neuroscience investigations provide a rigorous means of exploring intuitions from the humanities and allow these intuitions to be framed in processing terms. The humanities offer psychologists and neuroscientists a wealth of ideas about how full complex narratives are read, in particular about rhetorical issues such as the stylistic devices used in narratives and their experiential effects. We have brought together representative examples of the current state of knowledge in these different disciplines, and we hope that the research described also contributes to setting the agenda for future interdisciplinary explorations of mind, brain and narrative.

Appendix 1   Electroencephalography (EEG)

One important technique in estimating brain activity is EEG. If two electrodes are placed on the scalp, electrical activity within the brain can be measured in terms of a voltage between the electrodes. The voltages involved are very small indeed, sometimes measurable only in microvolts. Nevertheless, spontaneous rhythms can be readily detected through the use of amplifiers. By using an array of electrodes, up to 120 or even more, it is possible to observe activity localized to particular parts of the scalp, and many of these have an approximate correspondence to the parts of the brain where the electrical activity is generated.

Of particular interest to language researchers has been the use of so-called *event-related potentials* (ERPs). These are peaks of electrical activity that are time-locked to the onset of stimuli, such as flashes of light or sounds. Because these ERPs are easily hidden by the continuous, spontaneous activity of the brain, they are most readily recognized if a large number of stimuli are presented, and the voltage changes from the onset of the stimuli are averaged over presentations. That way the spontaneous activity becomes smoothed out, leaving only the ERP.

For research on language, the interesting discovery was that when words are presented as stimuli, particular forms of ERPs are observed. For example, there is a negative voltage peak about 400 ms after words are presented, with a characteristic spatial distribution over parts of the scalp, known for convenience as the N400. What is of special interest is that the N400 is larger when a word is presented that does not fit a context well, compared to one that does. The difference is known as the *N400 effect*. An example of the difference between a word that fits the context and one that does not is shown in Figure 2.1 of the main text.

The N400 is one of several ERPs that are observed in much language work, and is particularly associated with semantic processing (as discovered by Kutas & Hillyard, 1980). Another example is a positive voltage peak at around 600 ms after the onset of the stimulus word, known as the P600. The P600 is particularly associated with words that constitute syntactic violation of the sentences in which they appear. For an introduction to ERP effects associated with language studies, see Kutas, van Petten, and Kluender (2006), Samar (2006) and van Berkum (2004).

Appendix 2 Functional Magnetic Resonance Imaging (fMRI)

Functional MRI is one of the most important techniques for investigating the basis in the brain for various psychological phenomena. The technique makes use of the fact that when there is activity localized to particular areas of the brain, there are changes in blood flow there, which increase the supply of glucose and oxygen, essential for the metabolism. What fMRI measures is blood-oxygen-level dependence, or the BOLD response. Haemoglobin, the oxygen-carrying compound in the blood, has changes in its magnetic properties when there are changes in the extent to which it is oxygenated, and it is these magnetic changes that are detected in the MRI scanner. By using large magnetic fields in the MRI scanner, it is possible to localize brain volumes fairly accurately (using volumes, or voxels, of 2–4 millimetres). So, by comparing any two conditions in an experiment, it is possible to assess any activity that is localized in any respect to a particular part of the brain.

The localization of function is a seemingly simple and attractive way of making many comparisons. In this book, we illustrate several situations in which localization claims have been made. If, for instance, the same areas of the brain are similarly active when perceiving a real visual stimulus and imagining it, then there is a suggestion that perception and imagination are related. However, two caveats are necessary. First, the brain is a complex, diffuse system of neurons that interconnect in complex ways, so many important things may occur in the brain that are simply not localized. Second, it must be recognized as a leap of faith that when the same brain area shows activity with two different types of psychological event, this means that the neural computations are equivalent. However, it seems like a good start if two events (like visual perception and imagination) both produce similar activity in the same or closely related groups of voxels, to assume that there is something in common about the computations going on.

Detection of localized effects is the strength of fMRI, whereas uninvasive scalp-recorded EEG typical of studies with humans has very poor spatial resolution, and that resolution is restricted to the scalp. To infer a mapping in the brain relies on inferential methods, since many different types of activity in different areas of the brain can combine to give the same EEG pattern.

With fMRI, however, temporal resolution is very poor in comparison with EEG. Typically the BOLD response emerges after several seconds, and the millisecond accuracy of EEG is simply not possible. Sometimes both methods might be used together to form a fuller picture.

There are various descriptions of fMRI available through web searches. For further reading, see Cabeza and Kingstone (2006) and Skipper and Small (2006).

References

Abelson, R. P. (1963). Computer simulation of 'hot' cognition. In S. Tomkins & S. Messick (Eds.), *Computer simulation of personality: Frontier of psychological theory* (pp. 277–298). New York: Wiley.

Abercrombie, D. (1968). *Some functions of silent stress. Work in progress 2.* Edinburgh: Edinburgh University Press.

Adams, D. (1986a). *The hitchhiker's guide to the galaxy.* In *The hitchhiker's guide to the galaxy: A trilogy in four parts* (pp. 13–149). London: William Heinemann.

  (1986b). *The restaurant at the end of the universe.* In *The hitchhiker's guide to the galaxy: A trilogy in four parts* (pp. 151–308). London: William Heinemann.

Albrecht, J. E., & O'Brien, E. J. (1993). Updating a mental model: Maintaining both local and global coherence. *Journal of Experimental Psychology: Learning, Memory and Cognition, 19,* 1061–1070.

Alexander, J. D., & Nygaard, L. C. (2008). Reading voices and hearing text: Talker-specific auditory imagery in reading. *Journal of Experimental Psychology: Human Perception and Performance, 34,* 446–459.

Ali, M. (2004). *Brick Lane.* London: Black Swan.

Allbritton, D. W., & Gerrig, R. J. (1991). Participatory responses in text understanding. *Journal of Memory and Language, 30,* 603–626.

Allen, R. (2002). *Punctuation.* Oxford: Oxford University Press.

Allison, M., Brimacombe, C. A. E., Hunter, M. A., & Kadlec, H. (2006). Younger and older adult eyewitnesses' use of narrative features in testimony. *Discourse Processes, 41,* 289–314.

Almor, A. (1999). Noun-phrase anaphora and focus: The informational load hypothesis. *Psychological Review, 106,* 748–765.

Altmann, G. T. M., & Kamide, Y. (1999). Incremental interpretation at verbs: Restricting the domain of subsequent reference. *Cognition, 73,* 247–264.

Anderson, A., Garrod, S. C., & Sanford, A. J. (1983). The accessibility of pronominal antecedents as a function of episode shifts in narrative text. *Quarterly Journal of Experimental Psychology, 35A,* 427–440.

Anshel, M. H. (1988). The effect of mood and pleasant versus unpleasant information feedback on performing a motor skill. *Journal of General Psychology, 115,* 117–129.

Appel, M., & Richter, T. (2007). Persuasive effects of fictional narratives increase over time. *Media Psychology, 10,* 113–134.

  (2010). Transportation and need for affect in narrative persuasion: A mediated moderation model. *Media Psychology, 13,* 101–135.

Ariel, M. (1990). *Accessing noun-phrase antecedents*. London: Routledge.

Arnold, J. E. (2001). The effect of thematic roles on pronoun use and frequency of reference continuation. *Discourse Processes, 31*, 137–162.

Arnold, M. B. (1961). *Emotion and personality, Vol. 1*. London: Cassell.

Arzouan, Y., Goldstein, A., & Faust, M. (2007). Dynamics of hemispheric activity during metaphor comprehension: Electrophysical measures. *NeuroImage, 36*, 222–231.

Atkinson, J., & Drew, P. (1979). *Order in court: The organization of verbal interaction in judicial settings*. Atlantic Highlands, NJ: Humanities Press.

Attardo, S. (1994). *Linguistic theories of humour*. Berlin: Mouton de Gruyter.

Attardo, S., & Raskin, V. (1991). Script theory revis(it)ed: Joke similarity and joke representation model. *Humor: The International Journal of Humor Research, 4*, 293–348.

Atwood, M. (1996). *The handmaid's tale*. London: Vintage.

(2005). *Rude Ramsay and the roaring radishes*. London: Bloomsbury Publishing.

Auracher, J. (2006, August). *Biological correlates of suspense: An empirical introduction*. Paper presented at the meeting of the Society for the Empirical Study of Literature and Media (IGEL), Ludwig-Maximilians University, Munich.

Auracher, J., & van Peer, W. (Eds.). (2008). *New beginnings in literary studies*. Newcastle: Cambridge Scholars Press.

Aziz-Zadeh, L., Wilson, S. M., Rizzolatti, G., & Iacoboni, M. (2006). Congruent embodied representations for visually presented actions and linguistic phrases describing actions. *Current Biology, 16*, 1818–1823.

Baddeley, A. D., & Hitch, G. (1974). Working memory. In G. H. Bower (Ed.), *The psychology of learning and motivation, Vol. 8* (pp. 47–89). London: Academic Press.

Baddeley, A. D., & Lewis, V. (1981). Inner active processes in reading: The inner voice, the inner ear, and the inner eye. In A. M. Lesgold & C. A. Perfetti (Eds.), *Interactive processes in reading* (pp. 107–129). Hillsdale, NJ: Lawrence Erlbaum.

Baillet, S. D., & Keenan, J. M. (1986). The role of encoding and retrieval processes in the recall of text. *Discourse Processes, 9*, 247–268.

Baird, J. A., & Astington, J. W. (2004). The role of mental state understanding in the development of moral cognition and moral action. *New Directions for Child and Adolescent Development, 103*, 37–49.

Baker, L., & Wagner, J. L. (1987). Evaluating information for truthfulness: The effects of logical subordination. *Memory and Cognition, 15*, 247–255.

Baker, N. (1998). *The mezzanine*. London: Granta Books.

Bakhtin, M. M. (1981). Discourse in the novel. In M. M. Bakhtin, *The dialogic imagination: Four essays* (pp. 47–89). Austin, TX: University of Texas Press.

Bal, M. (1997). *Narratology: Introduction to the theory of narrative*. Toronto: University of Toronto Press. (First published in 1985.)

Bandura, A. (1977). *Social learning theory*. Englewood Cliffs, NJ: Prentice Hall.

Banfield, A. (1982). *Unspeakable sentences: Narration and representation in the language of fiction*. Boston, MA: Routledge and Kegan Paul.

Bargh, J. A., & Chartrand, T. L. (2000). The mind in the middle: A practical guide to priming and automaticity research. In H. T. Reis & C. M. Judd (Eds.), *Handbook of research methods in social and personality psychology* (pp. 253–285). New York: Cambridge University Press.

Bargh, J. A., & Tota, M. E. (1988). Context-dependent automatic processing in depression: Accessibility of negative constructs with regard to self but not others. *Journal of Personality and Social Psychology, 54*, 925–939.

Barker, S. (2006). Counterfactuals. In K. Brown (Ed.), *Encyclopedia of language and linguistics, Vol. 3* (pp. 259–261). Oxford: Elsevier.

Baron-Cohen, S. (2000). Autism: Deficits in folk psychology exist alongside superiority in folk physics. In Baron-Cohen, Tager-Flusberg, & Cohen (Eds.), (pp. 73–82).

(2002). The extreme male brain theory of autism. *Trends in Cognitive Sciences, 6*, 248–254.

Baron-Cohen, S., Tager-Flusberg, H., & Cohen, D. (Eds.). (2000). *Understanding other minds: Perspectives from developmental cognitive neuroscience.* Oxford: Oxford University Press.

Baron-Cohen, S., Wheelright, S., Hill, J., Raste, Y., & Plumb, I. (2001). The 'Reading the Mind in the Eyes' test revised version: A study with normal adults and adults with Asperger's syndrome or high-functioning autism. *Journal of Child Psychology and Psychiatry, 42*, 241–251.

Barsalou, L. W. (1999). Perceptual symbol systems. *Behavioral and Brain Sciences, 22*, 577–660.

Barsalou, L. W., Simmons, W. K., Barbey, A. K., & Wilson, C. D. (2003). Grounding conceptual knowledge in modality-specific systems. *Trends in Cognitive Sciences, 7*, 84–91.

Barthes, R. (1968). L'effet de réel. *Communications, 11*, 84–89.

(1977). Introduction to the structural analysis of narratives. In R. Barthes, *Image–music–text* (pp. 79–124). London: Flamingo.

Barton, S. B., & Sanford, A. J. (1993). A case study of anomaly detection: Shallow semantic processing and cohesion establishment. *Memory and Cognition, 21*, 477–487.

Bateman, J., & Delin, J. (2006). Rhetorical structure theory. In K. Brown (Ed.), *Encyclopedia of language and linguistics, Vol. 10* (pp. 588–596). Oxford: Elsevier.

Batson, D. C., Early, S., & Salvarani, G. (1997). Perspective taking: Imagining how another feels versus imagining how you would feel. *Personality and Social Psychology Bulletin, 23*, 751–758.

Bear, M. F., Connors, B. W., & Paradiso, M. A. (2007). *Neuroscience: Exploring the brain.* Baltimore, MD: Lippincott Williams & Wilkins.

Berlyne, D. E. (1960). *Conflict, arousal and curiosity.* New York: McGraw-Hill.

(1971). *Aesthetics and psychobiology.* New York: Appleton-Century-Crofts.

Berry, D. C., Michas, I., & Bersellini, E. (2003). Communicating information about medication: The benefits of making it personal. *Psychology and Health, 18*, 127–139.

Birch, S. L., Albrecht, J. E., & Myers, J. L. (2000). Syntactic focussing structures influence discourse processing. *Discourse Processes, 30*, 285–304.

Birch, S. L., & Garnsey, S. M. (1995). The effect of focus on memory for words in sentences. *Journal of Memory and Language, 34*, 232–267.

Birch, S. L., & Rayner, K. (1997). Linguistic focus affects eye movements during reading. *Memory and Cognition, 25,* 653–660.

Bohan, J. (2008). *Depth of processing and semantic anomalies.* Doctoral thesis, University of Glasgow, Glasgow.

Bohan, J., Filik, R., MacArthur, A., & McCluskey, C. (2009, September). *The effect of reading perspective on depth of processing.* Poster presented at the meeting on Architectures and Mechanisms for Language Processing (AMLaP), Universitat Pompeu Fabra, Barcelona.

Bohan, J., & Sanford, A. J. (2008). Semantic anomalies at the borderline of consciousness: An eyetracking investigation. *The Quarterly Journal of Experimental Psychology, 61,* 232–239.

Bohan, J., Sanford, A. J., Cochrane, S., & Sanford, A. J. S. (2008, September). *Direct and indirect speech modulates depth of processing.* Poster presented at the meeting on Architectures and Mechanisms for Language Processing (AMLaP), University of Cambridge, Cambridge.

Bohan, J., Sanford, A. J., Glen, K., Clark, F., & Martin, E. (2008, September). *Focus and emphasis devices modulate depth of processing as reflected in semantic anomaly detection.* Poster presented at the meeting on Architectures and Mechanisms for Language Processing (AMLaP), University of Cambridge, Cambridge.

Booth, W. C. (1991). *The rhetoric of fiction.* Harmondsworth: Penguin.

Bordwell, D., & Thompson, K. (2010). *Film art: An introduction.* New York: McGraw Hill.

Bornstein, B. H., & Wiener, R. L. (Eds.). (2010). *Emotion and the law: Psychological perspectives.* New York: Springer.

Bortolussi, M., & Dixon, P. (2003). *Psychonarratology: Foundations for the empirical study of literary response.* Cambridge: Cambridge University Press.

Bowdle, B. F., & Gentner, D. (2005). The career of metaphor. *Psychological Review, 112,* 193–216.

Bower, G. H., Black, J. B., & Turner, T. J. (1979). Scripts in memory for text. *Cognitive Psychology, 11,* 177–220.

Boyd, R., Gintis, H., Bowles, S., & Richerson, P. J. (2003). The evolution of altruistic punishment. *Proceedings of the National Academy of Sciences of the United States of America, 100,* 3531–3535.

Bradley, M. M., Codispoti, M., Sabatinelli, D., & Lang, P. J. (2001). Emotion and motivation II: Sex differences in picture processing. *Emotion, 1,* 300–319.

Bransford, J. D., & Johnson, M. K. (1972). Contextual prerequisites for understanding: Some investigations of comprehension and recall. *Journal of Verbal Learning and Verbal Behavior, 11,* 717–726.

Bray, J. (2007a). The effects of free indirect discourse: Empathy revisited. In M. Lambrou & P. Stockwell (Eds.), *Contemporary stylistics* (pp. 56–67). London: Continuum.

(2007b). The 'dual voice' of free indirect discourse: A reading experiment. *Language and Literature, 16,* 37–52.

Braze, D., Shankweiler, D., Ni, W., & Palumbo, L. C. (2002). Readers' eye movements distinguish anomalies of form and content. *Journal of Psycholinguistic Research, 31,* 25–44.

Brédart, S., & Docquier, M. (1989). The Moses illusion: A follow-up on the focalization effect. *Cahiers de Psychologie Cognitive (European Bulletin of Cognitive Psychology), 9*, 357–362.

Brédart, S., & Modolo, K. (1988). Moses strikes again: Focalisation effect on a semantic illusion. *Acta Psychologica, 67*, 135–144.

Brewer, W. F. (1996). The nature of narrative suspense and the problem of re-reading. In Vorderer, Wulff, & Friedrichsen (Eds.), (pp. 107–127).

Brewer, W. F., & Lichtenstein, E. H. (1981). Event schemas, story schemas and story grammars. In J. Long & A. Baddeley (Eds.), *Attention and performance, Vol. 9* (pp. 363–379). Hillsdale, NJ: Lawrence Erlbaum.

(1982). Stories are to entertain: A structural-affect theory of stories. *Journal of Pragmatics, 6*, 473–486.

Brewer, W. F., & Ohtsuka, K. (1988). Story structure, characterization, just world organization, and reader affect in American and Hungarian short stories. *Poetics, 17*, 395–415.

Brooks, P. (1996). The law as narrative and rhetoric. In P. Brooks & P. Gewirtz (Eds.), *Law's stories: Narrative and rhetoric in the law* (pp. 13–22). New Haven, CT: Yale University Press.

Brown, D. (2003). *The Da Vinci code.* London: Corgi.

Bruner, J. (1991). The narrative construction of reality. *Critical Inquiry, 18*, 1–21.

(2002). *Making stories: Law, literature and life.* New York: Farrar, Straus and Giroux.

Brunyé, T. T., Ditman, T., Mahoney, C. R., Augustyn, J. S., & Taylor, H. A. (2009). When you and I share perspectives: Pronouns modulate perspective-taking during narrative comprehension. *Psychological Science, 20*, 27–32.

Bühler, K. (1982).The deictic field of language and deictic words. In R. Jarvella & W. Klein (Eds.), *Speech, place and action: Studies in deixis and related topics* (pp. 9–30). New York: Wiley. (First published in 1934.)

Burke, M. (2006). Emotion: Stylistic approaches. In K. Brown (Ed.), *Encyclopedia of language and linguistics, Vol. 4* (pp. 127–129). Oxford: Elsevier.

(2010). *Literary reading, cognition and emotion: An exploration of the oceanic mind.* London: Routledge.

Burke, P. (2001). History of events and the revival of narrative. In P. Burke (Ed.), *New perspectives on historical writing* (pp. 283–300). Cambridge: Polity.

Bushnell, M. C., Duncan, G. H., Hofbauer, R. K., Ha, B., Chen, J. I., & Carrier, B. (1999). Pain perception: Is there a role for primary somatosensory cortex? *Proceedings of the National Academy of Sciences, 96*, 7705–7709.

Busselle, R., & Bilandzic, H. (2009). Measuring narrative engagement. *Media Psychology, 12*, 321–347.

Büttner, A. C. (2007). Questions versus statements: Challenging an assumption about semantic illusions. *The Quarterly Journal of Experimental Psychology, 60*, 779–789.

Cabeza, R., & Kingstone, A. (Eds.). (2006). *Handbook of functional neuroimaging of cognition.* Cambridge, MA: MIT Press.

Cacciari, C., & Glucksberg, S. (1994). Understanding figurative language. In M. A. Gernsbacher (Ed.), *Handbook of psycholinguistics* (pp. 447–477). San Diego, CA: Academic Press.

Cacioppo, J. T., Crites, S. L., Berntson, G. G., & Coles, M. G. H. (1993). If attitudes affect how stimuli are processed, should they not affect the event-related brain potential? *Psychological Science*, *4*, 108–112.

Cacioppo, J. T., Priester, J. R., & Berntson, G. G. (1993). Rudimentary determinants of attitudes: II. Arm flexion and extension have differential effects on attitudes. *Journal of Personality and Social Psychology*, *65*, 5–17.

Campbell, R. S., & Pennebaker, J. W. (2003). The secret life of pronouns: Flexibility in writing style and physical health. *Psychological Science*, *14*, 60–65.

Campion, N. (2004). Predictive inferences are read as hypothetical facts. *Journal of Memory and Language*, *50*, 149–164.

Campion, N., Martins, D., & Wilhelm, A. (2009). Contradictions and predictions: Two sources of uncertainty that raise the cognitive interest of readers. *Discourse Processes*, *46*, 341–368.

Carr, D. (1986a). Narrative and the real world: An argument for continuity. *History and Theory*, *25*, 117–131.

(1986b). *Time, narrative and history*. Bloomington, IN: Indiana University Press.

(2008). Narrative explanation and its malcontents. *History and Theory*, *47*, 19–30.

Carroll, N. (1996). The paradox of suspense. In Vorderer, Wulff, & Friedrichsen (Eds.), (pp. 71–91).

(2001). On the narrative connection. In van Peer & Chatman (Eds.), (pp. 21–41).

Carter, R. (2004). *Language and creativity: The art of common talk*. London: Routledge.

Chafe, W. L. (1994). *Discourse, consciousness and time: The flow and displacement of conscious experience in speaking and writing*. Chicago, IL: University of Chicago Press.

Chatman, S. (1978). *Story and discourse: Narrative structure in fiction and film*. Ithaca, NY: Cornell University Press.

Chen, M., & Bargh, J. A. (1999). Consequences of automatic evaluation: Immediate behavioral predispositions to approach or avoid the stimulus. *Personality and Social Psychology Bulletin*, *25*, 215–224.

Christianson, K., Hollingworth, A., Halliwell, J. F., & Ferreira, F. (2001). Thematic roles assigned along the garden path linger. *Cognitive Psychology*, *42*, 368–407.

Christie, A. (1955). *Sparkling cyanide*. London: Pan.

Clark, H. H., & Gerrig, R. J. (1990). Quotations as demonstrations. *Language*, *66*, 764–805.

Cockroft, R., & Cockroft, S. M. (1992). *Persuading people: An introduction to rhetoric*. London: Macmillan.

Cohn, D. (1978). *Transparent minds: Narrative modes for representing consciousness in fiction*. Princeton, NJ: Princeton University Press.

Colby, B. N. (1973). A partial grammar of Eskimo folktales. *American Anthropologist*, *75*, 645–662.

Constanzo, M., & Archer, D. (1989). Interpreting the expressive behaviour of others: The Interpersonal Perception Task. *Journal of Nonverbal Behavior*, *13*, 225–245.

Cook, A. E., Limber, J. E., & O'Brien, E. J. (2001). Situation-based context and the availability of predictive inferences. *Journal of Memory and Language*, *44*, 220–234.

Cook, G. (1994). *Discourse and literature: The interplay of form and mind*. Oxford: Oxford University Press.

Cooper, R. M. (1974). The control of eye fixation by the meaning of spoken language: A new methodology for the real-time investigation of speech perception, memory, and language processing. *Cognitive Psychology, 6*, 84–107.

Cooreman, A., & Sanford, A. J. (1996). *Focus and syntactic subordination in discourse* (Research Report No. RP-79). University of Edinburgh: Human Communication Research Centre.

Coplan, A. (2006). Catching characters' emotions: Emotional contagion responses to narrative fiction film. *Film Studies, 8*, 26–38.

Cotter, C. (1984). Inferring indirect objects in sentences: Some implications for the semantics of verbs. *Language and Speech, 27*, 25–45.

Coulmas, F. (Ed.). (1986). *Direct and indirect speech* (Trends in linguistics: Studies and monographs, *31*). Berlin: Mouton de Gruyter.

Coulson, S. (2001). *Semantic leaps*. Cambridge: Cambridge University Press.

(2008). Metaphor comprehension and the brain. In Gibbs (Ed.), (2008) (pp. 177–194).

Coulson, S., & van Petten, C. (2002). Conceptual integration and metaphor: An ERP study. *Memory and Cognition, 30*, 958–968.

(2007). A special role for the right hemisphere in metaphor comprehension? ERP evidence from hemifield presentation. *Brain Research, 1146*, 128–145.

Cowles, H. W., Walenski, M., & Kluender, R. (2007). Linguistic and cognitive prominence in anaphor resolution: Topic, contrastive focus, and pronouns. *Topoi, 26*(3), 3–18.

Craik, K. J. W. (1943). *The nature of explanation*. Cambridge: Cambridge University Press.

Crossman, A. R., & Neary, D. (2010). *Neuroanatomy: An illustrated colour text*. Edinburgh: Churchill Livingstone.

Cunningham, A. E., & Stanovich, K. E. (1997). Early reading acquisition and its relation to reading experience and ability 10 years later. *Developmental Psychology, 33*, 934–945.

Cutler, A., & Fodor, J. A. (1979). Semantic focus and sentence comprehension. *Cognition, 7*, 49–59.

Dahl, R. (1990a). Parson's pleasure. In *The best of Roald Dahl* (pp. 142–163). London: Vintage.

(1990b). Taste. In *The best of Roald Dahl* (pp. 53–65). London: Vintage.

Damasio, A. (2000). *The feeling of what happens: Body, emotion, and the making of consciousness*. London: Vintage.

(2003). *Looking for Spinoza: Joy, sorrow and the feeling brain*. Orlando, FL: Harcourt.

(2006). *Descartes' error: Emotion, reason and the human brain*. London: Vintage Books. (First published in 1994.)

Dancygier, B. (2012). *The language of stories: A cognitive approach*. Cambridge: Cambridge University Press.

Daneman, M., Lennertz, T., & Hannon, B. (2007). Shallow semantic processing of text: Evidence from eye movements. *Language and Cognitive Processes, 22*, 83–105.

Daneman, M., Reingold, E. M., & Davidson, M. (1995). Time course of phonological activation during reading: Evidence from eye fixations. *Journal of Experimental Psychology: Learning, Memory, and Cognition, 21*, 884–898.

Danto, A. C. (1985). *Narration and knowledge.* New York: Columbia University Press.

Dascal, M. (1987). Defending literal meaning. *Cognitive Science, 11,* 259–281.

Davis, M. H. (1980). A multidimensional approach to individual differences in empathy. *JSAS Catalogue of Selected Documents in Psychology, 33,* 934–945.

(1994). *Empathy: A social psychological approach.* Madison, WI: Brown and Benchmark.

(2007). Empathy. In J. E. Stets & J. H. Turner (Eds.), *Handbook of the sociology of emotions* (pp. 443–466). New York: Springer.

Davis, M. H., Coleman, M. R., Absalom, A. R., Rodd, J. M., Johnsrude, I. S., Matta, B. F., Owen, A. M., & Menon, D. K. (2007). Dissociating speech perception and comprehension at reduced levels of awareness. *Proceedings of the National Academy of Sciences of the United States of America, 104,* 16032–16037.

Davis, M. H., Soderlund, T., Cole, J., Gadol, E., Kute, M., Myers, M., & Weihing, J. (2004). Cognitions associated with attempts to empathize: How do we imagine the perspective of another? *Personality and Social Psychology Bulletin, 30,* 1625–1635.

de Araujo, I. E. T., Rolls, E. T., Kringelbach, M. L., McGlone, F., & Phillips, N. (2003). Taste-olfactory convergence, and the representation of the pleasantness of flavour, in the human brain. *European Journal of Neuroscience, 18,* 2059–2068.

de Graaf, A. (2010). *Narrative persuasion: The role of attention and emotion.* Doctoral thesis, Radboud Universiteit, Nijmegen, The Netherlands.

de Graaf, A., Hoeken, H., Sanders, J., & Beentjes, H. (2009). The role of dimensions of narrative engagement in narrative persuasion. *Communications: The European Journal of Communication Research, 34,* 385–405.

de Grauwe, S., Swain, A., Holcomb, P. J., Ditman, T., & Kuperberg, G. R. (2010). Electrophysiological insights into the processing of nominal metaphors. *Neuropsychologia, 48,* 1965–1984.

de Vega, M., Diaz, J. M., & Leon, I. (1997). To know or not to know: Comprehending protagonists' beliefs and their emotional consequences. *Discourse Processes, 23,* 169–192.

de Vega, M., Glenberg, A. M., & Graesser, A. C. (Eds.). (2008). *Symbols and embodiment: Debates on meaning and cognition.* Oxford: Oxford University Press.

de Wied, M., & Zillmann, D. (1996). The utility of various research approaches in the empirical exploration of suspenseful drama. In Vorderer, Wulff, & Friedrichsen (Eds.), (pp. 255–282).

Decety, J., & Ickes, W. (Eds.). (2011). *The social neuroscience of empathy.* Cambridge, MA: MIT Press.

Decety, J., Jeannerod, M., Durozard, D., & Baverel, G. (1993). Central activation of autonomic effectors during mental simulation of motor action in man. *Journal of Physiology, 461,* 549–563.

Decety, J., & Somerville, J. A. (2003). Shared representations between self and other: A social cognitive neuroscience view. *Trends in Cognitive Sciences, 7,* 527–533.

DelFattore, J. (2002). Controversial narratives in schools: Content, values, and conflicting viewpoints. In Green, Strange, & Brock (Eds.), (pp. 131–155).

Delin, J. (1992). Properties of *It*-cleft presupposition. *Journal of Semantics, 9*, 289–306.

DeLong, K. A., Urbach, T. P., & Kutas, M. (2005). Probabilistic word pre-activation during language comprehension inferred from electrical brain activity. *Nature Neuroscience, 8*, 1117–1121.

deQuervain, D. J. -F., Fischbacher, U., Treyer, V., Schellhammer, M., Schnyder, U., Buck, A., & Fehr, E. (2004). The neural basis of altruistic punishment. *Science, 305*, 1254–1258.

Dershowitz, A. M. (1996). Life is not a dramatic narrative. In P. Brooks & P. Gewirtz (Eds.), *Law's stories: Narrative and rhetoric in the law* (pp. 99–109). New Haven, CT: Yale University Press.

di Pellegrino, G., Fadiga, L., Fogassi, L., Gallese, V., & Rizzolatti, G. (1992). Understanding motor events: A neuropsychological study. *Experimental Brain Research, 91*, 176–180.

Diamond, M. C., Scheibel, A. B., & Elson, L. M. (1985). *The human brain coloring book*. New York: HarperPerennial.

Ditman, T., Brunyé, T. T., Mahoney, C. R., & Taylor, H. A. (2010). Simulating an enactment effect: Pronouns guide action simulation during narrative comprehension. *Cognition, 115*, 172–178.

Djikic, M., Oatley, K., Zoeterman, S., & Peterson, J. B. (2009). On being moved by art: How reading fiction transforms the self. *Creativity Research Journal, 21*, 24–29.

Doležel, L. (1989). Possible worlds and literary fictions. In S. Allén (Ed.), *Possible worlds in humanities, arts and sciences: Proceedings of the Nobel Symposium 65* (pp. 223–242). Berlin: Walter de Gruyter.

Dopkins, S. (1996). Representation of superordinate goal inferences in memory. *Discourse Processes, 21*, 85–104.

Douthwaite, J. (2000). *Towards a linguistic theory of foregrounding*. Turin: Edizioni dell'Orso.

Dove, G. (2009). Beyond perceptual symbols: A call for representational pluralism. *Cognition, 110*, 412–431.

Duchan, J. F., Bruder, G. A., & Hewitt, L. E. (1995). *Deixis in narrative: A cognitive science perspective*. Hillsdale, NJ: Lawrence Erlbaum.

Eagleton, T. (1983). *Literary theory: An introduction*. Oxford: Blackwell.

Eisenberg, N., & Strayer, J. (Eds.). (1987). *Empathy and its development*. Cambridge: Cambridge University Press.

Emmott, C. (1997). *Narrative comprehension: A discourse perspective*. Oxford: Oxford University Press.

    (2002). Responding to style: Cohesion, foregrounding and thematic interpretation. In Louwerse & van Peer (Eds.), (pp. 91–117).

    (2003). Reading for pleasure: A cognitive poetic analysis of 'twists in the tale' and other plot reversals in narrative texts. In J. Gavins & G. Steen (Eds.), *Cognitive poetics in practice* (pp. 145–159). London: Routledge.

    (2006). Reference: Stylistic aspects. In K. Brown (Ed.), *Encyclopedia of language and linguistics, Vol. 10* (pp. 441–450). Oxford: Elsevier.

Emmott, C., & Alexander, M. (2010). Detective fiction, plot construction, and reader manipulation: Rhetorical control and cognitive misdirection in Agatha Christie's

Sparkling Cyanide. In D. McIntyre & B. Busse (Eds.), *Language and style: In honour of Mick Short* (pp. 328–346). Houndmills: Palgrave Macmillan.

Emmott, C., Sanford, A. J., & Alexander, M. (2010). Scenarios, role assumptions, and character status: Readers' expectations and the manipulation of attention in narrative texts. In J. Eder, F. Jannedis, & R. Schneider (Eds.), *Characters in fictional worlds: Understanding imaginary beings in literature, film and other media* (pp. 377–399). Berlin: de Gruyter.

Emmott, C., Sanford, A. J., & Dawydiak, E. J. (2007). Stylistics meets cognitive science: Studying style in fiction and readers' attention from an inter-disciplinary perspective. *Style, 41*, 204–226.

Emmott, C., Sanford, A. J., & Morrow, L. I. (2006a). Capturing the attention of readers? Stylistic and psychological perspectives on the use and effect of text fragments in narratives. *Journal of Literary Semantics, 35*, 1–30.

(2006b). Sentence fragmentation: Stylistic aspects. In K. Brown (Ed.), *Encyclopedia of language and linguistics, Vol. 11* (pp. 241–251). Oxford: Elsevier.

Emmott, C., Sanford, A. J., & Smith, F. (2008, July). *'Then somebody appeared': Scenarios, character under-specification and narrative interest.* Paper presented at the meeting of the Society for the Empirical Study of Literature and Media (IGEL), University of Memphis, Memphis, TN.

Erickson, T. D., & Mattson, M. E. (1981). From words to meaning: A semantic illusion. *Journal of Verbal Learning and Verbal Behavior, 20*, 540–551.

Esrock, E. (2004). Embodying literature. *Journal of Consciousness Studies, 11*, 79–89.

(2010). Embodying art: The spectator and the inner body. *Poetics Today, 31*, 217–250.

Fadiga, L., Craighero, L., Buccino, G., & Rizzolatti, G. (2002). Speech listening specifically modulates the excitability of tongue muscles: A TMS study. *European Journal of Neuroscience, 15*, 339–402.

Fairclough, N. (2000). *New Labour, New language?* London: Routledge.

Farber, D. A., & Sherry, S. (1996). Legal storytelling and constitutional law: The medium and the message. In P. Brooks & P. Gewirtz (Eds.), *Law's stories: Narrative and rhetoric in the law* (pp. 37–53). New Haven, CT: Yale University Press.

Fauconnier, G. (1994). *Mental spaces: Aspects of meaning construction in natural language.* Cambridge: Cambridge University Press.

(1997). *Mappings in thought and language.* Cambridge: Cambridge University Press.

Fauconnier, G., & Turner, M. (1998). Conceptual integration networks. *Cognitive Science, 22*, 133–187.

(2002). *The way we think: Conceptual blending and the mind's hidden complexities.* New York: Basic Books.

(2008). Rethinking metaphor. In Gibbs (Ed.), (2008) (pp. 53–66).

Faust, M., & Weisper, S. (2000). Understanding metaphoric sentences in the two cerebral hemispheres. *Brain and Cognition, 43*, 186–191.

Feagin, S. L. (1996). *Reading with feeling: The aesthetics of appreciation.* Ithaca, NY: Cornell University Press.

Fehr, E., & Gächter, S. (2002). Altruistic punishment in humans. *Nature, 415*, 137–140.

Felten, D. L., & Shetty, A. N. (2009). *Netter's atlas of human neuroscience.* Teterbo, NJ: Icon Learning Systems.

Ferguson, H. J., Breheny, R., Sanford, A. J., & Scheepers, C. (2009, March). *Reading the minds of others: Disentangling the gender-specific mechanisms.*

Poster presented at the meeting of the Cognitive Neuroscience Society, San Francisco, CA.

Ferguson, H. J., & Sanford, A. J. (2008). Anomalies in real and counterfactual worlds: An eye-movement investigation. *Journal of Memory and Language, 58,* 609–626.

Ferguson, H. J., Scheepers, C., & Sanford, A. J. (2010). Expectations in counterfactual and theory of mind reasoning. *Language and Cognitive Processes, 25,* 297–346.

Ferreira, F. (2003). The misinterpretation of noncanonical sentences. *Cognitive Psychology, 47,* 164–203.

Ferreira, F., Bailey, K. G. D., & Ferraro, V. (2002). Good-enough representations in language comprehension. *Current Directions in Psychological Science, 11,* 11–15.

Ferreira, F., & Henderson, J. (1999, September). *Good-enough representations in visual cognition and language.* Paper presented at the meeting on Architectures and Mechanisms of Language Processing (AMLaP), University of Edinburgh, Edinburgh.

Ferretti, T. R., Kutas, M., & McRae, K. (2007). Verb aspect and the activation of event knowledge. *Journal of Experimental Psychology: Learning, Memory and Cognition, 33,* 182–196.

Filik, R., Hunter, C. M., & Leuthold, H. (2009, July). *Irony and embodiment: Evidence from the affect-movement compatibility effect.* Poster presented at the meeting on Embodied and Situated Language Processing, Erasmus University Rotterdam, Rotterdam.

Filik, R., & Leuthold, H. (2008). Processing local pragmatic anomalies in fictional contexts: Evidence from the N400. *Psychophysiology, 45,* 554–558.

Fillenbaum, S. (1974). Pragmatic normalization: Further results for some conjunctive-disjunctive sentences. *Journal of Experimental Psychology: General, 102,* 574–578.

Fischer, O., & Nänny, M. (Eds.). (2001). *The motivated sign: Iconicity in language and literature 2.* Amsterdam: John Benjamins.

Fludernik, M. (1993). *The fictions of language and the languages of fiction.* London: Routledge.

(1996). *Towards a natural narratology.* London: Routledge.

(2009). *An introduction to narratology.* London: Routledge.

Foraker, S., & McElree, B. (2007). The role of prominence in pronoun resolution: Active versus passive representations. *Journal of Memory and Language, 56,* 357–383.

Förster, J., & Strack, F. (1996). Influence of overt head movements on memory for valenced words: A case of conceptual–motor compatibility. *Journal of Personality and Social Psychology, 71,* 421–430.

Fowler, H. W., & Fowler, F. G. (1931). *The King's English.* Oxford: Clarendon Press. (First published in 1906 by H. W. Fowler.)

Fowler, R. (1996). *Linguistic criticism.* Oxford: Oxford University Press.

Francis, S., Rolls, E. T., Bowtell, R., McGlone, F., O'Doherty, J., Browning, A., Clare, S., & Smith, E. (1999). The representation of pleasant touch in the brain and its relationship with taste and olfactory areas. *Neuroreport, 10,* 453–459.

Fraurud, K. (1990). Definiteness and the processing of noun phrases in natural discourse. *Journal of Semantics, 7,* 395–433.

Frijda, N. (1986). *The emotions*. Cambridge: Cambridge University Press.

(2007). *The laws of emotion*. Mahwah, NJ: Lawrence Erlbaum.

Fukuda, Y., & Sanford, A. J. (2008, July). *The effects of personalization on shallow processing*. Poster presented at the meeting of the Society for Text and Discourse, University of Memphis, Memphis, TN.

Galloway, J. (1992). Blood. In J. Galloway, *Blood* (pp. 1–9). London: Minerva.

(2003). *Clara*. London: Vintage.

Gardam, J. (1984). Stone trees. In *The pangs of love and other stories* (pp. 47–68). London: Abacus.

Garnham, A. (1983). What's wrong with story grammars? *Cognition, 15*, 145–154.

Garrod, S. C., & Sanford, A. J. (1977). Interpreting anaphoric relations: The integration of semantic information while reading. *Journal of Verbal Learning and Verbal Behavior, 16*, 77–90.

(1981). Bridging inferences and the extended domain of reference. In J. Long & A. Baddeley (Eds.), *Attention and performance, Vol. 9* (pp. 331–346). Hillsdale, NJ: Lawrence Erlbaum.

(1983). Topic dependent effects in language processing. In G. B. Flores d'Arcais & R. J. Jarvella (Eds.), *The process of language understanding* (pp. 271–296). Chichester: John Wiley & Sons.

(1994). Resolving sentences in a discourse context: How discourse representation affects language understanding. In M. A. Gernsbacher (Ed.), *Handbook of psycholinguistics* (pp. 675–698). San Diego, CA: Academic Press.

Garvin, P. L. (Ed.). (1964). *A Prague School reader on esthetics, literary structure and style*. Georgetown, DC: Georgetown University Press.

Gavins, J. (2007). *Text world theory: An introduction*. Edinburgh: Edinburgh University Press.

Gearey, A. (2005). Law and narrative. In D. Herman, M. Jahn, & M.-L. Ryan (Eds.), *Routledge encyclopedia of narrative theory* (pp. 271–275). London: Routledge.

Genette, G. (1980). *Narrative discourse: An essay in method*. Ithaca, NY: Cornell University Press.

(1988). *Narrative discourse revisited*. Ithaca, NY: Cornell University Press.

Gentner, D., & Gentner, D. R. (1983). Flowing waters or teeming crowds: Mental models of electricity. In Gentner & Stevens (Eds.), (pp. 99–129).

Gentner, D., & Stevens, A. L. (Eds.). (1983). *Mental models*. Hilldsale, NJ: Lawrence Erlbaum.

Gerardin, E., Sirigu, A., Lehéricy, S., Poline, J.-P., Gaymard, B., Marsault, C., Agid, Y., & Le Bihan, D. (2000). Partially overlapping neural networks for real and imagined hand movements. *Cerebral Cortex, 10*, 1093–1104.

Gergen, M. M., & Gergen, K. J. (2007). Narratives in action. In M. Bamberg (Ed.), *Narrative: The state of the art* (pp. 133–143). Amsterdam: John Benjamins.

Gernsbacher, M. A. (1989). Mechanisms that improve referential access. *Cognition, 32*, 99–156.

(1990). *Language comprehension as structure building*. Hillsdale, NJ: Lawrence Erlbaum.

Gernsbacher, M. A., Goldsmith, H. H., & Robertson, R. R. W. (1992). Do readers mentally represent characters' emotional states? *Cognition and Emotion, 6*, 89–111.

Gernsbacher, M. A., & Jescheniak, J. D. (1995). Cataphoric devices in spoken discourse. *Cognitive Psychology, 29*, 24–58.

Gernsbacher, M. A., & Robertson, R. W. (1992). Knowledge activation versus sentence mapping when representing fictional characters' emotional states. *Language and Cognitive Processes, 7*, 353–371.

Gerrig, R. J. (1993). *Experiencing narrative worlds: On the psychological activities of reading.* New Haven, CT: Yale University Press.

(1996). The resiliency of suspense. In Vorderer, Wulff, & Friedrichsen (Eds.), (pp. 93–105).

Gerrig, R. J., & Bernardo, A. B. I. (1994). Readers as problem-solvers in the experience of suspense. *Poetics, 22*, 459–472.

Gerrig, R. J., & Prentice, D. A. (1991). The representation of fictional information. *Psychological Science, 2*, 336–340.

Gewirtz, P. (1996a). Narrative and rhetoric in the law. In P. Brooks & P. Gewirtz (Eds.), *Law's stories: Narrative and rhetoric in the law* (pp. 2–13). New Haven, CT: Yale University Press.

(1996b). Victims and voyeurs: Two narrative problems at the criminal trial. In P. Brooks & P. Gewirtz (Eds.), *Law's stories: Narrative and rhetoric in the law* (pp. 135–161). New Haven, CT: Yale University Press.

Gibbs, R. W. (1994). *The poetics of mind: Figurative thought, language, and understanding.* Cambridge: Cambridge University Press.

(2000). Making good psychology out of blending theory. *Cognitive Linguistics, 11*, 347–358.

(2002a). A new look at literal meaning in understanding what is said and implicated. *Journal of Pragmatics, 34*, 457–486.

(2002b). Feeling moved by metaphor. In S. Csábi & J. Zerkowitz (Eds.), *Textual secrets: The medium of the message* (pp. 13–28). Budapest: Eötvös Loránd University.

(2003). Nonliteral speech acts in text and discourse. In A. C. Graesser, M. A. Gernsbacher, & S. R. Goldman (Eds.), *Handbook of discourse processes* (pp. 357–394). Mahwah, NJ: Lawrence Erlbaum.

(Ed.). (2008). *The Cambridge handbook of metaphor and thought.* Cambridge: Cambridge University Press.

Gibbs, R. W., & Colston, H. L. (Eds.). (2007). *Irony in language and thought.* New York: Lawrence Erlbaum.

Gibbs, R. W., & Matlock, T. (2008). Metaphor, imagination and simulation: Psycholinguistic evidence. In Gibbs (Ed.), (2008) (pp. 161–176).

Giora, R. (2008). Is metaphor unique? In Gibbs (Ed.), (2008) (pp. 143–160).

Giora, R., & Fein, O. (1999). On understanding familiar and less-familiar figurative language. *Journal of Pragmatics, 31*, 1601–1618.

Glenberg, A. M., & Kaschak, M. P. (2002). Grounding language in action. *Psychonomic Bulletin and Review, 9*, 558–565.

Glenberg, A. M., Meyer, M., & Lindem, K. (1987). Mental models contribute to foregrounding during text comprehension. *Journal of Memory and Language, 26*, 69–83.

Glenberg, A. M., Sato, M., Cattaneo, L., Riggio, L., Palumbo, D., & Buccino, G. (2008). Processing abstract language modulates motor system activity. *The Quarterly Journal of Experimental Psychology, 61*, 905–919.

Glenberg, A. M., Webster, B. J., Mouilso, E., Havas, D. A., & Lindeman, L. M. (2009). Gender, emotion, and the embodiment of language comprehension. *Emotion Review*, *1*, 151–161.

Glucksberg, S. (2008). How metaphors create categories – quickly. In Gibbs (Ed.), (2008) (pp. 67–83).

Glucksberg, S., Gildea, P., & Bookin, H. B. (1982). On understanding nonliteral speech: Can people ignore metaphors? *Journal of Verbal Learning and Verbal Behavior*, *21*, 85–98.

Goatly, A. (1997). *The language of metaphors*. London: Routledge.

Goldstein, A., Arzouan, Y., & Faust, M. (2008). Timing the metaphoric brain: Contribution of ERPs and source localization to understanding figurative language. In Z. Breznitz (Ed.), *Brain research in language* (pp. 205–223). New York: Springer.

Goodwin, G. P., & Johnson-Laird, P. N. (2008). Transitive and pseudo-transitive inferences. *Cognition*, *108*, 320–352.

Gordon, P. C., Grosz, B. J., & Gilliom, L. A. (1993). Pronouns, names, and the centering of attention in discourse. *Cognitive Science*, *17*, 311–347.

Gordon, P. C., & Hendrick, R. (1998). The representation and processing of coreference in discourse. *Cognitive Science*, *22*, 389–424.

Gordon, P. C., Hendrick, R., & Johnson, M. (2001). Memory interference during language processing. *Journal of Experimental Psychology: Learning, Memory and Cognition*, *27*, 1411–1423.

Grady, J., Oakley, T., & Coulson, S. (1999). Blending and metaphor. In R. W. Gibbs & G. Steen (Eds.), *Metaphor in cognitive linguistics* (pp. 101–124). Philadelphia, PA: John Benjamins.

Graesser, A. C., Singer, M., & Trabasso, T. (1994). Constructing inferences during narrative text comprehension. *Psychological Review*, *101*, 371–395.

Gray, A. (1994). *Lanark: A life in 4 books*. London: Picador.

Graybeal, A., Sexton, J. D., & Pennebaker, J. W. (2002). The role of story-making in disclosure writing: The psychometrics of narrative. *Psychology and Health*, *17*, 571–581.

Green, M. C. (2004). Transportation into narrative worlds: The role of prior knowledge and perceived realism. *Discourse Processes*, *38*, 247–266.

Green, M. C., & Brock, T. C. (2000). The role of transportation in the persuasiveness of public narratives. *Journal of Personality and Social Psychology*, *79*, 701–721.

Green, M. C., Strange, J. J., & Brock, T. C. (Eds.). (2002). *Narrative impact: Social and cognitive foundations*. Mahwah, NJ: Lawrence Erlbaum.

Greene, S. B., McKoon, G., & Ratcliff, R. (1992). Pronoun resolution and discourse models. *Journal of Experimental Psychology: Learning, Memory and Cognition*, *18*, 266–283.

Gregory, W. L., Cialdini, R. B., & Carpenter, K. M. (1982). Self-relevant scenarios as mediators of likelihood estimates and compliance: Does imagining make it so? *Journal of Personality and Social Psychology*, *43*, 89–99.

Greimas, A. J. (1983). *Structural semantics: An attempt at a method*. Lincoln, NE: University of Nebraska Press.

Grice, P. H. (1975). Logic and conversation. In P. Cole & J. Morgan (Eds.), *Speech acts: Syntax and semantics, Vol. 3* (pp. 41–58). New York: Academic Press.

Guéraud, S., Tapiero, I., & O'Brien, E. J. (2008). Context and the activation of predictive inferences. *Psychonomic Bulletin and Review, 15*, 351–356.

Gundel, J. K. (1999). On three kinds of focus. In P. Bosch & R. van der Sandt (Eds.), *Focus: Linguistic, cognitive and computational perspectives* (Studies in natural language processing) (pp. 293–305). Cambridge: Cambridge University Press.

Gundel, J. K., Hedberg, N., & Zacharski, R. (1993). Cognitive status and the form of referring expressions in discourse. *Language, 69*, 274–307.

Gygax, P., Garnham, A., & Oakhill, J. (2004). Inferring characters' emotional states: Can readers infer specific emotions? *Language and Cognitive Processes, 19*, 613–639.

Gygax, P., Oakhill, J., & Garnham, A. (2003). The representation of characters' emotional responses: Do readers infer specific emotions? *Cognition and Emotion, 17*, 413–428.

Hakala, C. M., & O'Brien, E. J. (1995). Strategies for resolving coherence breaks in reading. *Discourse Processes, 20*, 167–185.

Hakemulder, J. (2000). *The moral laboratory: Experiments examining the effects of reading literature on social perception and moral self-concept*. Amsterdam: John Benjamins.

Halliday, M. A. K. (1967). Notes on transitivity and theme in English (Parts 1–3). *Journal of Linguistics, 3*, 199–244.

(1981). Linguistic function and literary style: An inquiry into the language of William Golding's *The inheritors*. In D. C. Freeman (Ed.), *Essays in modern stylistics* (pp. 325–360). London: Methuen.

Hamilton, J. M. E., & Sanford, A. J. (1978). The symbolic distance effect for alphabetic order judgements: A subjective report and reaction time analysis. *Quarterly Journal of Experimental Psychology, 30*, 33–41.

Hanauer, D. I., & Waksman, S. (2000). The role of explicit moral points in fable reading. *Discourse Processes, 30*, 107–132.

Hannon, B., & Daneman, M. (2001). Susceptibility to semantic illusions: An individual-differences perspective. *Memory and Cognition, 29*, 449–461.

(2004). Shallow semantic processing of text: An individual-differences account. *Discourse Processes, 37*, 187–204.

Harmon-Vukić, M., Guéraud, S., Lassonde, K. A., & O'Brien, E. J. (2009). The activation and instantiation of instrumental inferences. *Discourse Processes, 46*, 467–490.

Harnad, S. (1990). The symbol grounding problem. *Physica D, 42*, 335–346.

Harris, T. (1989). *The silence of the lambs*. London: Arrow Books.

Hart, H. L. H., & Honoré, A. M. (1959). *Causation in the law*. Oxford: Clarendon Press.

Hatfield, E., Cacioppo, J. T., & Rapson, R. L. (1993). Emotional contagion. *Current Directions in Psychological Science, 2*, 96–99.

Hauk, O., Johnsrude, I., & Pulvermüller, F. (2004). Somatotopic representation of action words in human motor and premotor cortex. *Neuron, 41*, 301–307.

Havas, D. A., Glenberg, A. M., Gutowski, K. A., Lucarelli, M. J., & Davidson, R. J. (2010). Cosmetic use of botulinum toxin-a affects processing of emotional language. *Psychological Science, 21*, 895–900.

Havas, D. A., Glenberg, A. M., & Rinck, M. (2007). Emotion simulation during language comprehension. *Psychonomic Bulletin and Review, 14*, 436–441.

Haviland, S., & Clark, H. H. (1974). What's new? Acquiring new information as a process in comprehension. *Journal of Verbal Learning and Verbal Behavior, 13*, 512–521.

Havránek, B. (1964). The functional differentiation of the standard language. In Garvin (Ed.), (pp. 3–16). (First published in Czech in 1932.)

Hedberg, N. (2000). The referential status of clefts. *Language, 76*, 891–920.

Herman, D. (2002). *Story logic: Problems and possibilities of narrative.* Lincoln, NE: University of Nebraska Press.

(2009). *Basic elements of narrative.* Chichester: Wiley-Blackwell.

Higgins, E. T., & Bargh, J. A. (1987). Social cognition and social perception. *Annual Review of Psychology, 38*, 369–425.

Hilton, D. J., & Slugoski, B. R. (1987). Knowledge-based causal attribution: The abnormal conditions focus model. *Psychological Review, 93*, 75–88.

Hirst, G. (1981). *Anaphora in natural language understanding.* Berlin: Springer.

Hobbs, J. R. (1985). Granularity. *Proceedings of the Ninth International Joint Conference on Artificial Intelligence*, 432–435.

Hoeken, H., & van Vliet, M. (2000). Suspense, curiosity and surprise: How discourse structure influences the affective and cognitive processing of a story. *Poetics, 26*, 277–286.

Hoey, M. (1983). *On the surface of discourse.* London: George Allen & Unwin.

(2001). *Textual interaction: An introduction to written discourse analysis.* London: Routledge.

Hoffman, M. L. (2008). Empathy and prosocial behavior. In M. Lewis, J. M. Haviland-Jones, & L. Feldman Barrett (Eds.), *Handbook of emotions* (pp. 440–455). New York: Guilford Press.

Hovland, C. I., Lumsdaine, A. A., & Sheffield, F. D. (1949). *Experiments on mass communication.* Princeton, NJ: Princeton University Press.

Hühn, P. (2009). Event and eventfulness. In P. Hühn, J. Pier, W. Schmid, & J. Schönert (Eds.), *Handbook of narratology* (pp. 80–97). Berlin: Walter de Gruyter.

(2010). *Eventfulness in British fiction.* Berlin: de Gruyter.

Hühn, P., Schmid, W., & Schönert, J. (Eds.). (2009). *Point of view, perspective and focalization: Modeling mediation in narrative.* Berlin: Walter de Gruyter.

Ingarden, R. (1973). *The literary work of art: An investigation on the borderlines of ontology, logic and theory of literature.* Evanston, IL: Northwestern University Press. (First published in German in 1931.)

Iser, W. (1978). *The act of reading: A theory of aesthetic response.* London: Routledge and Kegan Paul. (First published in German in 1976.)

Izard, C. E. (1971). *The face of emotion.* New York: Appleton-Century-Crofts.

Jackendoff, R. (1972). *Semantic interpretation in generative grammar.* Cambridge, MA: MIT Press.

Jackson, B. S. (1988). *Law, fact and narrative coherence.* Merseyside: Deborah Charles Publications.

(1990). Narrative theories and legal discourse. In C. Nash (Ed.), *Narrative in culture: The uses of storytelling in the sciences, philosophy, and literature* (pp. 23–50). London: Routledge.

Jackson, P. L., Brunet, E., Meltzoff, A. N., & Decety, J. (2006). Empathy examined through the neural mechanisms involved in imagining how I feel versus how you feel pain. *Neuropsychologia, 44*, 752–761.

Jahn, M. (1999). Speak, friend, and enter: Garden paths, artificial intelligence and cognitive narratology. In D. Herman (Ed.), *Narratologies* (pp. 167–194). Columbus, OH: Ohio State University Press.

James, W. (1890). *Principles of psychology, Vol. 2.* London: Macmillan.

Jeffries, L. (2001). Schema theory and white asparagus: Cultural multilingualism among readers of texts. *Language and Literature, 10*, 325–343.

John, O. P., & Srivastava, S. (1999). The Big Five trait taxonomy: History, measurement and theoretical perspectives. In L. A. Pervin & O. P. John (Eds.), *Handbook of personality: Theory and research* (pp. 102–138). New York: Guilford Press.

Johnson, M. (1987). *The body in the mind: The bodily basis of meaning, imagination and reason.* Chicago, IL: University of Chicago Press.

Johnson, S. C., Baxter, L. C., Wilder, L. S., Pipe, J. G., Heiserman, J. E., & Prigatano, G. P. (2002). Neural correlates of self-reflection. *Brain, 125*, 1808–1814.

Johnson-Laird, P. N. (1981). Mental models of meaning. In A. K. Joshi, B. L. Webber, & I. A. Sag (Eds.), *Elements of discourse understanding* (pp. 106–126). Cambridge: Cambridge University Press.

   (1983). *Mental models.* Cambridge: Cambridge University Press.

Jose, P. E., & Brewer, W. F. (1984). Development of story liking: Character identification, suspense, and outcome resolution. *Developmental Psychology, 20*, 911–924.

Joyce, J. (1960). *Ulysses.* Harmondsworth: Penguin. (First published in 1922.)

Just, M. A., & Carpenter, P. A. (1980). A theory of reading: From eye fixations to comprehension. *Psychological Review, 87*, 329–354.

Just, M. A., Newman, S. A., Keller, T. A., McEleney, A., & Carpenter, P. A. (2004). Imagery in sentence comprehension: An fMRI study. *NeuroImage, 21*, 112–124.

Kahneman, D., Krueger, A. B., Schkade, D., Schwarz, N., & Stone, A. A. (2006). Would you be happier if you were richer? A focusing illusion. *Science, 312*, 1908–1910.

Kahneman, D., Slovic, P., & Tversky, A. (Eds.). (1982). *Judgment under uncertainty: Heuristics and biases.* Cambridge: Cambridge University Press.

Kahneman, D., & Tversky, A. (1982). The simulation heuristic. In Kahneman, Slovic, & Tversky (Eds.), (pp. 201–208).

Kamas, E. N., Reder, L. M., & Ayers, M. S. (1996). Partial matching in the Moses illusion: Response bias not sensitivity. *Memory and Cognition, 24*, 687–699.

Kamide, Y., Altmann, G. T. M., & Haywood, S. L. (2003). The time-course of prediction in incremental sentence processing: Evidence from anticipatory eye movements. *Journal of Memory and Language, 49*, 133–156.

Kaschak, M. P., Madden, C. J., Therriault, D. J., Yaxley, R. H., Aveyard, M., Blanchard, A. A., & Zwaan, R. A (2005). Perception of motion affects language processing. *Cognition, 94*, B79–B89.

Kazmerski, V., Blasko, D., & Dessalegn, B. (2003). ERP and behavioural evidence of individual differences in metaphor comprehension. *Memory and Cognition, 31*, 673–689.

Keefe, D. E., & McDaniel, M. A. (1993). The time course and durability of predictive inferences. *Journal of Memory and Language, 32*, 446–463.

Keen, S. (2007). *Empathy and the novel.* Oxford: Oxford University Press.

Keenan, J. M., & Baillet, S. D. (1980). Memory for personally and socially significant events. In R. S. Nickerson (Ed.), *Attention and performance, Vol. 8* (pp. 651–669). Hillsdale, NJ: Lawrence Erlbaum.

Keenan, J. M., Baillet, S. D., & Brown, P. (1984). The effects of causal cohesion on comprehension and memory. *Journal of Verbal Learning and Verbal Behavior, 23*, 115–126.

Keenan, J. M., Potts, G. R., Golding, J. M., & Jennings, T. M. (1990). Which elaborative inferences are drawn during reading? A question of methodologies. In D. A. Balota, G. B. Flores d'Arcais, & K. Rayner (Eds.), *Comprehension processes in reading* (pp. 377–402). Hillsdale, NJ: Lawrence Erlbaum.

Kehler, A., Kertz, L., Rohde, H., & Elman, J. L. (2008). Coherence and coreference revisited. *Journal of Semantics, 25*, 1–44.

Kennison, S. M., & Gordon, P. C. (1997). Comprehending referential expressions during reading: Evidence from eyetracking. *Discourse Processes, 24*, 229–252.

Kessler, K., & Thomson, L. A. (2010). The embodied nature of spatial perspective taking: Embodied transformation versus sensorimotor interference. *Cognition, 114*, 72–88.

Keysar, B. (1989). On the functional equivalence of literal and metaphorical interpretations in discourse. *Journal of Memory and Language, 28*, 375–385.

Kintsch, W. (1974). *The representation of meaning in memory*. Hillsdale, NJ: Lawrence Erlbaum.

  (1988). The role of knowledge in discourse comprehension: A construction-integration model. *Psychological Review, 95*, 163–182.

  (1998). *Comprehension: A paradigm for cognition*. Cambridge: Cambridge University Press.

Kintsch, W., & Keenan, J. M. (1973). Reading rate and retention as a function of the number of propositions in the base structure of sentences. *Cognitive Psychology, 5*, 257–274.

Kintsch, W., Kozminsky, E., Stretby, W. J., McKoon, G., & Keenan, J. M. (1975). Comprehension and recall of text as a function of content variables. *Journal of Verbal Learning and Verbal Behavior, 14*, 196–214.

Kintsch, W., & van Dijk, T. A. (1978). Toward a model of text comprehension and production. *Psychological Review, 85*, 363–394.

Kjaer, T. W., Nowak, M., & Lou, H. C. (2002). Reflective self-awareness and conscious states: PET evidence for a common midline parietofrontal core. *NeuroImage, 17*, 1080–1086.

Klin, C. M., & Myers, J. L. (1993). Reinstatement of causal information during reading. *Journal of Experimental Psychology: Learning, Memory and Cognition, 19*, 554–560.

Kneepens, E. W. E. M., & Zwaan, R. A. (1994). Emotions and literary text comprehension. *Poetics, 23*, 125–138.

Knott, A., & Sanders, T. (1998). The classification of coherence relations and their linguistic markers: An exploration of two languages. *Journal of Pragmatics, 30*, 135–175.

Koski, L., Wohlschläger, A., Bekkering, H., Woods, R. P., Dubeau, M.-C., Mazziotta, J. C., & Iacoboni, M. (2002). Modulation of motor and premotor activity during imitation of target-directed actions. *Cerebral Cortex, 12*, 847–855.

Kosslyn, S. M., Alpert, N. M., Thompson, W. L., Maljkovic, V., Weise, S. B., Chabris, C. F., Hamilton, S. E., Rauch, S. L., & Buonanno, F. S. (1993). Visual mental imagery activates topographically organized visual cortex: PET investigations. *Journal of Cognitive Neuroscience*, *5*, 263–287.

Kosslyn, S. M., Pascual-Leone, A., Felician, O., Camposano, S., Keenan, J. P., Thompson, W. L., Ganis, G., Sukel, K. E., & Alpert, N. M. (1999). The role of Area 17 in visual imagery: Convergent evidence from PET and rTMS. *Science*, *284*, 167–170.

Kourtzi, Z., & Kanwisher, N. (2000). Activation in human MT/MST by static images with implied motion. *Journal of Cognitive Neuroscience*, *12*, 48–55.

Kövecses, Z. (2000). *Metaphor and emotion: Language, culture and body in human feeling*. Cambridge: Cambridge University Press.

(2002). *Metaphor: A practical introduction*. Oxford: Oxford University Press.

(2010). A new look at metaphorical creativity in cognitive linguistics. *Cognitive Linguistics*, *21*, 663–697.

Kraemer, D. J. M., Macrae, C. N., Green, A. E., & Kelley, W. M. (2005). Musical imagery: Sound of silence activates auditory cortex. *Nature*, *434*, 158.

Kuiken, D. (2008). A theory of expressive reading. In Zyngier, Bortolussi, Chesnokova, & Auracher (Eds.), (pp. 49–68).

Kuiken, D., Miall, D. S., & Sikora, S. (2004). Forms of self-implication in literary reading. *Poetics Today*, *25*, 171–203.

Kuiken, D., Phillips, L., Gregus, M., Miall, D. S., Verbitsky, M., & Tonkonogy, A. (2004). Locating self-modifying feelings within literary reading. *Discourse Processes*, *38*, 267–286.

Kumkale, G., & Albarracin, D. (2004). The sleeper effect in persuasion: A meta-analytic review. *Psychological Bulletin*, *130*, 143–172.

Kurby, C. A., Magliano, J. P., & Rapp, D. N. (2009). Those voices in your head: Activation of auditory images during reading. *Cognition*, *112*, 457–461.

Kutas, M., & Hillyard, S. A. (1980). Reading senseless sentences: Brain potentials reflect semantic incongruity. *Science*, *207*(4427), 203–205.

(1984). Brain potentials during reading reflect word expectancy and semantic association. *Nature*, *307*(5947), 161–163.

Kutas, M., van Petten, C., & Kluender, R. (2006). Psycholinguistics electrified II: 1994–2005. In M. J. Traxler & M. A. Gernsbacher (Eds.), *Handbook of psycholinguistics* (pp. 659–724). New York: Elsevier.

Lai, V. T., Curran, T., & Menn, L. (2009). Comprehending conventional and novel metaphors: An ERP study. *Brain Research*, *1284*, 145–155.

Laird, J. D., Alibozak, T., Davainis, D., Deignan, K., Fontanella, K., Hong, J., Levy, B., & Pacheco, C. (1994). Individual differences in the effects of spontaneous mimicry on emotional contagion. *Motivation and Emotion*, *18*, 231–247.

Lakoff, G. (1972). Structural complexity in fairy tales. *The Study of Man*, *1*, 128–190.

(1987). *Women, fire and dangerous things: What categories reveal about the mind*. Chicago, IL: University of Chicago Press.

Lakoff, G., & Johnson, M. (1980). *Metaphors we live by*. Chicago, IL: University of Chicago Press.

(1999). *Philosophy in the flesh: The embodied mind and its challenge to western thought*. New York: Basic Books.

Lakoff, G., & Turner, M. (1989). *More than cool reason: A field guide to poetic metaphor*. Chicago, IL: University of Chicago Press.

Lamb, C. (2002). *The sewing circles of Herat: A memoir of Afghanistan*. London: HarperCollinsPublishers.

Landauer, T. K. (1962). Rate of implicit speech. *Perceptual and Motor Skills, 15*, 646.

Landauer, T. K., & Dumais, S. T. (1997). A solution to Plato's problem: The latent semantic analysis theory of acquisition, induction, and representation of knowledge. *Psychological Review, 104*, 211–240.

Landauer, T. K., Foltz, P. W., & Laham, D. (1998). An introduction to latent semantic analysis. *Discourse Processes, 25*, 259–284.

Langacker, R. (1987). *Foundations of cognitive grammar, Vol. 1*. Stanford, CA: Stanford University Press.

(1991). *Foundations of cognitive grammar, Vol. 2*. Stanford, CA: Stanford University Press.

Larsen, S. F., & Seilman, U. (1988). Personal remindings while reading literature. *Text, 8*, 411–429.

Larson, D. L. (2009). Advancing entertainment education: Using *The Rosie O'Donnell Show* to recognise implementation strategies for saturated markets. *Communication Theory, 19*, 105–123.

Lassonde, K. A., & O'Brien, E. J. (2009). Contextual specificity in the activation of predictive inferences. *Discourse Processes, 46*, 426–438.

Lawrence, D. H. (1996). The woman who rode away. Harmondsworth: Penguin. (First published in 1928.)

Ledoux, K., Gordon, P. C., Camblin, C. C., & Swaab, T. Y. (2007). Coreference and lexical repetition: Mechanisms of discourse integration. *Memory and Cognition, 35*, 801–815.

Leech, G. (1981). *Semantics: The study of meaning*. Harmondsworth: Penguin.

(2008). *Language in literature: Style and foregrounding*. London: Longman.

Leech, G., & Short, M. (2007). *Style in fiction: A linguistic introduction to English fictional prose*. London: Longman. (First published in 1981.)

Leland, J. (1983). The last sandcastle. In J. Leland (Ed.), *The last sandcastle* (pp. 89–93). Dublin: O'Brien Press.

Leslie, A. M. (1994). Pretending and believing: Issues in the theory of ToMM. *Cognition, 50*, 211–238.

Levelt, W. J. M., Schreuder, R., & Hoenkamp, E. (1978). Structure and use of verbs of motion. In R. N. Campbell & P. T. Smith (Eds.), *Recent advances in the psychology of language, Vol. 2* (pp. 137–162). New York: Plenum Press.

Lewis, D. (1973). *Counterfactuals*. Cambridge, MA: Harvard University Press.

Lewis, R. L. (1996). Interference in short-term memory: The magical number two (or three) in sentence processing. *Journal of Psycholinguistic Research, 25*, 93–115.

Li, C. N. (1986). Direct and indirect speech: A functional study. In F. Coulmas (Ed.), *Direct and indirect speech* (Trends in linguistics: Studies and monographs, *31*) (pp. 29–45). Berlin: Mouton de Gruyter.

Linde, C. (1993). *Life stories: The creation of coherence*. Oxford: Oxford University Press.

(2005). Life story. In D. Herman, M. Jahn, & M.-L. Ryan (Eds.), *Routledge encyclopedia of narrative theory* (pp. 277–278). London: Routledge.

Louwerse, M., & van Peer, W. (Eds.). (2002). *Thematics: Interdisciplinary studies.* Amsterdam: John Benjamins.

MacDonald, M. C., Pearlmutter, N. J., & Seidenberg, M. S. (1994). Lexical nature of syntactic ambiguity resolution. *Psychological Review, 101,* 676–703.

Madden, C. J., & Therriault, D. J. (2009). Verb aspect and perceptual simulations. *Quarterly Journal of Experimental Psychology, 62,* 1294–1303.

Maio, G. R., & Esses, V. M. (2001). The need for affect: Individual differences in the motivation to approach or avoid emotions. *Journal of Personality, 69,* 583–615.

Majid, A., Sanford, A. J., & Pickering, M. J. (2007). The linguistic description of minimal social scenarios affects the extent of causal inference making. *Journal of Experimental Social Psychology, 43,* 918–932.

Mak, W. M., Vonk, W., & Schriefers, H. (2006). Animacy in processing relative clauses: The hikers that rocks crush. *Journal of Memory and Language, 54,* 466–490.

Malt, B. C., Gennari, S., Imai, M., Ameel, E., Tsuda, N., & Majid, A. (2008). Talking about walking: Biomechanics and the language of locomotion. *Psychological Science, 19,* 232–240.

Mann, W. C., & Thompson, S. A. (1988). Rhetorical structure theory: Toward a functional theory of text organization. *Text, 8,* 243–281.

Mar, R. A., & Oatley, K. (2008). The function of fiction is the abstraction and simulation of social experience. *Perspectives on Psychological Science, 3,* 173–192.

Mar, R. A., Oatley, K., Hirsh, J., dela Paz, J., & Peterson, J. B. (2006). Bookworms versus nerds: Exposure to fiction versus non-fiction, divergent associations with social ability, and the simulation of fictional social worlds. *Journal of Research in Personality, 40,* 694–712.

Marsolek, C. J. (1999). Dissociable neural subsystems underlie abstract and specific object recognition. *Psychological Science, 10,* 111–118.

Martel, Y. (2003). *Life of Pi.* Edinburgh: Canongate.

Masson, M. E. J., Bub, D. N., & Warren, C. M. (2008). Kicking calculators: Contribution of embodied representations to sentence comprehension. *Journal of Memory and Language, 59,* 256–265.

Mattenklott, A. (1996). On the methodology of empirical research in suspense. In Vorderer, Wulff, & Friedrichsen (Eds.), (pp. 283–299).

McCrum, R. (1999). *My year off: Rediscovering life after a stroke.* London: Picador.

McCutchen, D., & Perfetti, C. A. (1982). The visual tongue-twister effect: Phonological activation in silent reading. *Journal of Verbal Learning and Verbal Behavior, 21,* 672–687.

McElree, B., & Nordlie, J. (1999). Literal and figurative interpretations are computed in equal time. *Psychonomic Bulletin and Review, 6,* 486–494.

McGlone, M. S., Glucksberg, S., & Cacciari, C. (1994). Semantic productivity and idiom comprehension. *Discourse Processes, 17,* 167–190.

McHale, B. (2009). Speech representation. In P. Hühn, J. Pier, W. Schmid, & J. Schönert (Eds.), *Handbook of narratology* (pp. 434–446). Berlin: Walter de Gruyter.

McIntosh, D. N. (1996). Facial feedback hypotheses: Evidence, implications, and directions. *Motivation and Emotion, 20,* 121–147.

McKoon, G. (1977). Organization of information in text memory. *Journal of Verbal Learning and Verbal Behavior, 16,* 247–260.

McKoon, G., & Ratcliff, R. (1986). Inferences about predictable events. *Journal of Experimental Psychology: Learning, Memory and Cognition, 12,* 82–91.

(1990). Textual inferences: Models and measures. In D. A. Balota, G. B. Flores d'Arcais, & K. Rayner (Eds.), *Comprehension processes in reading* (pp. 403–421). Hillsdale, NJ: Lawrence Erlbaum.

McRae, K., Hare, M., Elman, J. L., & Ferretti, T. (2005). A basis for generating expectancies for verbs and nouns. *Memory and Cognition, 33,* 1174–1184.

Mellet, E., Tzourio-Mazoyer, N., Bricogne, S., Mazoyer, B., Kosslyn, S. M., & Denis, M. (2000). Functional anatomy of high-resolution visual mental imagery. *Journal of Cognitive Neuroscience, 12,* 98–109.

Mertz, E., & Yovel, J. (2005). Courtroom narrative. In D. Herman, M. Jahn, & M.-L. Ryan (Eds.), *Routledge encyclopedia of narrative theory* (pp. 86–88). London: Routledge.

Miall, D. S. (2007). *Literary reading: Empirical and theoretical studies.* New York: Peter Lang.

Miall, D. S., & Kuiken, D. (1994). Foregrounding, defamiliarization, and affect: Response to literary stories. *Poetics, 22,* 389–407.

(2002). A feeling for fiction: Becoming what we behold. *Poetics, 30,* 221–241.

Miller, G. A., & Johnson-Laird, P. N. (1976). *Language and perception.* Cambridge: Cambridge University Press.

Moens, M., & Steedman, M. J. (1988). Temporal ontology and temporal reference. *Computational Linguistics, 14,* 15–28.

Moggach, D. (2000). *Tulip fever.* London: Vintage.

Mouilso, E., Glenberg, A. M., Havas, D. A., & Lindeman, L. M. (2007). Differences in action tendencies distinguish anger and sadness after comprehension of emotional sentences. In D. S. McNamara & J. G. Trafton (Eds.), *Proceedings of the 29th Annual Cognitive Science Society* (pp. 1325–1330). Austin, TX: Cognitive Science Society.

Moyer-Gusé, E. (2008). Toward a theory of entertainment persuasion: Explaining the persuasive effects of entertainment-education messages. *Communication Theory, 18,* 407–425.

Mukařovský, J. (1964a). Standard language and poetic language. In Garvin (Ed.), (pp. 17–30). (First published in Czech in 1932.)

(1964b). The esthetics of language. In Garvin (Ed.), (pp. 31–69). (First published in Czech in 1932.)

Munslow, A. (2007). *Narrative and history.* Houndmills: Palgrave.

Murphy, F. C., Wilde, G., Ogden, N., Barnard, P. J., & Calder, A. J. (2009). Assessing the automaticity of moral processing: Efficient coding of moral information during narrative comprehension. *Quarterly Journal of Experimental Psychology, 62,* 41–49.

Murray, J. D., Klin, C. M., & Myers, J. L. (1993). Forward inferences in narrative text. *Journal of Memory and Language, 32,* 464–473.

Myers, J. L., O'Brien, E. J., Albrecht, J. E., & Mason, R. A. (1994). Maintaining global coherence during reading. *Journal of Experimental Psychology: Learning, Memory and Cognition, 20,* 876–886.

Myers, J. L., Shinjo, M., & Duffy, S. A. (1987). Degree of causal relatedness and memory. *Journal of Verbal Learning and Verbal Behavior, 26*, 453–465.

Naciscione, A. (2010). *Stylistic use of phraseological units in discourse.* Amsterdam: John Benjamins.

Nafisi, A. (2004). *Reading Lolita in Tehran: A memoir in books.* New York: Random House.

Nänny, M., & Fischer, O. (Eds.). (1999). *Form miming meaning: Iconicity in language and literature.* Amsterdam: John Benjamins.

Ni, W., Fodor, J. D., Crain, S., & Shankweiler, D. (1998). Anomaly detection: Eye movement patterns. *Journal of Psycholinguistic Research, 27*, 515–539.

Niedenthal, P. M. (2007). Embodying emotion. *Science, 316*, 1002–1005.

Niederhoff, B. (2009a). Focalization. In P. Hühn, J. Pier, W. Schmid, & J. Schönert (Eds.), *Handbook of narratology* (pp. 115–123). Berlin: Walter de Gruyter.

(2009b). Perspective/point of view. In P. Hühn, J. Pier, W. Schmid, & J. Schönert (Eds.), *Handbook of narratology* (pp. 384–397). Berlin: Walter de Gruyter.

Nieuwland, M. S., & van Berkum, J. J. A. (2006). When peanuts fall in love: N400 evidence for the power of discourse. *Journal of Cognitive Neuroscience, 18*, 1098–1111.

Niffenegger, A. (2005). *The time traveler's wife.* London: Vintage.

Nolan, C. (1988). My autobiography entitled 'A Mammy Encomium'. In *Dam-burst of dreams* (pp. 3–24). London: Pan.

Nummenmaa, L., & Niemi, P. (2004). Inducing affective states with success-failure manipulations: A meta-analysis. *Emotion, 4*, 207–214.

Oatley, K. (1992). *Best laid schemes: The psychology of emotions.* Cambridge: Cambridge University Press.

(1999). Why fiction may be twice as true as fact. *Review of General Psychology, 3*, 101–117.

(2002). Emotions and the story worlds of fiction. In Green, Strange, & Brock (Eds.), (pp. 39–69).

(2008). The mind's flight simulator. *The Psychologist, 21*, 1030–1033.

(2011). *Such stuff as dreams: The psychology of fiction.* Chichester: Wiley-Blackwell.

Oatley, K., & Johnson-Laird, P. N. (1987). Towards a cognitive theory of emotion. *Cognition and Emotion, 1*, 51–58.

Oatley, K., Keltner, D., & Jenkins, J. M. (2006). *Understanding emotions.* Oxford: Blackwell.

Oberman, L. M., Winkielman, P., & Ramachandran, V. S. (2007). Face to face: Blocking facial mimicry can selectively impair recognition of emotional expressions. *Social Neuroscience, 2*, 167–178.

O'Donnell, M. (1980). *The beehive.* London: Eyre Methuen.

O'Halloran, K. (2003). *Critical discourse analysis and language cognition.* Edinburgh: Edinburgh University Press.

Opdahl, K. M. (2002). *Emotion as meaning: The literary case for how we imagine.* Lewisburg, PA: Bucknell University Press.

Orwell, G. (1951). *Animal farm.* Harmondsworth: Penguin.

Osaka, N., Osaka, M., Morishita, M., Kondo, H., & Fukuyama, H. (2004). A word expressing affective pain activates the anterior cingulate cortex in the human brain: An fMRI study. *Behavioural Brain Research, 153*, 123–127.

Oxford English Dictionary, OED Online (2011), Oxford: Oxford University Press, www.oed.com.

Page, N. (1988). *Speech in the novel*. London: Longman.

Partee, B. (1973). The syntax and semantics of quotation. In P. Kiparsky & S. Anderson (Eds.), *A festschrift for Morris Halle* (pp. 410–418). New York: Holt.

Pascal, R. (1977). *The dual voice: Free indirect speech and its functioning in the nineteenth century European novel*. Manchester: Manchester University Press.

Pavel, T. G. (1986). *Fictional worlds*. Cambridge, MA: Harvard University Press.

Peake, M. (1985). *Gormenghast*. London: Methuen.

Pennebaker, J. W. (1997a). *Opening up: The healing power of expressing emotion*. New York: Guilford Press.

(1997b). Writing about emotional experiences as a therapeutic process. *Psychological Science*, *8*, 162–166.

Pennebaker, J. W., & Beall, S. K. (1986). Confronting a traumatic event: Toward an understanding of inhibition and disease. *Journal of Abnormal Psychology*, *95*, 274–281.

Pennebaker, J. W., & Chung, C. K. (2007). Expressive writing, emotional upheavals, and health. In H. Friedman & R. Silver (Eds.), *Handbook of health psychology* (pp. 263–284). New York: Oxford University Press.

Pennebaker, J. W., Mayne, T. J., & Francis, M. E. (1997). Linguistic predictors of adaptive bereavement. *Journal of Personality and Social Psychology*, *72*, 863–871.

Pennebaker, J. W., & Seagal, J. D. (1999). Forming a story: The health benefits of narrative. *Journal of Clinical Psychology*, *55*, 1243–1254.

Petty, R. E., & Cacioppo, J. T. (1986). *Communications and persuasion: Central and peripheral routes to attitude change*. New York: Springer.

Pichert, J. W., & Anderson, R. C. (1977). Taking different perspectives on a story. *Journal of Educational Psychology*, *69*, 309–315.

Pohl, R., Colonius, H., & Thüring, M. (1985). Recognition of script-based inferences. *Psychological Research*, *47*, 59–67.

Poldrack, R. A. (2006). Can cognitive processes be inferred from neuroimaging data? *Trends in Cognitive Sciences*, *10*, 59–63.

Polichak, J. W., & Gerrig, R. J. (2002). 'Get up and win!': Participatory responses to narrative. In Green, Strange, & Brock (Eds.), (pp. 71–95).

Polkinghorne, D. E. (1988). *Narrative knowing and the human sciences*. Albany, NY: State University of New York Press.

Potts, G. R., Keenan, J. M., & Golding, J. M. (1988). Assessing the occurrence of elaborative inferences: Lexical decision versus naming. *Journal of Memory and Language*, *27*, 399–415.

Pratt, N. L., & Kelly, S. D. (2008). Emotional states influence the neural processing of affective language. *Social Neuroscience*, *3*, 434–442.

Prentice, D. A., & Gerrig, R. J. (1999). Exploring the boundary between fiction and reality. In S. Chaiken & Y. Trope (Eds.), *Dual-process theories in social psychology* (pp. 529–546). New York: Guilford Press.

Prentice, D. A., Gerrig, R. J., & Bailis, D. S. (1997). What readers bring to the processing of fictional texts. *Psychonomic Bulletin and Review*, *4*, 416–420.

Preston, S. D., & de Waal, F. B. M. (2002). Empathy: Its ultimate and proximal bases. *Behavioral and Brain Sciences, 25,* 1–71.

Price, J. (2008). *The use of focus cues in healthy ageing.* Doctoral thesis, University of Glasgow, Glasgow.

Price, J., & Sanford, A. J. (2008, March). *Focus effects in healthy aging: Ease of reference and shallow processing.* Poster presented at the meeting of CUNY Conference on Sentence Processing, University of North Carolina at Chapel Hill, NC.

Prince, E. F. (1978). A comparison of wh-clefts and *it*-clefts in discourse. *Language, 54,* 883–906.

Prince, G. (1971). Notes toward a categorization of fictional 'narratees'. *Genre, 4,* 100–106.

Prinz, J. J. (2004). *Gut reactions: A perceptual theory of emotion.* Oxford: Oxford University Press.

Prochaska, J. O., DiClemente, C. C., & Norcass, J. C. (1992). In search of how people change: Applications to addictive behaviors. *American Psychologist, 47,* 1102–1114.

Propp, V. (1968). *Morphology of the folktale.* Austin, TX: University of Texas Press.

Puccetti, R. (1973). *The trial of John and Henry Norton.* London: Hutchinson.

Pulvermüller, F. (1999). Words in the brain's language. *Behavioural and Brain Sciences, 22,* 253–336.

    (2001). Brain reflections of words and their meaning. *Trends in Cognitive Sciences, 5,* 517–524.

    (2005). Brain mechanisms linking language and action. *Nature Reviews Neuroscience, 6,* 576–582.

Pulvermüller, F., Shtyrov, Y., & Ilmoniemi, R. (2005). Brain signatures of meaning access in action word recognition. *Journal of Cognitive Neuroscience, 17,* 884–892.

Pynte, J., Besson, M., Robichon, F., & Poli, J. (1996). The time-course of metaphor comprehension: An event-related potential study. *Brain and Language, 55,* 293–316.

Rabinowitz, P. J. (1987). *Before reading: Narrative conventions and the politics of interpretation.* Columbus, OH: Ohio State University Press.

Ramírez-Esparza, N., & Pennebaker, J. W. (2007). Do good stories produce good health? Exploring words, language, and culture. In M. Bamberg (Ed.), *Narrative: State of the art* (pp. 249–259). Amsterdam: John Benjamins.

Raposo, A., Moss, H. E., Stamatakis, E. A., & Tyler, L. K. (2009). Modulation of motor and premotor cortices by actions, action words and action sentences. *Neuropsychologia, 47,* 388–396.

Rapp, A. M., Leube, D. T., Erb, M., Grodd, W., & Kircher, T. T. J. (2004). Neural correlates of metaphor processing. *Cognitive Brain Research, 20,* 395–402.

Rapp, D. N., & Gerrig, R. J. (2006). Predilections for narrative outcomes: The impact of story contexts and reader preferences. *Journal of Memory and Language, 54,* 54–67.

Raskin, V. (1985). *Semantic mechanisms of humour.* Dordrecht: Reidel.

Reiterer, S., Erb, M., Grodd, W., & Wildgruber, D. (2008). Cerebral processing of timbre and loudness: fMRI evidence for a contribution of Broca's area to basic auditory discrimination. *Brain Imaging and Behavior, 2,* 1–10.

Ricoeur, P. (1983–1988). *Time and narrative, Vols. 1–3*, Chicago, IL: University of Chicago Press.

Rimmon-Kenan, S. (1983). *Narrative fiction: Contemporary poetics*. London: Methuen.

Rizzolatti, G., & Craighero, L. (2004). The mirror-neuron system. *Annual Review of Neuroscience, 27*, 169–192.

Rolls, E. T., & Scott, T. R. (2003). Central taste anatomy and neurophysiology. In R. L. Doty (Ed.), *Handbook of olfaction and gustation* (pp. 679–705). New York: Marcel Dekker.

Rolls, E. T., Scott, T. R., Sienkiewicz, Z. J., & Yaxley, S. (1988). The responsiveness of neurones in the frontal opercular gustatory cortex of the macaque monkey is independent of hunger. *Journal of Physiology, 397*, 1–12.

Ronan, F. (1994). *The men who loved Evelyn Cotton*. London: Sceptre.

Rooth, M. (1992). A theory of focus interpretation. *Natural Language Semantics, 1*, 75–116.

Rowling, J. K. (2003). *Harry Potter and the Order of the Phoenix*. London: Bloomsbury.

Rueschemeyer, S.-A., Glenberg, A. M., Kaschak, M., Mueller, K., & Friederici, A. D. (2010). Top-down and bottom-up contributions to understanding sentences describing objects in motion. *Frontiers in Psychology, 1, 183*, doi:10.3389/fpsyg.2010.00183.

Rumelhart, D. E. (1975). Notes on a schema for stories. In D. G. Bobrow & A. Collins (Eds.), *Representation and understanding: Studies in cognitive science* (pp. 211–236). New York: Academic Press.

Ryan, M.-L. (1980). Fiction, non-factuals and the principle of minimal departure. *Poetics, 9*, 403–422.

(1991). *Possible worlds, artificial intelligence and narrative theory*. Bloomington, IN: Indiana University Press.

(2007). Toward a definition of narrative. In D. Herman (Ed.), *The Cambridge companion to narrative* (pp. 22–35). Cambridge: Cambridge University Press.

Samar, V. J. (2006). Evoked potentials. In K. Brown (Ed.), *Encyclopedia of language and linguistics, Vol. 4* (pp. 326–335). Oxford: Elsevier.

Sanders, J. (1994). *Perspective in narrative discourse*. Doctoral thesis, Tilburg University, Tilburg.

Sanders, T., Spooren, W., & Noordman, L. (1992). Toward a taxonomy of coherence relations. *Discourse Processes, 15*, 1–35.

(1993). Coherence relations in a cognitive theory of discourse representation. *Cognitive Linguistics, 4*, 93–133.

Sanford, A. J. (1987). *The mind of man: Models of human understanding*. New Haven, CT: Yale University Press.

(1989). Component processes of reference resolution in discourse. In N. E. Sharkey (Ed.), *Models of cognition: A review of cognitive science* (pp. 113–140). Norwood, NJ: Ablex.

(1999). Word meaning and discourse processing: A tutorial review. In S. C. Garrod & M. J. Pickering (Eds.), *Language processing* (pp. 301–334). Hove: Psychology Press.

(2002). Context, attention and depth of processing during interpretation. *Mind and Language, 17*, 188–206.

(2008). Defining embodied processing of discourse. In de Vega, Glenberg, & Graesser (Eds.), (pp. 181–194).

Sanford, A. J., Clegg, M., & Majid, A. (1998). The influence of types of character on processing background information in narrative discourse. *Memory and Cognition, 26,* 1323–1329.

Sanford, A. J., Dawydiak, E., & Emmott, C. (2006, July). *External and internal sources of attention control: Findings from change detection.* Poster presented at the meeting of the Society for Text and Discourse, Minneapolis, MN.

Sanford, A. J., Filik, R., Emmott, C., & Morrow, L. I. (2008). They're digging up the road again: The processing cost of institutional *they. The Quarterly Journal of Experimental Psychology, 61,* 372–380.

Sanford, A. J., & Garrod, S. C. (1981). *Understanding written language: Explorations in comprehension beyond the sentence.* Chichester: John Wiley.

(1998). The role of scenario mapping in text comprehension. *Discourse Processes, 26,* 159–190.

(2005). Memory-based approaches and beyond. *Discourse Processes, 39,* 205–224.

Sanford, A. J., & Graesser, A. C. (2006). Shallow processing and underspecification. *Discourse Processes, 42,* 99–108.

Sanford, A. J., Leuthold, H., Bohan, J., & Sanford, A. J. S. (2011). Anomalies at the borderline of awareness: An ERP study. *Journal of Cognitive Neuroscience, 23,* 514–523.

Sanford, A. J., & McGinley, M. T. (1990). In search of a richer model of written language comprehension: Three fragments of evidence. In Ö. Dahl & K. Fraurud (Eds.), *The second Nordic conference on text comprehension in man and machine* (pp. 121–135). Stockholm: Stockholm University Institute of Linguistics.

Sanford, A. J., & Moxey, L. M. (1995). Aspects of coherence in written language: A psychological perspective. In M. A. Gernsbacher & T. Givón (Eds.), *Coherence in spontaneous text* (pp. 161–187). Amsterdam: John Benjamins.

(1999). What are mental models made of? In G. Rickheit & C. Habel (Eds.), *Mental models in discourse processing and reasoning* (pp. 57–76). North Holland: Elsevier.

Sanford, A. J., & Sturt, P. (2002). Depth of processing in language comprehension: Not noticing the evidence. *Trends in Cognitive Sciences, 6,* 382–386.

Sanford, A. J. S., Price, J., & Sanford, A. J. (2009). Enhancement and suppression effects resulting from information structuring in sentences. *Memory and Cognition, 37,* 880–888.

Sanford, A. J. S., Sanford, A. J., Filik, R., & Molle, J. (2005). Depth of lexical-semantic processing and sentential load. *Journal of Memory and Language, 53,* 378–396.

Sanford, A. J. S., Sanford, A. J., Molle, J., & Emmott, C. (2006). Shallow processing and attention capture in written and spoken discourse. *Discourse Processes, 42,* 109–130.

Sapolsky, R. M. (1994). *Why zebras don't get ulcers: A guide to stress-related diseases and coping.* New York: W. H. Freeman.

Scarry, E. (1996). Speech acts in criminal courts. In P. Brooks & P. Gewirtz (Eds.), *Law's stories: Narrative and rhetoric in the law* (pp. 165–174). New Haven, CT: Yale University Press.

Schank, R. C. (1999). *Tell me a story: Narrative and intelligence*. Evanston, IL: Northwestern University Press.

Schank, R. C., & Abelson, R. P. (1977). *Scripts, plans, goals and understanding: An enquiry into human knowledge structures*. Hillsdale, NJ: Lawrence Erlbaum.

Schlesinger, I. M. (1968). *Sentence structure and the reading process*. The Hague: Mouton.

Schlink, B. (2008). *The reader*. London: Phoenix. (First published in 1997.)

Schmitt, C. S., & Clark, C. (2007). Sympathy. In J. E. Stets & J. H. Turner (Eds.), *Handbook of the sociology of emotions* (pp. 467–492). New York: Springer.

Searle, J. (1980). Minds, brains and programs. *Behavioral and Brain Sciences, 3*, 417–457.

Semino, E. (1997). *Language and world creation in poems and other texts*. London: Longman.

(2006). Possible worlds: Stylistic applications. In K. Brown (Ed.), *Encyclopedia of language and linguistics, Vol. 9* (pp. 777–782). Oxford: Elsevier.

(2008). *Metaphor in discourse*. Cambridge: Cambridge University Press.

Semino, E., & Short, M. (2004). *Corpus stylistics: Speech, writing and thought representation in a corpus of English writing*. London: Routledge.

Semino, E., & Steen, G. (2008). Metaphor in literature. In Gibbs (Ed.), (pp. 232–246).

Shen, Y. (2006). Figures of speech. In K. Brown (Ed.), *Encyclopedia of language and linguistics, Vol. 4* (pp. 459–464). Oxford: Elsevier.

(2007). Foregrounding in poetic discourse: Between deviation and cognitive constraints. *Language and Literature, 16*, 155–168.

Shklovsky, V. (1965). Art as technique. In L. T. Lemon & M. J. Reis (Eds.), *Russian Formalist criticism: Four essays* (pp. 3–24). Lincoln, NE: University of Nebraska Press. (First published in Russian in 1917.)

Short, M. (1996). *Exploring the language of poems, plays and prose*. London: Longman.

Sillitoe, A. (1961). *The loneliness of the long distance runner*. London: Pan Books.

Simmons, W. K., Martin, A., & Barsalou, L. W. (2005). Pictures of appetizing foods activate gustatory cortices for taste and reward. *Cerebral Cortex, 15*, 1602–1608.

Simmons, W. K., Pecher, D., Hamann, S. B., Zeelenberg, R., & Barsalou, L. W. (2003, March). *fMRI evidence for modality-specific processing of conceptual knowledge on six modalities*. Poster presented at the meeting of the Society for Cognitive Neuroscience, New York.

Simmons, W. K., Ramjee, V., Beauchamp, M. S., McRae, K., Martin, A., & Barsalou, L. W. (2007). A common neural substrate for perceiving and knowing about color. *Neuropsychologia, 45*, 2802–2810.

Simons, D. J., & Levin, D. T. (1997). Change blindness. *Trends in Cognitive Sciences, 1*, 261–267.

(1998). Failure to detect changes to people during a real-world interaction. *Psychonomic Bulletin and Review, 5*, 644–649.

Simpson, P. (1993). *Language, ideology and point of view*. London: Routledge.

(2003). *On the discourse of satire: Towards a stylistic model of satirical humour*. Amsterdam: John Benjamins.

Singer, M. (1979). Processes of inference during sentence encoding. *Memory and Cognition, 7*, 192–200.

Singer, T., Seymour, B., O'Doherty, J. P., Kaube, H., Dolan, R. J., & Frith, C. D. (2004). Empathy for pain involves the affective but not sensory components of pain. *Science, 303* (5661), 1157–1162.

Singer, T., Seymour, B., O'Doherty, J. P., Stephan, K. E., Dolan, R. J., & Frith, C. D. (2006). Empathic neural responses are modulated by the perceived fairness of others. *Nature, 439* (7075), 466–469.

Singhal, A., Cody, M. J., Rogers, E. M., & Sabido, M. (2004). *Entertainment-education and social change: History, research and practice.* Mahwah, NJ: Lawrence Erlbaum.

Singhal, A., & Rogers, E. M. (1999). *Entertainment-education: A communication strategy for social change.* Mahwah, NJ: Lawrence Erlbaum.

(2002). A theoretical agenda for entertainment-education. *Communication Theory, 12,* 117–135.

Skipper, J. I., & Small, S. L. (2006). fMRI studies of language. In K. Brown (Ed.), *Encyclopedia of language and linguistics, Vol. 4* (pp. 496–511). Oxford: Elsevier.

Slater, M. D. (2002). Entertainment education and the persuasive impact of narratives. In Green, Strange, & Brock (Eds.), (pp. 157–181).

Sloan, D. M., & Marx, B. P. (2004). Taking pen to hand: Evaluating theories underlying the written disclosure paradigm. *Clinical Psychology: Science and Practice, 11,* 121–137.

Smith, G. M. (2003). *Film structure and the emotion system.* Cambridge: Cambridge University Press.

Smith, M. (1995). *Engaging characters: Fiction, emotion and the cinema.* Oxford: Clarendon Press.

Solarz, A. K. (1960). Latency of instrumental responses as a function of compatibility with the meaning of eliciting verbal signs. *Journal of Experimental Psychology, 59,* 239–245.

Song, H., & Schwarz, N. (2008). Fluency and the detection of misleading questions: Low processing fluency attenuates the Moses illusion. *Social Cognition, 26,* 791–799.

Sotillo, M., Carretié, L., Hinojosa, J. A., Tapia, M., Mercado, F., López-Martin, S., & Albert, J. (2005). Neural activity associated with metaphor comprehension: Spatial analysis. *Neuroscience Letters, 373,* 5–9.

Sotirova, V. (2006). Reader responses to narrative point of view. *Poetics, 34,* 108–133.

Speer, N. K., Zacks, J. M., & Reynolds, J. R. (2007). Human brain activity time-locked to narrative event boundaries. *Psychological Science, 18,* 449–455.

Stanovich, K. E., & West, R. F. (1989). Exposure to print and orthographic processing. *Reading Research Quarterly, 24,* 402–433.

Stanzel, F. K. (1984). *A theory of narrative.* Cambridge: Cambridge University Press.

Steen, G. (1994). *Understanding metaphor in literature.* London: Longman.

Sternberg, M. (1978). *Expositional modes and temporal ordering in fiction.* Baltimore, MD: Johns Hopkins University Press.

(1982). Proteus in quotation-land: Mimesis and the forms of represented discourse. *Poetics Today, 3,* 107–156.

(2003). Universals of narrative and their cognitivist fortunes (I). *Poetics Today, 24,* 297–395.

Stevenson, R. J., Crawley, R., & Kleinman, D. (1994). Thematic roles, focus and the representation of events. *Language and Cognitive Processes, 9,* 519–548.

Stockwell, P. (2002). *Cognitive poetics: An introduction*. London: Routledge.

(2009). *Texture: A cognitive aesthetics of reading*. Edinburgh: Edinburgh University Press.

Strack, F., Martin, L. L., & Stepper, S. (1988). Inhibiting and facilitating conditions of the human smile: A non-obtrusive test of the facial feedback hypothesis. *Journal of Personality and Social Psychology, 54*, 768–777.

Sturt, P., Sanford, A. J., Stewart, A., & Dawydiak, E. (2004). Linguistic focus and good-enough representations: An application of the change-detection paradigm. *Psychonomic Bulletin and Review, 11*, 882–888.

Suh, S. Y., & Trabasso, T. (1993). Inferences during reading: Converging evidence from discourse analysis, talk-aloud protocols, and recognition priming. *Journal of Memory and Language, 32*, 279–300.

Swann, J., & Allington, D. (Eds.). (2009). *Literary reading as a social practice*. Special issue of *Language and Literature, 18*(3).

Swinney, D., & Cutler, A. (1979). The access and processing of idiomatic expressions. *Journal of Verbal Learning and Verbal Behavior, 18*, 523–534.

Taboada, M., & Mann, W. C. (2006). Rhetorical structure theory: Looking back and moving forward. *Discourse Studies, 8*, 423–459.

Taleb, N. N. (2007). *The black swan: The impact of the highly improbable*. London: Penguin.

Talmy, L. (1988). Force dynamics in language and cognition. *Cognitive Science, 12*, 49–100.

Tan, E. S. (1994). Story processing as an emotion episode. In H. van Oostendorp & R. A. Zwaan (Eds.), *Naturalistic text comprehension* (pp. 167–188). Norwood, NJ: Ablex.

(1996). *Emotion and the structure of narrative film: Film as an emotion machine*. Mahwah, NJ: Lawrence Erlbaum.

Tan, E. S., & Diteweg, G. (1996). Suspense, predictive inference, and emotion in film viewing. In Vorderer, Wulff, & Friedrichsen (Eds.), (pp. 149–188).

Tanenhaus, M. K., Spivey-Knowlton, M. J., Eberhard, K. M., & Sedivy, J. E. (1995). Integration of visual and linguistic information in spoken language comprehension. *Science, 268*, 1632–1634.

Tannen, D. (1999). *The argument culture: Changing the way we argue and debate*. London: Virago.

Tartter, V. C., Gomes, H., Dubrovsky, B., Molholm, S., & Vala Stewart, R. (2002). Novel metaphors appear anomalous at least momentarily: Evidence from the N400. *Brain and Language, 80*, 488–509.

Taylor, L. J., Lev-Ari, S., & Zwaan, R. A. (2008). Inferences about action engage action systems. *Brain and Language, 107*, 62–67.

Taylor, L. J., & Zwaan, R. A. (2008). Motor resonance and linguistic focus. *The Quarterly Journal of Experimental Psychology, 61*, 896–904.

Tellegen, A. (1982). *Brief manual for the differential personality questionnaire*. Unpublished manuscript. Department of Psychology, University of Minnesota, Minneapolis, MN.

Terasaki, A. K. (2004). Pre-announcement sequences in conversation. In G. H. Lerner (Ed.), *Conversation analysis: Studies from the first generation* (pp. 171–219). Amsterdam: John Benjamins.

Tettamanti, M., Buccino, G., Saccuman, M. C., Gallese, V., Danna, M., Scifo, P., Fazio, F., Rizzolatti, G., Cappa, S. F., & Perani, D. (2005). Listening to action-related sentences activates fronto-parietal motor circuits. *Journal of Cognitive Neuroscience, 17*, 273–281.

Thomson, A. (2009). *Direct and indirect thought modulates depth of processing.* Unpublished undergraduate thesis, University of Glasgow, Glasgow.

Thorndyke, P. W. (1977). Cognitive structures in comprehension and memory of narrative discourse. *Cognitive Psychology, 9*, 77–110.

Tobin, V. (2009). Cognitive bias and the poetics of surprise. *Language and Literature, 18*, 155–172.

Tolkien, J. R. R. (2001). *The lord of the rings.* London: Harper-Collins.

Tomkins, S. S. (1962). *Affect, imagery and consciousness, Vol. 1.* New York: Springer.

Toolan, M. (1990). *The stylistics of fiction: A literary linguistic approach.* London: Routledge.

(2001). *Narrative: A critical linguistic introduction.* London: Routledge.

(2006). Speech and thought, representation of. In K. Brown (Ed.), *Encyclopedia of language and linguistics, Vol. 11* (pp. 698–710). Oxford: Elsevier.

Trabasso, T., & Magliano, J. P. (1996). Conscious understanding during comprehension. *Discourse Processes, 21*, 255–287.

Traxler, M. J., Morris, R. K., & Seely, R. E. (2002). Processing subject and object relative clauses: Evidence from eye movements. *Journal of Memory and Language, 47*, 69–90.

Traxler, M. J., & Pickering, M. J. (1996). Plausibility and the processing of unbounded dependencies: An eye-tracking study. *Journal of Memory and Language, 35*, 454–475.

Traxler, M. J., Sanford, A. J., Aked, J., & Moxey, L. M. (1997). Processing causal and diagnostic statements in discourse. *Journal of Experimental Psychology: Learning, Memory and Cognition, 23*, 88–101.

Tsur, R. (2008). *Toward a theory of cognitive poetics.* Brighton: Sussex Academic Press.

Tversky, A., & Kahneman, D. (1973). Availability: A heuristic for judging frequency and probability. *Cognitive Psychology, 5*, 207–232.

Uspensky, B. (1973). *A poetics of composition: The structure of the artistic text and the typology of a compositional form.* Berkeley, CA: University of California Press.

van Berkum, J. J. A. (2004). Sentence comprehension in a wider discourse: Can we use ERPs to keep track of things? In M. Carreiras & C. Clifton (Eds.), *The on-line study of sentence comprehension: Eye-tracking, ERPs and beyond* (pp. 229–270). New York: Psychology Press.

van Berkum, J. J. A., Brown, C. M., Zwitserlood, P., Kooijman, V., & Hagoort, P. (2005). Anticipating upcoming words in discourse: Evidence from ERPs and reading times. *Journal of Experimental Psychology: Learning, Memory and Cognition, 31*, 443–467.

van Berkum, J. J. A., Hagoort, P., & Brown, C. M. (1999). Semantic integration in sentences and discourse: Evidence from the N400. *Journal of Cognitive Neuroscience, 11*, 657–671.

van Berkum, J. J. A., Holleman, B., Nieuwland, M. S., Otten, M., & Murre, J. (2009). Right or wrong? The brain's fast response to morally objectionable statements. *Psychological Science, 20*, 1092–1099.

van den Broek, P., & Lorch, R. F. (1993). Network representations of causal relations in memory for narrative texts: Evidence from primed recognition. *Discourse Processes, 17*, 75–98.

van Dijk, T. A., & Kintsch, W. (1983). *Strategies of discourse comprehension.* London: Academic Press.

van Jaarsveld, H. J., Dijkstra, T., & Hermans, D. (1997). The detection of semantic illusions: Task-specific effects for similarity and position of distorted terms. *Psychological Research, 59*, 219–230.

van Oostendorp, H., & de Mul, S. (1990). Moses beats Adam: A semantic relatedness effect on a semantic illusion. *Acta Psychologica, 74*, 35–46.

van Peer, W. (1986). *Stylistics and psychology: Investigations of foregrounding.* London: Croom Helm.

(Ed.). (2007). *Foregrounding.* Special issue of *Language and Literature, 16*(2), 99–224.

van Peer, W., & Chatman, S. (Eds.). (2001). *New perspectives on narrative perspective.* Albany, NY: State University of New York Press.

van Peer, W., & Hakemulder, J. (2006). Foregrounding. In K. Brown (Ed.), *The encyclopedia of language and linguistics, Vol. 4* (pp. 546–551). Oxford: Elsevier.

van Peer, W., Hakemulder, J., & Zyngier, S. (2007). Lines on feeling: Foregrounding, aesthetics and meaning. *Language and Literature, 16*, 197–213.

van Peer, W., & Pander Maat, H. (1996). Perspectivation and sympathy: Effects of narrative point of view. In R. J. Kreuz & M. S. MacNealy (Eds.), *Empirical approaches to literature and aesthetics* (pp. 143–154). Norwood, NJ: Ablex.

Vonk, W., Hustinx, L. G. M. M., & Simons, W. H. G. (1992). The use of referential expressions in structuring discourse. *Language and Cognitive Processes, 7*, 301–333.

Vorderer, P. (1996). Toward a psychological theory of suspense. In Vorderer, Wulff, & Friedrichsen (Eds.), (pp. 233–254).

Vorderer, P., Wulff, H. J., & Friedrichsen, M. (Eds.). (1996). *Suspense: Conceptualizations, theoretical analyses, and empirical explorations.* Mahwah, NJ: Lawrence Erlbaum.

Voss, J. F., & van Dyke, J. A. (2001). Narrative structure, information certainty, emotional content, and gender as factors in a pseudo jury decision-making task. *Discourse Processes, 32*, 215–243.

Voss, J. F., Wiley, J., & Sandak, R. (1999). On the use of narrative as argument. In S. R. Goldman, A. C. Graesser, & P. van den Broek (Eds.), *Narrative, comprehension, causality and coherence: Essays in honor of Tom Trabasso* (pp. 235–252). Mahwah, NJ: Lawrence Erlbaum.

Wales, K. (1996). *Personal pronouns in present-day English.* Cambridge: Cambridge University Press.

(2001). *A dictionary of stylistics.* London: Longman.

Wallbott, H. G. (1988). Big girls don't frown, big boys don't cry: Gender differences of professional actors in communicating emotion via facial expression. *Journal of Nonverbal Behavior, 12*, 98–106.

Walton, K. L. (1978). Fearing fictions. *Journal of Philosophy, 75*, 5–27.

(1990). *Mimesis as make-believe: On the foundations of the representational arts.* Cambridge, MA: Harvard University Press.

Warren, T. (2001). *Understanding the role of referential processing in sentence complexity*. Doctoral thesis, Massachusetts Institute of Technology, Cambridge, MA.

Warren, T., & Gibson, E. (2002). The influence of referential processing on sentence complexity. *Cognition, 85*, 79–112.

Wason, P., & Reich, S. S. (1979). A verbal illusion. *Quarterly Journal of Experimental Psychology, 31*, 591–597.

Werth, P. (1999). *Text worlds: Representing conceptual space in discourse*. London: Longman.

West, R. F., Stanovich, K. E., & Mitchell, H. R. (1993). Reading in the real world, and its correlates. *Reading Research Quarterly, 28*, 34–50.

Wheeler, S. C., Green, M. C., & Brock, T. C. (1999). Fictional narratives change beliefs: Replications of Prentice, Gerrig and Bailis (1997) with mixed corroboration. *Psychonomic Bulletin and Review, 6*, 136–141.

White, H. (1973). *Metahistory: The historical imagination in nineteenth-century Europe*. Baltimore, MD: Johns Hopkins University Press.

(1980). The value of narrativity in the representation of reality. *Critical Inquiry, 7*, 5–27.

(1987). *The content of the form: Narrative discourse and historical representation*. Baltimore, MD: Johns Hopkins University Press.

Wicha, N. Y. Y., Bates, E. A., Moreno, E. M., & Kutas, M. (2003). Potato not Pope: Human brain potentials to gender expectation and agreement in Spanish spoken sentences. *Neuroscience Letters, 346*, 165–168.

Wicha, N. Y. Y., Moreno, E. M., & Kutas, M. (2003). Expecting gender: An event-related brain potential study on the role of grammatical gender in comprehending a line drawing within a written sentence in Spanish. *Cortex, 39*, 483–508.

(2004). Anticipating words and their gender: An event-related brain potential study of semantic integration, gender expectancy, and gender agreement in Spanish sentence reading. *Journal of Cognitive Neuroscience, 16*, 1272–1288.

Wicker, B., Keysers, C., Plailly, J., Royet, J.-P., Gallese, V., & Rizzolatti, G. (2003). Both of us disgusted in *my* insula: The common neural basis of seeing and feeling disgust. *Neuron, 40*, 655–664.

Winawer, J., Huk, A. C., & Boroditsky, L. (2008). A motion aftereffect from still photographs depicting motion. *Psychological Science, 19*, 276–283.

Winner, E., & Gardner, H. (1977). The comprehension of metaphor in brain-damaged patients. *Brain, 100*, 719–727.

Winter, E. O. (1977). A clause relational approach to English texts: A study of some predictive lexical items in written discourse. *Instructional Science, 6*, 1–92.

Wulff, H. J. (1996). Suspense and the influence of cataphora on viewers' expectations. In Vorderer, Wulff, & Friedrichsen (Eds.), (pp. 1–17).

Wuyam, B., Moosavi, S. H., Decety, J., Adams, L., Lansing, R. W., & Guz, A. (1995). Imagination of dynamic exercise produced ventilatory responses which were more apparent in competitive sportsmen. *Journal of Physiology, 482*, 713–724.

Yao, B., Belin, P., & Scheepers, C. (2011). Silent reading of direct versus indirect speech activates voice selective areas in the auditory cortex. *Journal of Cognitive Neuroscience, 23*, 3146–3152.

Yaxley, R. H., & Zwaan, R. A. (2007). Simulating visibility during language comprehension. *Cognition, 105*, 229–236.

Young, L., Cushman, F., Hauser, M., & Saxe, R. (2007). The neural basis of the interaction between theory of mind and moral judgment. *Proceedings of the National Academy of Sciences of the United States of America, 104,* 8235–8240.

Young, L., & Saxe, R. (2008). The neural basis of belief encoding and integration in moral judgment. *NeuroImage, 40,* 1912–1920.

(2009). An fMRI investigation of spontaneous mental state inference for moral judgment. *Journal of Cognitive Neuroscience, 21,* 1396–1405.

Zajonc, R. B., Murphy, S. T., & Inglehart, M. (1989). Feeling and facial efference: Implications of the vascular theory of emotion. *Psychological Review, 96,* 395–416.

Zaki, J., & Ochsner, K. (2011). You, me and my brain: Self and other representations in social cognitive neuroscience. In A. Todorov, S. T. Fiske, & D. A. Prentice (Eds.), *Social Neuroscience: Toward understanding the underpinnings of the social mind* (pp. 14–39). Oxford: Oxford University Press.

Zillmann, D. (1978). Attribution and misattribution of excitatory reactions. In J. H. Harvey, W. J. Ickes, & R. F. Kidd (Eds.), *New directions in attribution research* (pp. 133–163). Hillsdale, NJ: Lawrence Erlbaum.

(1991). Empathy: Affect bearing witness to the emotion of others. In J. Bryant & D. Zillmann (Eds.), *Responding to the screen: Reception and reaction processes* (pp. 135–167). Hillsdale, NJ: Lawrence Erlbaum.

(1994). Mechanisms of emotional involvement with drama. *Poetics, 23,* 33–51.

(1996). The psychology of suspense in dramatic exposition. In Vorderer, Wulff, & Friedrichsen (Eds.), (pp. 199–231).

(2003). Theory of affective dynamics: Emotions and moods. In J. Bryant, D. Roskos-Ewoldsen, & J. Cantor (Eds.), *Communication and emotion: Essays in honour of Dolf Zillmann* (pp. 533–567). Mahwah, NJ: Lawrence Erlbaum.

(2006a). Empathy: Affective reactivity to others' emotional experiences. In J. Bryant & P. Vorderer (Eds.), *Psychology of entertainment* (pp. 151–181). Mahwah, NJ: Lawrence Erlbaum.

(2006b). Dramaturgy for emotions from fictional narration. In J. Bryant & P. Vorderer (Eds.), *Psychology of entertainment* (pp. 215–238). Mahwah, NJ: Lawrence Erlbaum.

Zillmann, D., Hay, T. A., & Bryant, J. (1975). The effect of suspense and its resolution on the appreciation of dramatic presentations. *Journal of Research in Personality, 9,* 307–323.

Zunshine, L. (2006). *Why we read fiction: Theory of mind and the novel.* Columbus, OH: Ohio State University Press.

Zwaan, R. A. (1993). *Aspects of literary comprehension.* Amsterdam: John Benjamins.

(1996). Processing narrative time shifts. *Journal of Experimental Psychology: Learning, Memory and Cognition, 22,* 1196–1207.

(2004). The immersed experiencer: Toward an embodied theory of language comprehension. In B. H. Ross (Ed.), *The psychology of learning and motivation, Vol. 44* (pp. 35–62). New York: Academic Press.

Zwaan, R. A., Langston, M. C., & Graesser, A. C. (1995). The construction of situation models in narrative comprehension: An event-indexing model. *Psychological Science, 6,* 292–297.

Zwaan, R. A., Magliano, J. P., & Graesser, A. C. (1995). Dimensions of situation model construction in narrative comprehension. *Journal of Experimental Psychology: Learning, Memory and Cognition, 21*, 386–397.

Zwaan, R. A., Stanfield, R. A., & Yaxley, R. H. (2002). Language comprehenders mentally represent the shapes of objects. *Psychological Science, 13*, 168–171.

Zwaan, R. A., & Taylor, L. J. (2006). Seeing, acting, understanding: Motor resonance in language comprehension. *Journal of Experimental Psychology: General, 135*, 1–11.

Zwaan, R. A., Taylor, L. J., & de Boer, M. (2010). Motor resonance as a function of narrative time: Further tests of the linguistic focus hypothesis. *Brain and Language, 112*, 143–149.

Zwaan, R. A., & Yaxley, R. H. (2004). Lateralization of object-shape information in semantic processing. *Cognition, 94*, B35–B43.

Zyngier, S., Bortolussi, M., Chesnokova, A., & Auracher, J. (Eds.). (2008). *Directions in empirical studies: In honor of Willie van Peer*. Amsterdam: John Benjamins.

Author index

Subject index